Austrian Federalism in Comparative Perspective

Günter Bischof,
Ferdinand Karlhofer (Eds.)

CONTEMPORARY AUSTRIAN STUDIES | VOLUME 24

UNO PRESS

innsbruck university press

Printed in the United States of America

Book design by Allison Reu and Alex Dimeff

Cover photo © Parlamentsdirektion

Published in the United States by
University of New Orleans Press
ISBN: 9781608011124

UNO PRESS

Published and distributed in Europe
by Innsbruck University Press
ISBN: 9783902936691

iup

Publication of this volume has been made possible through generous grants from the the Federal Ministry for Europe, Integration, and Foreign Affairs in Vienna through the Austrian Cultural Forum in New York, as well as the Federal Ministry of Economics, Science, and Research through the Austrian Academic Exchange Service (ÖAAD). The Austrian Marshall Plan Anniversary Foundation in Vienna has been very generous in supporting Center Austria: The Austrian Marshall Plan Center for European Studies at the University of New Orleans and its publications series. The College of Liberal Arts at the University of New Orleans, the Vice Rectorate for Research, and the International Relations Office of the University of Innsbruck provided additional financial support.

Contemporary Austrian Studies

**Sponsored by the University of New Orleans
and Universität Innsbruck**

Table of Contents

NON-TOPICAL ESSAYS

FORUM: WORLD WAR I LITERATURE AND MEMORY

BOOK REVIEWS

Preface

In the United States, James Madison's, Alexander Hamilton's, and John Jay's famous eighty-five essays collected and printed in 1788 in *The Federalist* (later called *The Federalist Papers*) represent sacred texts of American political thought and define American thinking on a federal system. They were written to persuade Americans to ratify the newly written constitution in the heated constitutional debates of the late 1780s. They helped define the relationship between the central government in Washington and the (then) thirteen individual states of the Union. In Federalist # 45, James Madison wrote that "[t]he powers delegated by the proposed Constitution to the federal government are few and defined," while "[t]hose which are to remain in the State governments are numerous and indefinite." What has happened since 1789 is that "effective governing power flowed to the national government slowly in the first 80 years of the nation's history, somewhat more quickly in the next 80 and with dramatic speed from the middle of the twentieth century." This occurred without significant changes to the constitution's text, argues eminent constitutional historian Mark Tushnet, but through "a continuing constitutional convention" determining "how effective government is to be allocated."[1]

The Federalist Papers also address basic matters of political philosophy such as what constitutes "good government." So Federalist # 1 makes a case for American exceptionalism and ruminates: "It has been frequently remarked, that it seems to have been reserved to the people of this country, by their conduct and example, to decide the important question, whether societies of men are really capable or not, of establishing good government from reflection and choice, or whether they are forever destined to depend, for their political constitutions, on accident and force." The essays published in *The Federalist* are still today considered to constitute the basic political theory of federalism in the U.S. and the Western world. These ideas about factionalism in a democratic system, and central government-state relations,

1 Mark Tushnet, "The Evolution of Federalism in the United States: A Continuing Convention," in *Towards a European Constitution: A Historical and Political Comparison with the United States*, ed. Michael Gehler et al. (Vienna: Böhlau, 2005), 127-143, p. 127.

have helped keep the American Union together against all odds. In the 19th century (Southern) "states' rights" doctrine split the Union apart and unleashed the Civil War. In the 20th century anti-central government sentiment in large swaths of the American public has threatened the coherence of the American Union (ironically today often built on the ideas of anti-state "Austrian economists" so loved by the Tea Party).

Austrian federalism is a different cup of tea and a more recent phenomenon. Apart from the 1920 constitution, thinkers and writers on Austrian federalism cannot point to such a foundational and approachable text as the American *Federalist Papers*. Austrian federalism is historically constructed in the difficult post-World War I environment, when new states popped out of the Central European ground like mushrooms. Federalism was written into the 1920 constitution (revised 1929, suspended by the Dollfuß regime, and reinstituted after the period of Fascism/National Socialism in 1945).

With its ambiguous mix of weak federalist and strong centralist elements, the Austrian constitutional architecture has been subject to conflicting interpretations and claims from its very beginning. The written 1920 constitution has been paralleled by informal rules and forces making up for the imbalance of power between national and subnational authorities. Understanding these inherent weaknesses, virtually all political actors involved are well aware that reforming the allocation of rights and duties between the different levels in the federal state is urgently needed. In recent years, several initiatives of recalibrating the system of power-sharing between the different levels of government have been initiated. So far progress has been modest, yet the reform process is still underway.

Seen from an international perspective, the Austrian case is to be located at the edge of the comparative matrix of federal systems. Unlike the United States—and small Switzerland—Austria has no history of sovereign states coming together of their own free will to form a federation. Rather, the country's federal constitution was the result of a more or less chaotic process of cobbling together the German-speaking crown lands left over from the formerly massive multinational Habsburg Empire, which dissolved at the end of World War I.

The contributions to this volume shine a light on history, presence, and future aspects of the Austrian federal system from historical, juridical, economic, and political science perspective. The volume is also the first book in English ever devoted to the Austrian version of federalism. *Ferdinand Karlhofer* locates Austrian federalism in its historical context and the matrix of contemporary federalisms. *Anton Pelinka* views its failures through a larger Central European historical lense reaching back to the late Habsburg period. *Peter Bußjäger* locates the many levels of the functioning of Austrian cooperative federalism. *Franz Fallend* analyzes the role of the *Bundesrat*—the second constitutional chamber of the Austrian federal system—from a comparative perspective. *Margit Schratzenstaller* looks at the financial picture in the construction of a federal system, examining the complex system of Austrian fiscal federalism (the "*Finanzausgleich*") between the central and the *Länder* levels of government as well as those who are collecting the taxes. *Heinrich Neisser*, himself a former cabinet minister responsible for federalism, looks at various rounds of attempted administrative reforms of the federal system and analyzes why they were piece-meal and not very far reaching.

The final three essays deal with aspects of the "Europeanization" of Austrian federalism after Austria joined the European Union (EU) in 1995. *Annegret Eppler* and *Fritz Staudigl* shine a light on the augmented role of the *Länder* in the European Union after Austria's accession. Günther Pallaver provides a case study of the special role the state of Tyrol played after its division following World War I into North and South Tyrol and how that traumatic division has been overcome within the European Union with transnational regions like Tyrol moving closer together within the framework of EU-European regional policies. *Alice Engl* zooms in on the EU's regional policies and how the EU favors cross-border territorial cooperation among member states, providing a number of case studies of such groupings.

The two essays in the "non-topical" section are dedicated to aspects of Austrian visual history, following in the footsteps of recent articles in *Contemporary Austrian Studies* presenting case studies of visual history during World War I and after World War II. *Moran Pearl* from Hebrew University in Jerusalem presents a comparative study of the complicated history of Holocaust memorials built in Vienna and Berlin. *Ina Markova* from the University of Vienna looks at the emerging pictorial iconography and visual constructions of Austrian World War II memory right after the war in 1945/46.

As always, book reviews and the annual summary and update of Austrian politics in 2014 complete this volume. This volume, then, resumes a discourse on federalism that the University of New Orleans and University of Innsbruck partnership has touched on in their very first symposium in February 1982 in New Orleans.

A number of people have been instrumental in making the completion of this collection possible. Ferdinand Karlhofer in Innsbruck has conceptualized the "federalism-*Schwerpunkt*" and invited the contributors of the topical essays of this volume. We are sincerely thankful to all the contributing authors for submitting their essays and/or reviews on time and responding favorably to all editing suggestions from our production team. Ina Markova, the 2014/15 Austrian Ministry of Economics, Science, and Research Dissertation Fellow at UNO and PhD student in contemporary history at the University of Vienna, has done a superb job in tracking every manuscript through both the copy-editing and proof-reading processes and towards final publication. She has contributed an essay herself, in which she outlines preliminary results of her dissertation on Austrian visual history of the Nazi past. She has also corrected footnotes and humored authors towards completion of their manuscripts. Jen Hanks at UNO Publishing put her customary skills into the final round of copy-editing the individual manuscripts; Alex Dimeff skillfully type-set the final pdf of the volume. G.K. Darby and Abram Himelstein, the leadership team at UNO Publishing, have been hugely supportive to spirit this volume through to final publication. At Center Austria: The Austrian Marshall Plan Center for European Studies, Gertraud Griessner and David Messner conducted the Center's daily busy with superb efficiency to allow the co-editor to work on managing the completion of this volume. Without the dedicated teams at Center Austria and UNO Publishing there would be no CAS series. At innsbruck university press, Birgit Holzner was helpful with the production of the cover and the final round of proof-reading and then producing the volume for the European market. Cooperating with her has become a big bonus in the production of these volumes.

As always, we are happy in acknowledging our sponsors and supporters for making the publication of the Contemporary Austrian Studies series possible at all. At the Universities of Innsbruck and New Orleans our thanks go to Matthias Schennach of the International Relations Office as well as the Vice Recorate for Research along with Christina Antenhofer and Marion Wieser in the New Orleans Office. At UNO Kevin Graves, the interim dean of the College of Liberal Arts, and Robert Dupont, the chair of the History Department, have given us green lights and support when needed. We are also grateful to Rektor Tilmann Märk and President Peter Fos for their support of the entire UNO-University of Innsbruck partnership agenda, including its publication series. At the Austrian Cultural Forum in New York Christine Moser and Christian Ebner have supported our work as has their "boss" Martin Eichtinger, the chief of the Cultural Division of the Federal Ministry for Europe, Integration and Foreign Affairs in Vienna (we are looking forward working with his successor Wolfgang Waldner). In the Federal Ministry of Economics, Science, and Research and its student exchange office *Österreichischer Auslandsdienst* (ÖAD), we are grateful to Barbara Weitgruber, Christoph Ramoser, Felix Wilcek, Josef Leidenfrost and Florian Gerhardus. Markus Schweiger, the executive secretary, Ambassador Wolfgang Petritsch, the chairman of the board, as well as the board members of the Austrian Marshall Plan Foundation have been our strongest supporters for more than a decade now. It is a great pleasure and privilege to work with them all and acknowledge their unerring support of Center Austria: The Austrian Marshall Plan Center of European Studies at UNO and its activities.

Innsbruck, Tyrol—New Orleans, Louisiana, April 2015

Austrian Federalism in Comparative Perspective

Austrian Federalism: History–Properties–Change

Ferdinand Karlhofer

Introduction

In comparative research on federations, Austria ranks among the group of countries which "describe themselves as federations while being so centrally dominated in design and practice as to be little short of unitary states."[1] It is first and foremost the remarkable power asymmetry between the two houses of parliament that creates doubt as to whether the country should still be considered a federal, or rather a unitary country. The Federal Constitutional Law (*Bundesverfassungsgesetz* = B-VG) provides for supremacy of the *Nationalrat* (National Council) over the *Bundesrat* (Federal Council), markedly expressed in Article 10 which assigns the "exclusive federal competence in both legislation and administration" to the former, thus leaving only residual competences to the second chamber.[2]

Without question, from a merely institutional perspective the argument is definitely stringent. Closer inspection, though, reveals a more complex picture in that there are not only institutional provisions but also informal mechanisms and forces at work. As pointed out below, any approach disregarding the fact that the formal constitution is paralleled by a real one inevitably falls short in explaining Austrian federalism. Taking this in account, the approach chosen here draws upon the insights of historical institutionalism which allows for the assessment of the characteristics and work of institutions with reference to historical origins and path-dependent developments. Following Jörg Broschek, historical institutionalism is

> .... *historical* in that its proponents employ causal claims stressing timing and sequencing. Past choices, often made under

1 Thomas O. Hueglin and Alan Fenna, *Comparative Federalism: A Systematic Inquiry* (Toronto: Broadview Press, 2006), 34.

2 Peter Pernthaler, "The Impact of the New Cooperative and Tripartite Federalism on the Traditional Distribution of Competences in Austria," in *Decentralizing and Re-centralizing Trends in the Distribution of Powers within Federal Countries*, ed. Institut d'Estudis Autonòmics (Barcelona: El Tinter, 2010), 111-119, p. 112.

> conditions of uncertainty and involving contingent alternatives, are considered to delineate the boundaries within which future choices are made, and it is *institutional* in that past legacies manifest themselves most obviously in institutional trajectories. Unveiling the historically constructed "grammar" of institutional configurations can, therefore, illuminate exactly how past events are causally related to future development.[3]

Accordingly, the article begins with an outline of the origins of the federal republic, thereby focusing on foundational conditions shaping the system down to the present day. In the subsequent section institutional features and unwritten rules and arrangements that make up for structural shortcomings are described and analyzed. Afterwards, recent constitutional adaptations and amendments at state level are explained and discussed in detail. The article concludes with an examination of continuity and change in *Bund-Länder* relations as mirrored in constitutional politics.

The Making of the Austrian Federation

Until its collapse in 1918, the Habsburg Monarchy had been a multi-ethnic empire. The multinational composition inevitably implied some federal tradition, particularly in the wake of the Austrian-Hungarian *Ausgleich* ("Compromise") of 1867 through which the Dual Monarchy with Hungary had been fixed.[4] Notwithstanding, Austria-Hungary was not a federation in a strict sense, rather, the empire had moved in the direction of a decentralized unitary state.[5] As a matter of fact, though, the Habsburg regime increasingly had to cope with centrifugal forces fed by nationalist upheaval across the whole empire.[6] Unsurprisingly, with the empire in

---

3 Jörg Broschek, "Conceptualizing and Theorizing Constitutional Change in Federal Systems: Insights from Historical Institutionalism," *Regional and Federal Studies* 21, no. 4-5 (2011): 539-559, p. 541.

4 Michael Burgess, *Comparative Federalism: Theory and Practice* (London: Routledge, 2006), 93.

5 Karl Weber, "Die Entwicklung des österreichischen Bundesstaates," in *Bundesstaat und Bundesrat in Österreich*, ed. Herbert Schambeck (Vienna: Verlag Österreich, 1997), 37-64, p. 39.

6 It is noteworthy that the only political leaders theorizing about ways to federalize the multinational conglomerate came from within the ranks of an explicitly centralist force, namely the Social Democratic Party. Most prominent, though not adopted by the party leadership, was Otto Bauer's work *Die Nationalitätenfrage und die Sozialdemokratie* (Vienna 1907).

disarray as a result of the lost war, these peoples, with the support of the Entente, promptly founded sovereign states of their own.

What remained from the huge territorial superstate was no more than a small fraction of its original size of 677.000 km^2. No wonder that scarcely anybody supposed the 84.000 km^2 rump state would be able to survive unless it joined a larger state. Thus, the founding process took place under two premises: First, as for ethnicity, it was clear that the republic to be established would be confined to the German-speaking part of the former imperium (the expectation, German Bohemia and the Sudetenland would be included, too, soon turned out to have been a mere illusion). Second, not for no reason, the provisional republic established in 1918 called itself "Republic of German-Austria," hereby expressing its aim to ally with Germany sooner or later.

Reconstructing the process of establishing federalism in Austria is not an easy task to undertake. The abdicated imperial authority had left a political vacuum[7] with a prevailing mood of disorientation and a striking lack of prospects. At the very beginning, federalism was not on the agenda, on the contrary, the Provisional National Assembly convening in October 1918 aimed at founding a unitary state bound to become part of the German Reich. Soon, however, the debate revolved around the conflict centralism vs. federalism, with the latter targeted by the Christian Social Party, which dominated in the provinces, while the Social Democrats, with their stronghold Vienna, favored the centralist option.[8] The founding process became tension-filled and, while it should have taken around two years, was not finalized until November 1920 when the new—in the end—federal constitution came into effect.

As a matter of fact, on both sides there had been some misunderstanding about who had the real power to determine the country's fate. Eventually, the 1919 Treaty of St. Germain with Article 27 (stating that "[t]he frontiers of Austria shall be fixed as follows ....") in conjunction with Article 88 (forbidding Austria "any act which might directly or indirectly .... compromise her independence"), put an end to any ambition of pan-German unity. It was simply the victorious powers redrawing the boundaries, hereby leaving small Austria in the role of a henceforth minor, if not negligible player in European politics.

As for the envisaged internal structure of Austria the Entente did not care—it simply expected the country to accept the predetermined

7 Burgess, *Comparative Federalism*, 93.

8 Mandred Stelzer, *The Constitution of the Republic of Austria* (Oxford: Hart Publishing, 2011), 9.

boundaries. Along this line, any regional attempt to change the defined geography was brought to a halt. Bohemia and Sudeten were cut off while Burgenland which heretofore had belonged to Hungary was affiliated to Austria.

The debate on why and how Austria eventually was structured on a federal basis has been controversial up to the present time. One school of thought claims Austria was established in a first step toward a centralist unitary state which, in a second step, devolved competences to the *Länder*. In fact, the process was more challenging, as outlined in a recent historical study emphasizing that the first provisional constitution, adopted in October 1918, merely reconfirmed the imperial *Landesordnungen* (territorial law codes) of 1861 which assigned only rudimentary autonomy to the provinces.[9] However, within a short time the provinces, while accepting the constitution as kind of an indispensable "joint umbrella," started a debate around the question of whether the republic should be a federalist or a unitary one. Federalist claims rested upon the so-called *Kronländer* (crown lands), a quasi-federal Habsburg heritage comprising Vorarlberg, Tyrol, Salzburg, Carinthia, Styria, Upper Austria, and Lower Austria, with some of them tracing back as far as the late Middle Ages.[10] In November 1918, "most *Länder* declared their 'accession' to the newly created republic in order to demonstrate their original statehood and claim of autonomy."[11] Thus, all *Länder* constituted themselves as autonomous, albeit without arrogating sovereignty in the sense of an independent state but rather expressing the intent of linking to one another in a common state.[12]

What must be added, though, is that what appeared to become kind of a "coming-together federation" was actually orchestrated by Chancellor Karl Renner who provided pre-formulated, textually identical declarations of accession to the *Land* parliaments.[13] Notwithstanding, the states' commitment to the new republic remained fragile for a while, as revealed in the form of several attempts of secession: In 1919, Tyrol, in a hopeless effort to reunite with its southern part which had been annexed by Italy, declared itself a free state. In Vorarlberg, a referendum on acceding to Switzerland, held in 1921, was affirmed by ninety-nine percent of the voters. In the same

9 Ewald Wiederin, "Die verfassungspolitische Diskussion über die Einrichtung Österreichs als Bundesstaat," *Beiträge zur Rechtsgeschichte Österreichs* 1 (2011): 356-373.

10 Rudolf Palme, "Die Länderparlamente als Ausdruck der Identität der Länder," in *Die Länderparlamente als Ausdruck der Identität der Länder*, ed. Peter Pernthaler (Vienna: Braumüller, 2000), 29-46.

11 Joseph Marko, "Federalism, Sub-national Constitutionalism, and the Protection of Minorities," at <camlaw.rutgers.edu/statecon/subpapers/marko.pdf> (6 March 2015).

12 Wilhelm Brauneder, *Österreichische Verfassungsgeschichte* (Vienna: Manz, 1998), 202.

13 Wiederin, *Die verfassungspolitische Diskussion*, 361.

year, referenda in Tyrol and Salzburg on joining Germany were supported by strong majorities of voters. None of these initiatives had a reasonable chance of success.[14]

In 1945, the situation was quite the same as had been the case after WWI. The Allies definitely had no interest in considering regional interests in their strategic plans. The provisional government in Vienna was the only accepted authoritative interlocutor, albeit at the outset from the viewpoint of the Western forces suspected to be a tool of the Soviets. The fact that immediately after the defeat of the Nazi regime the country was divided into four "zones" (distributed among the U.S., the UK, France, and the Soviet Union) makes explaining the rebuilding of federalism in post-war Austria a bit difficult. For the Allied authorities in the provinces, the *Land* governors (in the beginning provisional only, since not elected) were welcome with regard to administrative matters. Thus, in the initial postwar time, with the central government not even in a position to communicate its decisions nationwide, the *Länder* managed to establish informal political and administrative structures they could build on when, in September 1945, the first *Länderkonferenz* (state conference) was to be held in Vienna.

To sum up, considering its historical development which has been characterized by ruptures and discontinuity, Austrian federalism does not fit into any of the categories of federal state-building as are provided by comparative research. Since, after the Habsburg Empire had fallen apart, virtually all actors, both the *Länder* and the political parties, had assumed the rump state would sooner or later join the German *Reich*, the outcome was not a "coming-together federation"; by the same reason, it wasn't a "holding-together federation" either.[15] And although state-building both in 1918 and 1945 took place under the control of external actors, a factor underlying the definition of "forced together federalism" given by Nancy Bermeo,[16] not even this latter category is adequate. It does not apply because the victorious powers, other than in Germany after WWII,[17] did not care whether or not Austria became a federation. As a matter of fact, Austrian federalism emerged in a more

14 Franz Fiedler, "Föderalismus als Gestaltungsprinzip," *IILP Sozialwissenschaftliche Schriftenreihe* 21 (2007): 5-17, p. 7-8.

15 Cf. the typology introduced by Alfred Stepan, "Federalism and Democracy: Beyond the U.S. Model," *Journal of Democracy* 10, no. 4 (1999): 19-34.

16 Nancy Bermeo, "The Importance of Institutions: A New Look at Federalism," *Journal of Democracy* 13, no. 2 (2002): 96-110, p. 110.

17 Cf. Klaus v. Beyme, *Das politische System der Bundesrepublik Deutschland* (Wiesbaden: VS-Verlag, 2010), 368; Burgess, *Comparative Federalism*, 95-97; Wilfried Swenden, *Federalism and Second Chambers* (Brussels: Peter Lang, 2004), 59.

or less chaotic process of cobbling together what already well before had been under a common roof, albeit now considerably smaller. There was no option other than assembling what had been left from former hugeness.[18] The inconsistencies of its foundation process have lived on to the present day in the Austrian federal state in that there is considerable regional identity among the citizens,[19] while at the same time a two-thirds majority of the population would not mind if federalism were to be abandoned, even if merely balancing an annual national budget were at stake.[20]

Institutional and Informal Framework: Properties and Ambiguities[21]

Basically, as expressed in the previous section, federations are to be regarded as historically constructed.[22] In principle, therefore, any change of a multi-layered system has to cope with path-dependency, inevitably generating all kinds of die-hard habits and routines. For historical reasons, in Austria policy-making "to a considerable extent aims at negotiated solutions."[23] The functional interaction of formal and informal negotiation rules under involvement of strong actors without explicit legal legitimation has, for instance, had a long tradition of cooperative relations between state and interest associations in connection with *Sozialpartnerschaft*, the Austrian version of corporatism.[24] The same holds true for the functioning of the federal system in that unwritten rules make up for the shortcomings of institutional provisions. The most characteristic features are:

18 Wiederin, *Die verfassungspolitische Diskussion*, 371.
19 See Peter Bußjäger, Ferdinand Karlhofer and Günther Pallaver, *Föderalistisches Bewusstsein in Österreich: Regionale Identitätsbildung und Einstellung der Bevölkerung zum Föderalismus* (Vienna: Braumüller, 2010).
20 "Zwei Drittel lehnen Föderalismus ab," opinion poll by Market Institute, in *Der Standard,* 21/22 June 2014, 6.
21 For a more detailed description see Ferdinand Karlhofer and Günther Pallaver, "Strength through Weakness: State Executive Power and Federal Reform in Austria," *Swiss Political Science Review* 19, no. 1 (2013): 41-59.
22 Broschek, *Conceptualizing and Theorizing,* 539.
23 Gerhard Lehmbruch, "Die korporative Verhandlungsdemokratie in Westeuropa," *Schweizerische Zeitschrift für Politische Wissenschaft* 19, no. 4 (1996): 19-41, p. 19.
24 For a detailed analysis see *Austro-Corporatism: Past–Present–Future*, ed. Günter Bischof and Anton Pelinka (Contemporary Austrian Studies 4) (New Brunswick: Transaction, 1996), and, more recently, *Sozialpartnerschaft: Österreichische und Europäische Perspektiven*, ed. Ferdinand Karlhofer and Emmerich Tálos (Vienna: LIT Verlag, 2005).

Weakness of the Second Chamber[25]

In the federal legislative process the *Bundesrat* possesses merely a suspensive veto (Article 42 B-VG) that can easily be overruled by the *Nationalrat*. What is more, in none of the (few) cases where the second chamber has an absolute veto—namely regarding bills affecting legislative or administrative *Länder* competences (Article 44 B-VG)—has it blocked a bill passed by the *Nationalrat*.[26] As a matter of fact, in the federal parties' hierarchical scale, the *Bundesrat* is subordinate and in practice almost insignificant. The modest prestige of *Bundesrat* deputies is best expressed by the fact that after every national election the government parties, when negotiating the coalition agreement, agree upon the voting behavior not only of the lower house members, but also of their respective members of the upper house—without consulting the latter.[27]

Indirect Federal Administration[28]

Regarding the division of competencies between *Bund* (federal state) and *Länder*, the constitution (Art 102 B-VG) distinguishes between direct and indirect federal administration, with the latter providing that a "significant proportion of federal administration is carried out by the *Länder* on behalf of the federation," a provision through which the constitution "compensates the *Länder* for their relative lack of power."[29] In practice, indirect federal administration (*mittelbare Bundesverwaltung*), other than the term suggests, is not hierarchical but rather a complex, in parts even stratarchical, negotiating system with the *Länder* controlling the execution of federal law. Austria's distinct system of indirect administration mirrors a special kind of "executive federalism" with the governors pulling the strings. With regard to the control of indirect administration through national authorities, the Federal Constitution is remarkably imprecise, with the result that "a substantial part of *Land* government activities remains without formal state supervision."[30]

25 For a detailed description and analysis of the *Bundesrat* see the contribution by Fallend to this volume.

26 Anna Gamper, "Republic of Austria," in *Legislative, Executive, and Judicial Governance in Federal Countries*, ed. Katy Le Roy and Cheryl Saunders (Montreal: McGill-Queen's University Press, 2006), 72-100, p. 79.

27 Jürgen Weiss, "Der Bundesrat und die Bundesstaatsreform," in *Bundesstaat und Bundesrat in Österreich*, ed. Herbert Schambeck (Vienna: Verlag Österreich, 1997), 497-525, p. 525.

28 See also the more detailed contribution by Bußjäger to this volume.

29 Gamper, "Republic of Austria," 82.

30 Franz Fallend, "Föderalismus–eine Domäne der Exekutiven?," in *Der Bund und die*

Land Governors: Gatekeepers in the Federal Architecture[31]

The office of a *Land* governor enjoys a special status in the country's federal setup. First of all, as outlined above, in the broad field of indirect federal administration it is the governor who has the final say. He/she alone is the central government's counterpart, and thus responsible neither to the *Landtag* nor to his cabinet. With the administrative apparatus directly subordinated to the governor and parliamentary decision-making to a high extent predetermined by the executive branch, the scope of influence of a *Landtag* is narrow, the more so as even as its formal right of creating and controlling the government is considerably restricted in practice. Not only is the governor head of the government, head of the bureaucracy, in charge with indirect federal administration and, last but not least, in all external relations "head of state." What is more, any candidate for governor is usually leader of his or her respective party and therefore enjoys strong intra-party authority—as a result, *Landtag* elections are primarily governor elections.[32]

"Partyness" of Federalism

In a multi-layered system, political parties are kind of integrative agents and, along with interest groups, important vehicles of centralization.[33] In Austria, due to their all-encompassing presence at all levels, political parties have represented a pivotal element for cohesion and unification. Being a country with "strong parties in a weak federal polity," [34] makes it a special case of *Parteienbundesstaat* (party federal state).[35]

For a long time, the structural architecture of the party federal state left little room for regional parties on a permanent basis. Until very recently, the

Länder: Über Dominanz, Kooperation und Konflikte im österreichischen Bundesstaat, ed. Herbert Dachs (Vienna: Böhlau, 2003), 17-68, p. 23.

31 Cf. Ferdinand Karlhofer, "Gestaltungskraft und Vetomacht: Funktion und Praxis der Landeshauptleutekonferenz," in *Im Dienste der Länder–im Interesse des Gesamtstaates: Festschrift 60 Jahre Verbindungsstelle der Bundesländer*, ed. Peter Rosner and Peter Bußjäger (Vienna: Braumüller, 2011), 311-326.

32 Karl Weber, "Politik und Verwaltung," in *Politik in Tirol*, ed. Ferdinand Karlhofer and Anton Pelinka (Innsbruck: StudienVerlag, 2004), 73-96, p. 78-80.

33 Klaus v. Beyme, *Das politische System der Bundesrepublik Deutschland* (Wiesbaden: VS-Verlag, 2010), 373.

34 Herbert Obinger, "Austria: Strong Parties in a Weak Federal Polity," in *Federalism and the Welfare State: New World and European Experiences*, ed. idem, Stephan Leibfried and Francis Castles (Cambridge: Cambridge University Press, 2005), 181-221.

35 Cf. Frank Decker, *Regieren im "Parteienbundesstaat": Zur Architektur der deutschen Politik* (Wiesbaden: VS-Verlag, 2011).

congruence of the party systems at national and provincial levels provided a welcome basis for policy coordination with the two dominant parties, the Social Democratic Party (SPÖ) and People's Party (ÖVP), which functioned as intermediary agencies between center and periphery.[36]

In the last two or three decades the Austrian party system, in accordance with international trends, has changed in a way that, among other issues, has manifested itself in a decline of the parties' capacity to reconcile conflicting interests.[37] Until the 1980s, given that the two dominant *Lager* parties SPÖ and ÖVP continuously received more than ninety percent of the votes, and the third largest Freedom Party (FPÖ) received between five and seven percent, Austria had a typical two-and-a-half-party system. Thereafter, the hitherto frozen party system entered into a stage of rapid change, with the newly emerging Greens on the one side and the FPÖ transforming into a radical right populist party on the other, and both capturing considerable shares of the *Lager* parties' electorates. At *Länder* level, however, the party systems have proved considerably resistant, with SPÖ and ÖVP having managed to maintain their supremacy. As of end-2014, SPÖ and ÖVP together hold a total of 302 out of 448 (i.e. sixty-seven percent) *Landtag* seats in the nine provinces, while holding merely ninety-nine out of 183 (fifty-four percent) seats in the National Council.[38] All things considered, the strength of the parties at state level appears to be the "most remarkable feature of real federalism [in Austria]."[39]

Conflicting Loyalties: Regional vs. Centralist Party Interests

For long periods of the Second Republic, the "partyness of government"[40] with regard to structures and processes in policy-making manifested itself in that *Land* election campaigns frequently were less determined by regional than by national issues, and quite often the outcome was considered a barometer of public opinion on national politics. For the SPÖ which focuses on centralism, this has always been beyond dispute;

36 v. Beyme, *Deutschland,* 376.

37 Cf. *Die Parteiensysteme Westeuropas*, ed. Oskar Niedermayer, Richard Stöss and Melanie Haas (Wiesbaden: VS-Verlag, 2006).

38 Official data by <www.bmi.gv.at/cms/bmi_wahlen> (1 February 2015).

39 Anton Pelinka, "Föderalismus für das 21. Jahrhundert: Perspektiven der Weiterentwicklung des politischen Systems Österreichs im Spannungsfeld zwischen Legitimität und Effizienz," in *Baustelle Bundesstaat: Perspektiven der Weiterentwicklung des politischen Systems Österreich*, ed. Friedrich Steger (Vienna: Braumüller, 2007), 119-154, p. 141.

40 Klaus v. Beyme, *Föderalismus und regionales Bewusstsein: Ein internationaler Vergleich* (Munich: Beck, 2007), 124.

and also the more federal-oriented ÖVP has emphasized a "dual" party structure, i.e. regional sub-units plus nation-wide *Bünde* ("leagues") along socio-economic lines in order to avoid or at least to mitigate centrifugal tendencies. Considerable change, though, has taken place since Austria's entry into the European Union (EU) in the mid-1990s. Since then, regional elections have tended to be more determined by regional issues than in the past. Inextricably, "vertical integration may become a burden" and "[r] egional politicians may tend to dissociate themselves from unpopular 'party friends' at the federal level."[41] The national government, on its part, tends to emphasize centralism more firmly in order to make up for losses coming along with ongoing Europeanization. With this background, in particular when reallocating competences is at stake, parties tend more and more to oscillate between promoting and blocking changes.[42]

It is noteworthy in this connection that the intra-party influence of the regional organizations varies strongly with both *Lager* parties: Vienna and Lower Austria have always been the centers of gravity, with power-conscious governors considering themselves anything but subordinate to their respective national party leadership. There has always been some kind of "asymmetry-in-symmetry" in Austria's federal system—symmetry understood as constitutional equality of the national subunits, while asymmetry mirrors the differences of population and wealth affecting the constitutional units' political power relations with each other as well as their varying degree of influence on federative institutions.[43]

Traditions and Modes of *Bund-Länder* Relations as Mirrored in Constitutional and Sub-Constitutional Politics

With regard to the historical development of the relations between *Bund* and *Länder* since the founding of the First Republic, three periods can be distinguished:[44]

41 Klaus Detterbeck, "Party Careers in Federal Systems: Vertical Linkages within Austrian, German, Canadian and Australian Parties," *Regional and Federal Studies* 21, no. 2 (2011): 245-270, p. 249.

42 See Arthur Benz, "Reformpromotoren oder Reformblockierer? Die Rolle der Parteien im Bundesstaat," *Aus Politik und Zeitgeschichte*, no. 29-30 (2003): 32-38.

43 Charles D. Tarlton, "Symmetry and Asymmetry as Elements of Federalism: A Theoretical Speculation," *The Journal of Politics* 27, no. 4 (1965): 861-874, p. 869; Ronald Watts, *Comparing Federal Systems* (Montreal: McGill Queen's University Press, 3rd ed. 2008), 123.

44 Friedrich Koja, *Das Verfassungsrecht der österreichischen Bundesländer* (Vienna: Springer, 2nd ed. 1988).

1) adjustment of state constitutions to the national constitution (a temporally uneven process, starting with Styria in 1918, and completed as late as 1930 when Upper Austria adopted its own constitution);

2) refoundation of the republic in 1945, followed by a long period of stagnation in which the *Länder* were essentially confined to replicating federal constitutional law with striking passiveness that did not change until the late 1960s;

3) significantly increased self-confidence of the *Länder* after the release of a constitutionalist's legal opinion attributing considerably more autonomy to the substates than initially thought.

As for phase three, it started in 1964 with a joint initiative of the *Länder* in which they claimed a strengthening of their competences in return for granting aid to the federation in a financially precarious situation.[45] The legal doctrine elaborated in this context, was drawing on the insight that state constitutions are not simply subordinated to the federal constitution,[46] but basically confined to implement federal law. Rather, notwithstanding the rule that state constitutions may in principle not affect the Federal Constitution, there has always been some "relative" constitutional autonomy largely neglected so far.[47] The opinion paved the way for a paradigm shift in constitutional politics, encouraging the *Länder* to address the federal government with further demands. The negotiations that followed did not really result in substantial changes but may provide an opening for significant revisions in times to come. Remarkably, by the way, the negotiations were conducted between federal government and state governors. The parliaments of both levels, though directly concerned when changing the rules is on the agenda, were not involved in the talks—a prime example of constitutional reality superimposing formal federalism.[48]

The change in the relations caused by the new doctrine of a relative autonomy has persisted down to the present day, naturally circling around the question of how to define the scope and limits of relative autonomy. Given that most federal systems provide just an "incomplete" framework, leaving more or less "space" for the federal architecture to be filled by sub-

---

45 Bernd-Christian Funk, "Die Bedeutung gliedstaatlichen Verfassungsrechts in der Gegenwart," *Veröffentlichungen der Vereinigung der Deutschen Staatslehrer* 46 (1988): 58-91, p. 71.

46 "The *Land* Constitution to be enacted by a *Land* constitutional law can, inasmuch as the Federal Constitution is not affected thereby, be amended by *Land* constitutional law" (Article 99 (1), Federal Constitutional Law).

47 Friedrich Koja, *Das Verfassungsrecht der österreichischen Bundesländer* (Vienna: Springer, 1st ed. 1967), 19-29.

48 Cf. Fallend, *Domäne der Exekutiven*, 28.

national provisions and arrangements,[49] identifying and analyzing scope, activities, and substance is both exciting and difficult.

Bearing in mind that filling the space is to a considerable extent not just a matter of options but also a matter of political culture, in some of the *Länder* regional identity is strong, underpinned with historical heritage, traditionalism, and patriotic sentiments, while in others citizens have a more rational view of the *Land* they live in. Comparative studies show that there is a difference between the Western and the Eastern *Länder*: in Vorarlberg, Tyrol, and Salzburg, emotional attachment to the *Land* is significantly higher than in the national average.[50] Obviously, there is a close correlation between regional identity and the attitude towards federalism: the citizens of Vorarlberg and Tyrol rank highest (seventy-five percent resp. seventy-four percent compared to fifty-nine percent nation-wide) in desiring a stronger role for the *Länder* in federal politics.[51]

Given the relevance of historical and cultural aspects, it makes sense to put them into consideration when comparing constitutions. In a recent empirically based thesis, Austria's nine *Land* constitutions are grouped in three categories:[52]

1) Styria and Vienna are states with pronounced positivistic constitutions which are decidedly confined to positive law provisions and abstain from inexact norms and promises that cannot be fulfilled, e.g., protecting and fostering marriage and family.[53]

2) Burgenland, Carinthia, and Lower and Upper Austria have constitutions with a mix of legal positivism and natural law, in part

49 Alan G. Tarr, "Explaining Sub-national Constitutional Space," *Penn State Law Review* 115, no. 4 (2011): 1133-1149, p. 1133.

50 Fritz Plasser and Peter Ulram, "Regionale Mentalitätsdifferenzen in Österreich," in *Der Bund und die Länder: Über Dominanz, Kooperation und Konflikte im österreichischen Bundesstaat*, ed. Herbert Dachs (Vienna: Böhlau, 2003), 421-440, p. 433.

51 Bußjäger et al., *Föderalistisches Bewusstsein*, 38.

52 Moritz Moser, "Die Verfassungen der österreichischen Länder und ihre Autonomie im Vergleich," PhD diss., Vienna University 2010, 69-72, at <http://othes.univie.ac.at/9739/1/2010-05-17_0502171.pdf> (6 March 2015). Although not addressing the political-cultural dimension directly, the study provides a valuable classification for comparative analysis drawing on key questions as outlined by Tarr: identifying differences and similarities of substate constitutions and, still more important, explaining the reasons for differences, i.e. "why sub-national units have made more or less use of the constitutional space available to them." Cf. Alan G. Tarr, Sub-national Constitutional Space: An Agenda for Research, prepared delivered at the *World Congress of the International Association of Constitutional Law in Athens* (2007), at <http://camlaw.rutgers.edu/statecon/workshop11greece07/workshop11/Tarr.pdf> (6 March 2015).

53 Peter Häberle, "Textstufen in österreichischen Landesverfassungen–ein Vergleich," in *Jahrbuch des öffentlichen Rechts der Gegenwart* 54 (Tübingen: Mohr Siebeck, 2006), 367-514, p. 381. See also Marko, *Federalism*, 3.

including provisions with imprecise norms, e.g., state goals, basic/civil rights, and the like.

3) Salzburg, Tyrol, and Vorarlberg have constitutions that are distinctly natural law oriented, i.e. expressing broad commitment to (vaguely defined) values such as human dignity, freedom, independence etc.

In the last three decades, all *Länder*, albeit much of the content of their constitutions is predetermined in detail by the Federal Constitution, have extensively adapted their constitutions. Recent studies even identify "contours of distinct Austrian constitutional profiles at member state level" which find expression in "spirited innovations."[54] It must be noted, though, that with regard to substance not every constitutional change earns the attribute "spirited." *Land* constitutions tend to focus on (nonbinding, because unenforceable) fundamental rights and "state goals" (*Staatsziele*) such as commitments to "family, marriage, equal treatment of housework and gainful employment, Sundays and legal holidays, regional patriotism, and subsidiarity."[55] For instance, the preamble of the Tyrolean constitution affirms, among other things, "trust in God," "spiritual and cultural unity of the whole *Land* [South Tyrol implied]" and the "well-ordered family as the basic element of people and state" (not entirely coincidental, Tyrol ranks among the group of *Länder* with natural law oriented constitutions). And all *Länder* have incorporated symbols into their basic laws in order to underline cultural identity and the claim of (regional) autonomy. As a rule, every *Land* has an anthem of its own, a flag, a patron saint celebrated at a feast day, and the like.[56]

While many changes fall primarily in the category of symbolic politics, others lead to far-reaching alterations of single elements of the political system. With regard to the topics such as direct democracy and lowering the voting age, the *Länder* are clearly forerunners compared to the federal level. As for direct democracy, Austria at national level has always been reluctant to extending participation rights. By contrast, it was the *Länder* which, in the 1970s, opened up for revisions of their constitutions in order to enhance civic participation. The new spirit was influenced by two factors: For one thing, the new legal doctrine of relative autonomy fostered an understanding of sub-national self-reliance. And for another thing, policymakers were increasingly faced with civil society activities, such as local initiatives and action groups which more or less explicitly put the enhancement of civic involvement on the agenda. Within a short time,

54 Author's translation.
55 Anna Gamper, "Allgemeine Bestimmungen des Landesverfassungsrechts," in *Das Recht der Länder*, ed. Erich Pürgy (Vienna: Jan Sramek, 2012), 61-85, p. 70.
56 Häberle, "Textstufen," 371-372.

broadening the scope for direct democracy became a nationwide topic, and none of the *Länder* could ignore the demand for more direct democracy. By the end of the 1990s virtually all *Länder* had amended their constitutions in this direction.[57] Today, there is both at *Land* and at local level a broad spectrum of provisions for citizen participation.

Regarding the voting age, Austria at present is the only EU member state, in fact the only developed democracy worldwide, that provides voter rights to its sixteen-year-old citizens.

What was introduced in 2007 in Austria nationwide, had been practiced in some of the *Länder* for a couple of years already. After in the 1990s in several German *Länder* the voting age for local elections had been lowered to sixteen years, Carinthia and Burgenland made a start in Austria by introducing "vote at 16" for municipalities in 2000, Burgenland extended the reform also to *Landtag* elections. By 2005, five *Länder* had lowered the voting age for local elections and three, additionally, for *Landtag* elections. Eventually, in 2007, the newly elected federal government, formed by SPÖ and ÖVP, followed suit and lowered the voting age for *Nationalrat* elections, too. As a consequence, due to the constitutional *Homogenitätsprinzip* (homogeneity rule) which provides that at no level the voting age may be higher than for the *Nationalrat*, all election laws—including not only the four remaining *Länder* but also referenda, the election of the federal president and even elections to the European Parliament—had to be adapted.

The most momentous change taking place at *Land* level, though, is the abandonment of *Proporz* as outlined in the following section.[58]

Reluctant Farewell to *Proporz* Rule

With regard to Austria's political system, the term *Proporz* has an ambivalent meaning: In an informal sense it is a well-established term inextricably linked with the concept of "consociationalism" defined as a societal arrangement typical for countries which in their historical development were unable or only insufficiently able to establish a viable,

57 Klaus Poier, "Sachunmittelbare Demokratie in Österreichs Ländern und Gemeinden: Rechtslage und empirische Erfahrungen im Überblick," in *Sachunmittelbare Demokratie im interdisziplinären und internationalen Kontext 2008/2009: Deutschland, Österreich, Schweiz*, ed. Peter Neumann and Denise Renger (Baden-Baden: Nomos, 2010), 31-56, p. 34.

58 For a detailed analysis see Ferdinand Karlhofer, "Wählen mit 16–Österreich als Vorreiter in Europa?," in *Entwicklungen des Wahlrechts am europäischen Fallbeispiel*, ed. Anna Gamper (Vienna: Springer, 2010), 175-193.

non-destructive system based on the ideal of competitive democracy.[59] The Austrian version of *Proporz* democracy is to be traced back to the late 19th, early 20th century when the Social Democratic Party and the Christian Social Party organized virtually the whole society in two big "camps" (therefore the term *Lagerparteien*). As is well known, the First Republic ended with civil war and the abolition of democracy. The Second Republic, then, was founded on the insight that none of the two forces was able to prevail. As a consequence the now renamed parties SPÖ and ÖVP established a system of proportional representation finding its expression in a long series of grand coalitions characterized by comprehensive mutual control and almost excessive clientilism in political, economic, social, and cultural affairs.

The informal post-WWII arrangement of mutual control had had a prelude already at the cradle of the democratic republic which was founded after 1918. After long disputes revolving around the question whether to establish a federation or a central state, a compromise was found in that the outcome was a federation with strong centralist elements. The crucial point was that Vienna and several industrial areas were clear domains of the Socialist while rural areas were controlled by the Christian Social party. The solution was that all *Land* constitutions, except for Vorarlberg and Vienna, drafted constitutions which provided for the composition of the *Land* government along the parties' vote shares in *Landtag* elections with executive positions to be filled proportionally. Thus, neither of the two *Lager* parties had to fear being excluded from government permanently.

However, although enshrined in provincial constitutions drafted in the First Republic already, the system of *Proporz* government could fulfill its purpose not before 1945. Only from then on, the two *Lager* parties in office could rely on a balance of power both at national and substate level.

Beginning with the late 1970s, and accelerating with economic crisis in the 1980s, the essentials of Austrian consociationalism based on two-party dualism increasingly eroded. At national level, entering a grand coalition had meanwhile become a risky game, and similar changes took place at *Länder* level as well. And as far as *Proporz* rule was concerned: It seemed, the Moor had done his duty, the Moor might go.

Proporz had not only become a burden for central parties, it had also become an ever-growing problem right for those parties that had been used to put majorities in proportionally composed *Land* governments. As long as a predominant party can easily push through its will vis-à-vis its junior

59 Cf. Manfred G. Schmidt, *Demokratietheorien: Eine Einführung* (Opladen: Leske+Budrich, 2010), 306-335.

partners, all's right with the world. And it can make use of its right that the *Land* bureaucracy is directly and exclusively subordinated to the *Land* governor—a privilege that frequently has caused criticism.[60] With shares of votes gradually shrinking and finally falling under the fifty percent mark, though, formerly power-conscious parties have lost ground. As of 2015, there is only one party at the provincial level left (the ÖVP in Lower Austria) still holding an absolute majority in parliament. As soon as the early 1990s, the *Land* Salzburg took the lead and started considering a change from proportional to majoritarian rule for government election. After years of fruitless negotiations, though, there was no end in sight.[61] Notwithstanding, in 1998, due to a political scandal—the FPÖ, holding a seat in government, had made public confidential computer data—all the other parties came to an agreement on changing the system at the very earliest. As a result, already in 1999, when provincial elections were to be held, the new government was built on the basis of majority rule. Simultaneously, in Tyrol following the example of Salzburg, the government was elected along the same pattern.[62]

For several years, no other *Land* got ready to follow suit and make a move in this direction. Most recently, however, Styria and Burgenland introduced majority rule, Carinthia is supposed to adapt the system by the end of 2015 while in Upper Austria ÖVP and Greens, building a coalition informally within the stipulated all-party government, are pronounced proponents of changing the rule but lack the required two-thirds majority in parliament.

Concluding this section, it must be noted that in connection with the shift from proportional to majority rule the parliamentary control rights had to be adapted. The reason for that was that in the relationship between government and opposition the logic of action is different. During the Second Republic, several *Länder* with *Proporz* system repeatedly lacked opposition in parliament due to the fact that all parties were in government.[63] The dominance of the leading party/parties in government has been secured through high thresholds for the use of parliamentary control instruments, thus inevitably resulting in a lack of accountability. For instance, in four

60 Kurt R. Luther, "Dimensions of Party System Change: The Case of Austria," in *Understanding Party System Change in Western Europe*, ed. Peter Mair and Gordon Smith, (Abingdon: Frank Cass, 1990), 3-27, p. 16.
61 Franz Schausberger, "Die Abschaffung des Proporzsystems in den Bundesländern Salzburg und Tirol," in *Österreichisches Jahrbuch für Politik 1998* (Vienna: Verlag für Geschichte und Politik, 1999), 257-270, p. 258.
62 Ibid.
63 In practice, though, frequently two or three of the parties conclude unofficial coalitions with the consequence that important portfolios are distributed among the contract partners while the others are restricted to minor spheres of influence.

Länder with *Proporz* governments (Burgenland, Carinthia, Lower and Upper Austria) a vote of no-confidence against a cabinet member requires either a two-thirds majority of his own party or of the total of MPs.[64] The same had been the case in Salzburg and Tyrol before *Proporz* had been abandoned; now, under majoritarian system, it requires merely simple majority of votes to force a cabinet member to resign.[65]

Conclusion: Federal Dynamics between Continuity and Change

During 1918 to 1920, as set out in the beginning of this chapter, along with the tension-filled formation of the democratic republic, a federal architecture developed whose shortcomings have persisted to the present day. The striking lack of constitutionally entrenched balance of power-sharing, markedly expressed in the relative insignificance of the *Bundesrat*, has even caused doubt whether Austria is to be seen as a federation or rather a unitary state. However, as has been argued in this article, a comprehensive analysis of Austrian federalism deserves closer attention to informal rules and power relations beyond the institutional framework. Moreover, in the long run, perceptions, interpretations and practice may be subject to change even if institutions remain unaltered.

Drawing on this consideration, the analysis of Austrian sub-national constitutional politics gives a different picture, all the more so as it is anything but static or unidirectional. A flash back to the immediate post-war decades seems to corroborate the assessment of Austria as a comparably "weak" federation. The *Länder* exhibited little individuality or distinct political cultures. For a long time, they more or less mirrored the logic of the national development. Not for no reason, the fact that federal law was mostly replicated one-to-one by state legislators was sarcastically labelled "rank-xerox federalism."[66]

From the late 1970s, with the new doctrine of "relative autonomy" unfolding, *Länder* politics have undergone major changes. Particularly with regard to government creation rules and direct democracy, both considered important issues to tackle, the *Länder* (with varying commitment) have become proactive in adapting their constitutions. It must be noted that the Federal Constitution still sets limits to overarching ambitions.

64 Franz Fallend, "Austria: From Consensus to Competition and Participation?," in *Local and Regional Democracy in Europe*, ed. John Loughlin, Frank Hendriks and Anders Lidström (Oxford: Oxford University Press, 2011), 173-195, p. 181.

65 Ferdinand Karlhofer, "Bruch, Kontinuität und neue Dynamik: Der Tiroler Landtag 2008-2013," in *Politik in Tirol: Jahrbuch 2013* (Vienna: StudienVerlag, 2013), 11-28, p. 17.

66 Theo Öhlinger, *Verfassungsrecht* (Vienna: Facultas, 8th ed. 2009), 52.

Notwithstanding, despite restrictions due to the *Homogenitätsprinzip*, one can agree with Tarr stating with reference to Germany and Austria that, although their constitutions "have limited constitutional experimentation in the *Länder*, they have not foreclosed it," such as generally the system of cooperative federalism "does not necessarily preclude significant use of sub-national constitutional space."[67] Taken as a whole, recent experience has shown that sub-national self-reliance has gained steam, and frequently changes in one *Land* serve as a model for others.

All things considered, sub-national as well as national adaptation to a changing environment is inherently a step-by-step process. Therefore, with good reason, the dynamics should not be overestimated.[68] Anyway, right at the substate level there is some potential of change: In course of the recalibration of the party systems at *Länder* level, coming along with the decline of the formerly predominant catch-all parties SPÖ and ÖVP, the "partyness" of federalism is withering. Heretofore, the stability of Austria's cooperative federalism has been seen in close connection with government congruence at national and sub-national level.[69] Long-term studies, though, suggest qualifying the assessment since congruence is no longer "a function of government formation at the national level."[70] As of early 2015, in six of the nine *Länder* governments there are coalitions formed between SPÖ resp. ÖVP and the Green Party—the latter not really prone to the logic of *Proporz* politics as has been characteristic for the Second Republic. The traditional pattern of government congruence has obviously already begun to disintegrate, thereby inextricably affecting top-down policy implementation and the premise of *Land* authorities being in the role of "agents" of the central government as identified by James Gardner.[71] Against this backdrop, change (albeit gradual) at sub-national level may eventually turn out to be more effective than the nationwide federal reform which has not really made progress in the past quarter-century. However, one should not overlook the fact that it is the same *Land* governors who,

67 Tarr, "Explaining Sub-national Constitutional Space," 1139.

68 Peter Bußjäger, "Between Europeanization, Unitarism and Autonomy: Remarks on the Current Situation of Federalism in Austria," in *Revista d'Estudis Autonomics i Federals*, n. 10 (2010): 11-39, p. 33, at <http://www10.gencat.cat/drep/binaris/_reaf10_Bussjager_tcm112-124464.pdf> (6 March 2015).

69 Nicole Bolleyer and Evelyn Bytzek, "Government Congruence and Intergovernmental Relations in Federal Systems," *Regional and Federal Studies* 19, no. 3 (2009): 371-397, p. 381.

70 Marcelo Jenny, "Austria: Regional Elections in the Shadow of National Politics," in *Regional and National Elections in Western Europe*, ed. Regis Dandoy and Arjan H. Schakel (Basingstoke: Palgrave Macmillan, 2013), 27-46, p. 44.

71 James A. Gardner, "In Search of Sub-National Constitutionalism," *European Constitutional Law Review* 4, no. 2 (2008): 325-343.

while reform-minded with regard to "domestic" politics, in their role of key players in Austria's real constitution apply the same skills when it comes to thwart initiatives aiming at changing the distribution of rights and duties between federation and states.[72]

72 Regarding the gridlock in federal reform see, among others: Fiedler, "Föderalismus als Gestaltungsprinzip"; Karlhofer and Pallaver, "Strength Through Weakness"; Steger, *Baustelle Bundesstaat*.

Topical Essays

From Habsburg to Communism to Democracy: Reflections on (Non-)Federalism in Central Europe

Anton Pelinka

This essay explains the lack of success federal concepts of state building have in Central Europe. One reason for this failure was the arrival at a consensus to provide the Habsburg Empire with a solid and consistent federal structure in 1867 and in the following years. The failure to construct the Habsburg Empire's successor states as solid federations is another experience we need to consider. The Holocaust and ethnic cleansing during and after World War II changed the multinational and multicultural character of Central European societies dramatically. It destroyed one decisive incentive for the federalization of states more than ever defined as nation states. The expiration of communist one-party systems after the end of the Cold War was also the end of two prominent communist case studies of federations—Yugoslavia imploded violently while the Czechoslovakian federation expired peacefully.

The Habsburg Legacy

The Austro-Hungarian "Dual Monarchy" established in 1867 was an asymmetric and unbalanced federation. The new constitution gave different nationalities different significance not as a result of their quantitative size but due to their traditional position in the Habsburg Monarchy. The Germans dominated the Austrian half—they comprised about one third of "Cisleithania," while the Magyars represented a little bit less than fifty percent of "Transleithania." Due to manipulations, especially in the Hungarian part of the empire, the other nationalities had very good reasons to feel discriminated against.

The Dual Monarchy's structural imbalance created an inherent political weakness. This was the main reason for the extraordinary belligerence demonstrated by the Austrian-Hungarian diplomatic and military authorities in their reactions to the assassination of Archduke Franz Ferdinand on 28 June 1914. When crucial decisions were made for war or peace during the decisive weeks of July 1914, the Austro-Hungarian government pushed for war—not out of strength but out of weakness.[1] The military and political factions argued for adopting an aggressive attitude towards Serbia, making war unavoidable; they acted out of political paralysis. The only possible reforms that could have strengthened the empire internally would have been one that rebuilt the strained system into a balanced federal union. However, such reforms were blocked by specific interests. In Cisleithania, the Pan-German parties prevented the Badeni reforms from being implemented, even though they had already been passed by the Austrian parliament. In Hungary, the overwhelming attitude of the Hungarian governing parties rested on not widening the electoral law to give the non-Magyar peoples a fair chance to participate in Hungarian politics. In both cases, then, the ethnic groups who considered themselves the core elites (Germans in Austria, Magyars in Hungary) blocked reforms which were designed to integrate the other ethnic groups into some type of federalized empire that all peoples could identify with.

In the end the Habsburg Monarchy was unable to transform the multinational empire into a consistent federal structure. All of its attempts to balance the ethnic power structure—like the *Ausgleich* with Hungary in 1867—were full of inconsistency and contradiction. The Habsburg Empire's decision to guarantee the Magyars specific rights it was unwilling and unable to guarantee the other (non-German) nationalities was the principal reason for its disruptive ethnic conflicts which overshadowed the last decades of the Dual Monarchy. Traditional (feudal) elites ruled the Hungarian half with an iron fist. They defined Hungary as a nation state, ruled by one nationality, tolerating the other nationalities. But these Hungarian elites in control of Transleithania did not permit the Croats and Slovaks, the Serbs and Romanians to see themselves as equal partners in a multinational state. The ruling elites considered the 1867 *Ausgleich* as a "reconciliation" of sorts between the Habsburg dynasty and Hungary. It was not an attempt to remake the Habsburg Empire—ruled until then by the dynasty in an absolutistic way—into a federation in which all the nationalities could claim their share of power.[2]

The elites and the dynasty constructed the Austrian half of the "Dual Monarchy" in a different way. They did not design it to be a nation state as Hungary saw itself. The constituent nationalities of Cisleithania were defined by their linguistic identity. The *Staatsgrundgesetz*—the constitution

1 Alexander Watson, *Ring of Steel: Germany and Austria-Hungary at War, 1914-1918* (London: Allen Lane, 2014), 14-20.

2 Paul Lendvai, *Die Ungarn: Ein Jahrtausend Sieger in Niederlagen* (Munich: C. Bertelsmann, 1999), 301-347.

of 1867—treated them as equals. Legally, no nationality could claim a dominant position in the Austrian half. When in 1907 parliament introduced universal male suffrage, conditions for transforming at least the Austrian half into a multinational federation seemed to be better than ever. But the social realities were quite different from the legal intent. The sometimes violent conflicts between the nationalities prevented not only such a federalization—it made governing as such more or less impossible. When the empire declared war in 1914, the Austrian parliament—the *Abgeordnetenhaus des Reichsrates*, elected in 1911—was not in session. Consequently, Emperor Francis Joseph and the imperial government ruled by emergency decree.

The Dual Monarchy might be seen as an unbalanced, asymmetric federation.[3] The two highly autonomous halves of the Dual Monarchy enjoyed only three common competencies—foreign policy, defense, and finance; in 1878, the administration of the newly occupied Bosnia-Herzegovina was added as the fourth task, and the two halves of the monarchy administered it jointly. The empire was governed by a body not responsible to any parliament—no Austrian-Hungarian parliament existed. The central decisions were made by executives, accountable to the emperor only, and representatives of the governments, accountable to two different parliaments, elected by different electoral systems and based on different national philosophies—the Hungarian nation state and the (incipient yet unfinished) transnational Austria.

At the end, the Hungarian nation state had to pay the price for its insistence on national dominance. Hungary as defined by the Treaty of Trianon lost most of its territory with ethnically mixed populations (such as Slovakia, Transylvania, and Croatia). These massive territorial losses in 1919 are still the reason for an ongoing national narrative of Hungary as victim. The Austria half of the old Dual Monarchy lost even more of its territories—to Poland and Czechoslovakia, Italy and Yugoslavia. German-Austria's efforts to define "the rest" as part of Germany were blocked by the peacemakers in St. Germain, creating another national narrative—the "Anschluss."

The Revisionist Legacy

The postwar order established by the peacemakers in Paris proved to be of remarkable instability. The victorious powers only respected their guiding

3 For the concept of asymmetric federalism, see Mikhail Filippov, Peter C. Ordeshook and Olga Shvetsova, *Designing Federalism: A Theory of Self-Sustainable Federal Institutions* (Cambridge: Cambridge University Press, 2004), 138-140.

principle of "self-determination" if it did not contradict their basic security interests.[4] The legacy of the Paris peace arrangements was an inbuilt geo-strategic conflict between powers who considered themselves victims and tried from the very beginning to undermine the Paris peace order and powers who were strongly motivated to defend the newly constructed status quo. This conflict between "revisionists" and "anti-revisionists" dominated European politics, especially the Central European arena, during the entire interwar period.

President Wilson's principle of self-determination was used to free the destructive forces of exclusive nationalism from its box. Ethnic nationalism seemed to be justified by defining "the people" (the *demos*) in a way which made it impossible to think of any transnational, federal structure. In Transylvania, the former Magyar overlords saw themselves dominated by Romanians as the new overlords. In Yugoslavia, the attempt to define the State of the Serbs, Croats, and Slovenians did not succeed—the nationalistic Croats perceived the Yugoslav kingdom as Greater Serbia. In Czechoslovakia, the majority of ethnic Germans and ethnic Hungarians rejected the liberal democratic structure. Moreover, the new state refused to implement the concept of a Czechoslovak federation, thus generating increasing Slovak resentment.

During the interwar era, Czechoslovakia served in many respects as the beacon of liberal democracy in Central Europe. Prague failed to bring the different nationalities to identify with their state. It was constitutionally based on an agreement between Czech and Slovak elites, but in actuality, significant parts of the Slovak population considered it to be a state dominated by Czech interests. Thus Czechoslovakia, more than any other of the new states of Central Europe, exemplified the failure of the Paris peace treaties, since Czechoslovakia did not fall into the trap of authoritarian rule, yet did not succeed as a state either.[5] Sound arguments can be made, of course, that a federal Czechoslovakia would only have strengthened German and Hungarian secessionism. But in the end, it happened to be such nationalistic secessionism that destroyed Masaryk's republic.

The fateful legacy of such ethnic nationalism unleashed in the region after 1918 was the tendency to refuse to assimilate—and in the end to expel and even murder—those considered to be not like "us." In the aftermath of the Greco-Turkish War (1919-22), following the breakup of the Ottoman Empire, ethnic cleansing was organized in a comparatively consensual

4 For the inherent structural deficits, see Margaret MacMillan, *Paris 1919: Six Months That Changed the World* (New York: Random House, 2003).

5 Mary Heimann, *Czechoslovakia: The State That Failed* (New Haven: Yale University Press, 2009), 48-86.

way. In a very different and murderous form, it soon became the dominant mode of dealing with ethnic diversity all over Central Europe. The creation of ethnic homogeneity by force was the purported intent. The case of Salonica in Northern Greece, which had been a model multicultural and multinational city over many centuries, shows us how history was rewritten. Once the Turks were expelled after World War I and the Jews were deported and murdered under the brutal German occupation in 1943/44, Salonica became an ethnically uniform Greek city.[6]

The case of Poland, more than any other Habsburg succession state, demonstrates the horrors of ethnic nationalism. After World War I, the Entente powers reestablished Poland out of the former Russian, German, and Austrian parts acquired during the Polish partitions in the late 18th century. During the interwar period, Poland was supposed to function as a multiethnic state but was defined as a nation state. As a result the non-Polish ethnic minorities—especially Germans, Ukrainians, White Russians, Lithuanians, and Jews—viewed themselves as second-class citizens.[7]

Nazi Germany cynically used Poland's multiethnic character and its national conflicts to justify its aggression in September 1939. Nazi Germany's even more cynical partnership with Soviet Russia ("the Hitler-Stalin Pact") led to the complete dissolution of Poland in 1939. Nazi-Germany's invasion and occupation of the Eastern parts of Poland controlled by the Soviets between 1939 and 1941, created fierce underground resistance movements by both Polish partisans (and regular military units) and Ukrainian national partisans. Both these guerilla movements fought the Nazis and each other and were in constant conflict with partisans loyal to the USSR. All these factions had to defend themselves against fierce anti-partisan German armed forces in this multi-polar conflict. Historian Timothy Snyder has characterized this multifront conflict as the defining character of what he calls the Central-East European "bloodlands."[8]

These "bloodlands" were also the region where Nazi Germany—with some collaboration by non-German segments of the local populations—implemented the bulk of the Holocaust. These "bloodlands" were the region where the Nazi-German policy of Germanization became responsible for systematic ethnic cleansing, affecting all ethnic non-German groups. These "bloodlands" were also the region where postwar Soviet policy created both ethnically "pure" Belorussia and Ukraine, following the expulsion of

6 Mark Mazower, *Salonica: City of the Ghosts, Christians, Muslims and Jews 1430-1950* (London: Harper Perennial, 2004), 332-355 and 421-442.

7 Adam Zamoyski, *Poland: A History* (London: Harper Press, 2009), 303-310.

8 Timothy Snyder, *Bloodlands: Europe between Hitler and Stalin* (New York: Basic Books, 2010).

millions of ethnic Poles and ethnic Germans once postwar Poland had been shifted to the West with its new borders established at Yalta and Potsdam.[9]

As a result of these massive and violent population transfers at the end of World War II, Poland became an almost entirely ethnically homogenous nation state. The Jews had been murdered during the war by the Nazi-German occupation. The Red Army, in cooperation with the newly established Polish communist regime ("Lublin Poles") forced through the unique policy of moving the entire country westward. According to the provisions of the 1939 Hitler-Stalin agreement, Eastern Poland became part of the Soviet Union. Moscow quickly integrated this Polish territory into the Lithuanian, the Belorussian, and the Ukrainian Soviet Republics. Millions of ethnic Poles were forced to leave these territories and resettled in formerly German Silesia, Pomerania, and Prussia in the West. In turn, millions of ethnic Germans were expelled from their farms and property in these territories. The final result of such brutal ethnic cleansing was a homogenous Polish state free of significant ethnic minorities.[10]

It may be seen as particularly ironic that a regime which claimed to have overcome nationalism built statehood on the understanding of an ethno-nationalistic monopoly. The "fires of hatred" which defined such murderous ethnic cleansing in 1945, were instrumentalized by a system which by its own official understanding was "post-national." De facto, then, Marxism-Leninism played the nationalistic card in the most murderous way.[11]

After World War I, the creation of new states in post-Habsburg Central Europe did not result in systematic ethnic cleansing, yet. Germans and Hungarians—defined by their language—established new states in East-Central Europe. Ordinary Germans and Hungarians did not yet leave Czechoslovakia, Yugoslavia, Romania, and Poland *en masse*. Most of the German and Hungarian speaking population stayed in their traditional homesteads and thus became the focus of revisionists' claims during the period between the two World Wars. Only the bureaucratic class in the police and armed forces left after 1919. Only at the end of World War II did these minorities—now seen as potential instruments of future revisionism—became the victims of systematic and violent expulsion.

Sociologist Rogers Brubaker has used the Central-, Eastern-, and South-Eastern regions of Europe as his prime examples for what he

9 Ibid., 313-338.

10 R. M. Douglas, *Orderly and Humane: The Expulsion of the Germans after the Second World War* (New Haven: Yale University Press, 2012); Keith Lowe, Savage Continent: Europe in the Aftermath of World War II (New York: St. Martin's Press, 2012), 187-270.

11 Norman M. Naimark, *Fires of Hatred: Ethnic Cleansing in the Twentieth-Century Europe* (Cambridge, MA: Harvard University Press, 2002).

terms the "un-mixing of people." As an indirect consequence of an ethnic interpretation of the catchphrase "self-determination," people were either being classified by their perceived national identity or classified themselves in such a way. After World War II people were forced to migrate or decided to flee to guarantee national "purity" and to prevent any challenges to the supremacy of a state's defining nation.[12]

The Turkish-Greek "population exchange" in the 1920s turned out to be the least catastrophic case of systematic ethnic cleansing. As a result of the Balkan Wars (1912-13), World War I (1914-18), and the Greco-Turkish War (1919-22) about one million ethnic Greeks were moved from the newly established Turkish Republic to Greece; almost the same number of ethnic Turks moved from Greece to Turkey. This process, however, was negotiated and controlled by the two governments with the cooperation of some segments of the affected populations. At the time such a population "exchange" was seen as a model for a peacefully negotiated and implemented modus of undoing ethnic complexity in a region. In reality, however, this did not become a model for population exchanges in the World War II era in Europe, which was characterized by ethnic cleansing and mass murder. The Greco-Turkish population exchange was seen at the time as a model of a consensual form of "ethnic cleansing"—the number of victims was comparatively small. After the massive ethnic cleansing of millions of people during World War II, in 1947, when British India was partitioned along religious lines, millions of Muslims left India for what became Pakistan, while millions of Hindus and Sikhs left Pakistan for India. Because population transfers were agreed on in principle by the two governments concerned, the mass migration in both directions got completely out of control. An unanticipated explosion of mass violence created an atmosphere in which more than one million of people were murdered. In India after the war, like in Europe during the war, the very idea of creating ethnic homogeneity and/or religious "purity," produced mass murder.

The history of Central Europe in the first half of the 20th century was dominated by an inability to accept ethnic, cultural, and religious diversity. States in Central Europe saw ethnic minorities as an unwelcome burden they had to get rid of in the interest of national homogeneity. It is a cautionary tale that demonstrates how the unwillingness to create federal structures to balance diversity and to integrate the different forms of national identity characterized this period—with catastrophic results.

12 Rogers Brubaker, *Nationalism Reframed: Nationhood and the National Question in the New Europe* (Cambridge: Cambridge University Press, 1996), 148-179.

The Post-Communist Legacy

During the communist era, the Red Army liberated and occupied Central Europe (with the exception of Austria); those countries were ruled by a Soviet-style one party system. As long as the absolute monopoly of power by the Marxist-Leninist unity party was guaranteed, aspects of centralized or decentralized forms of government came secondary. The Soviet Union demonstrated how a communist system allowed for the federalization of the state—as long as it concerned cultural but not political diversity.

Under the auspices of direct control by the Soviet Union, after the Warsaw pact military invasion of Czechoslovakia in August 1968, the country was transformed into a federal republic, balancing the Czech lands and Slovakia. Without interference from the Soviet Union, postwar Yugoslavia was reconstructed as a complex system of six republics and two autonomous regions—here was another case of communist federalism.

The three European federal systems established (or reestablished) within the framework of Marxist-Leninist communism did not survive the transformation of 1989-91. By the end of 1991 the Soviet Union, on the one hand, imploded (more or less peacefully) and the fifteen constituent republics of the Soviet Union declared their independence (more or less voluntarily). In a curious way, by allowing all republics the right to secede, this process lived up to the promise of the Soviet constitution.

Yugoslavia, on the other hand, imploded in an extremely violent form. The series of wars between Yugoslavia's different successor states lasted from 1991 to 1999. Democratic transformation signaled the end of the Yugoslav federation. Competitive elections were organized only on the level of the individual republics. The Yugoslav federation, still based on communism à la Tito, in the end was confronted by democratically legitimated republics. This internal conflict spelled the end of the federation.

Czechoslovakia happened to be the only communist federation with democratic roots in its pre-communist history. Czechoslovakia opted to end its federal structure on 1 January 1993 by "peaceful separation." The Czech lands and Slovakia negotiated a peaceful end to their republic, based on the liberal democratic understanding of Czechoslovakia's interwar period ("First Republic"), as well as on the communist inspired constitutional reforms based on the years of "normalization" after the Soviet occupation in 1968.

The only communist country successfully transformed into a democratic federal structure was the German Democratic Republic (GDR). The GDR happened to be a highly centralized state. Its federalized constitution served as a first step towards unification with the Federal Republic of Germany. As the next step, West Germany allowed the newly established East German states to join the (West) German federation.[13] The Cold War communist systems were brought down mostly by negotiated, peaceful transformations. Romania with its violent transformation during Christmas 1989 was the remarkable exception. Yugoslavia was a special case. There the civil war was the consequence of an already successfully implemented transformation on the level of the constituent republics. The peaceful transformation in Eastern Europe was first and foremost the result of a transformation attempt at the center of the communist world in Moscow. Mikhael Gorbachev's bold decision not to intervene in the affairs of the Soviet satellite countries robbed the Central European communist systems of their decisive pillar of regime stability, namely Soviet military power. The chain of events ending communist rule in Europe in 1989 was dramatic. The term "revolution" is fitting for this change.[14]

Yet these revolutions did not lead to the rise of post-communist federalism. On the contrary, while in the second half of the 20th century Western Europe experienced a wave of federalization, the equivalent did not occur in post-communist Central Europe. The rules of democracy had changed in Western Europe. Belgium was reborn after World War II as a highly decentralized state; post-Franco democratic Spain guaranteed Catalonia and the Basque Country high decrees of autonomy; British "devolution" gave the United Kingdom an almost completely new face. Instead of "devolving" power to the Slovakia as it had done after 1968, Czechoslovakia preferred to break up.

Instead of federalization, we are witnessing the fateful rebirth of the same national narratives that dominated the region during the interwar period. Why should Romania and Slovakia risk Hungarian revisionism by giving their Hungarian minorities specific political rights going beyond bilingual street signs in some municipalities? Beginning in 1938 the region experienced events, driven or at least encouraged by expansionist Nazi Germany, that (ab)used the very existence of minorities as an instrument to restructure the political landscape against the interests of the geopolitical design guiding the peacemakers in Paris in 1919. With the prominent exception of Poland, the Central Europe designed and established in Yalta and Potsdam mirrored the design of the peacemakers of Paris, some decades earlier.

13 Philip D. Zelikow and Condoleezza Rice, *Germany Unified and Europe Transformed: A Study on Statecraft* (Cambridge, MA: Harvard University Press, 1995).
14 Victor Sebestyen, *Revolution 1989: The Fall of the Soviet Empire* (New York: Pantheon Books, 2010), esp. 309f.

The post-communist states in Central Europe saw no reason for risking new kinds of revisionism, especially when remembering that the ethnic cleansing of 1945 had already taken care of much of the region's former diversity. In Central Europe, of course, the outlook of Hungary—the self-perceived perennial victim—is still different from the perspective if its neighbors. Creating autonomous regions in Romania and Slovakia may be seen as an advantage for the Magyar speaking minorities outside Hungary—but is still a potential threat for Hungary's neighbors.

Conclusion

The inability of the Dual Monarchy to create lasting federal institutions that might have given equal rights and satisfied the various nationalities in both the Austrian and Hungarian halves of the Habsburg Monarchy left a legacy of ethnic tensions in the post-Habsburg multiethnic succession states. Woodrow Wilson's principle of "self-determination" was a slippery concept the peacemakers in Paris only applied selectively in the post-Habsburg succession states in East-Central Europe. The growing ethnic tensions in the new Central European states were one cause to invite Nazi Germany into the region to "liberate" what the Nazis perceived to be suppressed German minorities. The Nazi policies of "ethnic cleansing" of Jews (and Slavs), in turn, produced ethnic cleansing of German ethnics on a massive scale by the Soviets and Poles (and Czechs/Slovaks and Hungarians) after the war. The final outcome of these successive waves of ethnic cleansing was the homogenization of the post-World War II Soviet satellite states in Eastern Europe. Of course, one cannot blame the German and Hungarian elites of the Dual Monarchy for subsequent ethnic cleansing in the region, but one can blame them for not working hard enough in building equitable federal structures that would have pacified the struggle between the nationalities in the multi-ethnic East-Central Europe. We have to admit, in an age of hyper-nationalism such equity between nationalities was hard to conceive of and build.

Austria's Cooperative Federalism

Peter Bußjäger

Introduction

Austria's federal system is commonly described as highly centralized with a dominant role played by the federation and restricted fields of legislative competences exercised by the *Länder*. Moreover, participation of the *Länder* in federal lawmaking is—officially—weak because the second parliamentary chamber, the Federal Council, has limited competences.

This description, which refers to the legal basis of the federal constitution, seems to be in contradiction with the prominent role of certain instruments of informal cooperation within the Austrian federation, specifically the Conference of *Land* Governors. Obviously, there is a gap between the provisions of the federal constitution and political reality. In fact, cooperative federalism, with its long tradition, shapes the practical operation of the Austrian federal system, acting as a counterweight to centralizing forces.[1] How this system works will be described as follows.

General Overview on Austria's Federal System

Historical Remarks

During the foundation of the new republic from 1918 to 1920, the *Länder* played an important role in building up administrative and political institutions at the *Land* level. In the so-called *Länderkonferenzen* (conferences of state government) held in 1919 between the *Länder* and the new central government in Vienna, it was agreed that the new republic should be constructed as a federation.

1 For further dimensions of Austrian federalism, especially with regard to intergovernmental relations, see Anna Gamper, "Republic of Austria," in *Legislative, Executive, and Judicial Governance in Federal Countries*, ed. Katy Le Roy and Cheryl Saunders (Montreal: McGill Queen's University Press, 2006), 71-100.

In 1945, after Austria's liberation from the Nazi regime, the *Länder* again exercised a prominent role in forming the new state. For the first few months following the Second World War, the first provisional government, led by Chancellor Karl Renner, was initially only recognized by the Soviets and not by the other occupying forces (i.e., the United States of America, France, and Great Britain). The government of Chancellor Renner acted on the basis of a "provisional constitution," which treated Austria as a unitary state. In September 1945, following further *Land* conferences, the *Länder* in those parts of Austria occupied by the Western Allies accepted the government of Renner but only after his government promised to re-establish Austria as a federation. The acceptance of the government of Renner by the *Länder* beyond the Soviet-occupied zone was a precondition for the recognition of the government by the other Allied powers.

Today, in discussions on Austrian federalism, political representatives of the *Länder* sometimes refer to the 1919 and 1945 conferences to emphasise that the republic was established twice "by the *Länder*" (although more precisely, one should say that the republic was established in both cases with strong involvement of the *Länder*).

General Features of the Federal System

The Austrian Federal Constitution (*Bundesverfassungs-Gesetz*, B-VG) of 1920—mainly drafted by the legal scholar Hans Kelsen—is based on a number of structural principles ("*Baugesetze*"). Art. 1 stipulates that Austria is a democratic republic (democratic and republican principle). Another of these basic principles is the federal principle in Art. 2 B-VG (the others being the rule of law, including the separation of powers, and the liberal principle, meaning respect for fundamental rights).

According to Art. 44 par 3 B-VG, the deletion of one of these principles or its serious violation would qualify as a total revision of the Federal Constitution. This would require a two-thirds majority in the National Council as well as approval by the citizens in an obligatory referendum. Moreover, in the case of the federal principle, this would also require the consent of the second federal chamber, the Federal Council, by a two-third majority. The only total revision of the Austrian Federal Constitution since 1945 occurred in 1994, with the treaty of Austria's accession to the European Union (EU).

The legislative branch is composed of the National Council and the Federal Council. The latter represents the *Länder* in the federal legislative branch, but is nevertheless an institution of the federation. The parliamentary bodies of the *Länder*—called *Landtage*—are unicameral.[2] The Federal Council is composed of deputies elected by the *Landtage* for their respective election period. Although there seems to be a strong linkage to *Land* politics, in practice, the members of the Federal Council usually vote along party lines. In other words, they consider themselves more as members of their party than as representatives of their respective *Länder*.

Municipalities play an important role in the constitutional system. There are about 2.100 municipalities, most of them with less than 10.000 inhabitants.[3] According to Article 118 B-VG, municipalities are autonomous in all matters of exclusive or predominant local interest, and which are suited for management by the community within its local borders. This is the case, for example, of the local public security police, the administration of municipal traffic areas, and the local traffic police. Overall, there are three orders of government. Some scholars speak of a "three-level-federalism."[4]

Distribution of Competences

By international comparison, Austria is a highly centralized federation.[5] On the one hand, Art. 10, 11, 12, 14, 14a and 14b B-VG explicitly list the competences of the federal order of government. On the other hand, Art. 15 par 1 B-VG provides that "in so far as a matter is not expressly delegated by the Federal Constitution to the legislation or also the execution of the Federation, it remains within the autonomous sphere of competence of the *Länder*."[6] In practice, these residual competences are rather limited because the enumerated list of federal matters is very long and detailed.

Public administration by the *Länder* acts both for the *Land* and for the execution of most federal laws. The *Land* governors are responsible to the federal government for the execution of federal laws in this so-called

2 Art. 95 B-VG.

3 Through some decades, the number of the Austrian municipalities ranged around 2.350. With the beginning of 2015, with the enforcement of the municipal reform in Styria, the number of the Styrian municipalities was reduced from 542 to 288.

4 Peter Bußjäger, "Local Government Cooperation in Austria: Options and Benefits for the Communities," in *Crossing the Line: Dealing with Cross-Border Communities*, ed. Bertus de Villiers (Johannesburg: Konrad-Adenauer-Stiftung, 2009), 81-91.

5 Cf. from a comparative perspective Daniel Halberstam and Mathias Reimann, "Federalism and Legal Unification: Comparing Methods, Results, and Explanations Across 20 Systems," in *Federalism and Legal Unification*, ed. idem (Dordrecht: Springer, 2014), 32-34; Ferdinand Karlhofer and Günther Pallaver, "Strength through Weakness: State Executive Power and Federal Reform in Austria," *Swiss Political Science Review* 19, no. 1 (2013): 41-59.

6 Federal Chancellery of the Republic of Austria, at <http://www.bundeskanzleramt.at/DocView.axd?CobId=3462> (21 April 2009).

"indirect federal administration,"[7] which affects a number of important matters such as water management, forestry, and industries. This system of indirect administration gives the *Länder* some influence over the implementation of federal laws and programs, and works as a compensation for the centralized division of competences. However, several important matters such as finances, public security, and the courts are directly administered by the federal government.[8]

Moreover, there are the *Land* governments, which carry out *Land* administration (with regard, for example, to social aid, building law, and town and country planning) as well as a few federal matters (such as environmental assessment).

There are thus four essential types of competences:[9]

– **Exclusive federal competences, both in legislation and administration** (Art. 10 B-VG). This covers more than 100 different areas, including foreign policy, all courts, civil and criminal law, labour law, laws relating to freedom of association and assembly, banking, industry, national road and rail transport, mining, forests, water supply, most matters related to the protection of the environment, health, social security, unemployment, education services (except for primary, professional, and some parts of agricultural training), high schools and universities, national economy and fiscal policy, radio and television, weapons, food, unfair competition, public security, all police forces, and armed forces;

– **Federal legislation, but with administration by the *Länder*** (Art. 11 B-VG), e.g., nationality, traffic regulation on roads, non-border rivers and lakes, subsidized housing, town planning, environmental assessment, and animal welfare);

– **Federal legislation for general principles, with the *Länder* being responsible for more detailed legislation and administration** (Art. 12 B-VG). These include basic social assistance, hospitals, land reform, electricity, school buildings, and the maintenance of

7 Art. 102 B-VG.

8 Art. 102 par. 2 B-VG.

9 Anna Gamper and Bernhard A. Koch, "Federalism and Legal Unification in Austria," in *Federalism and Legal Unification*, ed. Daniel Halberstam and Mathias Reimann (Dordrecht: Springer, 2014), 104-110; Peter Pernthaler, "Austrian Federalism," in *Federalism and Decentralization*, ed. Jürgen Rose and Johannes Ch. Traut (Münster: Lit Verlag, 2001), 130-132.

schools (except for high schools and universities). In the absence of relevant principles in federal legislation, *Länder* are free to legislate.

– **Exclusive competences of the *Länder* both with regard to legislation and administration** (Art. 15 B-VG). These include all matters that are not expressly delegated to the federation in legislation and/or administration. They comprise some aspects of environmental protection, construction law, town and country planning, hunting, fishing, some aspects of agriculture, areas of youth and child welfare, nursery schools, sports, tourism, local government, local police, laws on land transfers, acquisition of real estate, and the preservation of landscape and natural heritage.

The allocation of legislative competences is done on an exclusive basis, which means that either the federation or the *Länder* have the competence to regulate the different subject matters.

In addition to their formal competences described above, the *Länder* may act pursuant to private law in areas that are within the sphere of competence of the federal authority. For instance, they may finance any projects within the realm of the federation or the *Länder*. They can also use legal institutions such as companies, private law, or non-governmental administrations, without being restricted to their exclusive competences. This constitutional rule (Art. 17 B-VG) serves as a kind of "safety-valve" against the strong centralization of competences. It is very significant in terms of the *Länder's* political autonomy. For example the *Länder* may also establish and fund academic institutions even if they are not entitled to legislate with regard to education and science. Some important public services, for example public traffic, are funded by the federation and the *Länder* (on ground of Art. 17 B-VG) and the municipalities (on ground of Art. 116 par 2 B-VG, which allows municipalities to act as subjects of civil law).

Overview on Intergovernmental Relations in Austria

General Remarks

In general, Austrian federalism is characterised by a high degree of entanglement between the *Länder* and the federal order, as well as by a certain subordination of the *Länder* towards the federation. Several factors explain this fact: One is the complexity of the division of competences.

Another is the role played by the Federal Council. A third is the fact that *Land* governors are responsible for executing federal legislation. Finally, cooperation and hierarchical relations also derive from party politics because Austria's party system is rather integrated across jurisdictional lines, and party politics at the federal level may influence politics at the *Land* level, and vice versa.

Various vertical and horizontal cooperative instruments were introduced in the second half of the last century; in the given context, two of them must be mentioned.

The principal one is the Conference of *Land* Governors. It emerged in the late 1950s and early 1960s when centralizing tendencies strengthened the dominance of the federation and increasingly endangered the position of the *Länder* as entities of the federation. This horizontal mode of cooperation works as a relatively efficient counterbalance to the weight of the federal order of government. Indeed, despite a continuous process of centralization of legislative powers, the Conference of the *Land* Governors has developed into an important platform for the *Länder*, especially in the field of financial equalization and in negotiations concerning cost-sharing for the execution of federal law by the *Länder* and municipalities. For example in 2013, the Conference was very influential regarding the elaboration of new rules regulating speculative operations with public funds. The *Land* governors adopted rules in a cooperative way, thus successfully managing to set aside a planned uniform federal law.[10]

Other interesting multilateral models of "federalism by negotiation" have emerged as well. This is the case, for instance, of the so-called "consultation mechanism," a formal agreement based on Art. 15a B-VG. This was set into force 1999 between the federation, the *Länder*, and—on the basis of a specific constitutional law, which delegated these institutions to sign the agreement—the associations of cities and municipalities. It obliges the federal government and the *Länder* to consult each other and the municipalities if a draft law or a regulation of one entity imposes financial burdens on the other orders of government. A number of ground rules structure these consultations. If the tripartite negotiations do not lead to unanimous solutions or if the law-making entity does not follow the recommendation of the consultation committee, that legislative body will bear any additional costs incurred by others.

Officially, the Constitutional Court is competent to resolve disputes concerning this mechanism, although until recently, the Court had never

10 See 38. *Bericht über den Föderalismus in Österreich 2013*, ed. Institut für Föderalismus (Vienna: new academic press, 2014).

been called upon, as all disputes had been politically resolved. In 2014, however, the Court denounced a violation of the consultation mechanism by the federal government regarding costs for railway crossings for Austrian municipalities.[11] On the one hand, this consultation mechanism protects the *Länder* and the municipalities from federal laws that would have a financial impact on them. On the other hand, the *Länder* themselves run the risk of bearing additional costs if they enact laws against the will of others.

Mutual Participation of *Länder* and Federation on Law-Making

A number of constitutional provisions ensure *Länder* participation in the elaboration of federal legislation, either through the Federal Council or by direct involvement of *Land* governments in the federal legislative process.

The members of the Federal Council are elected by the *Landtage* (the *Länder*'s legislative assemblies) for the duration of the respective *Landtag* electoral period. These "representatives" are not bound by directives of the *Land* governments or the *Landtage*, by contrast to the *Bundesrat* in Germany, for instance. The tasks of the Federal Council are listed as follows:[12]

– Art. 42 par 2 B-VG provides a suspensive veto on all ordinary federal law, with some exceptions (such as federal financial laws or the National Council's Standing Orders which do not require any participation of the Federal Council). The National Council may overrule such a veto by readopting its original resolution;

– it has an absolute veto on all modifications in the constitutional allocation of the *Länder*'s legislative or executive competences (Art. 44 par 2 B-VG);

– it must approve international treaties concluded by the federation, which affect the sphere of competences of the *Länder* (Art. 50 par 1 B-VG).

Furthermore, the Federal Council delegates some of its members to a parliamentary committee that can make a final ruling on objections raised by the federal government against *Land* legislation concerning *Land*

11 Judgment of the Constitutional Court from 12 March 2014, F 1/2013-20.

12 See Anna Gamper, "The Austrian Bundesrat," in *A World of Second Chambers*, ed. Jörg Luther, Paolo Passaglia and Rolando Tarchi (Milan: Giuffrè Editore, 2006), 781-828.

or municipal taxes. Half of its twenty-six members are delegated by the National Council and half come from the Federal Council (§ 9 Financial Constitution, F-VG).[13]

In certain matters, the Federal Constitution provides for specific modes of interaction between the federation and the *Länder* in the context of lawmaking. Hence, the *Länder* (represented by the *Land* governors) have the right to examine the drafts of laws and regulations in the fields of public procurement of the federation and participate in preparing these drafts (Art. 14b par 4 B-VG). These laws also need the approval of the *Land* governments. In a mirror fashion, the federation must approve some Länder laws, especially those that alter the organization of the *Land* administration (Art. 15 par 10 B-VG). So far, there has been no refusal of consent by any *Land*, possibly as a result of cooperation during the preparation of these laws.

Another cooperative technique concerns *Land* laws that provide for the cooperation of federal authorities for their execution (Art. 97 par 2 B-VG). Such *Land* legislation must be approved by the federal government. This is the case, for instance, when laws of the *Länder* provide that the police, who are under exclusive federal authority, must support *Land* authorities in executing federal laws. In the past, the federal government has refused to give consent according to Art. 97 par 2 B-VG only in few cases.[14]

On the other hand, there is the *Berücksichtigungsprinzip* (principle of mutual consideration), which is not explicitly provided for in the Federal Constitution, but was developed by the Constitutional Court.[15] It is a similar instrument to the general principle of *Bundestreue* in Germany, which implies that in exercising their authority, the *Länder* as well as the federation are bound to respect each other's interests, even if this term is not used in Austria. The Austrian principle of mutual consideration is binding on both the federation and the *Länder* and only means that the legislatures of the federation and the *Länder* must not undermine each other. However, in most cases in which it has relied on the principle, the Constitutional Court has ruled in favour of the federal order. An example lies with the so-called "Semmering decision," which concerns a project to build a new railway tunnel connecting the *Länder* of Lower Austria and Styria under the Semmering mountain. The Court annulled Lower Austria's legislation on the protection of nature on the ground that it contradicted the principle

13 In German: *Finanz-Verfassungsgesetz* (F-VG).

14 See for example *38. Bericht über den Föderalismus*, ed. Institut für Föderalismus, 59.

15 Constitutional Court, VfSlg. 8831/1980, 10.292/1984, 14.403/1996, 15.281/1998, 15.552/1999, 16.452/2002, etc.

of mutual recognition because it failed to recognize the public interest of the country as a whole.[16]

According to the Federal Constitution, there are no formal institutions of cooperation between parliamentarians of the different *Länder* or between the federation and the *Länder*. However, informal cooperation takes place through the parties of the National Council, the Federal Council, and the *Landtage*. For instance, members of the various parties in the Federal Council participate in meetings of their respective party in the National Council or in working groups or committees of the National Council dealing with intergovernmental aspects, such as administrative reform.

Horizontal and Vertical Cooperation

As mentioned previously, the Federal Council does not work as an organ of the nine different *Länder*. It has a weak legal status and deputies consider themselves members of the national parliament rather than representatives of the *Länder* and depend on federal party organizations for their career. As a result, the Conference of the *Land* Governors fosters horizontal cooperation between all *Länder*.[17] This cooperation is informal, voluntary, and consensus-based.[18] The *Land* governors meet at least every six months. The Liaison Office of the Austrian *Länder*[19] works as office of the Conference and the chair rotates between the nine *Länder*. The Conference of the *Land* Governors adopts resolutions and passes recommendations to the federal government on any federal matters which are of interest to the *Länder* and also on issues of horizontal coordination between the *Länder*. Resolutions are prepared by the Conference of the Directors of the Offices of the *Land* Governments, who heads the administration in the respective *Länder* at the technical level.

The lack of a formal legal status has no impact on the efficiency and output of the institution. According to constitutional law doctrine, informal institutions follow the principle of unanimity.[20] Hence, decisions of the Conference of *Land* Governors are made unanimously. This principle is set out in the internal "Rules of Procedure of the Liaison Office of the

16 Constitutional Court, VfSlg. 15.552/1999.

17 See Ferdinand Karlhofer, "Gestaltungskraft und Vetomacht: Funktion und Praxis der Landeshauptleutekonferenz," in *Im Dienste der Länder–im Interesse des Gesamtstaates: Festschrift 60 Jahre Verbindungsstelle der Bundesländer*, ed. Andreas Rosner and Peter Bußjäger (Vienna: Braumüller, 2011), 311-326.

18 Andreas Rosner, *Koordinationsinstrumente der österreichischen Länder* (Vienna: Braumüller, 1999), 176.

19 Ibid., 15-34.

20 Ibid., 29.

Austrian *Länder*," which are not published in any official gazette. In theory, the unanimity requirement should be an obstacle to common action or positions, but in practice, decisions are rarely blocked by vetoes.

In fact, this decision-making rule is an efficient means of cooperation, because no member is forced to accept resolutions it finds objectionable. Furthermore, it strengthens decisions taken by *Länder* because it does not create two categories of decisions: those taken unanimously and others. Party politics does not seem to take precedence over the interests of the *Länder*, as they do in the Federal Council, where members tend to be seen as part of their respective party in the National Council.

The resolutions of the conference are submitted by the Liaison Office of the Austrian *Länder* to the federal government. The follow-up-procedure is usually very informal and depends on the political importance of the matter. Issues are often discussed within informal working groups, composed by members of the staff of the respective federal ministries and the *Land* governments before a bill is transferred to parliament.

Usually, the *Land* governors exert greater influence when matters are discussed at the governmental level, rather than in the parliamentary arena, which also illustrates the importance of "executive type" intergovernmental relations in Austria. Sometimes members of the federal government participate in the Conference if certain important matters falling into their sphere of competences are discussed. This happened, for example, in the recent discussions about the distribution of asylum seekers in Austria, a matter which turned out be an enormous challenge for cooperative federalism in Austria and showed the limits of decision-making by negotiations across two levels of government.[21]

There is also horizontal coordination involving legislative institutions. At the political level, another important institution, the Conference of the Presidents of the *Landtage*, coordinates positions and comments concerning federal legislation with impact on the *Landtage*. Its positions and views are prepared by the Conference of the Directors of the *Landtage* (heads of the civil service).[22]

There are numerous other institutions and conferences and instruments of horizontal cooperation, in addition to the Conference of the *Land* Governors.[23] At the political level, there are conferences of *Land* ministers

---

21 See for example *34. Bericht über den Föderalismus in Österreich 2009*, ed. Institut für Föderalismus (Vienna: Braumüller, 2010), 55-58.

22 These courts are institutions of the *Länder*. They act as organs of parliamentary control, especially of budgetary allocations, which are voted by the various parliaments.

23 Andreas Rosner and Robert Gmeiner, "Die Länderkonferenzen als Instrumente der Selbstkoordination der Länder und des kooperativen Bundesstaates," in *Kooperativer Föderalismus in Österreich*, ed. Peter Bußjäger (Vienna: Braumüller, 2010), 49-64, p. 60.

according to portfolio (e.g., for finances and social matters). At the official level, there are conferences of the directors of the offices of the *Land* governments as well as experts' conferences of the *Länder* (which bring together experts in certain policy matters, such as environment protection).

All those institutions are purely informal. Hence, federal law stipulates that the Conference of the *Land* Governors is entitled to make a number of recommendations and nominations.[24] The Conference of the *Land* Governors is therefore indirectly recognized by federal law as an institution representing the interests of the *Länder*. For example, the Conference of the *Land* Governors delegates one or two members to a number of institutions, such as the National Statistics Conference, the National Debt Committee, the National Security Council, the Committee for National Integration and Foreign Policy, the Environment Council, and the Development Cooperation Committee.

Through such participation, the *Länder* are able to share their views on various issues discussed in these conferences, whose purpose is mostly to provide unanimous recommendations to the federal or *Land* governments. The position of the respective members has a certain weight. There are no fixed rules for delegation; which persons represent the *Länder* differs from case to case and depends on specific interest of *Länder* or parties which influence these decisions.

Usually, the Conference of the *Land* Governors meets twice in year, sometimes with an additional extraordinary meeting.[25] Hence, there are also meetings of other members of the *Land* governments on a number of policy matters (e.g., agrarian issues). In addition to these conferences, numerous conferences of high-ranging representatives of the staffs of the *Land* administrations take place.

In particular, the experts' conferences of the *Länder* are very effective institutions to exchange information, prepare statements, and coordinate measures between the different *Länder*. Experts' conferences play a key role in coordinating positions of the *Länder* in areas that lay within the sphere of competences of the *Länder*, as well as in fields of federal competences (given the importance of indirect federal administration).

The following chart provides an overview of horizontal cooperation through the several conferences:[26]

24 See, for example, Art. 59b par. 1 B-VG.
25 See *37. Bericht über den Föderalismus in Österreich 2012*, ed. Institut für Föderalismus (Vienna: new academic press, 2013), 72-73.
26 Rosner, *Koordinationsinstrumente*, 26.

Conference of the Austrian Land Governors

⇓ instruction ⇓ ⇑ enactment recommendation ⇑

Conference of the Directors of the offices of the Land Governments

⇓ instruction ⇓ ⇑ draft ⇑

Experts – Conference of the Länder

⇓ joint secretary for all Conferences of the *Länder* ⇓

Liaison Office of the Austrian Länder

The Liaison Office of the Austrian *Länder* is the most important institution for coordinating matters between all the *Länder*. The head office is situated in Vienna and is part of the organization of the office of the *Land* government of Lower Austria. Its main tasks are the organization of all the *Land* conferences discussed above, as well as the reporting of the viewpoints of the different *Länder* and the issuing of joint statements by the *Länder*.

Concerning vertical cooperation, various platforms and institutions will be mentioned (see below). Vertical cooperation also takes place in various expert groups composed by members of the administrative staffs of federal ministries and *Land* governments.[27]

Finally, very important are the various working groups which are established ad hoc to discuss and elaborate proposals on specific matters. For example, the working group on deregulation and reform of administration was established in 2014; it is composed of the leading civil servants of federal ministries and heads of the offices of *Land* governments. Until December 2014, the working group had delivered two reports to the federal government with numerous proposals on measures implementing administration reform in Austria.[28]

The working group on deregulation and administrative reform was not the first in this field: In the past, various other reform groups, composed of representatives of the federal government and the *Länder*, had similar

27 See <http://www.aufgabenreform.at> (31 December 2014).

28 See the first report at <http://cdn.aufgabenreform.at/pdf/erster_bericht_adk_beschlusstext.pdf> (31 December 2014).

tasks and were more or less successful (see the administrative reform of 2001, the Austrian Convention 2003-2005, or the working group on state and administrative reform 2007).[29] In political opinion, all these working groups were not very successful. Actually, a general reform of the political and administrative system of Austria has not been realized until now, but nevertheless many single measures have been undertaken. For example, in the beginning of 2014, nine *Land* administrative courts and two federal administrative courts replaced about 120 authorities on federal and *Land* level functioning in administrative procedures as appellate councils. This reform can be counted as a success story in cooperative federalism in Austria.[30]

Recent working programs of the federal government, coalitions of the SPÖ and the ÖVP from 2008 to 2013 and from 2013 to 2018, are strongly promoting the idea of cooperation and coordination between the various orders of government by agreements between federation and *Länder* according to Art. 15a B-VG in matters such as child care, hospitals, and asylum seekers. The coalition program of 2013 established various working groups on administration reform, tax reform, and reform of financial equalization, composed by representatives of federation and *Länder*.[31]

Cooperative Federalism in European Matters

With regard to European matters in principle, the federation represents Austrian interests, but the *Länder* have an important impact on decision-making, as stipulated in Article 23d B-VG.[32]

In 1992, prior to Austria's accession to the EU, the Integration Conference of the *Länder* (IKL) and the Permanent Integration Committee of the *Länder* (SIL) were established. Up until now, these conferences have played no decisive role. They only convened twice in 1992 and 1997.[33] The Integration Conference of the *Länder* has not been effective because it is governed by too many detailed regulations. This kind

29 See Peter Bußjäger, "Der Einfluss von Experten in der österreichischen Bundesstaatsdiskussion," in *Politikberatung in Verfassungsreformen*, ed. Arthur Benz (Veröffentlichungen des Dimitris Tsatsos-Instituts für Europäische Verfassungswissenschaften 10) (Berlin: Berliner Wissenschafts-Verlag, 2012), 65-87.

30 See 37. *Bericht über den Föderalismus*, ed. Institut für Föderalismus, 17-21.

31 See for example "Das neue Regierungsprogramm aus föderalistischer Sicht," *Föderalismus-Info* 1 (2014), at <http://cdn.aufgabenreform.at/pdf/erster_bericht_adk_beschlusstext.pdf> (31 December 2014).

32 *37. Bericht über den Föderalismus*, ed. Institut für Föderalismus, 70-72.

33 Peter Bußjäger and Daniela Larch, *Grundlagen und Entwicklungen der bundesstaatlichen Instrumente in Österreich* (Innsbruck: Institut für Föderalismus, 2005), 33.

of institution turned out to be impracticable for decision-making by the nine *Länder* because it was difficult to organize such a large conference in a timely fashion. Participation in the European decision-making process demands efficient responses. The Conference of the *Land* Governors has been more effective because the positions and statements of the *Länder* are formulated by the executive staffs of the *Land* administrations before being simply approved by the Conference of the *Land* Governors in an informal way.[34]

Nevertheless, the European Union has an enormous impact on Austrian intergovernmental relations. Participation in the European decision-making process as well as the implementation of European law into national law accelerated and intensified cooperative mechanisms between the federation and the *Länder* as well as among the *Länder*.

The Liaison Office of the Austrian *Länder* also works in European matters with its sub-organization, the Liaison Office Brussels.[35] Their main task is to coordinate the interests of the *Länder* and to issue joint statements to the federal government. Article 23d B-VG stipulates that the federal government must inform the *Länder* without delay about all projects within the framework of the European Union, which either affect the *Länder*'s sphere of competences or could otherwise be of interest to them. In addition, the federal government must give the *Länder* the chance to comment on EU decision-making within a reasonable timeframe.

If the federal government receives a unanimous statement by the *Länder* regarding matters within the exclusive sphere of competences of the *Länder*, it is bound to adhere to this statement in negotiations at the European level. It may only deviate from it for compelling foreign and integration policy reasons, and it must inform the *Länder* of the reasons for its deviation without delay.

Statements by the *Länder* regarding EU matters are in most cases elaborated on within the various executive branches, without any participation by the *Land* parliaments. In other words, Europeanization has led to a strengthening of the position of the *Land* governors vis-à-vis the federal order and has weakened the position of the *Land* legislatures. The latter have to implement European law into the *Land* legal order without

34 Peter Bußjäger, "Mitwirkung der Länder an Vorhaben im Rahmen der EU," in *10 Jahre Mitgliedschaft Österreichs: Bilanz und Ausblick*, ed. Waldemar Hummer and Walter Obwexer (Vienna: Springer, 2006), 58-60.

35 See Klemens Fischer, "Die Verbindungsstelle der Bundesländer in Brüssel: Das föderale Doppelhutmodell," in *Im Interesse der Länder–im Interesse des Gesamtstaates: Festschrift 60 Jahre Verbindungsstelle der Bundesländer*, ed. Andreas Rosner and Peter Bußjäger (Vienna: Braumüller, 2011), 67-76.

participating in the European decision-making process in the same way as the *Land* governments. While the various *Landtage* have established committees for European matters, these have not been able to gain much influence concerning European legislation. This is even the case in *Länder* in which the *Land* constitution requires the executive to inform the *Landtag* about projects of European integration (i.e., Burgenland, Upper Austria, Salzburg, Styria, Tyrol, and Vorarlberg).

Until now it seems that the interests of the federation and the *Länder* in EU matters have so far been relatively close to one another. The statements of the *Länder* are often very vague and imprecise, thus imposing few restrictions on the federal government in EU negotiations. The joint statements of the *Länder* are often formulated in a cooperative way, with very rare objections by specific *Länder*. This suggests that the *Länder* share broad common interests.

Since 1995, the federal government has deviated from a joint statement by the *Länder* in EU matters only in three cases, which were not very important in terms of regional politics, as they concerned aspects of animal protection in zoos, information on environmental matters, and waste disposal, which affected *Land* competences only marginally.[36] This indicates that there have not been any serious conflicts between the federal government and the *Länder* in the past with regard to European matters. Moreover, there have been no cases in which the *Länder* have used the EU as an ally against the national government.

The *Länder* can also participate directly in EU negotiations. If issues within their legislative realm are discussed, the Austrian government may include a *Land* nominee in Austria's delegation. This representative may, however, only act in cooperation with the responsible member of the federal government (see Art. 23d par. 3 B-VG). In practice, the participation of a so-called common representative of the *Länder* in the European Council has little relevance. The participation of representatives of the *Länder* in the Austrian delegation within working groups of the Council is much more important.[37]

The Federal Council may formulate binding statements only if EU law must be implemented by a modification of the federal constitution in a way that would reduce the legislative or executive competences of the *Länder*. However, the *Bundesrat*'s role was recently strengthened with regard to monitoring the subsidiarity principle through a modification of the federal

36 Peter Bußjäger and Andreas Rosner, *Mitwirken und Mitgestalten: Europa und die österreichischen Länder* (Vienna: Braumüller, 2005), 62-67.

37 Ibid., 12.

constitution adopted in July 2010.[38] The Federal Council can submit statements to the European Commission and appeal to the European Court if the subsidiarity principle is violated by EU legislation. Moreover, the Federal Council has to take statements of the *Landtage* "into consideration" even if it is not bound by them. The *Landtage* are also allowed to send a representative to the relevant committee of the *Bundesrat*. There are further moves towards closer links between the *Bundesrat* and *Landtage* with regard to monitoring subsidiarity.

Finally, all the *Länder*, apart from Vorarlberg, have established Liaison Offices in Brussels. They are mainly contact points for information, lobbying, and service and have more symbolic than real influence.[39]

Joint Agencies and Other Platforms of Coordination and Cooperation

Several institutions are structured between the federal level, the *Länder* and the municipalities, which aim to facilitate coordination and cooperation. Vertical ones include the Austrian Conference on Spatial Planning (ÖROK) and the Federal Crisis Management Conference. Horizontal institutions include the Liaison Office of the Austrian *Länder*, the Austrian Institute of Construction Engineering, and the Commission for School Books of the Austrian *Länder*.[40]

ÖROK is a joint organization of the federal government, the *Länder*, representatives of the Economic Chamber and Workers' Chamber, the League of the Austrian Cities, and the League of the Austrian Municipalities for matters of the European regional policy and the European Spatial Development. The conference provides recommendations and has no regulatory authority.

With regard to crisis management, cooperation between the federation and the *Länder* is absolutely necessary because natural hazards do not stop at the frontiers of the different *Länder*. Efficient cooperation—without disputes concerning competences—is essential because the resources that

38 Federal Law Gazette, BGBl. I no. 57/2010; see on the participation of the Federal Council on the consultation process regarding the subsidiarity principle Peter Bußjäger, "Frühlingserwachen? Über die aufkeimende Liebe der regionalen und nationalen Parlamente an der Mitwirkung in der Europäischen Union," in *Jahrbuch des Föderalismus 2009*, ed. Europäisches Zentrum für Föderalismus-Forschung (Baden-Baden: Nomos, 2009), 511-512.
39 Cf. in detail Florian Mast, "Die Rolle der Regionen und ihrer Verbindungsbüros in Brüssel im europäischen Mehrebenensystem," in *Multi-Level-Governance im Alpenraum*, ed. Peter Bußjäger and Christian Gsodam (Vienna: Braumüller, 2013), 129-150.
40 *37. Bericht über den Föderalismus*, ed. Institut für Föderalismus, 74-76.

the *Länder* badly need in an emergency are within the competences of the federation (e.g., the military and the police). So far, cooperation between federation and *Länder* in this area has worked relatively well.

The Austrian Institute of Construction Engineering was set up in 1993 to coordinate technical matters relative to construction engineering. The main impetus for its creation was the implementation of the EU's Construction Products Directive by the *Länder*. It also provides assistance to the *Länder* for the harmonization of other technical aspects of building laws. All *Länder* are members of the institute, which has no direct regulatory authority but prepares regulations and decisions for the *Länder*.

In addition to these horizontal institutions in which all *Länder* participate, there is the Planning Community East whose function is to coordinate the regional development (planning) of Austria's Eastern *Länder*. Its functions are only advisory.

Municipality associations can be established according to Article 116a of the Federal Constitution. This provision allows the municipalities to transfer specific tasks within their spheres of competence to these associations.[41] Municipality associations can be established by voluntary agreement between the involved municipalities, by law, or by an executive act. Municipality associations are one of the most popular forms of cooperation. There are numerous municipality federations, established by *Land* legislation, in particular in the following areas: schools, civil registry offices, and waste and water management. Other associations are established on a voluntary basis in the field of tourism, for instance. Such an agreement requires the approval of the superior authority (in general the *Land* administration). Establishing an association of municipalities may not jeopardize individual municipalities' autonomy as self-administrative corporate bodies. Municipality associations often interact with the *Land* governments, as the *Länder* are responsible for legislation in matters that then have to be executed by the associations.

Agreements between Orders of Governments

In 1974, the Federal Constitution was amended to officially provide for the conclusion of horizontal agreements (between *Länder*), in addition to vertical ones between the federal order of government and the *Länder* (Art. 15a par 1 and 2 B-VG). These amendments permitted the *Länder* to enter into voluntary "treaty-like" cooperation with each other, as well as with the federal order, on matters within their respective spheres of competence.

41 See Bußjäger, "Local Government Cooperation in Austria," 81-91.

Agreements concluded pursuant to Article 15a B-VG are probably the most far-reaching legal instruments of cooperative federalism in Austria.[42] These agreements need the consent of the legislative assemblies of the federation and the *Länder* in order to have the binding character for legislation.

As of 1 January 2014, there were 108 agreements according to Article 15a par 1 B-VG between the federation and the *Länder* (this does not mean that all *Länder* participate in all agreements)[43] and forty-six agreements according to Article 15a par 2 B-VG between the *Länder* (this does not mean that all *Länder* participate in all agreements). Municipalities, which are usually not allowed to sign such agreements, take part in two agreements: the Austrian Pact of Stability and the agreement concerning the consultation mechanism, discussed earlier. The inclusion of municipalities, represented by the Austrian Association of Cities and the Austrian Association of Municipalities, required amendments to the Federal Constitution (see below).

According to the Constitutional Court, agreements based on Article 15a B-VG are not directly applicable.[44] Similar to international treaties, they require an implementation by legislation or, if the agreement does not modify any law, by regulations by each of the parties involved. This constitutional ruling has rendered coordination by agreements rather complicated. Citizens may not challenge the constitutionality or legality of agreements according to Article 15a B-VG; they may only appeal against legislative acts or regulations, which implement them before the Constitutional Court. So far, there has been no case law on conflicts arising between parties to such agreements.

A relatively recent development regarding Article 15a B-VG agreements deserves particular attention; § 24 par. 9 FAG 2008 (Law on Financial Equalization) stipulated that the *Länder* are (more or less) forced to ratify Article 15a B-VG agreements concerning the Austrian Stability Pact, otherwise they risk losing federal transfer payments. This contract-like instrument, which went in the meantime out of force, was the only formal means through which the federal order may exert influence on the *Länder* in this context.

The Constitutional Court has in a similar case ruled that such a process does not imply actual obligations for the *Länder*. They are—in legal terms—free to refuse to conclude the agreement, and their autonomy is

42 Gamper, "Republic of Austria," 20.

43 Source: Institute of Federalism. See Peter Bußjäger, Silvia Bär and Ulrich Willi, *Kooperativer Föderalismus im Kontext der Europäischen Union* (Innsbruck: Institut für Föderalismus, 2006), 61; *37. Bericht über den Föderalismus*, ed. Institut für Föderalismus, 120.

44 Constitutional Court, VfSlg. 9886/1983.

thus not violated.[45] This is a very restrictive view and the Constitutional Court should reconsider this issue since such forced agreements ("forced cooperative federalism") are not compatible with the requirement of voluntariness pursuant to Article 15a B-VG.

Intergovernmental Relations and Fiscal Federalism

Coordination of the various budgets of *Länder* and municipalities is structured through an internal stability pact and the financial constitution. Municipalities, which are represented by the League of the Austrian Cities and the League of the Austrian Municipalities, are able to join in agreements according to Article 15a B-VG on the Stability Pact and the Consultant Mechanism.[46]

Financial equalization (*Finanzausgleich*) results in a complex web of competences, accomplishment of tasks, and financial resources. A telling example is provided by the financing of hospitals. Hospitals are mostly institutions of the *Länder*, but they are financed by various sources of the *Länder*, the federation, and the institutions of social security. Furthermore, while no legal mechanism structure negotiations regarding financial equalization, agreements introducing a consultation mechanism in 1999[47] and the Stability Pact (the first in 1999,[48] the current one in 2008[49]) have a constitutional basis.

Since the beginning of Austrian federalism, intergovernmental relations concerning fiscal federalism have followed a simple and unmodified basic structure. For historical reasons, they are governed by very complex and detailed rules.[50] Financial equalization is the result of negotiations between representatives of the federal order, the *Länder*, and the municipalities through the following institutions: a consultation board, the Austrian Board of Coordination, various boards of coordination of the *Länder*, and the Mediation Board.

An important characteristic of all these boards is that municipalities are present along with the federal order and the *Länder*. This can be seen as an

45 Constitutional Court, VfGH 10 October 2008, G 5/07.
46 Federal Law Gazette, BGBl. I no. 1998/61.
47 Federal Law Gazette, BGBl. I no. 35/1999.
48 Federal Law Gazette, BGBl. I no. 101/1999.
49 Federal Law Gazette, BGBl. I no. 127/2008.
50 Erich Thöni, "Intergovernmental Fiscal Relations: Die Verteilung der finanziellen Mittel," in *Kooperativer Föderalismus in Österreich*, ed. Peter Bußjäger (Vienna: Braumüller, 2010), 113-120, p. 113ff.

example of the increasing importance of "tripartite federalism" in Austria. Members of all these boards are political representatives as well as experts.

The main revenues for all orders of government are generated through the so-called "joint taxation system." First, the total revenue of different forms of taxes is divided between the federation, the *Länder*, and the municipalities according to ratios negotiated for each tax (*Oberverteilung*). Then, the total shares for the *Länder* are divided between the nine *Länder* (*Unterverteilung*) and the shares are divided among the municipalities in each *Land*. In practice, tripartite negotiations take place between the three orders of the federal system (federal, *Land*, and municipal). These negotiations result in a compromise agreement on fiscal equalization. In reality, the *Länder* and the local governments have no real alternative but to accept the determination of fiscal relations by the federal government.[51] The federal laws on financial equalization are usually fixed for four to six years, and they implement the rules of the Financial Constitution. The present law on financial equalization covers 2008 to 2014 (originally it was foreseen that the law should run out in 2013, but in 2011 its validity was extended to 2014) and is a complex conglomeration of detailed rules regarding the vertical and horizontal allocation of financial resources. The F-VG contains two basic rules: 1) the cost-bearing rule pursuant to which each government has to finance its own expenditures (§ 2 F-VG) and 2) the principle of a justified distribution of finances, which stipulates that each order of government must receive as much as it is necessary to finance its current tasks (§ 4 F-VG).

As an exception to the first rule, some expenditures are transferred between orders of government. For example, the federation covers teachers' salaries and pensions, despite the fact that primary and lower secondary school teachers are employees of the *Länder*. Hospital financing offers another example of cost-transfer by *Länder*. Hence, municipalities must bear part of the deficits of public hospitals, which are under the responsibility of the *Länder* (this is not the case of all hospitals).[52] All in all, the health-care system is characterized by complex and opaque cost shifting.

Co-financing mechanisms lack transparency. They also have the effect of distorting fairness, which is one of the aims of financial equalization. Moreover, co-financing leads to the fiscal illusion that public expenditures

51 Peter Bußjäger, "Reforms on Fiscal Federalism in Austria," in *Reforming Federalism: Foreign Experiences for a Reform in Germany*, ed. Gerhard Robbers (Frankfurt a. M.: Peter Lang, 2005), 59-67.

52 See for financing of health care in Austria: Vereinbarung zwischen dem Bund und den Ländern gemäß Art. 15a B-VG über die Organisation und Finanzierung des Gesundheitswesens StF: BGBl. I No. 105/2008

are lower than they are in reality. Reforms of the Financial Constitution and of the rules governing financial equalization in order to increase responsibility and transparency should be a top priority. This seems to be difficult because the federation wants to supervise the budget decisions of the *Länder* and municipalities. For their part, most of the *Länder* are not interested in instruments of fiscal federalism because, until now, the tradition of bargaining prior to the new federal laws of financial equalization or within the framework of such laws was more comfortable than raising *Land* taxes.

Cooperative Federalism, Efficiency in Policy Making, and Accountability

Presently, it seems that the *Länder* have an informal veto power to the extent they manage to act unanimously. Austria operates as a "negotiated federal regime" with the Conference of the *Land* Governors as an instrument of mediation and coordination between the *Länder* and in bargaining with the federal government.

Essentially, decisions are made on the basis of federal party politics, and not primarily in the interests of the *Länder*. As previously mentioned, there are nearly no regional parties with an appreciable degree of influence.[53] Citizens have a comparatively strong feeling of regional identity, but there is a weak public awareness of the federal system.[54]

Apart from the usually consensus-driven practice of federal cooperation, there are also cases in which intergovernmental relations fail. For example, in the dispute over bilingual road signs (German and Slovenian) in Carinthia, the Carinthian governor refused to execute a federal law. In 2001, the Constitutional Court delivered a judgment stipulating that Carinthia had to place more bilingual traffic signs on its roads than had been provided by regulations of *Land* authorities so far.[55] However, the *Land* and its governor refused to comply.[56] Following the Constitutional Court's rulings, a widely accepted agreement was ratified in 2011 and safeguarded by constitutional

53 Ferdinand Karlhofer, "A Federation Without Federalism? Zur Realverfassung der Bund-Länder-Beziehungen," in *Kooperativer Föderalismus in Österreich*, ed. Peter Bußjäger (Vienna: Braumüller, 2010), 131-145.

54 See Peter Bußjäger, "Federalism without Federal Values? Austrian Citizens Attitudes towards Federalism and their Effects on Political Culture," *Federal Governance* 9, no. 2 (2012): 9-26; idem, Ferdinand Karlhofer and Günther Pallaver, *Föderalistisches Bewusstsein in Österreich* (Vienna: Braumüller, 2010); Günther Voith, "Schein und Sein im österreichischen Föderalismus," *Sozialwissenschaftliche Schriftenreihe*, no. 21 (2007): 37-38.

55 Constitutional Court, 13 December 2001, G 213/01-18.

56 Karlhofer, "A Federation without Federalism?," 131-145.

directives in the federal law on national minorities, which solved the conflict both politically and judicially.[57]

The current mode of governance reinforces the trend towards greater unitarism and centralization, although in specific conflicts, the political leaders of the *Länder* successfully oppose federal projects. Sometimes, however, they are not interested in getting more influence on certain matters: For example, in 2009 the *Länder* opposed the federal government's project to transfer competences in giving permissions of residence to asylum seekers under humanitarian aspects. The *Länder* stressed that the new regulations were very bureaucratic;[58] in fact, they were not interested in deciding the matter, which was rather contested in public opinion.

The political result is that issues discussed in parliamentary debates in both the federal and *Land* arenas often do not comply with the division of competences provided in the Federal Constitution. For citizens, this process is opaque because the distribution of competences is unclear. One example is the health-care system, which is financed by the federational government, agencies of social security, and the *Länder*. Public hospitals are often established by the *Länder*. The financing system is very complex, and many experts doubt its efficiency. Another example is the education system, which is marked by similar complexity. By contrast to health care, however, and by reference to international benchmarks, Austria's education system is expensive and, in terms of efficiency, ranks among the lowest of the OECD countries. However, decisions are made "behind closed doors" with no democratic legitimacy. In summary, this system also lacks transparency for outsiders.[59]

In public debates, Austrian federalism is often seen as complicated and inadequate in managing the great challenges of the future, especially in the context of the financial crisis. This being said, public attention given to debates on the future of federalism in Austria is minimal.

Summary

Austrian federalism is characterised by a high degree of integration through several institutions and organizations. Cooperative federalism

57 See Martin Hiesel, "Die Lösung des Kärntner Ortstafelstreites," *Europäisches Journal für Minderheitenfragen* 4, no. 3 (2011): 173-179.

58 See also *34. Bericht über den Föderalismus*, ed. Institut für Föderalismus, 52-53.

59 Peter Bußjäger, "Föderalismus durch Macht im Schatten? Österreich und die Landeshauptmännerkonferenz," in *Jahrbuch des Föderalismus 2003*, ed. Europäisches Zentrum für Föderalismus-Forschung Tübingen (Baden-Baden: Nomos, 2003), 79ff; Karl Weber, "Macht im Schatten? Landeshauptmänner-, Landesamtsdirektoren- und andere Landesreferentenkonferenzen," *Österreichische Zeitschrift für Politikwissenschaft*, no. 4 (1992): 405-418.

involves the federal order, the *Länder*, and the municipalities. The result is that competences are often unclear and the system seems to be clumsy. It may be, however, that cooperative federalism may only work in this way.

In fact, Austrian federalism is a mix of federalist and centralist tendencies. Though there are main federal institutions, in constitutional reality, they seem to have a dummy—artificial—character. Hence, the Federal Council is a political lightweight, which is mainly compensated by the Conference of the *Land* Governors. From the beginning, the federal system was characterised by a high degree of centralism, which has not really decreased with time. Although the *Länder* enjoy a degree of autonomy in terms of their internal organization, the substantive result of this autonomy—in policy terms—has diminished over time. Furthermore, because the allocation of competences is extremely complex and unclear, a modernization of the division of competences would be necessary.[60]

Unfortunately, while there is consensus about the need of far-reaching reforms, there is none concerning the measures that should be taken. Representatives from the federal order, especially in ministries, would probably strongly disagree that there is any need to strengthen the competences of the *Länder* and would prefer a strengthening of centralized powers. Many leaders of the *Länder* see things in exactly the opposite way.

60 Peter Bußjäger, "Der 'zentralistischste aller Bundesstaaten' als (Lehr)beispiel für Europa?," in *Föderalismus: Leitbild für die Europäische Union?*, ed. Michael Piazolo and Jürgen Weber (Munich: Olzog, 2004), 141-145.

A Redundant Second Chamber? The Austrian *Bundesrat* in Comparative Perspective

Franz Fallend

Introduction

In the comparative literature on federalist systems, Austria is usually qualified as a case of "weak" federalism, meaning that, in comparison to the central, national government, the sub-national entities or provinces (in Austria called *Länder*) have only limited policy responsibilities of their own (self-rule) as well as only limited influence on federal policy-making (shared rule). According to Thomas A. Hueglin and Alan Fenna, Austria belongs to those countries which "describe themselves as federations while being so centrally dominated in design and practice as to be little short of unitary states."[1] Similarly, Arend Lijphart places Austria into the category of federal, but centralized states.[2] Dietmar Braun seems to go even a step further when he asserts that in Austria "the power of the central state is so overwhelming .... that one can hardly speak of federalism."[3]

The status of the second chamber, the Federal Council (or *Bundesrat*), is often mentioned as a primary indicator for the weakness of the federal system in Austria. While formally designed to represent the interests of the provinces in the law-making process at the federal level, the Federal Council has neither equal powers with the first chamber, the National Council (or

1 Thomas O. Hueglin and Alan Fenna, *Comparative Federalism: A Systematic Inquiry* (Peterborough, Ont.: Broadview Press, 2006), 34.

2 Arend Lijphart, *Patterns of Democracy: Government Forms and Performance in Thirty-Six Countries* (New Haven, Conn.: Yale University Press, 1999), 189-190.

3 Dietmar Braun, "Hat die vergleichende Föderalismusforschung eine Zukunft?," in *Jahrbuch des Föderalismus 2002: Föderalismus, Subsidiarität und Regionen in Europa*, ed. Europäisches Zentrum für Föderalismus-Forschung Tübingen (Baden-Baden: Nomos, 2002), 97-116, p. 102 (author's translation). Similar assessments give Jan Erk, "Austria: A Federation Without Federalism," *Publius: The Journal of Federalism* 34, no. 1 (2004): 1-20, p. 2; Franz Fallend, "Bund-Länder-Beziehungen," in *Politik in Österreich: Das Handbuch*, ed. Herbert Dachs et al. (Vienna: Manz Verlag, 2006), 1024-1040, p. 1024; Ferdinand Karlhofer and Günther Pallaver, "Strength through Weakness: State Executive Power and Federal Reform in Austria," *Swiss Political Science Review* 19, no. 1 (2013): 41-59, p. 41.

Nationalrat), nor is it composed in a significantly different, incongruent manner—two criteria which, according to Lijphart, are essential for making a strong second chamber.[4] Ferdinand Karlhofer and Günther Pallaver estimate that "in the federal parties' hierarchical scale the Federal Council is subordinate and in practice almost insignificant."[5] The general public seems to share this view: an opinion poll in 2014 revealed that fifty-four percent of the interviewed Austrians preferred to abolish the Federal Council.[6]

However, the generally negative evaluation of the performance of the Federal Council should not lead to the premature conclusion that the Austrian second chamber is irrelevant and therefore does not merit to be investigated. "[A]ll second chambers exercise influence even if they are considered weak or insignificant," George Tsebelis and Jeannette Money have contended.[7] Even if the two chambers of parliament are composed in a congruent manner (i.e., are dominated by the same political parties or social groups) and even if their members display similar political preferences, like in Austria, a case has been made that "second legislative chambers can make informational contributions to the legislative process that result in qualitatively superior legislation being adopted than would have been adopted by a unicameral legislature."[8]

How and to what degree the Austrian Federal Council exercises political influence will be the topic of this contribution. While there are quite a few systematic overviews of the compositions, functions, and powers of second chambers in the world,[9] I will focus on a more qualitative analysis, based on Lijphart's theoretical argument about the strength of bicameralism. In section two, I elaborate the theoretical framework and explain the selection of the cases on which I focus the comparison (Belgium, Canada, and Switzerland). The comparison should help one better understand the reasons for and the conditions of the subordinate role of the Federal Council. At the same time, it should also show possible ways out of this role. Sections three and four deal with the composition and functions of

4 Lijphart, *Patterns of Democracy*, 205-211.

5 Karlhofer and Pallaver, "Strength through Weakness," 44.

6 *profil*, 27 January 2014, 12.

7 George Tsebelis and Jeannette Money, *Bicameralism* (Cambridge: Cambridge University Press, 1997), 211.

8 James R. Rogers, "An Informational Rationale for Congruent Bicameralism," *Journal of Theoretical Politics* 13, no. 2 (2001): 123-151, p. 143-144.

9 See, e.g., Samuel C. Patterson and Anthony Mughan, "Fundamentals of Institutional Design: The Functions and Powers of Parliamentary Second Chambers," *The Journal of Legislative Studies* 7, no. 1 (2001): 39-60; Meg Russell, "Elected Second Chambers and Their Powers: An International Survey," *The Political Quarterly* 83, no. 1 (2012): 117-129; John Coakley, "The Strange Revival of Bicameralism," *The Journal of Legislative Studies* 20, no. 4 (2014): 542-572.

the Federal Council and the other second chambers, respectively. In section five, I will try to draw tentative conclusions from the other examples as to possible reforms of the Federal Council, whose need to be reformed is recognized by nearly everybody who is concerned about federalism in Austria. The last section contains final remarks.

Theoretical Framework and Research Design: The Causes and Conditions of Strong/Weak Bicameralism

In 1997, when Tsebelis and Money published their study, about one-third of the countries in the world had bicameral legislatures.[10] While statistics, e.g. of the Inter-Parliamentary Union (IPU), claimed a steady decline of bicameralism in the late 20th century, later studies have suggested that this trend has at least been arrested and that second chambers have experienced a "revival" during the last two decades. In 2014, John Coakley counted seventy-seven second chambers; twenty-eight of them had been established between 1996 and 2014.[11] Among democracies, the ratio of bicameral versus unicameral legislatures is even higher than among all countries in the world: of the thirty-six democracies which Lijphart included in his book, twenty-three, i.e. about two-thirds, were characterized by a two-chamber system.[12] Still, the correlation between democracies and bicameralism seems not to be very strong: of the twenty-eight countries which set up new second chambers, Freedom House in 2012 classified only three as "free."[13] The correlation between federalism and bicameralism seems to be stronger: all nine federal countries Lijphart studied had bicameral legislatures.[14] Until 2014, this percentage even increased slightly: then nineteen out of twenty-five federal states had a second chamber (i.e., seventy-six percent), compared to fifty-eight out of 164 unitary states (i.e., thirty-five percent).[15]

Although second chambers are a reality in many democracies, they have often been criticized from a democratic point of view. Overrepresenting traditional social groups and interests, they are blamed as a "conservative brake on the more democratically elected 'lower' houses."[16] In Austria, it was the Social Democrats who warned in 1920, during the negotiations

10 Tsebelis and Money, *Bicameralism*, 1.
11 Coakley, "Revival of Bicameralism," 547-550.
12 Lijphart, *Patterns of Democracy*, 202.
13 Coakley, "Revival of Bicameralism," 561
14 Lijphart, *Patterns of Democracy*, 203.
15 Coakley, "Revival of Bicameralism," 550.
16 Lijphart, *Patterns of Democracy*, 203.

on the new democratic constitution after the breakdown of the Austro-Hungarian Monarchy, that the struggle over the composition and the powers of the second chamber was a "question of power of first order." With vehemence they spoke up against alleged attempts of their major ideological rival, the Christian Socials, to establish a "house of Lords" leading to "a rectification in a reactionary sense of the lower house" and to a "distortion of democracy."[17] With the steady expansion of democratic institutions, amounting to "a global surge towards democracy,"[18] second chambers were more and more accused of being "undemocratic," "not popularly accountable," "unrepresentative" or "elitist."[19]

Considering these controversies about the composition and the status of second chambers in modern democracies, it seems important to know which factors account for a strong (or weak) position of today's second chambers. According to Lijphart, there are three relevant factors: 1) the formal constitutional powers of the second chamber, 2) the method of its selection, and 3) the difference to the first chamber with respect to the methods of selection.[20] Regarding their formal constitutional powers, second chambers are typically subordinate to first chambers. Frequently, their vetoes against proposed legislation can be overridden, and the cabinet cannot be removed from office by a vote of no-confidence, as this instrument is reserved to the first chamber. Regarding the method of their selection, the members of second chambers, as opposed to those of first chambers, are usually elected indirectly or, more often, appointed. As a result, they lack the democratic legitimacy of the members of the first chamber, which in turn diminishes their political influence. A direct election of a second chamber may compensate for its limited powers, but creates the dilemma that it may simply duplicate the role of the first chamber and thereby make itself redundant.[21] On the basis of these two criteria, Lijphart classified chambers that have equal or only moderately unequal constitutional powers as well as democratic legitimacy as "symmetrical" chambers, and chambers which lack these qualities as "asymmetrical." Finally, regarding the difference to the first chamber with respect to the methods of selection, second chambers are

17 Cited and translated from Franz Fallend, "Der Bundesrat in Österreich," in *Zweite Kammern*, ed. Gisela Riescher, Sabine Ruß and Christoph Haas (Munich: Oldenbourg Verlag, 2nd revised and extended edition 2010), 165-188, p. 168.
18 Lawrence LeDuc, Richard G. Niemi and Pippa Norris, "Introduction: The Present and Future of Democratic Elections," in *Comparing Democracies: Elections and Voting in Global Perspective*, ed. idem (London: Sage, 1996): 1-48, p. 1.
19 Robert Hislope and Anthony Mughan, *Comparative Politics: The State and its Challenges* (Cambridge: Cambridge University Press, 2012), 113-114.
20 Lijphart, *Patterns of Democracy*, 205-208.
21 Coakley, "Revival of Bicameralism," 560.

important when the composition of the two chambers is incongruent, i.e., when they overrepresent certain minorities or, in case of federal states, the smaller component units.[22]

Table 1: Cameral Structure of Legislatures

	Symmetrical	Asymmetrical
Congruent	*medium-strength bicameralism* [3.0] e.g. **Belgium**	*weak bicameralism* [2.0] e.g. **Austria**
Incongruent	*strong bicameralism* [4.0] e.g. Australia, Germany, **Switzerland**, USA	*medium-strength bicameralism* [3.0] e.g. **Canada**, India, Spain

Source: adapted from Lijphart, *Patterns of Democracy*, 212 (table 11.2). Only the nine federal countries of Lijphart's study are included in the table; the countries on which this study focuses appear in **bold** letters. The numbers in square brackets indicate Lijphart's indices of bicameralism.

Based on these considerations, Lijphart constructed a classification of cameral structures and an index of bicameralism (see table 1). The index ranges from 1.0 to 4.0: 1.0 stands for unicameralism, 2.0 for weak bicameralism (characterized by asymmetrical and congruent chambers), 3.0 for medium-strength bicameralism (characterized by symmetrical and congruent chambers or by asymmetrical and incongruent chambers), and 4.0 for strong bicameralism (characterized by symmetrical and incongruent chambers). As table 1 reveals, Lijphart put Austria into the asymmetrical and congruent category, leading to only weak bicameralism.

To sum up, Lijphart argued that the (a)symmetrical and (in)congruent structure of the two-chamber system accounts for the strength, i.e., the political influence, of the second chamber. To examine whether, and under which conditions, this is true, I will take a closer look at the Austrian Federal Council, and I will compare it with one case each of the other three categories shown in table 1. The three cases chosen for comparison are Belgium, Canada (both cases of medium-strength bicameralism, but with an opposite combination of the two variables) and Switzerland (a case of strong bicameralism, which combines a symmetrical with an incongruent

22 Lijphart, *Patterns of Democracy*, 205-208.

bicameral structure).[23] The description, analysis, and comparison of the four cases is supposed to provide arguments for (or against) a strengthening of the Austrian Federal Council as well as to hint at more specific avenues for reform.

The Composition of the Second Chamber

Second chambers vary enormously in their composition. Coakley lists seven different principles of representation: direct election, indirect election, appointment, heredity, corporate representation, selection by the lower house, and ex-officio membership, with university representation and co-optation as partial approaches. In effect, two criteria have to be distinguished: the representation criterion, i.e., the social groups or interests whose representation in the second chamber is intended, and the selection formula, i.e., the specific electoral arrangement for this.[24] Typically, second chambers are less democratic than first chambers. The convention in parliamentary studies is "to regard the upper chamber as 'secondary' compared to the first or lower chamber, on the basis that the first chamber is 'lower' in the sense of closer to the people, with a scheme of representation credited with being more democratic because it reflects the population at large rather than geographical regions or social minorities."[25]

The Austrian Federal Council

The composition of the Austrian Federal Council is the result of a historical compromise between the major political parties, the Christian Socials, and the Social Democrats at the beginning of the democratic era in Austria. In 1920, both parties agreed on a new constitution, which established the federal system and gave the second chamber the structure it essentially has today. In the negotiations, the Christian Socials had argued for an incongruent composition of the Federal Council. While the first chamber, the National Council, was to be elected directly on the principle of proportional representation, they pleaded for the second chamber to be

23 Coakley comes to a similar, though not identical estimation as Lijphart concerning the strength of the second chamber: according to him, the power of the second chamber in Austria and Canada is "low," in Belgium "medium" and in Switzerland "high." See Coakley, "Revival of Bicameralism," 557-562 (appendix).

24 Coakley, "Revival of Bicameralism," 551.

25 John Uhr, "Bicameralism," in *The Oxford Handbook of Political Institutions*, ed. R. A. W. Rhodes, Sarah A. Binder and Bert A. Rockman (Oxford: Oxford University Press, 2006), 474-494, p. 478.

composed after the model of the U.S. Senate and the Swiss Council of States (*Ständerat*), i.e., all provinces, irrespective of size and population, should be represented by an equal number of delegates. The Social Democrats, on the other side, advocated a strictly proportional composition, according to the strengths of the political parties in the provincial legislatures. The final compromise was that the province with the highest number of inhabitants should delegate twelve members to the Federal Council, the province with the lowest number three members, and the rest of the provinces a number in-between, dependent on their relative population share. In addition, it was agreed that the second-strongest party be entitled to nominate at least one of the members from each province.[26] The over-all number of Federal Council members can change slightly, as the ratios between the provinces are calculated anew after every national census, which takes place once in ten years. At the moment, the second chamber consists of sixty-one members.

As a result of this electoral arrangement, the Austrian Federal Council is only indirectly democratically legitimized and composed more or less congruently to the National Council. The same parties that dominate the first chamber also dominate the second chamber, even though the party strengths in both chambers do not completely mirror each other. The Social Democratic Party of Austria (SPÖ), for example, was the strongest party at the national level from 1970 till 2002. In the second chamber, however, it was usually confronted with a relative or even absolute majority of the Christian Democratic Austrian People's Party (ÖVP), due to the fact that the SPÖ managed to reach a majority only in three out of the nine provinces: Burgenland, Carinthia (until 1999), and Vienna. The relatively small number of members the single provinces delegate to the Federal Council also entails that, compared to the National Council, smaller parties have smaller chances to enter the Federal Council.[27]

The method of selection of the members of the Federal Council, in particular the fact that they are not directly elected by the people of the respective province, but indirectly by the provincial parliament, has consequences for their autonomy. In fact, their nomination and their further political careers depend on the party leaderships of "their" parties, at first at the regional level and then at the national level. Formally, they enjoy a free mandate, enshrined in the Federal Constitution; neither the provincial parliament which nominated them nor the national party headquarters have the right to give them instructions or to recall them. However, this

26 Wilfried Swenden, *Federalism and Regionalism in Western Europe: A Comparative and Thematic Analysis* (Basingstoke: Palgrave Macmillan, 2006), 195; Fallend, "Der Bundesrat in Österreich," 167, 170-172.

27 Fallend, "Der Bundesrat in Österreich," 173.

very right not only allows them to free themselves gradually from "their" provincial party organization, it also makes it easier for the national party organization and the party group in parliament to bring the preferences of the members of the Federal Council in line with those of the members of the National Council.[28] The fact that the seats of the members of the Federal Council are grouped by parties, not by provinces, is a striking indicator to whom their primary loyalty goes. Not being dependent on successful election campaigns, they are also much less present in their electoral districts than their counterparts in the National Council.[29]

Other Second Chambers

According to Lijphart's theoretical framework, the Belgian second chamber, called Senate (*sénat, senaat*), is expected to be stronger than the Austrian Federal Council. Traditionally, the Senate, which was established in 1830, represented the upper social classes. At first, the right to vote and the right to be elected depended on the payment of high taxes, a requirement which was only lifted in the 1920s. Since then, the electoral systems both for the first chamber (the House of Representatives = *chambre des représentants*) and the second chamber have been based on proportional representation. As a consequence of the democratization process, the differences between the two chambers were leveled more and more. In fact, the social and the party composition of the two chambers became very much alike, putting (similar to the Austrian case) the *raison d'être* of the Senate into question.[30]

In 1970, a process of federalization of the Belgian state was started, which divided the country into three regions (Dutch- or Flemish-speaking Flanders, French-speaking Walloon, and the bilingual Brussels region) as well as three communities (the Flemish, the Walloon, and the German), with regions and communities not being completely identical. The composition of the Senate was also changed. Since the elections of 1995, after Belgium had finally been transformed into a federal state (1993), it consisted of seventy-one members, of whom forty (twenty-five Flemish, fifteen French) were elected directly by the regional voters, twenty-one

28 Ibid.
29 Barbara Steininger, "Der Bundesrat," in *Die österreichischen Abgeordneten: Individuelle Präferenzen und politisches Verhalten*, ed. Wolfgang C. Müller et al. (Vienna: WUV-Universitätsverlag, 2001), 421-454, p. 433-434.
30 Swenden, *Federalism and Regionalism in Western Europe*, 193, 195; Wolfgang Zink, "Der belgische Senat: Institution unter Denkmalschutz?," in *Zweite Kammern*, ed. Gisela Riescher, Sabine Ruß and Christoph Haas (Munich: Oldenbourg Verlag, 2nd revised and extended edition 2010), 211-243, p. 213-218, p. 224.

(ten Flemish, ten French, one German) indirectly by the three community colleges, and ten (six Flemish, four French) were co-opted by the directly and indirectly elected members. What did not change, however, was that the two chambers resembled each other very closely, regarding both their social and their party composition. As the political parties designed their candidate lists for elections from a "national" perspective, that integrated both chambers, the legitimacy of the second chamber was not enhanced by the reform.[31] A constitutional reform in 2011 abolished the direct election of the senators. In the next election, 2014, twenty-nine senators were to be elected by the Flemish electoral colleges, twenty by the French, one by the German; ten senators were co-opted.[32] However, the congruence between the first and the second chamber was not altered much. The debate on the legitimacy of the second chamber will continue.

Compared to the Belgian Senate, the Canadian Senate, established in 1867, is characterized by the opposite combination of Lijphart's central variables. Its composition, which is based on regional weighting, is incongruent to the first chamber, the House of Commons. The majority of the 105 senators, twenty-four each, come from four regions (Ontario, Québec, Maritime provinces, Western provinces); the rest come from smaller territories.[33] Repeated demands, usually from the Western provinces, to reorganize Senate recruitment on the basis of the ten provinces, have failed so far as they would have endangered the special status of the French-speaking region of Québec.[34] Incongruence is also produced by the fact that members of certain minorities, who have little chance to enter the House of Commons because of its majority system, like Catholics, Protestants from Québec, members of trade unions or indigenous people, are represented to a higher degree in the Senate than in the House of Commons, as are members of the economic elite.[35]

While the incongruent composition of the two parliamentary chambers may, from a certain perspective, justify the existence of the Canadian Senate, its asymmetrical recruitment procedure does not. The Senate lacks the democratic legitimacy of the House of Commons, whose

31 Zink, "Der belgische Senat," 224-228.
32 Belgium–Sénat/Senaat/Senat (Senate), in *PARLINE Database of National Parliaments*, ed. Inter-Parliamentary Union, at <http://www.ipu.org/parline-e/reports/2030_B.htm> (20 February 2015).
33 Canada–Senate, in *PARLINE Database of National Parliaments*, ed. Inter-Parliamentary Union, at <http://www.ipu.org/parline-e/reports/2056_B.htm> (20 February 2015); Hueglin and Fenna, *Comparative Federalism*, 190-192.
34 Tanja Zinterer, "Der kanadische Senat: Ungeliebt, undemokratisch, unreformierbar?," in *Zweite Kammern*, ed. Gisela Riescher, Sabine Ruß and Christoph Haas (Munich: Oldenbourg Verlag, 2nd, revised and extended edition 2010), 245-263, p. 257.
35 Ibid., 248-249, 253.

members are directly elected on the basis of a majority (first-past-the-post) system in single-member districts. The senators, on the other hand, are not directly elected, but appointed from representatives of major cultural, social, and regional groups by the governor general (the representative of the British monarch) on the proposal of the prime minister.[36] Its unelected status precludes redundancy, but at the same time it contradicts democratic principles and "has reduced its role to that of a provider of 'sober second thought'."[37] Traditionally, the Canadian prime minister nominates elder party officials, mostly of his or her own party, so that most senators belong to one of the two major Canadian parties, the Conservative Party or the Liberal Party. The senators usually put party above regional considerations; especially in the case of polarizing issues, the chamber is split along party lines. Thus, the party-political cleavage also translates into the Senate, even if party discipline is somewhat lower there.[38] The public does not appreciate the recruitment procedure in the Senate; senatorial appointments are widely seen as "plum job rewards for party faithfuls heading for semi-retirement."[39] As in Austria and Belgium, the dominance of party aspects in the composition of the Canadian Senate reduces the democratic legitimacy of the second chamber and will ensure that the political debate about its usefulness will go on.

The Swiss second chamber, the Council of States (*Ständerat*), is expected to be the most powerful in our sample. Regarding its composition, it meets Lijphart's criterion of incongruence. As opposed to the Austrian Federal Constitution of 1920, the Swiss Federal Constitution of 1848 followed the U.S. model. The first chamber, the National Council (*Nationalrat*), is elected in twenty-six single- or multi-member electoral districts (mostly on the basis of proportional representation, with the number of seats varying according to population). The second chamber, the Council of States, on the other hand, is, due to the strong cantonal traditions in Switzerland, composed of two representatives of each of the twenty cantons (mostly elected on a majority basis) and one representative of the former six half-cantons. The link of the members of the Swiss Council of States to their cantons is also expressed by the fact that the electoral rules are set by the cantonal parliaments and vary from canton to canton.[40] On the other hand,

36 Canada–Senate, in *PARLINE Database of National Parliaments*, ed. Inter-Parliamentary Union, at <http://www.ipu.org/parline-e/reports/2056_B.htm> (20 February 2015).
37 Hueglin and Fenna, *Comparative Federalism*, 193.
38 Zinterer, "Der kanadische Senat," 248, 250-253.
39 Hueglin and Fenna, *Comparative Federalism*, 193.
40 Adrian Vatter, "The Transformation of Access and Veto Points in Swiss Federalism," *Regional & Federal Studies* 15, no. 1 (2005): 1-17, p. 4; Gisela Riescher, "Der Schweizer Ständerat," in *Zweite Kammern*, ed. idem, Sabine Ruß and Christoph Haas (Munich: Oldenbourg Verlag, 2nd revised and extended edition 2010), 61-75, p. 63-64.

like their Austrian counterparts, the members of the Swiss Council of States hold a free mandate and are not subject to instructions from the cantonal parliaments or governments.[41] In fact, as federal party organizations in Switzerland are weak and as neither chamber is entitled to a vote of no-confidence against the government, the members of parliament are relatively independent from their parties and parliamentary factions.[42] Thus, the direct election and the relative autonomy of the members of the Council of States vis-à-vis their parties and their party leaderships contribute to the democratic legitimacy of the second chamber.

The different rules of composition bring about different party majorities in the two chambers of the Swiss parliament. The Social Democratic Party (SPS) and the right-wing populist Swiss People's Party (SVP) have been regularly underrepresented in the Council of States, while the Christian Democratic People's Party (CVP), which still dominates in the Catholic, thinly populated cantons of central Switzerland, and the moderately right Free Democrats (FDP) have been overrepresented. Thus, the Council of States has a high capacity, quoting Lijphart's statement from above, to act as a "conservative brake," preventing the Protestant, German-speaking majority in the National Council from constantly outvoting the rest of the Swiss and mitigating its centralizing tendencies.[43] However, the dominant interpretation is that

> the Council of States has not primarily subscribed to the federal ideal of maintaining decentralization or the prerogatives of the cantons. A more convincing perspective is that different political forces—the Catholics, the bourgeois coalition, and the rural cantons—used their overrepresentation in the Council of States to their own advantage. Thus, the Council of States has often in the past played a conservative role, protecting the status quo against innovations proposed by the government and the other chamber. Yet this is an effect of the specific political composition of its majority, and not of the system itself.[44]

41 Riescher, "Der Schweizer Ständerat," 67.
42 Wolf Linder and Adrian Vatter, "Institutions and Outcomes of Swiss Federalism: The Role of the Cantons in Swiss Politics," *West European Politics* 24, no. 2 (2001): 95-122, p. 101; Swenden, *Federalism and Regionalism in Western Europe*, 195.
43 Hanspeter Kriesi, "The Federal Parliament: The Limits of Institutional Reform," *West European Politics* 24, no. 2 (2001): 59-76, p. 64; Riescher, "Der Schweizer Ständerat," 73.
44 Linder and Vatter, "Institutions and Outcomes of Swiss Federalism," 101.

Thus, even if regional considerations seem not to be the only or at least primary motivation of the members of the Council of States, the fact that the second chamber does not simply duplicate the composition and the preferences of the first chamber has prevented an intensive debate about its general usefulness or abolition so far—contrary to the situation in Austria.

The Powers and Functions of the Second Chamber

As far as the powers and functions of second chambers are concerned, a radical view could follow the famous dictum of Abbé Sieyès during the French Revolution: "If a second chamber dissents from the first, it is mischievous; if it agrees with it, it is superfluous."[45] Taking a more differentiated view, which goes beyond a simple dichotomy of dissent and agreement, second chambers in the comparative literature are usually described as exhibiting the following (or similarly expressed) functions: 1) legislative review (based on the provision of additional perspectives and/or professional expertise), 2) mutual veto (based on the necessity of a countervailing power to minimize the danger of institutional hegemony of the first chamber or, put more directly and less friendly, of "mob rule"), and 3) federal representation (designed as a safeguard against a majority-based, tyrannical government, which subjugates individual rights).[46] The third point, federal representation, has been discussed in part already in the foregoing section.

The Austrian Federal Council

No matter whether one takes the radical or the more differentiated view, the status of the Austrian Federal Council is usually described in very critical terms. The relatively congruent composition of first and second chamber, enhanced by strong parties and high party discipline, translates into high levels of agreement between the party groups of the same party in the two chambers. The question therefore arises what the Federal Council genuinely contributes to the main functions which parliaments typically have, i.e. law-making and control of the executive.

45 Cited in Coakley, "Revival of Bicameralism," 546.
46 Michael Lusztig, "Federalism and Institutional Design: The Perils and Politics of a Triple-E Senate in Canada," *Publius: The Journal of Federalism* 25, no. 1 (1995): 35-50, p. 39-41; cf. Meg Russell, "What are Second Chambers for?," *Parliamentary Affairs* 54, no. 3 (2001): 442-458; Uhr, "Bicameralism," 485-488.

Constitutionally, the Federal Council was designed to represent the provinces (Article 34 of the Austrian Federal Constitution). However, in practice it is not very active. Until 1970, it had not once used its right to submit a bill to the first chamber, the National Council. Since then, it has done so on the average one to two times a year.[47] The main reason for this lack of initiative is the asymmetrical status of the second chamber in relation to the first chamber. All bills approved by the National Council have to be submitted to the Federal Council. Important exceptions are financial bills, which are beyond the influence of the second chamber. What is more, only if the composition of the Federal Council is to be changed or if responsibilities of the provinces are to be transferred to the national parliament or government, the Federal Council has an absolute veto.[48] Neither of these veto rights has ever been used so far. Strikingly, according to statistics of the Institute of Federalism, from 1985 (when this right was given to it) until 2011, the second chamber has agreed in no less than 233 cases to federal laws interfering in the distribution of responsibilities between the federal state and the provinces.[49]

In all other cases, the Federal Council can only delay bills, which have been sent over from the National Council, for eight weeks. If the National Council insists on its original decision with a simple absolute majority, the suspensory veto of the Federal Council is overridden. Being a blunt weapon, the veto is seldom if ever used—in some legislative periods not even once. In times of coalition governments, which have become the rule since 1983, coalition agreements usually contain provisions binding the members of the Federal Council (and the National Council) to support government proposals, further curbing the autonomy of the members of the second chamber. Only in periods when the parties standing in opposition to the national government have a majority in the Federal Council, have they used the veto instrument more often (mainly for party-political and/or symbolic reasons, not because provincial interests would have been at stake).[50]

As a result of these restricting provisions, the Federal Council mainly acts as a "reworking" institution, and its members often comment on their political work as frustrating.[51] They attribute significantly less importance to committee meetings than the members of the National Council. The meetings are usually rather short, and their information character markedly

47 Fallend, "Der Bundesrat in Österreich," 177.
48 Ibid., 177-178.
49 Institut für Föderalismus, *36. Bericht über den Föderalismus in Österreich* (2011) (Vienna: new academic press, 2012), 34.
50 Fallend, "Der Bundesrat in Österreich," 179-180.
51 Steininger, "Der Bundesrat in Österreich," 439.

dominates over the decision-making character.[52] This is a result of the fact that the Federal Council is involved in the law-making process only at a late stage and that the positions of its members are to a high degree predetermined by the foregoing meetings of the factions of the respective party groups. The members of the Federal Council may voice their thoughts in these meetings, but afterwards they are expected to abide by party discipline.[53] Not surprisingly, the contents of the speeches in the Federal Council resemble those in the National Council to a high degree.[54]

The asymmetrical relationship between the first and second chambers does not get better when we turn to the possibilities of the Federal Council to control the federal government. The Federal Council, in contrast to the National Council, has no rights to pass a vote of no-confidence on the government, to install investigative committees or to instruct the audit office to inquire into suspicious government actions. It can only ask questions to members of the cabinet and pass (non-binding) resolutions, expressing its wishes for what the government should do. As a result, it is mainly the opposition which uses the forum of the Federal Council to replicate its criticisms on government policies; however, all in all the control initiatives in the Federal Council are distinctly less extensive than in the National Council.[55]

The fact that the members of the Federal Council, as opposed to those of the National Council, are not granted resources to hire professional assistants is a further indication of the subordinate role of the second vis-à-vis the first chamber. When the Federal Council submitted a bill to the National Council to extend this right, which was established for the National Council in 1992, to the Federal Council, the proposal was rejected, officially because of the need to save money. Not surprisingly, the Federal Council also lacks a legal service, which could support it in devising substantive bills.[56]

The asymmetrical constitutional status of National Council and Federal Council persists until today. However, recently the Federal Council has tried to prove its usefulness in a new field and thereby to counter repeated calls for its abolition because of redundancy: that is, regarding matters of the European Union (EU). In 1992, the Conference of the Provincial Governors, and not the Federal Council, was bestowed with the right to

52 Ibid., 426-427.
53 Fallend, "Der Bundesrat in Österreich," 175.
54 Günther Schefbeck, "Das Parlament," in *Politik in Österreich: Das Handbuch*, ed. Herbert Dachs et al. (Vienna: Manz Verlag, 2006), 139-167, p. 154.
55 Fallend, "Der Bundesrat in Österreich," 180-182.
56 Ibid., 176.

submit binding statements of the provinces to the federal government in EU matters. However, in 1994, both chambers got the right to submit binding statements to the federal government if new EU regulations were planned which would affect federal laws (in the case of the National Council) or require a change in the distribution of responsibilities between the federal and the provincial level (in the case of the Federal Council). In 2010, both chambers received additional rights in the context of the subsidiarity control established by the Treaty of Lisbon in the year before. In particular, the Federal Council has increased its respective activities and managed to emancipate itself somewhat from the National Council since then.[57]

Other Second Chambers

While the Belgian Senate resembled the Austrian Federal Council in its congruence with the first chamber, they differed markedly with respect to their status in the law-making process, in particular before the constitutional reform of 1993 in Belgium. From 1920/21 onwards, the Belgian Senate was equipped with the same powers as the House of Representatives. Bills had to generally pass both chambers to become law; a conciliation committee did not exist.[58] The practice of law-making was very similar in both chambers. Since the reform of 1993, there are still areas in which both chambers have to agree (notably concerning the institutional order and cultural matters), but these areas were noticeably reduced. In other areas, the first chamber was given the right to override decisions of the second chamber. In particular, the federal budget is now a prerogative of the first chamber (and the king or queen). Despite these changes, however, conflicts or even deadlocks in law-making between the two chambers are seldom, due to the relatively identical party composition. The logic of government versus opposition dominates over the logic of federal state versus regions or communities. Basically, the Senate lacks resources to play a more active role in law-making, but also seems to have accepted its secondary role.[59]

Regarding the control of the executive, the House of Representatives and the Senate in Belgium had the same rights and similar records before the reform of 1993. By the reform, however, the Senate was deprived of its right to pass a vote of no-confidence, thereby losing its most effective weapon (until 1995, two governments were overthrown by the Senate). Since then, the prime minister has given his government statement only before the

57 Institut für Föderalismus, *36. Bericht über den Föderalismus*, 34.
58 Zink, "Der belgische Senat," 228-229.
59 Ibid., 229-237.

House. While still active in debates about fundamental issues, the Senate has lost its capacity to steer day-to-day politics. Similar to its Austrian counterpart, however, it has intensified its international activities.[60] To sum up, the symmetry between the two Belgian chambers was not sufficient to provide for a strong second chamber, above all because of the party-political congruence between them, and the recent downgrading of the powers of the second chamber has further weakened its influence.

In Canada, the two chambers, the House of Commons and the Senate, are organized asymmetrically in Lijphart's terms, although the Senate has more powers than the Austrian Federal Council. It has to agree to all bills so that they become law, including financial bills. There is nothing like a conciliation committee. Since 1982, however, the Senate can only delay, but not prevent constitutional amendments any more. In addition, it has no right to expel the government from office by a vote of no-confidence.[61] The last aspect is a clear indicator of "the uneasy relationship between parliamentary majority rule and federalism";[62] the Canadian founding fathers were reluctant to give a chamber which was not directly elected the right to throw out a government.

In practice, the Canadian Senate only rarely introduces bills of its own and it does not alter proposals by the House of Commons substantively (as studies have shown, in recent years only about four percent of them). Even in cases when the opposition had a majority in the Senate, bills passed by the House of Commons were usually not rejected. However, the Senate has acquired some profile as a chamber that brings in "sober second thought" so that "quick shots" of badly designed, ineffective laws can be fended off. In the 1960s and 1970s, the Senate was also able to influence law-making indirectly when it set up special committees to debate major issues of the public debate. However, this influence has decreased in recent years as the governing parties have strived to relocate these debates into the House of Commons, which is easier for them to control. With respect to its function to control the executive, the Senate has in general acted very cautiously in order not to endanger the legitimacy of government[63]—similarly to the Austrian Federal Council.

In contrast to the Austrian Federal Council, the Swiss Council of States has powers that are symmetrical to those of the first chamber. Both chambers have to agree on bills before they become law. As a consequence, the Council of States is a real working parliament, with intensive committee

60 Ibid., 237-239.
61 Zinterer, "Der kanadische Senat," 247.
62 Hueglin and Fenna, *Comparative Federalism*, 67.
63 Ibid., 193; Zinterer, "Der kanadische Senat," 250-252.

work; indeed, the number of initiatives is higher in the Council of States than in the National Council. In case the two chambers fail to reach an agreement, at first a shuttle procedure and then a conciliation conference between the two chambers are utilized. Between 1992 and 2008, in all but three cases an agreement was reached;[64] in general, the two chambers are regarded as highly consensus-oriented.[65]

Due to the overrepresentation of the bourgeois parties, the Swiss Council of States has traditionally shown a preference for more liberal economic and social policies than the National Council.[66] However, the power of the Council of States should not be overestimated. There are other elements of the complex Swiss political system, like the extensive consultation mechanisms, the direct-democratic instruments and the cross-cutting confessional, language, and urban-rural cleavages, which influence policy-making and relativize the conservative bias as well as the overall importance of the Council of States.[67] Thus, the constraining effect on social policies in Switzerland was exercised by the conservative and liberal parties and the business organizations above all through the instrument of the referendum, only partly through the Council of States.[68] However, it acts as "*chambre de réflexion*"[69] and performs a vital role in balancing heterogeneous interests, minimizing conflicts and political integration.[70]

Reform of the Second Chamber?

A substantial reform of the Austrian Federal Council, though deemed unavoidable by many political observers, seems far-off. As was already clear at the time of its establishment, its construction was ill-conceived, triggering reform proposals by constitutional lawyers and political scientists as well as political parties.[71] The congruent nature of the Federal Council, and the dependence of its members on their parties, have led to proposals

64 Riescher, "Der Schweizer Ständerat," 68-72.
65 Kriesi, "The Federal Parliament," 63; Vatter, "Transformation of Access and Veto Points," 5; Riescher, "Der Schweizer Ständerat," 69.
66 Linder and Vatter, "Institutions and Outcomes of Swiss Federalism," 100; Herbert Obinger et al., "Switzerland: The Marriage of Direct Democracy and Federalism," in *Federalism and the Welfare State: New World and European Experiences*, ed. Herbert Obinger, Stephan Leibfried and Francis G. Castles (Cambridge: Cambridge University Press, 2005), 263-304, p. 270.
67 Riescher, "Der Schweizer Ständerat," 65-66.
68 Obinger et al., "Switzerland," 300, 302.
69 Linder and Vatter, "Institutions and Outcomes of Swiss Federalism," 101.
70 Riescher, "Der Schweizer Ständerat," 72.
71 For a short list of reform proposals see the references in Fallend, "Der Bundesrat in Österreich," 182-184.

(in the past mostly coming from the Social Democratic side) to change the recruitment procedure from indirect to direct election. Alternatively, it has been suggested (often by provincial politicians of the ÖVP) to bind the members of the Federal Council to an imperative mandate by the parliament or government of their provinces. Regarding its powers, it was suggested, among other things, to involve the Federal Council earlier in the parliamentary negotiations, not only at the end of the process, to extend its veto rights (especially concerning financial matters affecting the provinces) as well as its control rights. For sure, the political legitimacy of the Federal Council would have been raised by all those measures. However, as they would have changed the balance of power between the major political institutions and the major political parties, none of the proposals has ever come close to being realized, pointing to the "durability of constitutional arrangements once in place. Because they are the result of negotiated compromise, federal constitutions are like puzzles: taking one piece out of its familiar place is likely to affect too many others."[72] That is why political actors usually shy away from substantial reforms, which frequently bear the danger of cutting deeply into their spheres of influence.

Even if the political will, especially among the major political parties, were strong enough to allow for a substantial reform, the comparison of the Austrian Federal Council with its counterparts in Belgium, Canada, and Switzerland has demonstrated that it is not easy to make straightforward recommendations as to the direction in which a reform should go. Regarding the composition of the second chamber, it seems clear that it must not be congruent to the composition of the first chamber. Otherwise, it will be regarded as redundant. "Congruent" in this context refers not only to social groups, but to the political parties as well. A second chamber which is obviously dominated by the same parties as the first chamber will not be accepted by the public as useful or necessary (see the case of Belgium). The highest democratic legitimacy, and as a consequence the potentially highest political influence, would obviously be connected with a direct election of the members of the second chamber, while a recruitment by appointment seems unacceptable in an era of democratization (see the case of Canada). A recruitment by indirect election (like in Austria), which lies somewhere halfway between the other two recruitment procedures, lacks full democratic legitimacy and would have to be compensated by other features, e.g. an equal representation of the provinces or a (near-)symmetrical status in the law-making process, to avoid fundamental criticisms. Whether an equal representation of the provinces (like in the cases of Canada and Switzerland)

72 Hueglin and Fenna, *Comparative Federalism*, 196.

is a realistic goal for a reform of the Austrian Federal Council, is more than doubtful, however, considering the positions of the major political parties.

Regarding the powers and functions of the second chamber, a fundamental problem arises, which has been mentioned in the case studies. While a symmetrical status of the two parliamentary chambers is usually demanded by convinced federalists and seems necessary to warrant the existence of a second chamber, this symmetry can at the same time be questioned when it undermines the popular will, i.e., the will of the majority, as it is expressed in the first chamber (see the quoted dictum by Abbé Sieyès). The practical consequences of this becomes clear in the case of Canada, where the Senate has almost equal powers to the House of Commons, but has retreated in the background and does not question the supremacy of the first chamber. Likewise, the Belgian Senate has accepted its secondary role; the recent reform of its recruitment procedure, from direct to indirect election, seems to reproduce this fact. Switzerland, with its powerful Council of States, in which the provinces are represented equally, is different. Interestingly, the strong bicameralism in Switzerland does not lead to deadlock. Intensive consultation and accommodation mechanisms provide for a high degree of political consensus. Because of its rootedness in long traditions and its complexity, however, the Swiss political system is also one which is almost impossible to copy.

Partly as a consequence of the difficulties and unpredictabilities which are connected with far-reaching constitutional reforms, partly out of practical necessities, in many federal countries regional actors have sought for alternative channels, besides the second chambers, to influence federal policies. Often, these alternative channels have been governmental ones, leading to a downgrading of parliamentary institutions. So the Conference of the Provincial Governors (*Landeshauptleutekonferenz*) is "to be considered as the key player in Austria's real constitution."[73] Likewise, in Belgium, the Concertation Committee, which consists of the prime minister, six federal ministers and six ministers from the regions/communities, has become more important for streamlining inter-governmental relations than the Senate.[74] In Canada, the First Ministers' Conferences, chaired by the prime minister and attended by the provincial premiers, provide for the necessary political coordination in a highly regionalized federal state.[75] Also, in Switzerland, the Conference of Cantonal Governments has gained in importance, especially in the context of European integration.[76]

73 Karlhofer and Pallaver, "Strength through Weakness," 42.
74 Swenden, *Federalism and Regionalism in Western Europe*, 202.
75 Hueglin and Fenna, *Comparative Federalism*, 68-69.
76 Linder and Vatter, "Institutions and Outcomes of Swiss Federalism," 105.

Conclusions

Several conclusions can be drawn from the foregoing description, analysis, and comparison of the second chambers in the four parliamentary, federal states of Austria, Belgium, Canada, and Switzerland. First, all four cases are cases of parliamentary systems and it has been shown that "[t]he logics of parliamentarism and strong bicameralism do not fit well together."[77] Parliamentary systems are based on the support of government by the majority in parliament, and with "parliament," in this context, usually only the first chamber, which is directly elected on the basis of the principle "one person, one vote" is referred to. If a second chamber is, like the first chamber, directly elected, then "[b]y contrast with the presidential system, a difference or deadlock between the two houses would threaten the executive government itself."[78] On the other hand, in non-parliamentary or presidential systems, which have not been studied here, upper houses are rarely if ever regarded as secondary.[79]

Second, as fundamental reforms of political or federal systems (e.g. from parliamentary to presidential) are very unlikely, reforms of the composition or the powers of the second chamber within the parliamentary system have to steer a delicate course between the aspired democratic legitimacy (requiring almost inevitably a direct election of its members) and the legitimate representation of specific social groups or interests (necessary to counter objections of "redundancy"). Legitimacy is essential: "When push comes to shove, none of the alignments of symmetry or congruence will make much difference to the real institutional strength of a bicameral system if the system lacks public legitimacy."[80]

Third, to get the full picture a more detailed analysis would be necessary, which focuses on the relationships between the second chamber on the one hand and the type of federalism (dual versus functional), the degree of self-rule and shared rule, the degree of (de-)centralization (indicated by, among other things, the share of sub-national tax revenues and public expenditures), extra-constitutional channels of inter-governmental relations (conferences of executives, political parties, interest groups etc.) and other central elements of the political system on the other hand.

77 Swenden, *Federalism and Regionalism in Western Europe*, 192.

78 Hueglin and Fenna, *Comparative Federalism*, 192.

79 Uhr, "Bicameralism," 478.

80 Ibid., 490.

Reforming Austrian Fiscal Federalism: Options, Obstacles, and Pitfalls

Margit Schratzenstaller

Introduction[1]

The call for fundamental reforms in the Austrian system of fiscal federalism is far from being new; on the contrary, national experts and think tanks as well as international organizations have been demanding substantial reforms for several decades now.[2] So far, there is far-reaching consensus on the deficits of the current system as well as on the strategic thrust and the cornerstones of the reforms required to overcome these deficits.[3] However, this consensus, as well as a continuous push for fundamental reforms, which has been going on practically for several decades now, for a long time has been restricted almost exclusively to academia. It is only since the outbreak of the financial and economic crisis that public awareness and pressure for reform have increased considerably in Austria, as reforming federal

1 This article draws heavily on Helfried Bauer and Margit Schratzenstaller, "Ausgewählte Reformerfordernisse im österreichischen Finanzausgleich," in *Koordinierung der Finanzpolitik im Bundesstaat*, ed. Peter Biwald et al. (Vienna: Neuer Wissenschaftlicher Verlag, 2011), 114-131.

2 See, for example, *Finanzverfassung und Finanzausgleich: Herausforderungen und Anpassungserfordernisse*, ed. Beirat für Wirtschafts- und Sozialfragen (Vienna: Ueberreuter, 1992); Andrés Fuentes, Eckhard Wurzel and Andreas Wörgötter, "Reforming Federal Fiscal Relations in Austria," *OECD Economics Department Working Paper*, no. 474 (2006), at <http://dx.doi.org/10.1787/880241418571> (10 February 2015); Hans Pitlik, "Fiscal Federalism, Austrian Style: Fear of Competition," in *Fiscal Federalism and Fiscal Decentralization in Europe: Comparative Case Studies on Spain, Austria, the United Kingdom and Italy*, ed. Stefan August Lütgenau (Innsbruck: StudienVerlag, 2014), 41-59.

3 See, for example, the following studies commissioned by the Austrian Ministry of Finance: Helfried Bauer et al., *Grundsätzliche Reform des Finanzausgleichs: Verstärkte Aufgabenorientierung* (Vienna: Institut für Höhere Studien, 2010); Hans Pitlik, Klaus Wirth and Barbara Lehner, *Gemeindestruktur und Gemeindekooperation* (Vienna: WIFO, 2010); Peter Biwald et al., *Grundlegende Reform des Finanzausgleichs: Transfers und Kostentragung* (Vienna: KDZ, 2010); Johann Bröthaler et al., *Grundlegende Reform des Finanzausgleichs: Reformoptionen und Reformstrategien* (Vienna: TU Wien, 2011); Markus Achatz, *Zur Stärkung der Abgabenautonomie subnationaler Gebietskörperschaften (der Länder)* (Linz: Universität Linz, 2010).

fiscal relations is key to implementing expenditure-saving and efficiency-enhancing reforms in central policy areas such as health, subsidies, or the education/school system to reach the government's fiscal consolidation goals.[4]

This article provides a brief overview of the most important problem areas in the Austrian system of fiscal federalism and the direction of future reform efforts.[5] This overview is embedded into some fundamental deliberations on the premises and principles as well as a targeted and effective approach to a reform of the Austrian system of fiscal federalism.

Premises, Principles, and Approach of a Fundamental Reform of the Austrian System of Fiscal Federalism

General Framework and Aims

A substantial reform of the Austrian system of fiscal federalism should take off from three central premises. First, a broader understanding of fiscal federalism is indispensable. Considering the structural deficits within the current system of fiscal federalism and in view of the long-term challenges (e.g. demographic and climate change) Austria is facing, reform efforts must include the assignment of tasks and competencies to, as well as the dynamics of revenues and expenditures on the respective governmental levels. Second, the future architecture of the Austrian system of fiscal federalism should allow for an effective coordination among the governmental levels to achieve a macroeconomic and budgetary balance. Third, the size of the public sector (as measured, e.g., by the tax-to-GDP-ratio) should not be increased by implementing a new system of fiscal federalism.

There is a broad consensus among experts that a reform of federal fiscal relations in Austria should be motivated by the following central goals and corresponding reform requirements:[6]

– reform of the assignment of competencies and tasks to the governmental levels, explicitly taking into account the municipal level, to react adequately to technological and economic change and changing international relations, obligations, and commitments;

4 Hans Pitlik, Kristina Budimir and Norbert Gruber, "Optionen einer ausgabenseitigen Budgetkonsolidierung," *WIFO-Monatsberichte* 83, no. 3 (2010): 247-267.

5 For a brief overview of Austria's fiscal framework and fiscal equalization scheme see Pitlik, "Fiscal Federalism," 41-59; Fuentes, Wurzel and Wörgötter, "Reforming Federal Fiscal Relations."

6 See Bröthaler et al., *Grundlegende Reform des Finanzausgleichs.*

– strengthening the goal-orientation of the system of fiscal federalism, particularly with regard to central economic and political goals (e.g. climate protection);

– supporting efficient fulfillment of tasks by aligning task, spending, and financing responsibilities, as required by the principle of "connexity" (*Konnexität*) on all governmental levels;

– achieving transparency as well as responsibility and accountability of public actors for inputs and outputs/outcomes;

– creating a certain degree of interjurisdictional competition at the subnational governmental levels by strengthening expenditure and financing responsibility and by increasing transparency of locational advantages and disadvantages;

– strengthening fiscal equivalence;

– extending subnational fiscal autonomy, particularly tax autonomy, and a corresponding reduction of the amount of shared taxes;

– reducing the number of policy fields resting on mixed financing, joint responsibilities, and fragmented decision-making;

– radical retrenchment of intragovernmental transfers to strengthen accountability of decision-makers and to increase transparency;

– creating incentives for subnational levels to exploit own resources;

– increasing task-orientation of the allocation of funds (particularly revenues from shared taxes) to subnational levels;

– encouraging reforms of municipal structures and inter-municipal cooperation to exploit economies of scale and scope by promoting cooperations and fusions;

– separation of allocative and distributive goals within the allocation of revenues from shared taxes and within the system of intra-/intergovernmental transfers to increase transparency, effectiveness, and efficiency.

Altogether, a reform of Austrian federal fiscal relations, which currently are characterized by strong, albeit unsystematic redistribution effects and contain only weak incentives for subnational levels (particularly the states) to assume responsibility and accountability for financing and an efficient fulfillment of their tasks, should primarily enhance efficiency and performance-orientation.

Graph 1 displays the principles of the allocation of tasks and funds in a federal state.[7]

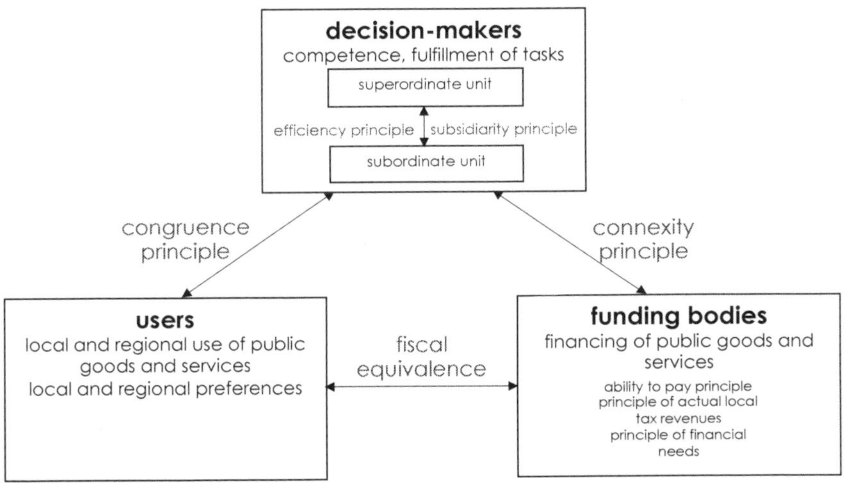

Graph 1: Principles of the allocation of tasks and funds in a federal state. Source: Bröthaler et al., *Grundlegende Reform.*

A reform of the system of federal fiscal relations requires a fundamental discussion about the design of the federation itself and its federalism model as well as about the assignment of tasks and competencies. Hereby various principles must be considered which aim at efficiency as well as equity (in the sense of inter-jurisdictional financial equalization).

Departing from the subsidiarity principle, according to which the responsibility for the fulfillment of a task and the provision of public goods and services, respectively, should be transferred to the lowest possible governmental level, the achievement of fiscal equivalence and connexity is of utmost importance. According to the principle of fiscal equivalence, those individuals and firms benefitting from a public good or service should be identical to those individuals and firms who contribute (in addition to

7 See ibid.

user fees) via taxes to financing this public good or service. The principle of connexity requires that decision-makers not only determine tasks and expenditures, but also the revenues required to finance these. Institutional and spatial congruence is a crucial prerequisite for these efficiency-oriented principles, i.e. direct accountability of decision-makers towards users (the electorate). The allocation of funds within the system of fiscal equalization should be guided by further principles, whose respective weights should be determined politically (inter alia the principle of actual local tax revenues, the principle of financial needs, the principle of task orientation, the principle of equity).

Strategic Elements of a Reform of Austrian Federal Fiscal Relations

A substantial reform of the Austrian system of fiscal federalism should rest on several strategic elements.

Planning and Design of the Reform Process

Several recent international examples (e.g. Switzerland or Germany) for substantial reforms of federal fiscal relations suggest that the focus of such reforms should be on the whole architecture of the system of federal fiscal relations. Restricting reforms to selected reform areas or to marginal reforms would not solve the fundamental problems, but may instead increase the complexity of an already non-transparent system even further. Moreover, a consistent redesign of the overall architecture of federal fiscal relations may also convince skeptical actors, and it is the only approach that is appropriate to cope with the manifold interdependencies between the various sub-areas of the whole system of federal fiscal relations.

An indispensable success factor for a fundamental reform of the overall system of federal fiscal relations is to decouple it from the regular renegotiations of the concrete Fiscal Equalization Law (*Finanzausgleichsgesetz*) between the governmental levels (the so-called financial equalization partners), which normally covers a period of four years and then expires automatically to be renegotiated again for the next four-years-period.[8] The renegotiations of the Fiscal Equalization Laws normally take place within a rather short time frame and have a limited focus, as they concentrate on the detailed financial flows between and

8 The current Fiscal Equalization Law is an exception insofar as originally it was stipulated for the period from 2007 to 2013; afterwards it was prolonged twice—first for another year, then for another two years until the end of 2016. This unusually long validity of the Fiscal Equalization Law in some respect reflects the increasing inability of the financial equalization partners to find long-term and (fiscally) sustainable solutions in important policy areas.

on the respective levels of government within the existing architecture of federal fiscal relations, which is taken as given. Thus these renegotiations only allow for incremental changes in selected sub-areas of the fiscal equalization scheme.

In addition, an appropriate design of transitional provisions is required: On the one hand, transitional provisions help to secure the acceptance of reforms by the governmental levels affected by them. On the other hand, transitional provisions should be limited to rather short time periods and should only partially compensate losses. Otherwise, there is the danger they may be taken for customary rights, and thus weaken incentives for jurisdictions' own efforts to improve the situation which has been negatively affected by the reforms beforehand.

A Federalism Model for Austria

One of the most important building blocks of substantial reforms within the Austrian system of federal fiscal relations is the decision for a modern federalism model to be achieved by the reform. A redesign of the allocation of tasks and revenues to the layers of government should rest on a federalism model that should be defined and made explicit from the outset. Departing from basic models of federalism[9]—competitive federalism, cooperative federalism, solidarian competitive federalism and administrative federalism—Austria's state and governance structure and political system as well as the efficiency problems of the current system of federal fiscal relations suggest pursuing a model of a "solidarian interregional competitive federalism."[10] Such a federalism model aims at a moderate increase of yard-stick competition between the states, to support political decisions which match citizens' preferences as closely as possible. In this way, namely by extending subnational revenue autonomy, by a clear distribution of tasks, competencies and expenditures, and by the possibility to compare benefit-cost-relations, the prerequisites for a solidarian and innovative development process should be created. Thus, the practices of interjurisdictional comparisons and learning from the best (best practice) will move more to the fore, resulting in increasing quality (structural efficiency) and decreasing costs (cost efficiency) of public goods and services. By contrasting public goods and services and outcomes/performance on the one hand and the financial burden they imply for users on the other hand, citizens should be enabled to discern "good" from "bad" governance.

9 See Bröthaler et al., *Grundlegende Reform des Finanzausgleichs*.

10 Erich Thöni, "Finanzierung öffentlicher Aufgaben–einige grundlegende Bemerkungen zum ungenutzten Beitrag der österreichischen Länder," in *Innovation im öffentlichen Sektor*, ed. Peter Biwald, Elisabeth Dearing and Thomas Weninger (Vienna: Neuer Wissenschaftlicher Verlag, 2008), 210-222, p. 221; author's translation.

Positioning the Reform of Federal Fiscal Relations towards Other Reform Areas

Another strategic challenge is to position the reform of federal fiscal relations towards other reform areas and to identify interdependencies. Before starting the reform of federal fiscal relations, those reform areas which are indispensable for a successful reform of federal fiscal relations have to be identified. It should be clarified which reform areas

– represent important elements of a reform of federal fiscal relations,
– form strategic push factors and incentives or rather act as essential barriers of a reform of federal fiscal relations, or
– are not related to a reform of federal fiscal relations at all.

A state reform is a central precondition insofar as it is necessary to disentangle the assignment of tasks to the governmental levels as well as to realize the principle of connexity. The same is true for an administrative reform across all layers of government. Tax reforms and the domestic stability pact are important reform areas which are closely connected to the system of federal fiscal relations. Other reform areas—for example the budgeting and accounting system or the structure of municipalities—can be treated and addressed separately from a reform of federal fiscal relations, even if they go in the same direction. Graph 2 illustrates the position of the reform of federal fiscal relations in relation to other reform areas.

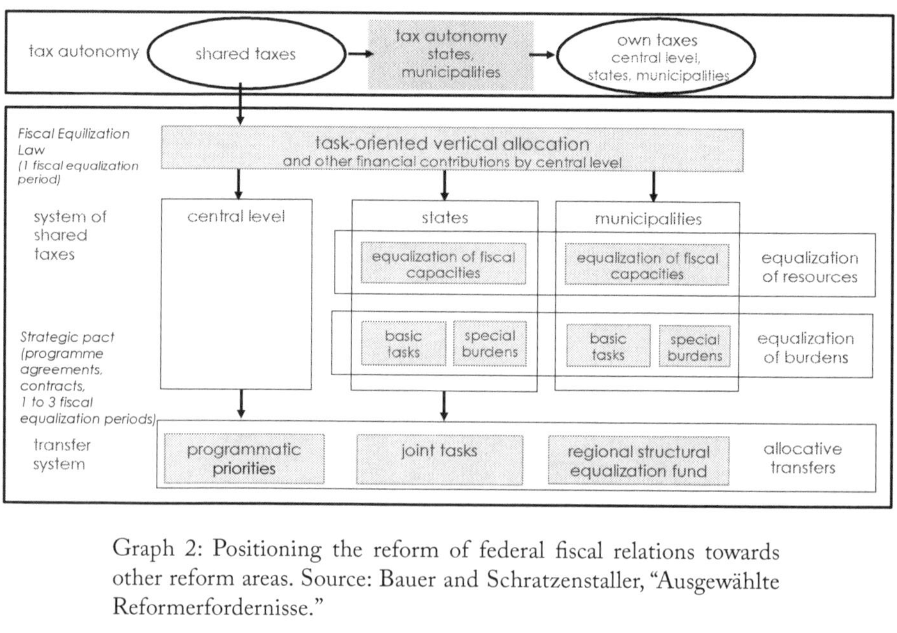

Graph 2: Positioning the reform of federal fiscal relations towards other reform areas. Source: Bauer and Schratzenstaller, "Ausgewählte Reformerfordernisse."

Related is the fundamental decision about whether the reform should be based on a broad or rather on a narrow understanding of the system of federal fiscal relations. The system of federal fiscal relations in a broad sense determines the allocation of funds across governmental levels in close connection to their tasks, which may vary over time due to political, economic, or social reasons or due to inter-/intragovernmental shifts of priorities. The system of federal fiscal relations in a narrow sense takes the assignment of tasks as well as the tasks themselves as given and focuses exclusively on the allocation of funds.

Overall Architecture of the System of Federal Fiscal Relations

A fundamental reform of the system of federal fiscal relations (in a narrow sense) should include a redesign of the overall architecture of the system of federal fiscal relations. Subnational tax autonomy, task-oriented vertical allocation of funds, a system of equalization of resources (bundling of all existing transfers) and of burdens (for basic tasks and special burdens) as well as a few allocative transfers which are granted temporarily and with a narrow thematic focus are core areas of this new architecture.

Graph 3 depicts the overall architecture of a substantially reformed system of federal fiscal relations.

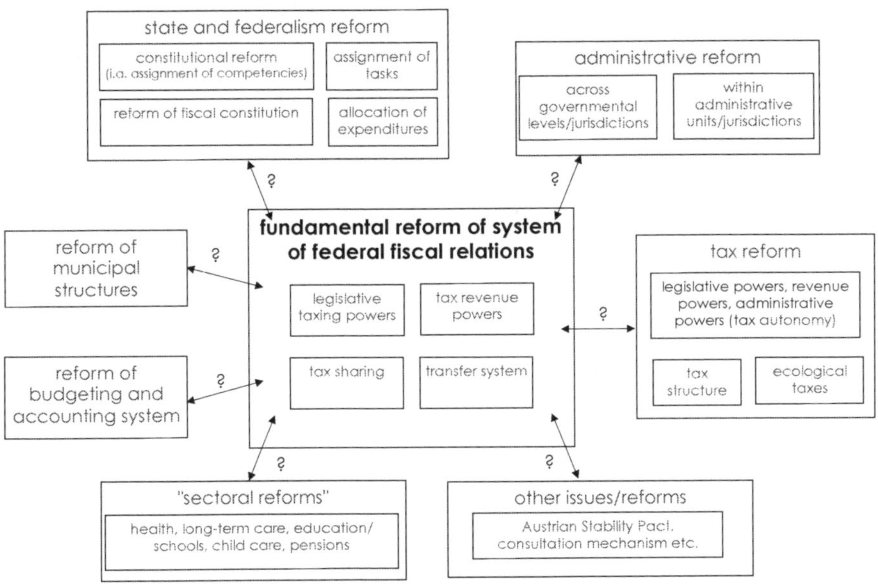

Graph 3: Perspective of a new overall architecture of the system of federal fiscal relations. Source: Bauer and Schratzenstaller, "Ausgewählte Reformerfordernisse."

Functional Analyses

Functional analyses are a central precondition for the redesign of federal fiscal relations in important policy fields. They analyze the responsibilities for tasks, expenditures, and revenues of the different governmental levels. At the core of functional analyses is the analysis of decision-makers and of transactions and structural links with other governmental levels as well as actors. Such functional analyses are particularly necessary for the health sector, for public transportation, for the education/school sector, for long-term care, and for social policy and the needs-based minimum benefit system. On the one hand, in these policy fields the (financial) links between the involved levels of government are complex and non-transparent and therefore very much in need of reform. On the other hand, these policy fields will gain in importance in the long run due to foreseeable long-term socioeconomic developments and challenges (e.g. ageing).

Evaluation

Finally evaluations are of utmost importance. First, the reform process itself as well as the effects of the reform compared to the status quo should be evaluated regularly. This makes it possible to identify possible weaknesses of the reform measures and to take appropriate countermeasures in time, as well as the assessment of the allocative and distributive effects of the reform measures. Hereby not only the immediate financial effects are of interest, but also medium- and long-term perspectives under the conditions of extended autonomy and self-responsibility as well as changes in the general framework conditions. Second, regular evaluations of the system itself should constitute an important element of a new system of federal fiscal relations. Regular evaluations create the information basis required for the assessment of the overall effects of the system of federal fiscal relations, and they are an important precondition for efficient political decisions.

Central Reform Areas

Interdependencies between the Core Elements of the System of Federal Fiscal Relations

A system of federal fiscal relations normally comprises several core elements and instruments that are characterized by certain interdependencies. The design elements related to the distribution of tasks may affect changes in the assignment of tasks (centralization versus decentralization) or in the intensity of their fulfillment (build-up of additional capacities, expiry of programs), but may also relate to the redesign of tasks which up to now have been fulfilled jointly by more than one level of government. Obviously, larger shifts within competencies or the actual ownership of tasks will require corresponding changes in the allocation of financial resources. The main instruments for allocation and distribution of funds across governmental and jurisdictions, respectively, are "own taxes" (*eigene Steuern*) of the governmental levels and jurisdictions, respectively (i.e. the right to determine tax rates and/or tax bases) and shared taxes (i.e. shares of the respective governmental levels in shared taxes determined by the central level and allocated to the governmental levels based on an allocation key). Intragovernmental transfers between the jurisdictions at one governmental level (horizontal, i.e. between the states or the municipalities) and/or between the governmental levels (vertical) are additional instruments. Assuming an upper limit for the overall tax ratio, own taxes determined by and accruing to the individual governmental levels and shared taxes are characterized by a complementary relationship. In the same vein, strengthening responsibility/accountability of the layers of government and thus the principle of connexity implies cutting back mixed financing and extending subnational tax autonomy, which, again, requires some equalization mechanism to compensate differences in potential own tax revenues (fiscal capacity) via horizontal transfers.

Extending Subnational Tax Autonomy and Corresponding Reduction of Shared Taxes

Strengthening subnational tax autonomy is a crucial element of a redesign of Austrian federal fiscal relations. It is an indispensable precondition to realize the principle of financial autonomy of jurisdictions as well as fiscal equivalence, i.e. a larger contribution of citizens, the business sector and owners of real estate to financing those goods and services at state and municipal level they are using. Currently, own taxes make up for less than two percent of overall revenues of the states and about twenty percent of overall revenues of municipalities.[11] Hereby, it is remarkable that most of these own taxes accruing to the subnational levels cannot be varied by these, as tax rates and bases are determined by the central level. The only significant exception is the real estate tax (*Grundsteuer*) accruing to the municipalities, for which these can vary the tax rate up to an upper limit.

In the last few years, several studies have analyzed several options to extend subnational tax autonomy: by transforming shared federal taxes into own taxes of the states (e.g. car taxes); by giving states or municipalities the right to levy surcharges on federal taxes (e.g. the income tax); or by extending the right of states and municipalities to find new tax sources and to increase existing own taxes, respectively (e.g. the real estate tax).[12]

Reforming the tax sharing arrangement is another cornerstone of a fundamental reform of federal fiscal relations. The tax sharing system was extended substantially during the last decades, at the cost of a corresponding reduction of the weight of own taxes of states and particularly municipalities. Graph 4 shows that the fraction of shared taxes as percent of total tax revenues has increased from seventy-five percent to ninety-three percent between 1990 and 2013, while own taxes of the governmental levels lose in importance. This development implies considerable consequences for horizontal fiscal equalization on the municipal level: While own taxes accrue to municipalities according to actual local tax revenues (which may result in considerable differences in per-capita-revenues between economically prospering municipalities and those with less favorable economic structures), revenues from shared taxes are allocated not only based on actual local tax revenues, but also based on population size and on the weighted population key (*abgestufter Bevölkerungsschlüssel*), respectively.

Past reforms within the vertical allocation of revenues from shared taxes include the harmonization of the allocation keys applied to allocate the revenues from shared taxes to governmental levels. Moreover, the horizontal allocation of the municipalities' share in shared taxes to individual

---

11 For details see Helfried Bauer, "Fiscal Decentralization: Trends, Unsolved Problems and Possible Reforms in Austria," in *Fiscal Federalism and Fiscal Decentralization in Europe: Comparative Case Studies on Spain, Austria, the United Kingdom and Italy*, ed. Stefan August Lütgenau (Innsbruck: StudienVerlag, 2014), 289-320.

12 See, e.g., Achatz, *Zur Stärkung der Abgabenautonomie*; Helfried Bauer et al., *Optionen zur Stärkung der Abgabenautonomie der österreichischen Gemeinden* (Vienna: WIFO, 2012). See also the contributions in *Stärkung der subnationalen Steuerautonomie und intragovernmentale Transfers*, ed. Helfried Bauer and Margit Schratzenstaller (Vienna: Neuer Wissenschaftlicher Verlag, 2007).

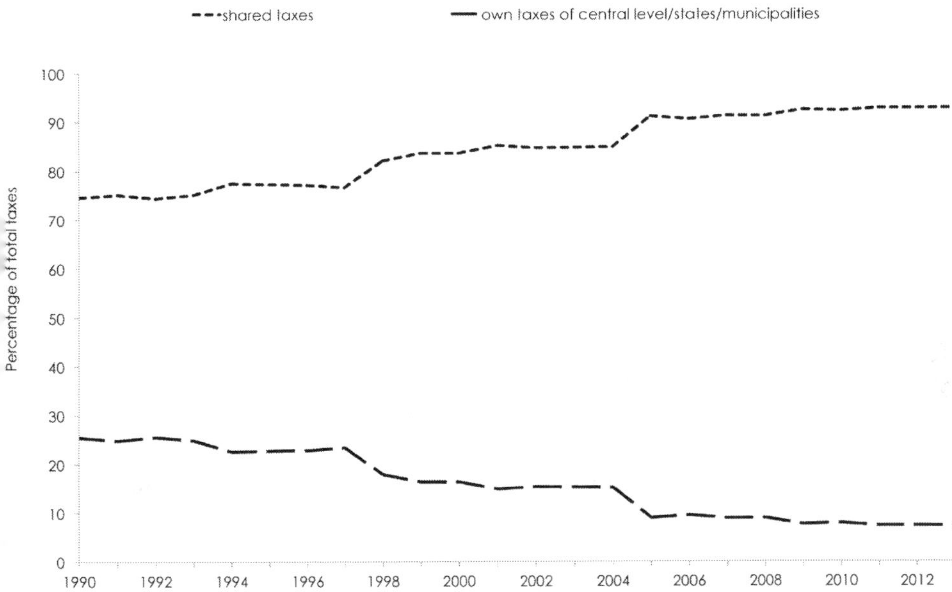

	shared taxes	own taxes of central level/states/municipalities	
1990	74.6	25.4	100.0
1991	75.2	24.8	100.0
1992	74.4	25.6	100.0
1993	75.1	24.9	100.0
1994	77.4	22.6	100.0
1995	77.3	22.7	100.0
1996	77.2	22.8	100.0
1997	76.6	23.4	100.0
1998	82.1	17.9	100.0
1999	83.6	16.4	100.0
2000	83.6	16.4	100.0
2001	85.2	14.8	100.0
2002	84.7	15.3	100.0
2003	84.8	15.2	100.0
2004	84.9	15.1	100.0
2005	91.2	8.8	100.0
2006	90.6	9.4	100.0
2007	91.2	8.8	100.0
2008	91.2	8.8	100.0
2009	92.4	7.6	100.0
2010	92.2	7.8	100.0
2011	92.8	7.2	100.0
2012	92.8	7.2	100.0
2013	92.8	7.2	100.0

Graph 4: Relation between own taxes of governmental levels and revenues from shared taxe. Source: *Statistik Austria*

municipalities is increasingly determined by the weighted population key, at the cost of weakening allocation according to actual local revenues from these taxes. In addition, at the municipal level, the differentiation of the allocation of funds according to population size by applying weighted population keys has been weakened significantly. Thus the system of allocation of funds is increasingly less adequate for the differing tasks of municipalities with different structures and different intensities of spending. This problem could be alleviated by basing the allocation of funds more on actual tasks.

Task-Orientation of the Allocation of Revenues from Shared Taxes

Allocating revenues from shared taxes based on the principle of task-orientation within vertical and horizontal allocation of funds can create a stronger connection to differing tasks and unit costs across differing jurisdictions than the current allocation of funds, which is primarily based on population size.[13] Task-orientation must be the guiding principle for the vertical allocation of funds to secure financing of new priorities laid down in strategic agreements between the governmental levels (e.g. expansion of long-term care, harmonization, and increase of means-tested minimum benefit system).

Within the vertical allocation of funds, task-orientation can rest on programs and/or on a change of allocation keys. Recently, some elements of task-orientation have been introduced via certain programs and their financial endowment. For example, the Fiscal Equalization Law 2008 contains several task-oriented financing arrangements, e.g. for the twenty-four hours nursing care program and for the means-tested minimum benefit system.

The principle of task-orientation can be integrated also into the horizontal allocation of funds: Besides basic tasks which are similar across jurisdictions and imply similar financial burdens (which are financed primarily based on population size accordingly), above-average special burdens for individual states and/or municipalities or groups of municipalities resulting from specific socio-demographic or geographic-topographic characteristics or from a function as a central location should be identified. This requires analyses whether in clearly defined policy fields there is on average a similar basic provision of public goods and services with regard to population size, so that population size (as one of the currently used indicators) can be applied. Or whether there are structurally

13 See Bauer et al., *Grundsätzliche Reform des Finanzausgleichs.*

induced special burdens that require specific indicators for the allocation of funds. Such special burdens may be caused by above-average unit costs (for example in the case of low population density for certain infrastructure networks or for pre-school day-care); by above-average levels of services necessary for functional reasons; or by some backlog demand.

To consider special burdens and different tasks and task intensities, respectively, of central locations on the one hand and small rural municipalities on the other hand, some countries apply structure- and performance-based indicators for the allocation of revenues from shared taxes or of financial transfers from higher governmental levels to states/regions/municipalities. Also in Austria, strengthening task-orientation within the allocation of funds could be achieved by the application of such indicators.

Examples for criteria/indicators to achieve task-orientation of the horizontal allocation of funds within subnational levels are:

> – Denmark: A part of the financial funds going to municipalities is allocated based on demographic indicators (population size, shares of different age groups in the overall number of inhabitants, etc.) and on socioeconomic indicators (e.g. share of low-income households, number of recipients of social assistance, number of patients in psychiatric treatment, etc.).
>
> – Switzerland: Within the equalization of burdens between the cantons, transfers for socioeconomic (special) burdens of urban cantons (indicators for poverty, e.g. number of long-term unemployed, shares of foreigners; indicators for core cities—high population density) and for geographical-topographical burdens of thinly populated mountainous cantons (burdens of sea level, of steepness of the terrain, share of inhabitants in very small municipalities) are granted.
>
> – Austria: Some interjurisdictional equalization of burden, for example, could be established between the states in the area of education partially based on the criterion population size, partially based on the number of pupils in vocational secondary schools (special burden). Within the area of health, an interjurisdictional equalization of burden could mainly be based on population size; additionally, special burdens (equalization of risks) captured by the structure of the population with regard to age and gender could be considered.

Disentangling and Cutting-Back Transfers

In federal systems transfers serve to close fiscal gaps. In practice, such fiscal gaps mostly result from an inadequate assignment of tasks, from centralizing taxation powers to avoid harmful tax competition between subnational governmental levels, and/or from a lack of taxing power on subnational governmental levels (e.g. lacking right to vary subnational tax rates). These reasons for fiscal gaps apply more or less also for Austrian federal fiscal relations. Hereby, transfers include earmarked deductions from total revenues from shared taxes before their distribution (*Vorwegabzüge*) to finance specific tasks;[14] earmarked grants from the central level to subnational governmental levels; a levy on the municipalities to the states (*Landesumlage*) mostly based on the municipalities' potential own revenues (fiscal capacities); and discretionary grants from the states to the municipalities to cofinance municipal investment projects. Besides these transfers, which are stipulated within the system of secondary fiscal equalization (i.e. based on the Fiscal Equalization Law), there is the system of tertiary fiscal equalization, which forms an additional area of fiscal links primarily between states and the respective municipalities, but also horizontally across municipalities. These transfers include, for example, the payments the municipalities in most states are obliged to make to the states to cofinance tasks of the states (e.g. social assistance or state hospitals). Altogether, this dense system of transfers within the systems of secondary and tertiary fiscal equalization results in a number of problems; just to name a few: When municipalities cofinance tasks of the state without having a say in states' decision-making, the principle of fiscal equivalence is violated, which is a source of inefficiency of states' performance. Levies on the municipalities to the states are mostly based on fiscal capacities (*Finanzkraft*) and do not consider differing financial burdens the municipalities may carry due to differing tasks; thus the allocation of funds (shares in shared taxes) within the system of primary fiscal equalization may be counteracted. Moreover, grants from states to municipalities are not always based on clear goals and criteria. Overall, the manifold transfers and fiscal links between governmental levels within the system of secondary and tertiary fiscal equalization make the Austrian system of federal fiscal relations very complex and non-transparent; their total distributionary and allocative effects are impossible to determine; and they make it rather difficult to efficiently manage the respective policy areas (e.g. health or education/schools).

14 For example, a fraction of personal income tax is deducted beforehand and transferred to the family burden equalization fund to finance family benefits.

Disentangling task and spending responsibilities of the governmental levels and reducing the number of policy areas with joint responsibilities and mixed financing and extending subnational tax autonomy and task-oriented allocation of revenues from shared taxes would make it possible to considerably scale back the transfers flowing within the systems of secondary and tertiary fiscal equaliziation. Thus basic principles of fiscal federalism—the connexity principle, the principle of fiscal equivalence, and fiscal autonomy—would be strengthened. A fundamental reform of transfers would leave three kinds of transfers: transfers aiming at the equalization of differing fiscal capacities of subnational governmental levels; allocative transfers aiming at the exploitation of economies of scale between municipalities and neighboring states and at the equalization of special burdens due to the function as a central location; and transfers to finance subnational joint tasks (e.g. public transportation).

Conclusions

Due to manifold interdependencies a fundamental reform of the system of federal fiscal relations is a complicated—but at the same time rather easy task, as actually it has to be based on some fundamental principles only, which build on one another. In face of the scientific foundation of the existing reform concepts, which—as several examples for best practices show—have proven as useful and applicable elsewhere, such a systemic reform requires a significant increase of overall willingness for reform among political decision-makers and important stakeholders. Up to now changes within the Austrian system of federal fiscal relations have been restricted to what is absolutely necessary and to single reforms in detail. This narrow policy approach has led a formerly rather balanced system into a significant imbalance which cannot be remedied by smaller repairs, quite on the contrary: selective, limited reforms bear the danger of increasing the complexity and non-transparency of the existing system even further. In the medium-to long-term, significant advantages can be expected from renewing the system of federal fiscal relations, which should overcompensate the efforts of a fundamental reform. Moreover, the reform may be divided into two or three steps, which focus on the disentanglement of certain tasks and their financing. Finally, transitional provisions should alleviate the practical implementation.

Federalism and Administrative Reform

Heinrich Neisser

Public Administration in Federal States

The term federalism denotes an organizational principle of a political system, emphasizing both vertical power-sharing across different levels of governance (center–region); at the same time it also means the integration of different territorial and socioeconomic units, and cultural and ethnic groups in one single polity.[1] Federal political systems are combining "unity with diversity." Federal states are different as far the autonomy and diversity of the corresponding units is concerned. Austria is a federal system where the integration of different units and the sharing of competencies are a special type of decentralization. The Austrian case of federalism can be considered a decentralized unitary state, or a form of centripetal federalism.

Austria is formally a federal state. Its two main levels of governance are the central state (*Bund*) and the *Länder*. The Austrian Constitution is based on the Federal Constitutional Law of 1920, which has been modified numerous times. Article 2 stipulates: "Austria is a federal state. It consists of the autonomous *Länder*: Burgenland, Carinthia, Lower Austria, Upper Austria, Salzburg, Styria, Tyrol, Vorarlberg, and Vienna."

But the federative element in the constitution is rather a "mixed" one. The constitution ensures the general power of the nine states. This means that all powers and responsibilities not expressly given to the federal administration are automatically in the purview of the states. But there are so many responsibilities that the Austrian case of federalism can be regarded as underdeveloped: Austria may be considered a "centralistic federation."[2] The Austrian federalism laid down in the constitution of 1920 was a compromise between the two principal political camps: the Social Democrats were pleading for a centralized state while the Christian Social

1 *Oxford Concise Dictionary of Politics*, ed. Iain McLean and Alistair McMillan (Oxford: Oxford University Press, 2nd ed. 2003), 194.

2 Anton Pelinka, *Out of the Shadow of the Past* (Boulder: Westview Press, 1998), 39.

Party was in favor of establishing a federal system. The final compromise was the "mixed" case of Austrian federalism that we have come to know.

The classical theory of federalism has been focusing on the relationship between federation and constituent units (= dual system of government). Nowadays, it is widely acknowledged that local government is a distinctive part of a multi-tiered system. The role of municipalities became more important because the needs of public services have been increasing over time at the level of governance that is closest to the citizens.[3] Therefore the Austrian federal system is a multi-level system consisting of three tiers:

– a federal tier representing the whole state of the Republic of Austria;

– a *Länder* tier consisting of nine constituent *Länder*;

– a tier of municipalities—the lowest tier in Austria—comprising more than 2.300 municipalities; this is both a territorial body of its own enjoying the right of autonomy, and self-government, and recognized as an administrative unit.

Every Austrian municipality belongs at least to one of two associations that serve as lobbies for their common interests. The Federation of Austrian Municipalities (*Österreichischer Gemeindebund*) represents the smaller municipalities (more than 2.300), and is traditionally dominated by the Austrian People's Party (ÖVP). The Federation of Austrian Cities (*Österreichischer Städtebund*) represents the larger municipalities (the bigger cities), and here the Austrian Social Democratic Party (SPÖ) is dominant. Both associations play an essential role in coordinating administrative reform activities.

As mentioned above, the federative element in the Austrian Constitution is a "mixed" one. Three main federal elements define the Austrian Constitution: the distribution of the competences between the central state and the *Länder*; the second chamber of the federal parliament (the *Bundesrat*); and the indirect federal administration by the *Länder* (exercised by the governor, e.g. *Landeshauptmann*).[4]

The distribution of competences laid down in the Federal Constitution reveals a prevailing position of the central state. The important competences

3 See Anna Gamper, "Local Government in Austria," in *Local Government in the Member States of the European Union: A Comparative Legal Perspective*, ed. Angel Manuel Moreno (Madrid: National Institute of Public Administration, 2012), 23-44, p. 23.

4 Kurt Richard Luther and Wolfgang C. Müller, *Politics in Austria: Still a Case of Consociationalism?* (London: Frank Lars, 1992), 122-127.

are allocated to the central state. In 1964, the *Länder* addressed a program of demands to the central state (*Forderungsprogramm der Bundesländer*), asking mainly for an extension of competences.[5] Some others such programs followed, where the *Länder* have continued to push for more power. This has led to few constitutional amendments changing single competences between the central state and the *Länder*. Yet the gains and losses of both sides did not produce more of a balance in the federal system.[6] Until today, the distribution of competences has been an issue and must eventually be solved. A modern distribution of competences is an inevitable prerequisite for any serious effective administrative reform.

Another federal element in the Austrian Constitution is the *Bundesrat* (Federal Council). The prime role of a second chamber in a federal system is to permit the constituent units to take part in the decision-making process of the center, and thus to represent the interests of everyone concerned.[7] The Austrian *Bundesrat* has always been very weak both constitutionally and politically. For most matters it only enjoys a veto to suspend legislation (but not to entirely stop it). In matters of the federal budget, it has no chance to influence the structures of the budgetary process. In practice, the *Bundesrat* has never played the role of serving as a warden for the *Länder's* interests. Its party composition is similar to that of the first chamber, the *Nationalrat*. The *Bundesrat* does not actually fulfill its constitutionally intended function, which is to represent the interests of the states in the legislative process on the federal level. The *Bundesrat*'s powers are insufficiently developed to do so. Debates on the role of the public administration in the *Länder* do not happen in the second chamber.

A third federal element is the so-called "indirect federal administration" (*mittelbare Bundesverwaltung*), serving as a special link between the *Länder* and the central state. Some important matters such as citizenship and traffic policing legislation rest with the central state; yet the *Länder* administration is entrusted with their execution. In the system of indirect federal administration, the governors enjoy a dual function.[8] On the one hand, they are the chairpersons of the *Land* governments and thus politically responsible to the *Länder* parliaments. On the other hand, governors also serve as the top representatives of the federal government in the *Länder*. Governors in their role as indirect federal administrators are

---

5 Peter Pernthaler, *Das Forderungsprogramm der österreichischen Bundesländer* (Vienna: Braumüller, 1980).

6 Klaus Berchtold, *Die Verhandlungen zum Forderungsprogramm der Bundesländer seit 1956* (Vienna: Braumüller, 1984).

7 Luther and Müller, *Politics in Austria*, 123.

8 Ibid., 124.

directed to follow federal ministers' directives; in this role, they must use all their resources (including those of the *Land* government) to implement the policies of the federal government. In case of not following instructions by the federal ministers, governors may be dragged before the constitutional court. This court has three kinds of sanctions at its disposal:[9]

– to declare the behavior of the governor unconstitutional;

– to dismiss the governor from this office;

– to deprive the governor temporarily of his or her political rights.

There is no doubt that this dual role of governors within the system of the indirect federal administration make them essential relay stations in the relationship between the central state and the *Länder*; this accrues them powerful positions. Thus, the regular Governors' Conferences (*Landeshauptleutekonferenz*) serve as the center of federal power and the hard core of federal interests being represented throughout the land.

A general assessment of Austrian federalism shows, then, that according to the constitution federalism is relatively underdeveloped.[10] The nine states have no jurisdiction of their own; all major financial decisions are made at the federal level. Federal Constitutional Law expressly gives prevailing power in terms of legislative and executive power to the federal and not the state level.

This situation gives the central state institutions overwhelming power as far as matters of administrative reforms are concerned. Effective reform strategies can only be developed by means of cooperation between the central state government and the *Länder*; hitherto all efforts to engender such cooperation have failed. Reestablishing a more equitably balanced federal system in the state is the great challenge to the Austrian federalism. This is particularly a serious mandate given that Austria, too, is facing the new regionalism so important in the European integration process. A new order of Austrian federalism therefore must be developed as a result of this new regionalism in the European Union (EU).

It is correct, then, to speak of reforms in Austrian federalism as the *Bundesstaatsreform* (i.e. reform of central state institutions), since the mandate is both an adaptation of federal structures and a total reform of the affairs of state. One of the main challenges is a comprehensive and profound

9 Article 142 par 2 lit e of the Austrian Federal Constitution.

10 Pelinka, *Out of the Shadow*, 65.

implementation of the principle of subsidiarity (*Subsidiaritätsprinzip*). Subsidiarity is always high on the list and mentioned in political statements and declarations but has never been put into place in a serious manner in shaping the relations between the three tiers of the Austrian political system. The notion of subsidiarity is characterized by a hierarchy of organs. Subsidiarity is a constitutional concept in some federal systems to provide a rationale for the allocation of powers between various levels of government. Wherever possible, powers are given to the least aggregated level of government. And only when a particular task cannot be taken care of adequately by a "lower" level of government will it be handed to a higher level.[11] Strangely, a fundamental debate on the principle of subsidiarity never happened in the arena of Austrian politics. Even the membership of Austria in the European Union did not generate essential impulses for an innovative reform of the distribution of competences in the Austrian federal system. One may arrive at the following conclusion: as long as basic reforms of the federal competences are not addressed, any effort to address administrative reforms in Austria will be fragmented and non-systematized.

Governance in the *Länder*

In the Austrian Federal Constitution, the federal system consists of nine states (*Bundesländer*). The nine states have no jurisdiction of their own. A great reform of the system of administrative justice established *Landesverwaltungsgerichte* as an element of federal jurisdiction in the states.[12] In the Austrian federal system all major financial decisions are made at the level of central government in Vienna. Given prevailing powers in terms of legislation and execution, formally federal constitutional law expressly delegates these powers to the central government and not the states. The *Länder* enjoy relative "constitutional autonomy" within the framework of the Federal Constitution. The nine Austrian states are organized along the lines of the principles of democratic systems. A directly elected state diet appoints the governor and the other members of the state government (e.g. state councilors or *Landesräte*). They are accountable to the state diet only. Only a few of the states maintain a "system of proportional government," requiring that the composition of the state governments reflects the proportional strength of the parties represented in the state diet.[13]

---

11 *Oxford Concise Dictionary of Politics*, ed. McLean and McMillan, 522.
12 See later remarks about administrative reform.
13 Pelinka, *Out of the Shadow*, 67.

The bureaucratic system within the *Länder* is dominated by the state governments' central office (*Amt der Landesregierung*). This office comprises departments and subdivisions. The civil servants work under the leadership of the government's office director (*Landesamtsdirektor*); he or she represents the top level of the state central office and the highest representative of the bureaucratic system of the *Länder*. The distribution of the competences within this top-level state governmental office is laid down in the so-called *Geschäftsverteilung*—a regulation adopted by the government of the *Länder*.

Below the top level of bureaucracies in the *Länder* is the level of political districts (*Bezirke*). They are administrative entities where no democratic elements exist. The district administration is to be carried out by the district administration agency (*Bezirksverwaltungsbehörde*), working under the leadership of the district governor (*Bezirkshauptmann*); these district governors are directly subordinated to the state government. The district administration agency is the first governmental instance, then, citizens would approach in the Austrian public administration system.

The only exception to this basic system of the *Länder's* district administration agencies is a group of mostly larger cities with a status of their own (so called *Städte mit eigenem Statut*). These cities are not integrated into or subject to the political district administration and enjoy the powers of both a municipality and political administrative district. These *Städte mit eigenem Statut* enjoy the constitutional liberty of maximizing their autonomy as municipalities—at the cost of weakening state power.[14] No district governor may stand between the mayors of such cities and the state government.

Moreover, the capital city Vienna has a special status in the Austrian administrative system. It enjoys the status of being both one of the nine states and a city. It is also the federal capital (*Bundeshauptstadt*). The governor of the state of Vienna also serves as the mayor of the City of Vienna; the members of the directly elected state diet in the state of Vienna simultaneously act as members of the city council.

What this essay is trying to show is the fact that the public administration in a federal political system such as Austria's operates on a multi-tiered structure and is at the same time determined by a high degree of differentiation. The three tiers of the federal system mentioned above all harbor their own structures—all of them to be kept in mind when trying to push administrative reforms. This complex federal organizational structure forms the basis for public decision-making as well as the implementation of public services being delivered to the citizenry.

14 Ibid., 69.

All three tiers of administration in the federal system enjoy certain degrees of autonomous responsibility. Therefore, any efforts at effective administrative reforms would require an intense system of coordination between these three tiers. One might say, in other words, that administrative reforms in a federal system are based on the demand of coordination of policies.

Administrative Reform in Austria

Reform processes of public administration in Austria since the end of the World War II—namely during the Second Republic—have happened in three stages:

– first, during the era of postwar reconstruction and recovery (1945 until the end of the 1960s);

– secondly, during an era of "modernization" of the public administration (starting at the end of the 1960s);

– and thirdly during the period of what may be termed the "Europeanization" of the public sector (starting with the Austrian application process to the European Economic Community/ European Union) from the end of the 1980s to the end of the 20th century.

During the first stage, starting in 1945, Austria was confronted by many difficulties. The forces of the victorious Allied powers occupying the territory of Austria after the war interfered numerous times in the Austrian public administration; the Soviet occupation element, for examples, tried to seize control of a vital sector of public administration—police forces. Only when the Austrian State Treaty of 1955 restored full independence and sovereignty to Austria did the Austrian government at last have the opportunity to establish a free and independent system of public administration.

At the end of the 1960s, Austria embarked on deeper reforms in public administration, especially in the fields of secondary and higher education. New federal ministries were founded then, such as the environmental ministry and the ministry of science. During this time, the process of modernization of public administration started. Years later, the federal government tried to organize a dialogue between public administration and businessmen in order to improve the information flow to the public and private economic sectors. The government was aiming to find new methods that might be transferred from the private sector to public administration practices, such as private methods of personnel recruitment and training, administrative leadership, etc.). Such private sector practices represented new strategies for the hidebound public sector, steeped in age old traditional bureaucracy. The buzz word then was "administrative management" (*Verwaltungsmanagement*). The strategy was based on new communicative channels furthering a permanent dialogue between public sector administration and the most prestigious representatives of the business world. Austria was trying to imitate an interesting project developed by Ronald Reagan, the president of the United States for much of the 1980s. When Reagan became president he established a special commission led by the businessman Peter Grace ("Grace Commission"). The members of that commission were all recruited from the business world, not from people working in public administration. Reagan's public administration reform project turned out to be successful. Hundreds of business people elaborated on thousands of new proposals for improving public administration. President Reagan put many of those proposals into action in a relatively short period of time.

This U.S. "Grace-Commission" became a model for other countries, in particular for Austria.[15] Under the rubric *Verwaltungsmanagement* broad discussions were unleashed on both the state and the *Länder* levels of government.

In the entire reform debate, the main topics have been the distribution of competences, a better control and awareness for the costs of the administrative system, improving the training system of the civil servants, involving the civil servants in the reform process, tempering the rigidity and inflexibility of the law, as well as providing better information for citizens ("*leichterer Zugang zum Recht*"). One of the main purposes of the *Verwaltungsmanagement* discourse centered around motivating civil servants to embrace cooperation within the process of administrative reform. Yet the ultimate outcome of the administrative reform debate was never a grand concept for reinventing the public sector. Still, many small steps towards reform have been elaborated and implemented. We may conclude that the idea behind and strategy towards *Verwaltungsmanagement* contributed more or less to the modernization of Austrian public administration at large.

15 Heinrich Neisser, "Verwaltungsreform: Anpassung und Strukturreform," *Das öffentliche Haushaltswesen in Österreich* 29 (1988): 83-94.

At the beginning of the 1980s, the Austrian government unleashed an intense debate about the privatization of parts of the public sector. The overall political goal was to develop a strategy for determining the limits of state power. "More privacy, less state" ("*Mehr privat–weniger Staat*") was a catchphrase at the time that seemed to signal a new era of administrative reform. In a broader sense, privatization can be understood as a transfer of public assets to the private sector, either by direct sale or by contracting out.[16] Privatization of the public sector means taking property and power from civil servants and politicians and transferring it to local or foreign businesses. It signifies a decrease of state ownership and state management and control of public economic assets.[17] The strategy may be the government choosing to retain ownership while contracting the management of the enterprise (or administrative unit) to a private company, or a sale of the public assets.

Privatization can be understood in terms of either its goals or its modalities. The goals normally are:

– increasing economic efficiency and competitiveness;

– reducing the burden of inefficient public state enterprises (in Austria that meant the huge sector of industries nationalized after World War II);

– attracting foreign investments;

– satisfying the demands of multilateral lenders (such as the International Monetary Fund).

In the Austria of the 1980s, privatization became a distinct strategy of administrative reform. At the time the central government developed different types of outsourcing (*Ausgliederung*), namely:[18]

– transferring public tasks to private companies (e.g. ending very old state monopolies such as the salt and tobacco monopolies, privatizing the public media radio and television = *Aufgabenprivatisierung*);

16 *Oxford Concise Dictionary of Politics*, ed. McLean and McMillan, 441.

17 Ernest J. Welsen, "Privatization," in *The Oxford Companion to Politics of the World*, ed. Joel Krieger (Oxford: Oxford University Press, 1998), 744-746.

18 Heinrich Neisser, "Verwaltung," in *Politik in Österreich: Das Handbuch*, ed. Herbert Dachs et al. (Vienna: Manz, 2006), 201-212, p. 205.

– transferring limited tasks to newly established private companies, but retaining the financial and organizational influence of state institutions over them (e.g. the ASFINAG for public highways; post offices and telecommunication = *Organisationsprivatisierung*);

– transferring property from the state to the private sector (state banks, the national airlines AUA = *Vermögensprivatisierung*);

– outsourcing special tasks to private companies (e.g. public sector security duties to sector to private security firms = *Funktionsprivatisierung*).

In the process of privatization special agreements were made between the government and the private sector to ensure the maintenance of public services and basic infrastructure. These arrangements aimed at bringing together the state priorities in maintaining social equality with the managerial skills of the private sector, as well as relieving the government of the burden of large capital expenditures and transferring the risks of cost overruns to the private sector. These "public-private partnerships" were designed to ensure that government and private businesses worked together in providing vital services to citizens rather than completely transferring public assets to the private sector hook, line, and sinker, as was the case with privatization.

The strategy of privatization was an important element in the restructuring of the entire public sector. The central state government and the *Länder*, even the municipalities, worked out programs for privatization and public-private partnerships. The central state presented about sixty different such projects altogether. Privatization and economic liberalization impacted the Austrian membership in the internal market of the European Union; it also influenced the structures of the public sector and modified many procedures and methods within public administration. Additional cooperation and more coordination became necessary between the three tiers of the Austrian federal system to cope with economic and financial problems. Measures limiting administrative expenditures have been of special significance in the realm of administrative reform. After a long period of legislation the representatives of the three tiers signed two agreements influencing the different levels of administration—the first one adhering to a so-called "consultation-mechanism," the second one being an Austrian "stability pact."

In May 1998, representatives of the three tiers of Austrian federalism signed a treaty establishing a consultation mechanism and a future stability pact of the *Gebietskörperschaften* (territorial authorities).[19] The consultation mechanism is based on a consultative body between the federal chancellor, vice chancellor, federal minister of finance, three representatives of the governments of the *Länder*, and one representative each of the Federation of Austrian Cities and the Federation of Austrian Municipalities. Subject to negotiations in this body are draft bills, legislative initiatives, draft regulations—all these prepared by federal ministries or administration offices of the *Länder* (such as the *Amt der Landesregierung*). All the draft documents had to include an analysis of their financial impact on the federal budget in accordance with guidelines adopted by the federal minister of finance. The representatives of the *Gebietskörperschaften* were permitted to inquire about negotiations regarding additional costs of projects. The consultative body might have adopted additional recommendations about the financial impact of projects. In case the recommendations of the consultative body were ignored, the territorial authority involved in the project was required to pay for the additional costs. Such additional expenditures would become part of the consideration in the next round of financial adjustment (*Finanzausgleich*) between the central government and the *Länder*.

Related to this consultative mechanism, an agreement was signed by representatives of the three tiers of the federal system. This agreement was called the Austrian Stability Pact[20] and impacted the coordination of the budgetary policy between the territorial authorities—it also had to be in conformity with the existing provisions of the European Union. With regard to the budgetary coordination process a special committee was established. Budgetary coordination included the adoption of common goals and principles for budgetary policies oriented towards the medium term. The three tiers developed a system of mutually informing each other and combined it with special measures of controlling and supervising budgetary developments, particularly when it affected budget deficits and the extensions of public debts. The federal minister of finance was committed to elaborate on a stability program, adopted by the federal government and the national assembly; the respective institutions of the European Union had to be informed too.

Finally, the Austrian Stability Pact determined deficit quotas and sanctions of the European Union. One can say that the consultative mechanism treaty, as well the stability pact, have been the most important and effective steps towards a new strategy of administrative reform.[21]

19 The treaty is published in Bundesgesetzblatt I 1999/35.
20 The Stability Pact is published in Bundesgesetzblatt I 1999/101.
21 Art 126 of the European Union treaty stipulates that member states must avoid excessive budgetary deficits, and can be penalized if they exceed the ceiling.

Austria has experienced a long history of the administration reform processes. Hundreds of commissions, conventions, and committees have been set up to elaborate proposals for improving public administration—namely improving the quality of citizen services, bringing additional efficiencies into a hidebound bureaucratic system, simplifying procedures, and adding economies to public expenditures. The overall goal was to establish an administrative system oriented towards citizens—where ordinary people were treated as partners in public administration. A lot of incremental change occurred in small areas, while a great reform was not possible.

Since the recent crisis of the Euro-Zone has ended, Austrian politics has been facing new challenges. The European Commission has gathered new ways for the budgetary monitoring of its member states. Austria, too, must respect these additional guidelines made in Brussels. This is amounting to a new situation for the central state government and the Austrian *Länder*. Austria has been asked to demonstrate more transparency in the relations between the central state and the *Länder*. Among other areas, the federal financial system needs to be changed, giving the *Länder* more autonomy in the field of taxation. Following the Swiss example, tax autonomy and full responsibility in financial issues is the new name of the game. Moreover, additional harmonization between the *Länder* is mandatory. The limits of liability (*Haftungsobergrenzen*) have been reduced drastically.

The General Accounting Office (*Rechnungshof*) has become an essential player in the public debate about administrative reform. The *Rechnungshof* serves as an auxiliary agency of the National Council and checks the legal records and general accounting of all offices of public administration. The General Accounting Office is acting under the leadership of a president elected by the National Council for a twelve-year term. In the past five years, the president of the *Rechnungshof* has presented literally hundreds of proposals for public discussion and thus has impacted reform efforts for administrative system. Predictably, the government bureaucracy has reacted reluctantly to implement such reforms suggested by the *Rechnungshof*.

The *Volksanwaltschaft* (Office of People's Attorneys) is another public institution that has acted as a player in the field of public administrative reform—but with less emphasis than the General Accounting Office. Modeled after the Scandinavian *Ombudsman*, the Austrian office, acting as the "people's attorney" (*Volksanwalt)*, is an office where people can voice their grievances against abuses in public administration. The *Volksanwaltschaft* serves as a public institution that is investigating citizens' complaints against maladministration in specified areas of public administration. The three public attorneys are elected by the National Council for six-year terms in office. The Office of People's Attorneys oversees the administration of both the central state government and the *Länder*, with the exception of Tyrol and Vorarlberg, which operate their own *Volksanwaltschaft*, responding to individual complaints of their citizens. The Austrian *Volksanwaltschaft* presents regular special reports to the federal parliament and the state diets, showing problems in law enforcement in particular cases of injustice.

This essay is trying to make clear that there are many different ways and approaches to effecting reforms of the public sector and the administrative system in Austria. Effective and sustainable reforms require a high degree of cooperation of all the relevant players in the public administration, be it on the level of the central state government (e.g. the federal chancellor and the minister of finance), or on the level of the *Länder* (the Governor's Conference or *Landeshauptleutekonferenz*), or the level of the representatives of the municipal sector; moreover, as has been argued here, the federal institutions of control (*Rechnungshof*, *Volksanwaltschaft*) are crucial players in the reform process, too. All these representatives and institutions should form a permanent platform for dealing with the reform of the administrative sector. The future mandate for administrative reform, then, might be "less commissions, more political decisions." This is a perspective for the future of administrative reforms advocating for more flexibility, efficiency, and citizens' confidence in the political system and process.

Public Administration and Citizen Participation

Democracy is usually understood as a system where parliament—legitimized by democratic elections—is the legislator. Democracy—representative democracy that is—serves as a process to legitimate parliamentary decisions by the voters. Public administration, in contrast, in a traditional sense focuses only on the implementation of the laws adopted by parliament. Laws are usually enforced by way of administrative systems, namely systems organized hierarchically, giving citizens no opportunity to influence the implementation process. The classical Austrian legal theorist Adolf Merkl has expressed it this way: "legislation is democratic, public administration [= law enforcement] must be autocratic."

In the 1970s, a host of citizens' movements cropped up to fight for the participation of people in the arena of public administration, for example in the field of environmental policy, which became a highly sensitive area of public administration. New legislation provided particular instruments for citizens' participation; the most essential of these new laws was the

Environmental Compatibility Act (*Umweltverträglichkeitsgesetz*). This law calls for a special screening process of big industrial projects to investigate whether such projects are compatible with existing environmental standards and requirements. Special provisos were included for the construction of road and railways.

The Austrian debate over the role of citizens in the arena of public administration was further incentivized by way of demands to improve the instruments of direct democracy. Contemporary debates about the extension of instruments of direct democracy in Austria involve more and better possibilities for citizen participation, especially in the areas of urban planning and municipal local politics. Strengthening and improving the participation of citizens in all issues substantially impacting their lives can be considered the essence of modern democracy. Administrative reforms, therefore, must give priority to all the ideas and proposals supporting the cooperation between administrative authorities and the citizens that might be affected. In essence, administrative cultures must be changed from a system of hierarchy to a system of cooperation.

European Perspectives

Austria became a member of the European Union on 1 January 1995. Ever since the Republic of Austria was fully integrated in the institutional framework of the EU, many competences from both the central and the state level of government have been transferred to Brussels. European community law became part of the national legal system. The Austrian government is responsible for transposing EU directives into national law by a certain deadline and in compliance with the adopted statutes. To comply with EU law, Austria needs to have the bureaucratic capacity to implement the legislation in a timely and correct manner.[22]

For a federal state, the opportunities for regional representation in Brussels are relevant. In the 2001 White Paper, the European Commission recognized the need to "organize a systematic dialogue with European and national associations of regional and local government, while respecting national and constitutional and administrative arrangements…. The principal responsibility for involving the regional and local level in EU policy remains and should remain with national administrations."[23] This

22 Simon Hix and Björn Höyland, *The Political System of the European Union* (Basingstoke: Palgrave MacMillan, 3rd ed. 2011), 33.

23 European Commission, European Governance: A White Paper COM (2001) 428 final, Brussels, 25 July, 12-13.

reflects the tension between the Commission's aim to involve regions to a greater degree and the national governments, which in a formal sense remain autonomous when deciding how their states are organized and how their regions participate in European level activities.

The institution where the regions have the right to directly contact the European Union is the Committee of the Regions. The Committee of Regions is an advisory body bringing together representatives of local and regional authorities.[24] Created in 1994 by the Maastricht Treaty, its main tasks are to give local and regional authorities a voice in EU governance. The Commission and the Council seek the Committee of Regions advice whenever new legislative proposals are initiated that have regional and/or local implications. In practice, this is the case whenever the policy fields economic and social cohesion, trans-European transportation networks, energy and telecommunications, public health, as well as employment and the environment are concerned. The 344 members of the Committee of Regions are appointed for four year-terms by the EU Council. The Austrian delegation is made up of twelve members, nine from the *Länder*, and three from the municipalities.

Apart from the Committee of Regions there are many other representations of the Austrian *Länder* in Brussels.[25] Each of the nine states has their own representation in Brussels. Since Austria's accession to the EU in 1995, many associations and networks have been created. Many of them are operating as lobbyists. A special role is played by the common representation of Tyrol, South Tyrol and Trento; this constitutes a special cross-border activity where three regions have a joint representation of regional interests in Brussels.[26]

Setting up such regional representations for furthering the process of European integration is part and parcel of the Europeanization process unleashed by Austria's EU membership. Europeanization signals a vast process of adaptations and adjustments. Austria's membership in the European Union augmented the existing Austrian three-tier federal system (central state—*Länder*—municipalities) with additional two levels of government. On the one hand there is the level European-regional relations (e.g. the transnational regional cooperation), on the other hand there is the

24 Michelle Cini and Nieves Pérez-Solórzano Borragien, *European Union Politics* (Oxford: Oxford University Press, 3rd ed. 2010), 302.

25 Stefan Mayer, "From Cooperation to Integration: The Foreign Policy/ies of the Austrian Länder," in *Austrian Foreign Policy in Historical Context*, ed. Günter Bischof, Anton Pelinka and Michael Gehler (Contemporary Austrian Studies 14) (New Brunswick: Transaction, 2006), 186-206.

26 On the special regional transnational status of the Tyrol issue, see also the essay by Günther Pallaver in this volume.

overall EU-European level. Therefore, new types of horizontal and vertical coordination are necessary for preparing political decisions. This process of Europeanization began as early as during the period of when Austria was an applicant in the European integration process. The negotiations (1 February 1993 to March 1994) were the most challenging period for calling on the expertise of the Austrian bureaucracy. During this period, the future implementation of the *acquis communautaire* had to be prepared by the governmental bureaucracy.

In the following years the so-called "special foreign policy" (*Fachaußenpolitik*) came into being. It comprised all the cooperation and communication of the foreign ministry with international organizations, in particular with the institutions in Brussels as well as the administrative systems of the member states of the European Union. In all federal ministries, departments, and governors' offices in the *Länder*, the internal organization had to be changed. A host of new departments, groups, and sections mushroomed in public administration in order to cooperate and communicate with the institutions in Brussels or with administrations in other member states. The Austrian "Ministry of Foreign Affairs" has since been renamed "Federal Ministry for Europe, Integration, and Foreign Affairs."

EU membership exercises a significant impact on the administrative systems of individual member states. The entire body of national bureaucracies must be trained to qualify for dealing with European issues. First and foremost, all training systems had to be "Europeanized." All bureaucrats had to demonstrate profound knowledge of the intricate political system of the European Union and all the impacts of EU membership. This also produced a new type of bureaucrat in so-called "mixed-bureaucracies." Officials of national administrations work in the staffs of the European Commission and Council. In the European External Action Service—the office formulating a quasi-joint EU foreign policy—experts and officials from the various national foreign services of EU member states work together. In the numerous committees and commissions of the European Council and the Commission, then, the civil servants of individual member states join staff in preparing joint programs and political concepts. This ongoing process of the Europeanization of national administrative systems will in the future increasingly foster tendencies to discuss problems of administrative reform on a European level.

Europeanization of Austrian Federalism: The Case of *Länder* Rights in EU Affairs

Annegret Eppler/Fritz Staudigl

Federalism is, on the one hand, regarded as a "dynamic system."[1] This is the case because formal and informal changes occur regarding tensions between unity and plurality in federal systems. Federal systems can therefore react to pressures to adapt, which are imposed by exogenous and endogenous influences as well as changing framework conditions. On the other hand, an extraordinary inertia constitutes an immanent characteristic of federal states.[2] Changes and reforms in federal systems are challenged by the fact that decisions are only made if all or at least a majority of the affected stakeholders at the national and subnational level agree to them.[3]

Austrian federalism has been subject to a variety of internal and external impulses during the last few decades. In the following, the changes of the federal system resulting from Austria's accession to the European Union (EU) will be analyzed on the basis of the participatory rights of the *Länder* in EU affairs.[4] We distinguish between indirect EU impacts that exist merely through the embedding of the Austrian federal system in the framework of the bigger EU multi-level governance system on the one hand and direct EU impacts in the subsidiarity control and early warning mechanism on the other hand. We analyze the changes these

---

1 Arthur Benz, *Föderalismus als dynamisches System: Zentralisierung und Dezentralisierung im föderativen Staat* (Opladen: Westdeutscher Verlag, 1985).

2 Gerhard Lehmbruch, "Der unitarische Bundesstaat in Deutschland: Pfadabhängigkeit und Wandel," *MPIfG Discussion Paper* no. 2 (2002), at <http://www.mpi-fg-koeln.mpg.de/pu/mpifg_dp/dp02-2.pdf> (3 March 2015).

3 Fritz W. Scharpf, "Die Politikverflechtungs-Falle: Europäische Integration und deutscher Föderalismus im Vergleich," *Politische Vierteljahresschrift* 26, no. 4 (1985): 323-356.

4 See Peter Pernthaler and Anna Gamper, "National Federalism within the EU: The Austrian Experience," in *The Changing Faces of Federalism: Institutional Reconfiguration in Europe from East to West*, ed. Sergio Ortino, Zagar Mitja and Vojtech Mastny (Manchester: Manchester University Press, 2005), 134-155.

different impulses have caused in the case of the rights of the *Länder* in EU affairs. We argue that in both cases essential characteristics of Austrian federalism have been strengthened or even redoubled as a result of these adaptations.

In the following, we will, first, provide an overview of the literature which addresses the Europeanization of federal systems, connect the Europeanization approach to the concept of path dependency, and formulate our thesis against this theoretical background. In a second step, we will illustrate the impacts imposed by EU accession on Austrian federalism, in particular the general framework the EU provides for the Austrian system (indirect influence) and the system of subsidiarity control that had to be implemented (direct influence). In a third step, we are going to analyze the adaptation of Austrian federalism exemplified through the participatory rights of the *Länder* in EU matters in the *Länderbeteiligungsverfahren* (procedure for *Länder* participation) and subsidiarity control.

Europeanization Approaches, Path Dependency, and Austrian Federalism

Europeanization Approaches and Federalism

More recent approaches in research on Europeanization focus on the feedback effects of European integration on national political systems. Ladrech sees Europeanization as an "incremental process re-orienting the direction and shape of politics to the degree that EU political and economic dynamics become part of the organisational logic of national politics and policy-making."[5] In contrast, Radaelli and Bulmer define it as follows: "Europeanization consists of (a) construction, (b) diffusion, and (c) institutionalization of formal and informal rules, procedures, policy paradigms, styles, 'ways of doing things,' and shared beliefs and norms which are first defined and consolidated in the EU policy process and then incorporated in the logic of domestic (national and subnational) discourse, political structures, and public policies."[6] Although the federal structures, as a polity dimension, do not touch upon the main question in Europeanization

5 Robert Ladrech, "Europeanization of Domestic Politics and Institutions: The Case of France," *Journal of Common Market Studies* 32, no. 1 (1994): 69-88, p. 69.

6 Simon Bulmer and Claudio Radaelli, "The Europeanization of National Policy," in *The Member States of the European Union*, ed. Simon Bulmer and Christian Lequesne (Oxford: Oxford University Press, 2005), 338-359, p. 341.

research,[7] the definitions indicate that Europeanization approaches are an appropriate instrument to capture and explain the influences of European integration on Austrian federalism.

Europeanization research is divisible into the different mechanisms that are ascribed to national adaptation. The "goodness of fit" approach[8] assumes that Europeanization occurs when European regulations cannot be adopted smoothly at the national level. A "misfit," i.e. an incompatibility between European and national policies, leads to pressure to adapt, to which the nation states involved react. It is frequently argued that the EU must not define binding guidelines for the structural organization of the member states, such as federalism, and that ascertainment of a misfit may therefore be difficult.[9] Although this approach is especially suited to explain Europeanization in the case of hierarchical intervention on the part of the EU, in several studies, for example on Spain and Germany,[10] the approach was applied to federal relations.

Indeed, few direct requirements of the EU exist that have a direct, quasi hierarchical, impact on Austrian federalism and its individual system of national state organization. This is the case, for example, when the rights of the Committee of the Regions (CoR), of subnational representatives in the Council, or of national parliaments within the subsidiarity control system—including representatives of subnational entities—are strengthened and their rights have to be implemented, within the scope of European law, at the national level. Such regulations create a direct impulse for the federal order. Pressure to adapt is also exerted by the European Union on the federal system via its policies in some policy fields, for example in the fields of structural, regional, and environmental policies.[11]

7 Peter Bursens, "State Structures," in *Europeanization: New Research Agendas*, ed. Paolo Graziano and Maarten P. Vink (New York: Palgrave, 2007), 115-127.

8 Tanja Börzel and Thomas Risse, "Conceptualizing the Domestic Impact of Europe," in *The Politics of Europeanization*, ed. Kevin Featherstone and Claudio M. Radaelli (Oxford: Oxford University Press, 2003), 57-80.

9 Florian Grotz, *Europäisierung und nationale Staatsorganisation: Institutionenpolitik in föderalen und unitaristischen EU-Staaten* (Baden-Baden: Nomos, 2007), 51-52; Kevin Featherstone, "Introduction: In the Name of 'Europe'," in *The Politics of Europeanization*, ed. idem and Claudio M. Radaelli (Oxford: Oxford University Press, 2003), 3-26, p. 16; Arthur Benz, "Conclusion: Linking Research on Europeanization and National Parliaments," *The Journal of Legislative Studies* 11, no. 3/4 (2005): 508-521, p. 512-513.

10 Tanja A. Börzel, "Institutional Adaption to Europeanization in Germany and Spain," *Journal of Common Market Studies* 37, no. 4 (1999): 573-596.

11 Roland Sturm and Jürgen Dieringer, "Theoretische Perspektiven der Europäisierung von Regionen im Ost-West Vergleich," in *Jahrbuch des Föderalismus 2004: Föderalismus, Subsidiarität und Regionen in Europa*, ed. Europäisches Zentrum für Föderalismus-Forschung Tübingen (Baden-Baden: Nomos, 2004), 21-35.

However, the misfit approach disregards the fact that, empirically, Europeanization occurs even without specific pressures to adapt. Europeanization can be not only a reaction to European pressure but also a result of active policies on the part of national actors.[12] The "bottom-uppers"[13] see the supranational sphere as an extension of decision makers' framework for action.[14] European integration constitutes an external frame of domestic preference formation and decision-making, which can influence them. The challenge of Europeanization is in this case not an alien element in the national political decision-making process.[15] The competition mechanism, as one of the bottom-up mechanisms, assumes that European policy provides a new common framework for action, thus changing the strategic positions of national actors. The actors adapt to the new situation, because they wish to improve or retain their positions, or because it seems easier to adopt already existing solutions from others. Competition may lead to learning effects and to the spread of innovations. Which actors are strengthened or weakened as a result of the influence of the EU has a significant influence on the direction and extent of Europeanization. The competition mechanism originally explains the impacts of European policies in the field of negative integration. For example, when the EU tries to remove barriers, the actors operate in a larger space and adjustments take place through horizontal competition.

The above situation is similar to that of the *Bund* (federal level) and *Länder* (state/regional/subnational level) in federal states, in which the boundaries become increasingly vague. Not only national actors but also the different national governmental systems are competitors of a sort in the European context. They have to assert themselves in a larger political space and can make use of the extended political framework for action under new conditions for their own political goals. In the framework of the development of the European architecture and European formulation

12 Simon Hix and Klaus H. Goetz, "Introduction: European Integration and National Political Systems," *West European Politics* 23, no. 4 (2000): 1-26; Christoph Knill and Dirk Lehmkuhl, "The National Impact of European Union Regulatory Policy: Three Europeanization Mechanisms," *European Journal of Political Research* 41, no. 2 (2002): 255-280.

13 Claudio M. Radaelli and Romain Pasquier, "Conceptual Issues," in *Europeanization: New Research Agendas*, ed. Paolo Graziano and Maarten P. Vink (New York: Palgrave, 2007), 35-45, p. 41.

14 Beate Kohler-Koch, "Europäisierung: Plädoyer für eine Horizonterweiterung," in *Deutschland zwischen Europäisierung und Selbstbehauptung*, ed. Michèle Knodt and idem (Frankfurt a. M.: Campus, 2000), 11-31.

15 Heinrich Pehle and Roland Sturm, "Die Europäisierung der Regierungssysteme," in *Die EU Staaten im Vergleich: Strukturen, Prozesse, Politikinhalte*, ed. Oscar Gabriel and Sabine Kropp (Wiesbaden: VS Verlag für Sozialwissenschaften, 2008), 155-178.

of policies including their timely implementation, federal states, with both the federal and the subnational levels, compete with central states and decentralized and regionalized systems. The idea of competition can also be a characteristic of the specific situation of national actors when negotiating on their own federal structure. From this bottom-up perspective, the extended European framework for action provides rather indirect impulses for the development of Austrian federalism.

Intervening Variables: Path Dependency as an Explanation for Concrete Changes

Despite the same European framework, the member state systems which are part of it show diverse reactions. The internal transformations are not only the results of European pressure to adapt and the new European framework for action but also of internal, domestic factors. These aforementioned endogenous variables are often derived from neo-institutionalism.[16] Internal domestic factors which influence the impact of European integration on national federal developments are derived from actor-centered neo-institutionalism. Such actor-oriented factors may be the number of actors involved, the rules of their interaction, for example representation and voting models, composition and rights of the second chamber etc. Beside actor-centered intervening factors other variables may intervene, e.g. specific characteristics of the political system, like certain central ideas and political culture.[17]

With regard to the specific shape of adaptation processes in federal systems, (rational) historical institutionalism, as another type of neo-institutionalism, may deliver some explanations. With the concept of "path dependency," it provides an explanation for the specific character of changes, as well as for the inability to reform. It assumes that all institutions—including federal systems—are difficult to change. The original character of institutions can be traced back to preferences of actors and their utility-maximization calculations. However, institutional changes become increasingly difficult over time. Even if other solutions seem to be more appropriate at a later point in time, fundamental reforms are prevented by "lock-in effects."[18] This means that, even if existing institutions are

16 Peter A. Hall and Rosemary Taylor, "Political Science and the Three New Institutionalisms," *Political Science* 44, no. 5 (1996): 936-957.

17 Fritz W. Scharpf, *Interaktionsformen: Akteurzentrierter Institutionalismus in der Politikforschung* (Opladen: Leske und Budrich, 2000).

18 Johan P. Olsen, "Change and Continuity: An Institutional Approach to Institutions of Democratic Government," *Europan Political Science Review* 1, no. 1 (2009): 3-32, p. 3.

suboptimal, institutional reforms are unlikely. Once a path of development is adopted in an initial situation—at a "critical juncture"—it is likely to be followed thereafter. Room for change is possible, but only taking account of existing developments. Major change is only possible when a path reproduction mechanism ceases to function or when a crisis situation (for example as a result of external pressure, "external shocks") forces change. Minor changes may strengthen the existing structure or even reinforce the existing parameters. For Germany, it has been illustrated that many focal points of the existing federal system are structures that have evolved over time[19] and that European influence has led to a reduplication of structures, interaction modes, and mechanisms.[20]

EU Impact on Austrian Federalism

An analysis of Austrian federalism shows that, as in all federal states, there are some central features.[21] In Austria,[22] first of all, the *Länder* have tiered rights in terms of policies and legislative competences. According to Art. 10-15 B-VG (*Bundesverfassungs-Gesetz* = the Austrian Federal Constitution), there are four different ways of allocating legislative competences to the federal and *Länder* levels. Nonetheless, there are typical legislative competences that are of significant interest to the *Länder*, especially agricultural, environmental, and transport issues.[23] Second, executive federalism is strongly developed in Austria. In view of the predominant role of federal legislation and the important role of the *Länder* in the execution of laws at all political levels, the governments of the *Länder* have a very strong position in the whole political system. Parliaments at all levels, especially at the subnational level, are rather weak, while the *Landeshauptleute* (governors) have a strong political and constitutional

19 See Lehmbruch, "Der unitarische Bundesstaat."

20 Annegret Eppler, "60 Jahre deutscher Föderalismus in Europa: Anpassungen im Bereich der Kompetenzordnung und der Entscheidungsstrukturen," in *Jahrbuch des Föderalismus 2009: Föderalismus, Subsidiarität und Regionen in Europa*, ed. Europäisches Zentrum für Föderalismus-Forschung Tübingen (Baden-Baden: Nomos, 2009), 189-207.

21 Ronald L. Watts, *Comparing Federal Systems* (Kingston: McGill-Queen's University Press, 2008); Daniel J. Elazar, *Federal Systems of the World: A Handbook of Federal, Confederal and Autonomy Arrangements* (Essex: longman group uk ltd.,1991).

22 Cf. Roland Sturm, "Austria," in *Handbook of Federal Countries*, ed. Forum of Federations (Montreal: McGill-Queen's University Press, 2005), 45-57.

23 Jan Erk, "Austria: A Federation without Federalism," *Publius: The Journal of Federalism* 34, no. 1 (2004): 1-20; Anna Gamper, "Österreich–das Paradoxon des zentralistischen Bundesstaats," in *Jahrbuch des Föderalismus 2000: Föderalismus, Subsidiarität und Regionen in Europa*, ed. Europäisches Zentrum für Föderalismus-Forschung (Baden-Baden: Nomos, 2000), 251-265.

position. Their conference, the *Landeshauptleutekonferenz*, plays an important role with regard to coordination among the *Länder* themselves and between the *Länder* and the federal authorities.[24] Third, Austria's federal state is one in which the political system is quite homogeneous and consensus-oriented.[25] Cooperative federalism comes with "informal, but very efficient"[26] ways to coordinate between the *Länder* themselves.[27] Coordination is achieved through formal bodies like the *Landeshauptleutekonferenz* and its liaison offices in Vienna and Brussels as well as through a multiplicity of informal working groups.

In the following, we argue that Austrian federalism faced indirect and direct impacts caused by EU membership. The adaptations the Austrian federal system went through in the course of integration into the EU system are path-dependent. Many of these changes constitute a strengthening or doubling of existing structures in Austrian federalism and its main characteristics, the specific allocation of competences, and executive and cooperative federalism.

We wish to demonstrate this point with reference to the rights of the *Länder* in EU affairs. The two cases we shall analyze are the *Länderbeteiligungsverfahren* and implementation of the subsidiarity control mechanism. While the *Länderbeteiligungsverfahren* is an example of bottom-up Europeanization, which is solely a result of the new framework of the EU, subsidiarity control is indebted to the top-down impact of the EU, introducing the early warning mechanism. In both cases, of bottom-up and top-down induced changes, the Austrian federal system changed itself by strengthening its main characteristics.

The EU's Indirect and Direct Impact on Austrian Federalism

Indirect EU Influence: Austria and Its Federal System in a "Pool" of Twenty-Eight Member States

Even before Austria officially became a member of the European Union in 1995, all Austrian political actors were confronted with the fact

24 Anna Gamper, *Legislative and Executive Governance in Austria* (Vienna: Braumüller, 2004).

25 Peter Bußjäger, *Homogenität und Differenz: Zur Theorie der Aufgabenverteilung zwischen Bund und Ländern in Österreich* (Vienna: Braumüller, 2006).

26 Pernthaler and Gamper, "National Federalism," 139.

27 Peter Bußjäger, *Kooperativer Föderalismus in Österreich: Beiträge zur Verflechtung von Bund und Ländern* (Vienna: Braumüller, 2010); see also the contribution of Bußjäger in this volume.

that the EU would necessitate changes to the political system.[28] Before EU membership, *Bund* and *Länder* were able to decide for themselves, with only the need to arrive at an agreement with the other *Länder* and the national arena. It was clear that, after EU membership, they would find themselves in a by far bigger political "pool" in which—today—twenty-eight member states with heterogeneous interests meet and make binding decisions.

By virtue of its legislative power, the EU can pass European law that suppresses national and subnational legislation. Therefore, to avoid sanctions, it must be implemented in national legislation once enacted at the European level.[29] Authority to implement this legislation is located at the political level that would also be competent for purely Austrian legislation on the same subject. Quantitatively at least, the major share of national legislation is determined by European law.

The scope of what *Bund* and *Länder* governments can regulate independently when it comes to legislation below the EU level has been narrowed down intensely. Not only matters that were nominally transferred to the EU contribute to this development. The European Union affects almost all areas de facto in some way—whether competences have been nominally transferred or not. As a consequence, the areas in which independent legislation can be enacted have shrunk for all national and subnational actors, even in those fields in which their own competences persist de jure. Policymakers at both *Bund* and *Länder* levels tend to be involved less in independent policy-making and more and more in the management of interdependencies with other actors in the EU framework and the implementation of EU policies.

As the Council is the EU institution where the member states' governments negotiate, the most effective formal channel for advocacy within the European institutional structure for all Austrian actors is usually via the Austrian federal government. Another direct path for impacting the EU's decision making processes leads via the European Parliament. Over the decades, it has gained a stronger influence on EU law-making, but the directly elected Austrian representatives are—at least formally—responsible to the whole of the EU population.

Against this background, almost all political institutions and actors in Austria have witnessed changes to their political influence. Legislative powers have been transferred from the national to the EU level, while

28 Many more references to texts written in German can be found in: Annegret Eppler and Fritz Staudigl, "Tirol als Akteur im EU-Mehrebenensystem," in *Jahrbuch Politik in Tirol*, ed. Ferdinand Karlhofer and Günther Pallaver (Innsbruck: StudienVerlag, 2015), 79-102.

29 Christian Ranacher and Fritz Staudigl, *Einführung in das EU-Recht: Institutionen, Recht und Politiken der Europäischen Union* (Munich: C.H. Beck, 2010).

Austria has acquired reciprocal participation rights in EU policy-making at the same time. While there is thus a form of vertical compensation between the Austrian federal level and the EU level, the shift towards the EU also affects the legislative powers of subnational actors. Moreover, the "upward" displacement of legislative powers to the EU level is to the detriment of the parliaments, i.e. the *Nationalrat* (first chamber), the *Bundesrat* (second chamber) and the *Landtage* (subnational parliaments). The "winner" is the federal government, which has benefitted from the acquisition of participation rights and is thereby able to act as a quasi-legislative actor at the higher EU level. This strengthening of executive federalism is compensated horizontally through the strengthening of the monitoring functions of the parliaments in relation to the European policy of the executive.

The Austrian *Länder* are directly affected by EU membership, as much of their legislative power has also been transferred de facto to the EU. Prior to EU membership, the Austrian *Länder* were confronted with the fact that the EU was going to have legislative powers in several policy fields that were of special interest to them and that they were going to lose the authority to regulate matters in those fields to a substantial extent—a right that had so far been guaranteed by the Austrian constitution. The fields concerned were nature protection, agriculture, regional development, spatial planning, land acquisition law for foreigners, construction law, traffic planning, business development, procurement, and employment policies, among others.

One Example of the EU's Direct Impact on Austrian Federalism: The Subsidiarity Control Mechanism

While EU membership provided a new framework for Austrian federalism, which stimulated changes without direct EU impacts on the national political system, with the system of subsidiarity control the EU introduced a procedure which gave it a direct influence on Austrian federalism. The subsidiarity control mechanism was introduced a few years after Austria joined the EU.

With the Treaty of Maastricht in 1993, the EU introduced the principle of subsidiarity and has since gradually developed it at increasing levels of detail. This has happened in the wake of growing criticism of the "regional blindness" of European integration and discussions on the model of a "Europe of the regions." With the Treaty of Lisbon in 2009, the subsidiarity principle was made justiciable. Therefore, an early warning system was also introduced, which for the first time explicitly includes not only the subnational actors, i.e. regional and local authorities (which had been mentioned already in the Maastricht Treaty), but also the subnational parliaments of member states in EU primary law: "[I]t is for each national parliament or each chamber of a national parliament to consult, where appropriate, regional parliaments with legislative powers," Article 6 of Protocol No. 2 on Subsidiarity and Proportionality of the Lisbon Treaty.

The system of subsidiarity control obliges the European Commission—the institution holding the right of initiative for the vast majority of legislative proposals—to inform the national parliaments of all plans for forthcoming legislation. In Austria, the *Nationalrat* and the *Bundesrat* receive information on all planned regulations and directives, as well as green and white papers, etc., before they are processed in the context of EU policy-making by the Council and the European Parliament. The national parliaments have eight weeks to consider the proposals and make any objections if they detect a violation of the principles of subsidiarity and proportionality. Each national parliament or chamber may involve regional parliaments with legislative powers, as is done in many EU member states.[30] If one third of the national parliaments lodges a complaint (one quarter in the areas of freedom, security, and justice), the Commission is obliged to review its plan and deliver an opinion in detail. So far, these parliamentary "yellow cards" have only been shown twice: namely for the proposal of a European Public Prosecutor and for planned EU rules on the right to go on strike (a proposal that was subsequently withdrawn by the Commission). If half of the national parliaments raise a complaint in the context of the ordinary legislative procedure, the Commission must explain its decision to insist on the proposal. Furthermore, the Council and the European Parliament have to "overrule" the national parliaments' complaint. De facto, the relevant Commission department has so far defined the rules in favor of the member states and their national and subnational parliaments: First, concessions are being made with respect to the eight week period, for example when it falls in the summer break.[31] Second, each objection is being examined, whether the one-third mark is reached or not. In practice, this control mechanism not only acts as an "exercise of powers barrier"[32]

30 *Subnational Parliaments in an EU Multi-level Parliamentary System: Taking Stock of the Post-Lisbon Era*, ed. Gabriele Abels and Annegret Eppler (Innsbruck: StudienVerlag, 2015).
31 Carmen Preising, "Der Umgang nationaler Parlamente mit den neuen Rechten des Vertrags von Lissabon–die Perspektive der Europäischen Kommission," in *Auf dem Weg zum Mehrebenenparlamentarismus? Funktion von Parlamenten im politischen System der EU*, ed. Gabriele Abels and Annegret Eppler (Baden-Baden: Nomos, 2011), 149-157.
32 Christian Ranacher, "Rechtliche Aspekte der Subsidiaritätskontrolle unter Berücksichtigung der Lissabon-Begleitnovelle," in *Im Dienste der Länder–im Interesse des Gesamtstaates: Festschrift 60 Jahre Verbindungsstelle der Bundesländer*, ed. Andreas Rosner and Peter Bußjäger (Vienna: Braumüller, 2011), 387-411, p. 390.

but is also used by the member states and regions to introduce their own substantive interests into the decision-making process of the EU at the earliest stage possible. As soon as a legal act has entered into force, national parliaments have the right of action before the European Court of Justice. They can now file a suit for compliance with the principles of subsidiarity and proportionality, regardless of whether they previously lodged a complaint or not.

Hence, through the system of subsidiarity control, the national parliaments have the opportunity to participate in the EU legislation process and exercise their parliamentary control function with regard to the EU level. They furthermore have the right to directly contact the Commission and are encouraged to collaborate. In recent years, extension of the subsidiarity control mechanism in EU primary law has also found a counterpart in most member states in national regulations and triggered a comprehensive discussion and reform process. This is a direct EU influence on the polity of its member states, as the latter have to establish rules for the integration of their national parliaments in the early warning mechanism. It also touches on the relationship between federal and state levels, as subnational parliaments may be integrated in the subsidiarity control system.

Changes in Austrian Federalism due to EU Impacts: The Case of the Rights of the *Länder* in EU Matters

In the previous chapter, two different kinds of EU impact on Austrian federalism have been illustrated: the embedding of the Austrian federation in the bigger EU multi-level system as an indirect impact and the introduction of the system of subsidiarity control as a direct impact. How did the Austrian federalism react to these different impacts? The *Länderbeteiligungsverfahren* (procedure for *Länder* participation) is a change the system made due to the indirect EU impact, while the implementation of the system of subsidiarity control is affected by direct EU impact.

The *Länderbeteiligungsverfahren*

It was the *Landeshauptleute* (*Land* governors) who, as the first politically significant force, urged the federal government in the mid-1980s to aspire to accession to the EU. Even then they knew that they were maneuvering themselves into greater dependency. But their strong position within the Austrian political system enabled them to impose certain conditions.

Hence their continuing political support for EU membership was more or less openly dependent on a satisfactory degree of participation in EU affairs for the *Länder*.[33] The logic of "competence levy against participation rights" between federal and *Länder* levels resembles the balance between national and European levels, and while the *Länder* lose competences to the EU, they have a say at the national level on how Austrian representatives vote in the Council. It is the indirect impact of the EU framework which forced *Bund* and *Länder* to find new modes of interaction in EU matters. Since the Austrian *Länder* have specific interests in areas with a high density of EU regulations especially, they considered it essential to be able to effectively lodge their concerns at an early stage within the EU decision-making system. This adaptation of the federal system is a result of EU membership but has not been effected through direct EU influence.

The cornerstone of *Länder* participation in European politics through the federal government is the *Länderbeteiligungsverfahren*[34] as provided for in Article 23d of the Federal Constitution (B-VG). This procedure was introduced in 1992, before Austria became a member of the European Union.[35] Subsequent agreements between the *Bund* and the *Länder* (Bu/Lä-Vb) and the *Länder* among themselves (Lä/Lä-Vb) on the participation rights of the *Länder* apply in parallel to the provisions of the constitution.

In detail, the federal government has to inform the *Länder* immediately of all EU projects which affect their autonomous sphere of competence or could otherwise be of interest to them (Art. 23d (1) B-VG). Since "projects" are not defined and everything could basically be "of interest" for the *Länder*, the right of the *Länder* to information is to be construed broadly. In practice, the transmission of information through the federal government works smoothly. According to Article 23d (1), the *Länder* are also provided with an opportunity to comment. Such comments have to be addressed to the *Bundeskanzleramt* (Federal Chancellery). The status of such opinions depends on the number of *Länder* intervening, the uniformity of their opinions, and the relevance of the issue for the *Länder* level. A

33 Fritz Staudigl, "Zur Rolle der österreichischen Länder im europäischen Integrationsprozess," *Österreichische Zeitschrift für öffentliches Recht und Völkerrecht* 46, no. 1 (1993): 41-66, p. 55.

34 Cf. Andreas Kiefer, "European and External Relations of the Austrian Länder–with a Specific Reference to Land Salzburg," in *Regional Autonomy and International Relations: New Dimensions of Multilateral Governance*, ed. Carlos Pacheco Amaral (Paris: L'Harmattan, 2011), 155-193.

35 Martina Büchel-Germann and Harald Kraft, "Länderbeteiligungsverfahren dargestellt an der Patientenmobilitätsrichtlinie," in *Im Dienste der Länder–im Interesse des Gesamtstaates: Festschrift 60 Jahre Verbindungsstelle der Bundesländer*, ed. Andreas Rosner and Peter Bußjäger (Vienna: Braumüller, 2011), 539-572.

uniform opinion on a project concerning a subject of subnational legislation constitutes a bound mandate, and the federal government may only deviate from the *Länder* opinion for reasons of integration and foreign politics and must immediately notify the *Länder* of those reasons (Art. 23d (2) B-VG). This allows the federal government to differ only in cases where flexible negotiation is necessary for the incorporation of the Austrian position in the result in some form, for example in the case of typical European package solutions.

The *Länderbeteiligungsverfahren* strengthens some of the characteristics that are already immanent in Austrian federalism. One of those characteristics is the tiered rights of the *Länder* with regard to policies and legislative competences. The *Länder* only have such a strong voice in EU affairs in policy fields in which they have legislative competences. Power sharing between *Bund* and *Länder* along policy lines, which has its roots in the distribution of legislative competences in the Austrian constitution, has therefore been redoubled and applied to the rights of the *Länder* in EU affairs. The gradation of *Länder* influence on federal EU politics reflects federal Austrian law: The opinion of just a single *Land* or only a few *Länder* has the lowest binding force. Where the legislative affairs of the *Länder* are involved and all *Länder* express a common opinion, the highest binding effect is achieved. Especially in those areas where they have a strong self-interest and legislative power according to the federal constitution, the *Länder* can thus have a particularly strong influence on federal EU politics.

Another focal point of Austrian federalism is the strong position of the executives, while parliaments at all levels are rather weak. Before Austria joined the European Union, the question of who was to coordinate the opinions of the *Länder*—the *Bundesrat* (second chamber), the *Landtage* (subnational parliaments) or the *Landeshauptleutekonferenz* (Governors' Conference)—was a subject of much debate among the *Länder* themselves. However, although the *Bundesrat* as the second chamber of parliament formally represents the *Länder* in federal politics, its legal weakness and political unimportance limit its scope. And while the subnational parliaments would have been strengthened through European policy coordination, which might have counteracted the ongoing process of de-parliamentarization resulting from EU integration, they still share this fate. This is because political, administrative, and technical know-how about all policies has always been a strong point of the *Länder* governments and administrations themselves. As a consequence, the *Landeshauptleute* were chosen to represent and lobby for the *Länder* interests. A major factor in this decision was the fact that EU coordination was seen by the actors as a government function best exercised by the executives, while the subnational parliaments should be involved mainly through their control function.

All Austrian *Länder* have similar rules on the involvement of their regional parliaments. As directly elected representatives, these subnational parliaments can at least formally influence their *Land*'s position. For example, in the Tyrol the *Land* government has made a commitment to report to its parliament on matters of European integration. In parallel with the *Länder* participation procedure, the subnational parliaments can use the instrument of resolutions to express an opinion on currently discussed European policy processes. An appropriate decision can be made either in the plenary or in the committee responsible for European integration. Usually, a *Land* government is the institution representing the *Land* in European politics. Therefore, it is the *Länder* government's task to represent the *Länder* parliament's position to the federal government and/or other *Länder*. However, in some *Länder* it is possible for the government to differ from the parliamentary vote only in cases of compelling integration policy or for *Land*-specific political reasons. In practice, the subnational parliaments rarely make use of these formal rights—their administrative resources for familiarizing themselves with the European political contexts are very limited, mostly one director of the *Landtag* and one staff member. But nevertheless, existing structures have again been doubled: The way legislative and executive powers interact horizontally in EU affairs has been transposed from the national to the subnational level, and executive federalism has been strengthened once again.

In all matters of internal policy-making, the *Landeshauptleutekonferenz* plays a crucial role. This construction is also being applied to the coordination of *Länder* interests in EU affairs. The forwarding of information from the federal government and its ministries to the *Länder* governments, and the coordination, collection, and transfer of *Länder* opinions to the federal government is the main function of the Liaison Office of the Austrian *Länder* (*Verbindungsstelle der Bundesländer*) in Vienna. The Liaison Office was established in 1951 and since then has played a very important role in terms of practical coordination between *Länder* executives and the federal government. However, the tasks of the Liaison Office are primarily organizational, whereas the content-related work continues to be handled by the administration of the *Länder*. When the *Länder* or the federal government learn about new relevant EU projects, they usually decide in each individual case which *Land* will be primarily responsible for examination of the content and possible *Länder*-specific interests. All the *Länder* participate approximately to the same extent depending on their long-standing regional and local interests. The Tyrol, for example, has been primarily involved in matters concerning transport, mountain farming, and the environment. A draft opinion formulated by one *Land* on an EU project is subsequently edited by various coordinating bodies of the *Länder*: In highly political cases it is usually the Governors' Conference. In some cases, especially urgent cases, the voting procedure is handled electronically by the Liaison Office of the *Länder*. The choice of procedure employed by the *Länder* to reach a uniform or common opinion that will be forwarded from the Liaison Office to the *Bundeskanzleramt* (Federal Chancellery), the Foreign Office, the responsible federal ministry, and the administrative office of the national parliament is subject to the right of the *Länder* to organize their own affairs.

The coordination meetings of the *Länder* directors of European affairs at the working level prior to the plenary sessions of the Committee of the Regions (CoR) play an important role for a detailed exchange about the short-, medium-, and long-term need for action in the field of European politics, even though they have not been formally assigned such a broad range of tasks. The task of the group, which meets six times a year, is to prepare the sessions of the CoR. However, these sessions include a second, informal part, in which the directors discuss and inform each other about recent developments, define positions and distribute tasks and responsibilities for producing specific dossiers. The members of this expert group cooperate continually and very closely without any red tape.[36] Issues which would usually have been discussed in a separate session are therefore quickly processed.

This is probably the reason why other bodies with a formal mandate to coordinate European policies have gained hardly any importance. An example of that is the *Integrationskonferenz der Länder* (IKL), which was established by the *Länder* in 1993 as platform for taking a vote on common positions on EU statements. Every *Land* was to be represented by the *Landeshauptmann* and the *Landtagspräsident* (president of the *Land* parliament); the Presidium of the *Bundesrat* was also entitled to participate. Decisions were to be taken by a majority vote, requiring the votes of five *Länder* (to be cast by the *Landeshauptmann*) with no votes against. The chairperson of the *Landeshauptleutekonferenz* was to chair the IKL, and the Liaison Office in Vienna was to serve as its staffed office. It was planned that, at the civil service level, the SIL (*Ständiger Integrationsausschuss der Länder*) should counsel and support the IKL. In fact, both the IKL and

36 Fritz Staudigl and Harald Büger, "Die österreichische Delegation im Ausschuss der Regionen," in *Im Dienste der Länder–im Interesse des Gesamtstaates: Festschrift 60 Jahre Verbindungsstelle der Bundesländer*, ed. Andreas Rosner and Peter Bußjäger (Vienna: Braumüller, 2011), 205-248, p. 239.

the SIL have met only twice. They proved to be too cumbersome and must be considered a dead letter. The same applies to the *Rat für Fragen der österreichischen Integrations- und Außenpolitik* (Council for Questions of Austrian Integration and Foreign Policy) introduced in 1989 and consisting of the chancellor, deputy chancellor, minister of foreign affairs, minister of defense, parliamentary groups, social partners, and the Austrian Association of Cities and Towns as well as the *Länder* represented by two governors and two presidents of the regional parliaments. In practice, it never played its intended role to coordinate Austrian European politics.

The fact that formal EU coordination bodies like IKL, SIL, and the *Rat für Fragen der österreichischen Integrations- und Außenpolitik* exist only on paper while coordination functions smoothly through informal channels and bodies mirrors another crucial characteristic of Austrian federalism: a cooperative style of interaction. Nevertheless, the codification rights of all actors are crucial since informal cooperation and political compromise is taking place quasi "in the shadow"[37] of these rights.

In practice, both *Länder* and *Bund* understand the need for compromise in order to speak with a unified voice in Brussels. Therefore, Austria's well-known and well-developed style of "cooperative federalism" is mirrored in the composition of the groups interacting in EU affairs. The opinions of the *Länder* often differ only in nuances. Even when Jörg Haider, an outspoken EU sceptic, was governor of Carinthia (between 1989 and 1991 and again from 1999 to 2008), unanimity among the *Länder* prevailed regarding factual EU policies. This is related to the federal government's practice of usually communicating the position of the *Länder* to Brussels unchanged. Since 1993, the federal government has only departed from the *Länder* position in four out of ninety-six uniform *Länder* opinions[38] on the grounds of compelling integration policies.[39] Thus, the Achilles heel of Article 32d B-VG[40] is legally significant in principle but has been of no real practical meaning so far. While

37 Arthur Benz, Fritz W. Scharpf and Reinhart Zintl, *Horizontale Politikverflechtung* (Frankfurt a. M.: Campus, 1992).

38 The annual "Report on Federalism in Austria" (*Bericht über den Föderalismus in Österreich*), published by the *Institut für Föderalismus* in Innsbruck, includes a list of the uniform *Länder* opinions for the respective year.

39 The four cases related to the Directive on Measures Facilitating the Exercise of Rights Conferred on Workers in the Context of Freedom of Movement for Workers, the Directive on Public Access to Environmental Information, the Waste Incineration Directive, and the Directive on the Keeping of Wild Animals in Zoos.

40 Christian Ranacher, "Die österreichischen Länder als Akteure im Prozess der europäischen Rechtsetzung: Erfahrungen und Perspektiven," in *Die Konstitutionalisierung der Verbandsgewalt in der (neuen) Europäischen Union: Rechtliche, politische und ökonomische Konsequenzen der neuen Verfassung der EU*, ed. Erhard Busek and Waldemar Hummel (Vienna: Böhlau, 2006), 217-246.

a petition to impeach a minister could be submitted to the Constitutional Court in the case of disregard of the binding effect of a *Länder* opinion, this has never occurred to date. Hence, the features of Austrian policy-making are transmitted in practice to the level of European politics, where political cooperation is also characterized by cooperative federalism. The federal government fulfils its duty of information and normally takes the rules of unified opinions into account. The *Länder* work cooperatively and use their power to comment extensively. That strengthens cooperative federalism.

The Subsidiarity Monitoring Mechanism

A few years after the *Länderbeteiligungsverfahren* had been introduced Austrian federalism was faced with the need to implement the subsidiarity control system. The increase in subsidiarity control within EU primary law has a direct influence on the polity of the member states, as it forces them to introduce new formal rules for the interaction of national parliaments and national governments in order to comply with the principle of subsidiarity control. In all member states, the EU's rules on subsidiarity control have been translated into national regulations, and most member states have responded by engaging in comprehensive discussions and setting reform processes in motion. In Austria, implementation of the Lisbon Treaty became effective in 2010, when Articles 23f and 23h B-VG were added to the federal constitution. These articles regulate the duty of cooperation of the federal government with the *Nationalrat* and the *Bundesrat* in order to organize subsidiarity control.

EU primary law only allows for the *Länder* to be formally integrated through their regional parliaments. Protocol no. 2 of the Lisbon Treaty stipulates that it is for the national parliaments to decide whether or not to involve subnational parliaments in subsidiarity monitoring. When subsidiarity control was introduced, the *Länder* executives had many years of experience with the *Länderbeteiligungsverfahren*. Therefore, the political actors in Austria argued that the executives were more accustomed than the *Länder* parliaments to coordinating and positioning themselves in European politics. According to the EU top-down rule, however, the subnational parliaments are formally at the centre of subnational subsidiarity control.

Austria duly implemented the EU requirements. According to Article 23g (3) B-VG, the *Bundesrat* must inform the subnational parliaments on all EU projects and give them the opportunity to issue an opinion.[41] The

41 Susanne Bachmann, "Bundesrat und Landtage," in *Im Dienste der Länder–im Interesse des Gesamtstaates: Festschrift 60 Jahre Verbindungsstelle der Bundesländer*, ed. Andreas Rosner and Peter Bußjäger (Vienna: Braumüller, 2011), 193-203.

Bundesrat has to consider these opinions with regard to the context and inform the subnational parliaments of its decision. Not all subnational parliaments in Austria have so far made use of this opportunity for subsidiarity control, relying on their governments' administration expertise.[42] The sheer numbers of the EU documents received daily are difficult for the Austrian subnational parliaments to cope with, quite apart from their lack of staff and specific know-how to process them. And there are further difficulties: The *Bundesrat*'s opinion has to reach the Commission in Brussels within eight weeks and therefore the position of the subnational parliaments must be in Vienna before the meeting of the European Committee of the *Bundesrat*. The *Bundesrat* must thus inform the *Länder* parliaments about its session plans and agenda to allow them to adopt their positions accordingly. That is tight schedule, which is why most Austrian subnational parliaments work closely with their *Länder* governments and administrations in matters of subsidiarity control.[43] The new potential and requirements for subsidiarity monitoring have other implications, too. In this respect, the subnational parliaments' ties have increased: at the national level via the Conference of Presidents of the subnational parliaments and their Directors Conference, and at the European level within the Conference of European Regional Legislative Assemblies (CALRE) and the Committee of the Regions. Additionally, there is also cross-border cooperation. For example, the Tyrolean *Landtag* works closely with the parliaments of South Tyrol and Trento in Italy.

In addition to the subsidiarity control mechanism of the subnational parliaments, the *Länder* executives created their own platform for subsidiarity control.[44] An expert conference was set up by the *Landeshauptleutekonferenz* and has since played a significant role in subsidiarity control at the national and European levels. This group of experts of the *Länder* administrations performs several tasks. They analyze the annual work program of the European Commission, involving the *Länder* administration and the

42 Eric Miklin, "Towards a More Active Role in EU Affairs: Austrian State Parliaments after Lisbon," in *Subnational Parliaments in an EU Multi-level Parliamentary System: Taking Stock of the Post-Lisbon Era*, ed. Gabriele Abels and Annegret Eppler (Innsbruck: StudienVerlag, 2015).

43 Gracia Vara Arribas and Delphine Boudrin, *Die Rolle der regionalen Parlamente bei der Subsidiaritätsanalyse im Rahmen des im Vertrag von Lissabon vorgesehenen Frühwarnsystem* (Brussels: Europäisches Institut für öffentliche Verwaltung und Europäisches Zentrum der Regionen, 2011), 9.

44 Andreas Kiefer, "Mehr Länderzusammenarbeit durch die Subsidiaritätskontrolle: Das arbeitsteilige Modell im Rahmen bestehender Kooperations- und Beteiligungsstrukturen," in *Im Dienste der Länder–im Interesse des Gesamtstaates: Festschrift 60 Jahre Verbindungsstelle der Bundesländer*, ed. Andreas Rosner and Peter Bußjäger (Vienna: Braumüller, 2011), 413-432.

administration of the subnational parliaments. The experts also assign responsibility for subsidiarity control to specific *Länder* in specific cases. Their task is to examine, on behalf of all the *Länder*, EU initiatives that are potentially relevant for subsidiarity monitoring. As in the case of *Länderbeteiligungsverfahren*, the national coordination group of the Committee of the Regions again plays an important role at the civil-service level, since it is this group that nominates the responsible *Land*. Finally, the joint representative of the Austrian *Länder* in the Permanent Representation of Austria to the EU is also involved in this coordination process. Among other things, he maintains a database with relevant information, which he provides to the Austrian *Länder* in a password-protected format. The Liaison Office of the Austrian *Länder* in Vienna sends the subsidiarity control opinions received from the *Länder* governments to all relevant Austrian and European authorities.

On paper, two independent channels have developed that allow the *Länder* to participate in subsidiarity control: one parliamentary and one executive. But while involvement of the subnational parliaments is a top-down provision of EU law, the Austrian subnational parliaments' lack of capacity limits their work, and hence, this channel of subsidiarity control. The procedures of the executives are closely aligned with the existing patterns of the *Länderbeteiligungsverfahren*. In practice, however, the *Länder* executives and legislatives work together very closely as is common in cooperative federalism. As the *Bundesrat* cannot be bound by any position of the *Länder* parliaments or executives, fruitful cooperation is also needed between the *Länder* and the *Bundesrat* in the preparation of subsidiarity complaints. So far, there have been no disagreements between the federal government and the *Länder* concerning specific instances of subsidiarity control.

The Treaty of Lisbon also provides for ex-post monitoring of the principle of subsidiarity. In Austria, the decision to implement it can only be taken by a joint plenary of the two parliamentary chambers. With regard to the legal standing of the *Länder* in matters of subsidiarity, Bu/Lä-VB specifies the federal government's duty to appeal to the European Court of Justice at the request of a *Land*. The preconditions for such a step are that the wrongful act or omission of an EU institution affects a matter of *Länder* legislation, that no other *Land* objects, and that no compelling reason against it exists.

Conclusion

In principle, the EU has only an indirect impact on the polity dimension of the political systems of its member states. The individual member states and their actors have to interdependently manage their relations with the different levels and actors within the EU multi-level system. Changes caused by new framework conditions are typically made bottom-up. Austria was faced with the challenge of changing its federal system to enable *Bund* and *Länder* to make use of their competences and their room for maneuver in the larger EU system and accordingly introduced the *Länderbeteiligungsverfahren* (procedure for *Länder* participation). In some cases, EU primary law induces direct impacts on the polity dimension of its member states. One example is the introduction of the subsidiarity control mechanism. The EU conferred new rights on the national and subnational parliaments of its member states, and the member states had to implement those rights within their political systems. This top-down impact led to changes in the positions of parliaments and executives inside the political systems of the member states and also touched upon the federal order.

We have analyzed the changes the Austrian federal system has made due to the various forms of EU impacts. With reference to the rights of the *Länder* in EU affairs, we have illustrated one case of bottom-up Europeanization (*Länderbeteiligungsverfahren*) and one case of top-down Europeanization (subsidiarity control). The adaptations which Austria's federal system went through in the course of integration into the EU system are path-dependent. Many of these changes strengthen or redouble existing structures of Austrian federalism and its main characteristics, the specific allocation of competences, and executive and cooperative federalism. Through rights to participate in EU affairs, the competences and interests of the *Länder* in specific policies have been doubled as the *Länder* now have a bigger say in policies within their autonomous field of action. Executive federalism has been strengthened, as the administrations of the *Länder*, the *Landeshauptleutekonferenz*, and the Liaison Offices of the *Länder* in Vienna and Brussels play a crucial role while parliaments, especially *Bundesrat* and *Landtage*, remain more or less de facto marginalized. As a result of executive federalism, even the role of subnational parliaments in subsidiarity control induced by the EU has shrunk, with the subsidiarity control mechanism managed mainly by the executives of the *Länder*.

The homogeneity of the federal system is also present in EU affairs. *Bund* and *Länder* have worked together on a very cooperative basis from the beginning. Hardly any disputes have occurred, neither during the establishment of the rules of cooperation nor later in the phase of practical cooperation in everyday European life. In the interest of optimum advocacy for their vital concerns, both *Länder* and *Bund* focus on speaking with one voice in Brussels. Cooperative federalism is strengthened as informal coordination structures are functioning much more efficiently than the old and new formal ones. Some formal coordination bodies that were created in the course of EU integration are not working in practice, while management of EU politics between the *Länder* themselves and between *Bund* and *Länder* are functioning very satisfactorily for all actors via informal bodies and channels.

Territorial Cooperation in a Federal Framework: Austria's Involvement in European Groupings of Territorial Cooperation

Alice Engl

Introduction[1]

The European Grouping of Territorial Cooperation (EGTC) is a legal instrument designed to promote territorial cooperation between entities from different states.[2] It was created in 2006 by a European Union (EU) regulation, and allows public entities and authorities related to the public sector to associate and act together with a legal personality in order to enhance territorial cooperation.

Cooperation between sub-state authorities from different states has developed since the 1950s as a concrete initiative to foster local and regional development, especially in border regions, and has become a widespread practice in Europe over the past few decades.[3]

As a cooperation that crosses the boundaries of political and legal systems of different states, it marks a clash between two fundamental principles: the opening up of state boundaries due to increased cooperation and common European policies on the one hand, and state control over

1 The author is grateful to Dr. Johannes Maier for his valuable comments and additions to the present article.

2 This article uses the term "territorial cooperation" to refer to the cooperation between regional and local authorities from different states. It covers cross-border cooperation between neighboring entities, interregional cooperation between non-neighboring entities and transnational cooperation on a larger geographical scale. This term corresponds to the terminology used by the European Union and is chosen because the present article focuses on the European Grouping of Territorial Cooperation, which is a legal instrument for territorial cooperation based on EU secondary law. Synonyms that may as well be used as generic terms are "cross-border cooperation" and "transfrontier cooperation." The latter is, for example, used within the related conventions of the Council of Europe. Overall, these terms generally refer to all kinds of cooperation acting beyond state borders.

3 Charles Ricq, *Handbook of Transfrontier Co-Operation* (Council of Europe: Strasbourg, 2006), 41-42; Markus Perkmann, "Cross-Border Regions in Europe: Significance and Drivers of Regional Cross-Border Co-operation," *European Urban and Regional Studies* 10, no. 2 (2003): 153-171; Derya Zeyrek, "Formen grenzüberschreitender Zusammenarbeit in Europa," in *Politisches Handeln in transnationalen Räumen, Zusammenarbeit in europäischen Grenzregionen*, ed. Almut Kriele, Urs Lesse and Emanuel Richter (Baden-Baden: Nomos, 2005), 55-64.

the territorial organization and the division of competences within a state on the other. Thus, the legal framing of territorial cooperation encounters major legal and political difficulties that derive from both state reluctance and state dominance over this issue. State reluctance has often impeded the development of a regulatory framework for territorial cooperation. Consequently, the adoption of the EGTC Regulation is a major achievement because it is the first common legal instrument anchored in EU secondary law.

In Austria, there are several factors that could favor the use of the EGTC as an instrument for territorial cooperation. Firstly, the implementation of the instrument is decentralized and the states have much room for self-rule. Secondly, Austria is a small country and eight out of its nine states share a border with a foreign state (the only exception being Vienna). Third, Austria has eight neighboring states and is therefore confronted with a huge political, economic, cultural and social diversity in its immediate neighborhood. As a small country, it has many common interests with its neighbours, particularly regarding infrastructure, science, health, and environmental protection. Since these factors both imply necessities and possibilities for territorial cooperation and since sub-state authorities are the primary drivers and beneficiaries of cross-border cooperation activities, one could assume that the EGTC instrument is of particular interest to the Austrian states.

The present article focuses on Austria's involvement in EGTCs. For that purpose, the article first gives a general overview on the EGTC as an instrument for territorial cooperation and explains its development and purpose. Then it analyzes the legal implementation of the EGTC Regulation in Austria, embedded in a brief comparison with other states. This analysis of the legal implementation is complemented by a short study of existing EGTCs that involve Austrian public authorities, done from an institutional and functional perspective. The aim is to assess whether certain legal and political conditions in Austria, as its federal structure and the fact that many of its regional authorities border foreign states, favor the application of the EGTC in practice. The article concludes by drawing the results on the Austrian involvement in existing EGTCs and by discussing reasons for possible reluctance and, on the basis of established EGTCs, further conditions for a successful and effective application of the instrument.

The European Grouping of Territorial Cooperation (EGTC): A Common Legal Instrument to Promote Cooperation Across State Borders

Cooperation across state borders between local and regional authorities from different states has become an important instrument for supporting the regional development of a certain territory, for improving services, and for remaining competitive within a common economic area. Already since the early 1980s, the Council of Europe attempted to support cross-border cooperation and create a suitable legal basis for it through international conventions and recommendations for the conclusion of corresponding bi- or multilateral agreements.[4]

But also within the European Union, in particular within the EU cohesion policy, territorial cooperation gained increasing significance as tool to promote cross-state integration and cohesion at a regional and local level and as a measure for reducing economic and social disparities between the member states. A key initiative was the creation of the European Regional Development Fund (ERDF)[5] in 1975 to accompany national measures and programs for the support of economically underdeveloped regions, and the launch of the ERDF-funded INTERREG program in 1990 to specifically support cross-border, transnational, and interregional cooperation.

The need for measures to promote integration and reduce economic and social fragmentation within the Community, especially in view of the

4 Particularly significant in this context are the European Outline Convention on Transfrontier Cooperation between Territorial Communities or Authorities (in force since 1981, also known as the "Madrid Convention") and its three Additional Protocols (in force since 1998, 2001, and 2013, respectively). Examples of bi- or multilateral agreements that are based upon this framework convention include the Isselburg-Anholt agreement between Germany and the Netherlands (in force since 1993), the Karlsruhe agreement between France, Germany, Luxembourg and Switzerland (in force since 1995), the framework agreement between Italy and Austria (in force since 1995) and the Treaty of Bayonne between France and Spain (in force since 1997). See Alice Engl, "Future Perspectives on Territorial Cooperation in Europe: The EC Regulation on a European Grouping of Territorial Cooperation and the Planned Council of Europe Third Protocol to the Madrid Outline Convention concerning Euroregional Co-Operation Groupings," *European Diversity and Autonomy Papers*, no. 3 (2007): 5-42; Francesco Palermo and Jens Woelk, "Grenzüberschreitender Regionalismus als Konfliktlösungsinstrument? Die Entwicklung der Brennerkooperation," in *Jahrbuch des Föderalismus 2003*, ed. Europäisches Zentrum für Föderalismusforschung (Baden-Baden: Nomos, 2003), 381-393.

5 Regulation (EEC) no. 724/75 of the Council establishing a European Regional Development Fund, Official Journal L 37, 18 March 1975. As the legal basis for the establishment of this fund, Art. 235 of the Treaty Establishing the European Economic Community (TEEC) was enlisted. This gave the Community the possibility of resorting to "extraordinary" measures when necessary for the functioning of the Common Market.

upcoming enlargement in 2004, was further underlined in the Commission reports on economic and social cohesion of 2001 and 2004 as well as in the Commission's White Paper on governance of 2001.[6] In these documents, the Commission mentioned territorial cooperation as a key priority for promoting integration and networking of local and regional authorities, as well as reducing economic and social fragmentation. Furthermore, the Commission affirmed its intent to improve the framework for territorial cooperation and to supplement the financial support by a new legal instrument.

At the same time, other EU institutions also proposed to provide legal support to territorial cooperation between local and regional authorities. Among these are the Committee of the Regions which recommended the development of framework regulation to allow for the creation of so-called European Cooperation Areas,[7] and the European Court of Auditors which reported on the INTERREG program, criticizing the administration, the programs, and the projects, and requiring further work on legal instruments of cooperation to facilitate the administration.[8]

Furthermore, mainly due to the 2004 enlargement, the criteria to allocate the EU European Structural and Investment Funds were to be reorganized at the end of the funding period 2000-2006.[9] Until 2006, the fund distribution was primarily linked to the applicant's economic output. With the start of the 2007-2013 programming period, convergence, regional competitiveness, and European territorial cooperation were defined as the three main cohesion policy goals required to guarantee a funds distribution to both old and new member states.[10]

---

6 European Commission, Second Report on Economic and Social Cohesion, Brussels, 31 January 2001, COM (2001) 24 final; European Commission, Third Report on Economic and Social Cohesion (2004), at <http://ec.europa.eu/regional_policy/sources/docoffic/official/reports/cohesion3/cohesion3_en.htm>, xxxi (24 November 2014); Communication from the Commission of 25 July 2001 "European governance–A White Paper" COM (2001) 428 final, Official Journal 2001 C 287, 12 October 2001.

7 Opinion of the Committee of the Regions on Strategies for Promoting Cross-border and Inter-regional Cooperation in an Enlarged EU–A Basic Document Setting out Guidelines for the Future, Official Journal C 192, 12 August 2002, 37.

8 Court of Auditors, Special Report no. 4/2004 on the Programming of the Community Initiative Concerning Trans-European Cooperation–Interreg III, together with the Commission's Replies, Official Journal C 303, 7 December 2004, 18, para. 98(i).

9 In most candidate countries, the gross domestic product (GDP) per capita was significantly below the EU average at the time. That had two effects: on one hand, significantly more states were now competing for the same funds, and on the other hand, hardly any new financial inflows were being generated. See Roland Sturm, "Welches Europa soll es sein? Interessenkonflikte im Vorfeld der Erweiterung," *Internationale Politik*, no.1 (2003): 3-10, p. 4.

10 See Committee of the Regions, The European Grouping of Territorial Cooperation, January 2007, CdR 117/2007 Study, 23.

In view of these strategic priorities and functional pressures, the European Council and the European Parliament adopted on the eve of the funding period 2007-2013 the above-mentioned regulation on the European Grouping of Territorial Cooperation (EGTC).[11] It has to be noted that Austria considerably supported the adoption of this instrument. Whereas most of the state delegations in the Council were skeptical, the Austrian presidency of the Council in the first half of 2006 succeeded to conclude the EGTC dossier together with the other five structural funds regulations that governed the funding period 2007-2013.[12]

The main purpose of the EGTC is to foster territorial cooperation beyond borders in order to enhance economic, social, and territorial cohesion. Possible members of an EGTC are member states or authorities at state level, regional authorities, local authorities, public projects, and programs entrusted with services of general economic interest of different EU member states, regional, or local authorities, or even bodies or public projects from third countries.[13] The EGTC instrument is a major achievement since it is the first legal instrument anchored in EU secondary law that provides a legal framework for territorial cooperation in all twenty-eight EU member states.

The participating members of an EGTC adopt a unanimous convention which designates among others the name of the grouping, its headquarters, members, period of existence, the extent of its territory, its objectives and tasks, the list of the EGTC's organs, and their respective competences as well as the applicable Union law and members state's law.

Furthermore, members adopt a common statute, which contain the operating provisions of its organs and their respective competencies, provisions on decision-making processes and working languages, on the

11 Regulation (EC) no. 1082/2006 of the European Parliament and of the Council of 5 July 2006 on a European Grouping of Territorial Cooperation (EGTC), Official Journal L 210, 31 July 2006; and Regulation (EU) no. 1302/2013 of the European Parliament and of the Council of 17 December 2013 amending Regulation (EC) no. 1082/2006 on a European grouping of territorial cooperation (EGTC) as regards the clarification, simplification, and improvement of the establishment and functioning of such groupings, Official Journal L 347, 20 December 2013.

12 Johannes Maier, "Rechtliche Hindernisse für die Implementierung des EVTZ-Instruments in die föderale Verfassungsstruktur Österreichs," in *Jahrbuch des Föderalismus 2009*, ed. Europäisches Zentrum für Föderalismusforschung (Nomos: Baden-Baden, 2009), 455-468, p. 455; Alice Engl, "The European Grouping of Territorial Cooperation (EGTC): Origin, Content and Member State Implementation," in *Functional and More? New Potential for the European Grouping of Territorial Cooperation*, ed. idem and Carolin Zwilling (Bozen: Eurac, 2014), 11-37, p. 18.

13 The conditions for a participation of entities from third countries are set forth in Article 3a of Regulation no. 1302/2013.

financial contributions by the members, as well as on issues of personnel management. Mandatory organs of an EGTC are an assembly and a director. Any additional organs may be defined in the convention and the statute.

The establishment of or participation in an EGTC must be approved by the corresponding state authorities in charge, which are designated by the member states (Art. 4). The state authority can reject the participation in or the establishment of an EGTC if does not conform with the EGTC Regulation, with other Union law or with national law, if it contradicts public interest or public policy, or if the statute is inconsistent with the convention. If the state authority does not approve the participation in or establishment of an EGTC, it shall declare its reasons for withholding approval and shall, where appropriate, suggest the necessary amendments to the convention. As a final step in the establishment procedure, an EGTC has to be officially registered in the state where it has headquarters, and its convention and statute have to be officially published.

EGTCs have a legal personality that is based on Union law and complemented by respective national legal provisions. In every member state, EGTCs have the broadest legal capacity and the same capacity to conduct business as is granted to legal persons under the domestic law of the respective member state (Art. 1). EGTCs may acquire property, employ staff and appear in court. At an international level, EGTCs are treated as institutions of the member state in which they have their headquarters.

The possible tasks of an EGTC cover different kinds of activities. An EGTC can implement projects of territorial cooperation that are financed by EU funds, such as the EGTC Greater Region, which is the managing authority of parts of the INTERREG IVA Program Greater Region and was established with partners from France, Germany, Belgium, and Luxembourg. EGTCs may also be founded independently of EU programs and may be active without the financial participation of the Union.[14] In these cases, EGTCs either pursue general cooperation purposes, such as the EGTC *Eurométropole Lille-Kortrijk-Tournai* with partners from France and Belgium, or specific cooperation goals, such as the EGTC *Hospital*

14 According to Art. 7(3) of the EGTC Regulation, the member states may in fact limit the tasks that the EGTC may carry out without any financial contribution from the Community, but certain measures of cooperation in areas such as tourism, culture, health, education, nature conservation and transport must always be allowed. See Walter Obwexer and Esther Happacher, "Rechtsfragen der Gründung eines Europäischen Verbundes für territoriale Zusammenarbeit (EVTZ) am Beispiel der Europaregion Tirol," *Europäisches Journal für Minderheitenfragen* 3, no. 2 (2010): 75-99, p. 84.

of Cerdanya that was created by Spanish and French partners to jointly manage a cross-border hospital.

The activities of an EGTC may however not concern the exercise of public powers such as police, justice, or foreign policy (Art. 7 (4)) nor violate public order, public security, or public interest of a member state (Art. 13). The only exception is that the assembly of an EGTC may define the terms and conditions to which a service of general economic interest is provided or to which an infrastructure may be used, including the tariffs and fees to be paid by the users. If the actions of an EGTC contravene these provisions, the national authorities of a member state may prohibit the activity in question on its territory or require its EGTC members to withdraw from the grouping.[15] Such decisions, by the national authority may, however, be reviewed by a domestic judicial authority (Art. 13).

As a final remark, it should be added that the EGTC Regulation is bound to a state obligation for implementation, as the final provisions require the member states to adopt appropriate provisions to ensure the effective application of the regulation (Art. 16). The member states must designate the corresponding national authorities to receive requests for the establishment of EGTCs; they must determine the institutions that carry out financial audits; and they can restrict the tasks that EGTCs may carry out without the financial participation of the Union. The laws of the member states also have a complementary function, because they supplement the EGTC Regulation in all areas that are not (or are only partially) encompassed by the regulation. The next section will analyze the implementation of the EGTC Regulation in Austria.

The Legal Dimension: Austria's Implementation of the EGTC Regulation

The enforcement of regulations with a state obligation for implementation is a complex process that requires the consideration of specific procedures and principles under Union law. Certain implementation measures can be contrary to EU law, for example if they prevent the immediate validity of the directly applicable parts of such a regulation and thus interfere with its simultaneous and unified application,[16] or if they impermissibly modify the scope of a regulation or supplement its

15 Such prohibitions shall not constitute a means of arbitrary or disguised restriction on territorial cooperation between the EGTC's members (Art. 13).

16 ECJ, Case 39/72 Commission/Italy (1973), ECR101. See Committee of the Regions, *The European Grouping of Territorial Cooperation*, 123.

provisions.[17] Consequently, the actions of the member states must adhere to the precept of efficiency of Union law and be restricted to the permitted framework.[18]

The national provisions with regard to the application of the EGTC Regulation were to be enacted by August 2007, but most states did not meet this deadline and adopted their laws between 2008 and 2009.[19] The responsibility and competence to adopt the respective implementation laws differ between central, decentralized, and federal states. In central or unitary states, the competence to adopt the implementation laws is reserved to the central state authorities. In decentralized and federal states, the competence to adopt implementation provisions is either centralized or shared between the central authorities and the decentralized or federal units, depending on which policy area the EGTC is assigned, and whether that policy area falls under state competence or under federal or decentralized competence. Spain, for example, treats the EGTC as part of international relations and public administration and, therefore, the adoption of the implementation provisions falls under state competence.[20] In Belgium, as an opposing example, according to the division of competences under constitutional law, the federation and the federative entities (regions and language communities) share the power of adopting respective implementation provisions. Therefore, each authority adopts respective laws or decrees in order to regulate the implementation of the EGTC Regulation for those entities that fall under its competence (the federation for state entities, the Walloon region for entities of that region, the Flemish community for entities of that community, etc.).[21]

In Austria there were diverging opinions on the constitutional basis and competence for enacting the provisions to implement the EGTC regulation.

17 ECJ, Case 74/69 Hauptzollamt Bremen/Krohn (1970), ECR 451. See Michael Schweitzer, Waldemar Hummer and Walter Obwexer, *Europarecht: Das Recht der Europäischen Union* (Vienna: Manzsche Verlags- und Universitätsbuchhandlung, 2007), 194-198.

18 Christiane Columbus and Meinhard List, "Vollzugsprobleme 'hinkender Verordnungen'," *Briefe zum Agrarrecht: Zeitschrift für Agrar- und Unternehmensrecht*, no. 6 (2008): 227-230.

19 Only Hungary and the United Kingdom met the deadline. For a closer analysis of this implementation process and selected EGTC laws see Alice Engl, "Ein Instrument zwischen Gemeinschaftspolitik und nationalem Recht: Die Durchführung der Verordnung über den Europäischen Verbund für Territoriale Zusammenarbeit in ausgewählten EU-Mitgliedstaaten," *Zeitschrift Europarecht*, no. 3 (2013): 285-306; Idem, *Zusammenhalt und Vielfalt in Europas Grenzregionen: Der Europäische Verbund für territoriale Zusammenarbeit in normativer und praktischer Dimension* (Baden-Baden: Nomos, 2014), 217-273.

20 idem, *Zusammenhalt und Vielfalt*, 228.

21 Ibid., 251-254.

First, both the federation (*Bund*) and the states (*Länder*) followed the so-called "9+1" model, according to which the nine Austrian states and the federation itself should each enact an EGTC application law.[22]

This approach is based on the argumentation that the federal constitution contains some elements that refer to legal forms of cross-border cooperation, also related to public law, and that constitutional references on the responsibility to govern such legal instruments of cooperation are mainly related to competences that are constitutionally assigned to the states.[23] In the autumn of 2007, a draft law was drawn up as the legislative basis for individual states as well as federal law.[24]

However, in April 2008 the federation presented its own draft law, which differed from the joint 2007 draft. Following an expert assessment of some draft states' EGTC laws, the federation changed its legal opinion and assigned the regulation of EGTC matters to civil law (Art.10(1), Sec. 6 of the Austrian Constitution) or foreign affairs (Art.10(1), Sec. 2 of the Constitution), which both fall under the competence of the federation.[25] This federal EGTC law was presented to parliament. In May 2009, parliament assigned it to the Constitutional Committee, which never followed it up.

The states, on the other hand, were of the view that according to Art. 15(1) of the Austrian Constitution the implementation of the EGTC Regulation was in their area of competence and continued their work on the state EGTC laws.[26] In December 2008, the Carinthian state assembly adopted the Carinthian EGTC law. The new federal government of December 2008 declared no objection to the Carinthian law and approved the official announcement of the state law.[27] In doing so, the federation signaled its consent to the state EGTC laws and other

22 See Idem, "Die Nutzung neuer Instrumente europarechtlicher Zusammenarbeit für eine engere Kooperation zwischen Nord- und Südtirol," in *Rechtsvergleichung an der Sprachgrenze*, ed. Peter Hilpold, Walter Steinmair and Christoph Perathoner (Frankfurt a. M.: Peter Lang, 2011), 115-156, p. 138-143; Maier, "Rechtliche Hindernisse," 463.

23 See Maier, "Rechtliche Hindernisse," 463-465.

24 Ibid., 463.

25 Institut für Föderalismus, "EVTZ-Gesetz und Kompetenzverteilung," *Föderalismus Info*, no. 6 (2008); Vorblatt und Erläuterungen zur Regierungsvorlage Bundesgesetz über Europäische Verbünde für Territoriale Zusammenarbeit (EVTZ-Bundesgesetz), 3, at <http://www.parlament.gv.at/PAKT/VHG/XXIV/I/I_00175> (24 November 2014); Engl, *Zusammenhalt und Vielfalt*, 246-251.

26 Art. 15(1) of the Austrian Constitution reads: "To the extent that a matter is not expressly transferred by the Federal Constitution to legislation or else to the execution by the federation, it remains in the separate domain of the states." See Vorblatt und Erläuterungen zur Regierungsvorlage EVTZ-Bundesgesetz, 5.

27 Maier, "Rechtliche Hindernisse," 467.

states followed Carinthia's example.[28] These state EGTC laws regulate the implementation of the EGTC Regulation at state level, provided that no contrary federal provisions are adopted.[29]

Apart from that, the enactment of a federal law is still necessary to regulate the EGTC participation of the federation or public entities that fall under the federal competence (*Bundeskompetenz*) because, as already mentioned before, state laws are restricted to the area of competence of the states. Without the enactment of a federal law, the federation or any entity that falls under federal competence cannot participate in an EGTC. However, this legal gap may be bypassed by a pragmatic approach. In such a case, the request to approve the participation in an EGTC would be submitted to the federal chancellor or the competent federal minister who would have to decide on the request by directly applying the EGTC Regulation despite the absence of a federal EGTC application law. The registration of such an EGTC could be handled at state level because the EGTC would locate its headquarters and thus also its official registration in one of the states.

In the following part, the Carinthian example illustrates the implementation of the EGTC at state level.

The Carinthian EGTC Law

The Carinthian EGTC law was adopted on 18 December 2008 and amended on 25 September 2014.[30] It regulates the approval process, registration, and auditing of EGTCs within the framework of the areas of competence of the state of Carinthia. This includes registration and auditing of an EGTC with headquarters in Carinthia, as well as the approval of the participation of the state of Carinthia, Carinthian municipalities, or other institutions under public law that are subordinated to state competence in a grouping with headquarters in a different Austrian state or in a different country. The Carinthian EGTC application law designates the Carinthian state

28 The states of Lower Austria, Salzburg, Styria, Tyrol, and Vorarlberg all adopted their respective EGTC laws by mid-2010. The state laws are oriented toward the model drawn up in 2007 and are, therefore, similarly structured. They are divided into five sections, which regulate the following aspects: scope of application or validity, authorization of participation in an EGTC, registration of an EGTC, supervision and dissolution of an EGTC, and auditing of the EGTC's finances.

29 The state laws contain a clause, which affirms that they regulate the implementation of the EGTC insofar as this falls under state competence. Thus, a law at federal level that opposes this clause could cause again a discussion on the legal competence to regulate this matter. See Maier, "Rechtliche Hindernisse," 466.

30 Law of 18 December 2008 on the European Grouping of Territorial Cooperation, LGBl. no. 20/2009; Law of 25 September 2014, LGBl. no. 51/2014.

government as the competent authority for approval, registration, and control of EGTCs. As the supervising body, it can also decide the dissolution of an EGTC, prohibit its activity, and request withdrawal of an EGTC member.

As the other Austrian state EGTC laws, the Carinthian EGTC law differentiates between approval to participate in an EGTC (Art. 2, Carinthian EGTC law) and registration of an EGTC (Art. 3, Carinthian EGTC law). The latter presupposes the approval of the establishment of the EGTC with its headquarters on the territory of Carinthia. The approval provisions concern participation of the state of Carinthia, a Carinthian municipality (or an association of municipalities), or another institution qualified for membership in an EGTC with headquarters in Austria or abroad. Prospective members obtain the approval to participate in an EGTC by notification, with appeal to the Administrative State Court of Carinthia if the approval is not granted. If an EGTC intends to set up its headquarters in Carinthia, additional "registration conditions" must be observed. To register an EGTC in Carinthia, the prospective members have to submit to the Carinthian government the EGTC convention and statutes as well as a notification that the participation of the single entities was approved by the respective competent authority or an appropriate confirmation that the terms and conditions of the approval process defined in Art. 4(3) of the EGTC Regulation have been respected. The Carinthian state government can indicate denial of registration by notification to the Administrative State Court of Carinthia which also handles any appeals. A denial of registration blocks the formation of an EGTC, as its prospective members would not obtain the status of a legal personality, as it is granted with the date of registration by Art. 5 of the EGTC Regulation.

Finally, the Carinthian state government is responsible for auditing the management of public funds (Art. 5, Carinthian EGTC law). The Carinthian state government must conduct audits if a competent authority under Art. 2(4) of the EGTC Regulation requests one on the grounds of suspicious circumstances, or if the Carinthian state government considers that an audit would be justified. The Carinthian state government may also conduct audits on a random basis, and may appoint an external, independent auditor to be paid by the EGTC.

Overall, the Austrian federal states have considerable room for self-rule with regard to the establishment and supervision of an EGTC. Compared to centralized processes applied, for example, in unitary states, in which the competence to act as decision-making authority rests with central government authorities, such a decentralized decision-making process can be an additional incentive to make use of the EGTC instrument. It implies a more "direct" control of the establishing process by those entities that at the same time might have more interest in enhancing an institutionalized territorial cooperation.

The Practical Dimension: Austrian Involvement in European Groupings of Territorial Cooperation

By the end of 2014 Austrian authorities formally participated in two established EGTCs.[31] Both are Euroregions with very general cooperation purposes: the *European Region Tyrol-South Tyrol-Trentino* and the *Euregio senza Confini / Euregio ohne Grenzen*. In both cases, the EGTC serves as a legal framework to institutionalize cooperation initiatives between regional authorities from Austria and Italy that already preceded the formal establishment of the EGTC, as outlined below. Also other cooperative networks that involve Austrian authorities took into consideration the foundation of an EGTC, such as the *Alps-Adriatic Working Community*, *Ökologie/Naturraum March-Thaya-Auen*, the *Euregio Salzburg-Traunstein-Berchtesgadener Land*, the *Euregio Weinviertel-Südmähren-Westslowakei*, the *Geopark Karawanken*, or the City Network *DonauHanse*. A further, most advanced initiative is the EGTC *Alpine Pearls*, which held its founding meeting on 12 October 2014 in Ratschings, South Tyrol, deciding on its convention and statute. It groups about twenty-five municipalities, municipal associations as well as "public" tourism organizations from Austria, Germany, Slovenia, Italy, Switzerland, and France and will be one of the first EGTCs of interregional cooperation operating jointly in the field of sustainable tourism. The partners plan to set up the official seat of this EGTC in Werfenweng, Salzburg. Thus, it would be the first EGTC officially registered in Austria. The comprehensive process for obtaining the needed approvals for the participation of the entities from five EU member states and from one third of the country has already started.

By the end of 2014, none of those planned EGTCs had been officially created. Therefore, the following sections analyze and compare the two established EGTCs.

31 Compared to the EGTC-involvement of sub-state authorities of other federal states, such as Germany and Belgium, this number is rather low. German public authorities are involved in five EGTCs and Belgian public authorities in six EGTCs. See Metis GmbH, *EGTC Monitoring Report 2013: Towards the New Cohesion Policy (2014)*, at <http://cor.europa.eu/en/documentation/studies/Documents/EGTC-monitoring-report-2013/EGTC-monitoring-report-2013.pdf> (24 November 2014). The EGTC instrument is therefore used despite the existence of previous bi- or multilateral state treaties that regulated cross-border cooperation already before the adoption of the EGTC (see note 3). For a closer assessment of political and legal factors that incentivize the use of the EGTC despite already existing bi- or multilateral state treaties on cross-border cooperation see Engl, *Zusammenhalt und Vielfalt*, 356-357.

The EGTC *European Region Tyrol-South Tyrol-Trentino* and the EGTC *Euregio senza Confini / Euregio ohne Grenzen*

In both these cases, regional authorities decided to use the EGTC instrument to legally institutionalize already existing Euroregional platforms and activities of cross-border cooperation.[32] The EGTC served as a tool to establish a legal and political framework that allows the involved regional authorities to work together in the frame of a Euroregion, and to pursue general cooperation purposes relevant to strengthening economic, social, and territorial cohesion on the respective territory.

These EGTCs were officially founded in 2011 and 2012 and are both officially registered in Italy. Therefore, Italian law governs all the aspects that are not (or are only partially covered by the EGTC Regulation. In both cases, the formal cooperation remains restricted to the regional level and the EGTC partners do not use the instrument to formally involve local authorities and other public entities.

The following table summarizes the main data of the EGTCs, before assessing in more detail the EGTCs' institutional and functional dimensions of cooperation.

EGTC	**EGTC European Region Tyrol-South Tyrol-Trentino**	**EGTC Euregio senza Confini / Euregio ohne Grenzen**
Members	Austria: Land Tyrol Italy: Autonomous Province of Bozen/Bolzano-South Tyrol, Autonomous Province of Trento	
Year of foundation	2011	2014
Working languages	German, Italian, if necessary Ladin	German and Italian
Organs according to the convention and the statute	1. Assembly (12 members) 2. Board (3 members) 3. President 4. General Secretary 5. Board of Auditors	1. Assembly (3 members) 2. Director 3. Board of Auditors
Registered seat	Bozen/Bolzano, Italy	Trieste, Italy

Table 1: EGTCs involving Austrian authorities

32 See Alice Engl and Birgit Oberkofler, "Europäische Verbünde territorialer Zusammenarbeit im Alpenraum," in *Multi-Level-Governance im Alpenraum*, ed. Peter Bußjäger and Christian Gsodam (Vienna: New Academic Press, 2013), 151-175; Alice Engl and Carolin Zwilling, "Herausforderungen für den Brennerraum: Der Europäische Verbund für territoriale Zusammenarbeit (EVTZ) Europaregion Tirol-Südtirol-Trentino," in *Politik in Tirol, Jahrbuch 2013*, ed. Ferdinand Karlhofer and Günther Pallaver (Innsbruck: StudienVerlag, 2013), 133-155.

The Institutional Dimension of Cooperation

A comparison of the number and type of the statutory organs of both EGTCs shows that the institutional framework of cooperation is at first glance quite different. The *Euregio senza Confini / Euregio ohne Grenzen* just follows the requirements of the EGTC Regulation and appoints an assembly and a director, which according to the EGTC Regulation are the mandatory organs of an EGTC, and only adds a board of auditors as third organ. The *European Region Tyrol-South Tyrol-Trentino,* by contrast, has five organs: an assembly and a president who takes over the function of the director, and in addition a board, a general secretary and a board of auditors.

A fundamental difference in the EGTCs' institutional set-up regards their administrative backing, which is organized as a permanent directorship in the *Euregio senza Confini / Euregio ohne Grenzen* and a rotating general secretary in the *European Region Tyrol-South Tyrol-Trentino.* The director of the *Euregio senza Confini / Euregio ohne Grenzen* is nominated by the board. The candidates can either be from the public or private sector and must have five years of relevant work experience. The director is the legal representative of the EGTC and has the following responsibilities: preparation of regulations, implementation of the work program, management of funds and personnel, preparation of administrative acts, and organization of the structure. He or she has a three-year mandate that is renewable only once. For the administration of the EGTC and its projects, the EGTC may employ outside personnel, either paid for by the EGTC or seconded by the EGTC members. However, by the end of 2014 the EGTC did not yet have any additional personnel.

The *European Region Tyrol-South Tyrol-Trentino* is administratively backed by a general secretary and a common office in Bozen/Bolzano. The position of the general secretary, who directs the common office, is not permanently assigned but rotates among the EGTC members in compliance with the rotation of the EGTC presidency. Thus, each EGTC member seconds one senior official to the administrative office. These senior officials hold the function of the EGTC's general secretary for two years when it is the respective member's turn and sustain the respective EGTC member's representatives in the assembly and in the board.[33] Apart from these three senior officials, the common office has further staff who in most

33 The general secretary organizes the meetings of the board and the assembly and proposes the respective agenda. Furthermore, he or she ensures that the decisions of the EGTC are prepared and carried out, concludes contracts and agreements to ensure the EGTC's day-to-day operation, and exercises any other duties that are assigned to him or her by the president.

cases are also seconded to the EGTC, or employed directly by third-party funding when working for specific projects. In addition, a certain degree of multilingualism is formally required. According to the internal rules of procedure, a good knowledge of Italian or German as a second language as well as a good knowledge of English are preconditions to work in the common office.

A commonality of the EGTCs' institutional set-up is the dominant position of the executive heads of the involved regions, which the cooperation needs on the one hand to secure its political backing and guiding. On the other hand, this dominating position of the executive heads can also be counterbalanced by other participatory mechanisms, which in the present cases is however not provided at all or to a limited extent, as outlined further below. The steering and decision-making organs of the EGTCs are the assembly in the *Euregio senza Confini / Euregio ohne Grenzen* and the board and the assembly in the *European Region Tyrol-South Tyrol-Trentino*.

The assembly of the *Euregio senza Confini / Euregio ohne Grenzen* is composed of the three presidents of the regional governments of Carinthia, Friuli-Venezia Giulia, and Veneto.[34]

Thus, it has the same structure and size as the board of the *European Region Tyrol-South Tyrol-Trentino*, which is also formed by the three regional presidents.[35] In both cases, the function to act as members of these steering committees is assigned automatically to the regional presidents of the participating regional entities. Thus, the political leadership of the EGTC is divided between the three regional presidents. Due to the restrictions on the number of members in these two organs and the absence of bargaining appointment procedures, a diversified participation is not envisaged.

In the *European Region Tyrol-South Tyrol-Trentino*, the dominance of the regional executive heads is partly counterbalanced by the creation of an assembly as second leading organ. The assembly of the *European Region*

34 The assembly meets at least once a year and approves the annual and pluri-annual programs, yearly budgets, balance sheets, and financial reports. It also determines the annual membership fee.

35 According to the statute, the board is responsible for the following tasks: decide upon the annual work program of the EGTC; approve agreements and contracts that do not concern the day-to-day operation of the EGTC; adopt the annual and multi-annual budget; define the annual financial contribution by the EGTC-members; and adopt other necessary provisions to ensure proper procedures in the EGTC. In addition, the statute stipulates that the board is empowered to take decisions on all matters that are not allocated to the other organs. The board can take its decisions by a two-thirds majority, with the exception of those areas where the statutes provide for unanimity, such as in the determination of annual financial contributions of the EGTC-members. The decisions of the board are only be valid if all members are present at the vote.

Tyrol-South Tyrol-Trentino consists of twelve members and ensures that in addition to government representatives also representatives of the regional parliaments are formally involved in the cooperative framework and decision-making process.[36] According to the EGTC statute, each EGTC partner sends two governmental representatives and two parliamentary representatives to the assembly. However, the possibilities to debate and bargain whom to send as a representative are limited because both the presidents of the three regional governments and the presidents of the three regional parliaments are appointed ex officio. The appointment of the second assembly member falls under the responsibility of the respective governmental or parliamentarian president, and the statute does not further regulate this nomination process.[37]

Furthermore, the steering and decision-making organs of both EGTCs are not embedded in a further institutionalized framework of cooperation that ensures a wider participation of other relevant players, such as administrative authorities, other public authorities, or non-governmental actors. Possibilities for an institutional and permanent involvement of other relevant actors in the cooperation framework and in the designing of cooperation projects, such as by creating permanent thematic working groups or other consultative bodies, are not used in both cases. The participation of other stakeholders is organized ad hoc and occasionally in individual projects.[38]

Finally, both EGTCs have a board of auditors which performs the economic and financial supervision according to the respective auditing rules. That board consists of one expert per member.

36 According to the EGTC statute, the assembly has the following tasks: establish the EGTC's guidelines and monitor the achievement of the respective objectives; decide upon the resolution of the EGTC, the inclusion of a new member and on amendments of the convention and the statute; approve the annual and multi-annual budget; and adopt internal rules of procedure. The assembly can adopt its decisions by a two-thirds majority provided that the absolute majority of the assembly members are present. For certain decisions, such as admission of new members, delegation of tasks of the EGTC to a member, amendments to the convention and statute as well as dissolution of the EGTC, unanimity is prescribed.

37 Within the regional parliament of Trentino, it was agreed that the opposition parties shall have the right to propose whom to nominate as a second parliamentary representative in the EGTC assembly.

38 The importance of a formal and institutionalized participation of a diversified range of actors for achieving an integrated and cohesive cross-border policy space is assessed in Alice Engl, "Von Kooperation zu Kohäsion: Die Europaregion Tirol-Südtirol-Trentino als transnationaler Handlungsraum," in *Politik in Tirol, Jahrbuch 2015*, ed. Ferdinand Karlhofer and Günther Pallaver (Innsbruck: StudienVerlag, forthcoming); and Engl, *Zusammenhalt und Vielfalt.*

The Functional Dimension of Cooperation

The general objective of both EGTCs is to promote territorial cooperation and to enhance the economic and social cohesion among its members. For that purpose, the EGTC statutes define the following basic objectives of cooperation: strengthening economic, social and cultural relations among the population of EGTC members; fostering territorial development and cooperation of the EGTC members according to their respective competences, for instance in the policy fields education, culture, energy, mobility, research and innovation, economy and environment; enhancing common participation in EU funded programs and projects, especially under the cohesion policy funds; representing the interests of the EGTC vis-à-vis national and European institutions; as well as taking other specific measures to foster territorial cooperation.

To achieve these objectives, the EGTC can pursue the following tasks: develop and implement common projects (with or without financial contribution by the EU); represent the EGTC's interests vis-à-vis national and European institutions; join organizations, associations and networks that pursue objectives that correspond to the ones of the EGTC; implement programs funded by the European Regional Development Fund; and take and implement any other measures that can contribute to the achievement of the EGTC's objectives.

The main instrument to develop and implement projects is the annual work program, elaborated and approved either by the assembly as in the *Euregio senza Confini / Euregio ohne Grenzen*, or by the president and by the board as in the *European Region Tyrol-South Tyrol-Trentino*. The annual program lists both general objectives and measures as well as specific projects that the partners want to implement in the respective year.

From a functional perspective, the *European Region Tyrol-South Tyrol-Trentino* has already more cooperation experiences and ongoing projects than the *Euregio senza Confini / Euregio ohne Grenzen*. Whereas the latter is still in the phase to start up its functional cooperation and concrete activities, the former already launched some initiatives and projects. For instance, there are several projects focused on multilingualism, migration and intercultural understanding. In November 2011, the EGTC partners signed an agreement to foster the cooperation and the exchange of experiences in intercultural policies in order to develop a cross-border approach. It was agreed to implement common projects and initiatives to enhance cross-border networking and to assess topics related to intercultural dialogue and integration. On the basis of this agreement, several conferences have already been organized and a common Interreg project on the intercultural dialogue in elementary schools has been successfully submitted and launched.[39] Furthermore, the EGTC has organized the elaboration of a bilingual history book that gives an overview on the history of the border area in both languages German and Italian. The book was distributed to schools, municipalities, and other public entities to ensure that it may be used for education and training throughout the European region.

Other projects and activities of the *European Region Tyrol-South Tyrol-Trentino* tackle issues such as health, energy, innovation and research. On the one hand, the basis for a long-term cooperation shall be provided by developing clearer concepts and "roadmaps" for cooperation, such as a common concept to expand the European Region's autonomy in the energy sector, which is currently under elaboration. Furthermore, the EGTC organizes regular thematic conferences that tackle legal conditions and challenges for cooperation. On the other hand, the EGTC is partner in several Interreg projects to promote renewable energies and organizes cross-border seminars to foster the networking among relevant actors and provide opportunities for developing further common projects.

Overall, the output of both EGTCs still lags behind the defined goals and tasks and the benefits of having an institutionalized cooperation structure as the EGTC are not yet fully exploited, both in functional and institutional terms.

Comparing Law and Practice: Results on the Austrian EGTC Involvement

The assessment of the legal dimension and the practical dimension in the previous sections leads to two main results with regard to the Austrian EGTC involvement. Firstly, there is a significant gap between legal opportunities and practice, and, secondly, the types of established EGTCs are very similar.

The gap between legal opportunities and practice is evident from the legally favorable conditions due to the decentralized implementation of the instrument on the one hand and the low number of EGTCs on the other hand. This is despite the high number of Austrian states that share external borders, and the high number of neighboring countries. Although the federal structure of Austria definitely facilitates the legal application of the instrument, especially compared to other states such as Spain or

39 Interreg IV Project Diversity4Kids, at <http://www.diversity4kids.eu> (24 November 2014).

Italy where the legal implementation of the EGTC is centralized, this facilitated application is not reflected in practice. By the end of 2014, only two EGTCs exist in which Austrian authorities participate, and only one EGTC with Austrian partners has taken significant steps to prepare its official creation. In other words, the decentralized legal implementation does not necessarily lead to a high number of EGTCs. As possible reasons for this gap, the following four provide a preliminary albeit incomplete explanation.

First, as mentioned before, Austria still lacks a federal implementation law that regulates the EGTC participation of authorities that fall under federal competence. This may impede the creation of EGTCs that envisage a formal involvement of any entities that fall under federal competence. However if the will to participate in an EGTC is given, pragmatic solutions can help to overcome this legal gap, as mentioned before.

Second, the EGTC is not the only instrument of cross-border cooperation. Many cooperation activities started two or three decades ago and are organized informally or with private law instruments. Such other forms of territorial cooperation, created for example as working community based on private law, are often already well-established and do not need to change their legal and organizational set-up into an EGTC. The Austrian example further underlines this.

Third, the legal frame that defines the application of the EGTC instrument is not the only factor that determines its use in practice. Any kind of cross-border cooperation is never a one-sided process but requires political, legal, and economic conditions on both sides of a border that generate the needs and opportunities for cooperation. Hesitation towards the establishment of an EGTC may root in too many differences regarding administrative structures and legal competences between entities from different states, lacking political will and support and concerns that permanent cooperation structures are too costly.

Formal and long-term cooperation structures such as the EGTC need political and economic sustainability, which means that both the given political and economic conditions must self-sustain the cooperation and its organizational set-up. Formally institutionalized cooperation procedures, as within an EGTC, certainly enhance the continuity of cooperation activities. However, the effectiveness of such cooperation structures is not guaranteed. A formal institutionalization without a solid political and economic basis for cooperation and without suitable organizational mechanisms that provide for an elaboration of cooperation strategies and projects by the relevant actors must therefore be considered critically.

The second result with regard to the Austrian involvement in existing EGTCs is that the types of EGTCs with Austrian authorities as partners that have been established so far are very similar. Austrian authorities are neither involved in any EGTCs that operate at local level and are composed of local authorities as partners, nor in any EGTCs that follow a specific purpose of cooperation (except for the planned EGTC *Alpine Pearls*), such as the administration of an EU territorial cooperation program, or the administration of a cross-border service.

Instead, Austrian authorities are involved in two EGTCs with general cooperation purposes whose organizational set-up is characterized by the dominant position of the regional authorities end their executive heads and presidents on the one hand, and limited other participatory mechanisms on the other hand. Such a broad-based and multi-functional collaboration, as envisaged in these two EGTCs, needs institutionalized cooperation processes and structured responsibilities, because the cooperation—due to the objectives laid down in the convention—intends to go beyond a mere coordination of political statements and exchange of experience, and should ensure the mandatory implementation of common strategies and projects.[40] A mere exchange of information and experiences can also be carried out within informal and non-binding cooperation platforms. Legal instruments such as the EGTC have the advantage of having a legally binding character, a clear structure and responsible institutions, which are a conditional framework for a long-term, strategic and efficient cooperation in various policy areas. Such facilitating formal institutions provide procedures and resources as well as leadership, which are necessary to back the cooperation.

However such a strong political and symbolic dimension of cooperation must be linked to functional and purpose-oriented incentives. Cross-border relationships must not only be guided by political and cultural proximity and by a few dominant actors, but need be organized along synergies as well as economic and social benefits.

Overall, cross-border cooperation and integration risks to stagnate if either only the political or only the functional dimension is dominant. A political-symbolic cooperation lacks the functional-pragmatic incentive for cooperation and thus the motivation for the involvement of various relevant actors in the cooperation structures. Conversely, purely functional and purpose-oriented cooperation, on the contrary, lacks political and cultural ties that are equally important for the development of sustainable cooperation structures.

40 Maier, "Rechtliche Hindernisse," 458.

Conclusions

The present article started by outlining the aim of territorial cooperation and the development as well as the general purpose of the EGTC instrument. It pointed out that according to EU policies, institutionalized territorial cooperation, as within an EGTC, can be a key strategy to promote integration and networking of local and regional authorities and to enhance cohesion in border areas.

Furthermore, the article highlighted the added values of the EGTC instrument which, briefly summarized, are its legal anchoring in EU secondary law and its flexibility with regard to membership, organizational set-up and tasks. But despite the added value of this instrument as well as the geographical and the legally favoring conditions in Austria, deriving from the decentralized implementation of the EGTC instrument and the fact that most of the Austrian sub-state authorities share borders with foreign states, the instrument so far is rarely used in practice.

To trigger the establishment of an EGTC or any other form of cross-border cooperation, laws are obviously not enough. Other important conditions must be fulfilled that favor an institutionalized cooperation, which are the political will, the functional need, and the economic capacity to sustain such cooperation structures. The EGTC is a strong and European-wide applicable cooperation tool, but it cannot generate those conditions.

Nevertheless, Austria's favorable conditions can still facilitate the implementation of EGTCs in future. EGTCs can develop as viable instruments for Austrian regional and local authorities to promote their networking and cooperation with foreign entities, provided that aims and visions of cooperation are developed beyond mere self-interest, and that institutions and rules are envisaged to frame and sustain the cooperation.

Confederalizing via European Integration: South Tyrol from Habsburg to the Present

Günther Pallaver

Introduction

South Tyrol is an autonomous province within the Trentino-South Tyrol region of Italy. The German and Ladin linguistic groups of South Tyrol enjoy far-reaching minority protection with international guarantees, serving as an example in Europe. South Tyrol also possesses an extensive legislative and executive territorial autonomy and a well-endowed budget to cover the costs incurred by the conferred competences. South Tyrol's per capita income is the highest in Italy, and the province ranks among the twenty richest regions in Europe.[1]

The South Tyrol conflict was sparked at the end of World War I and the following implosion of the Austro-Hungarian Empire. South Tyrol was annexed by Italy in exchange for entering the war on the side of the *Entente* powers (see table 1 for the development of the ethnic groups in South Tyrol).

Fascism tried to forcefully assimilate the German-speaking population, and an agreement between Mussolini and Hitler (1939) was to bring German speakers "home" to the German Reich in the framework of an alleged option. Despite attempts to rejoin Austria after World War II, South Tyrol remained part of Italy. However, the 1946 Paris Agreement between Italy and Austria guaranteed major minority protection provisions for the German-speaking population, thus constituting the basis for the passage of the First Autonomy Statute of 1948, South Tyrol's provincial constitution.

The central government of Italy, however, largely sabotaged the implementation of the autonomy provisions and minority protections,

1 Martin Larch, "Autonomie und Ökonomie: War die Selbstverwaltung ein Segen für die Wirtschaftsentwicklung? Möglich wär's," in *Politika12: Jahrbuch für Politik/ Annuario di politica/Annuar de politica*, ed. Günther Pallaver (Südtiroler Gesellschaft für Politikwissenschaft/Società di Scienza Politica dell'Alto Adige/Sozietà de scienza politica de Sudtirol) (Bozen: Edition Raetia, 2012), 327-342.

causing Austria to present the South Tyrol problem at the United Nations Organization (UN), which passed resolutions in 1960 and 1961 urging both parties to the agreements to come to a solution by means of negotiating. Far into the 1960s, these negotiations were accompanied by bomb attacks, the perpetrators of which did not pursue substantial autonomy, but the return to Austria.

In 1972 the Second Autonomy Statute was successfully passed. The revised province constitution ensured a significantly improved territorial autonomy for South Tyrol and a generous minority protection for German speakers and Ladins alike, thus being internationally praised today as an exemplary model of how to solve a minority problem through granting a high degree of minority protection.[2] The dispute pending within the UN framework was formally settled in 1992.[3]

Table 1: Population development in South Tyrol (1900-2011) by language groups (%)

Year	German	Italian	Ladin
1900	88.8	4.0	4.0
1910	89.0	2.9	3.8
1921	75.9	10.6	3.9
1961	62.2	34.3	3.4
1971	62.9	33.3	3.7
1981	64.9	28.7	4.1
1991	67.9	27.6	4.3
2001	69.1	26.4	4.3
2011	69.4	26.0	4.5

Source: *Statistisches Jahrbuch für Südtirol*, ed. Astat (Bozen, 2013), at <www.provinz.bz.it/astat/download/JB2013_K3.pdf> (27 January 2015).

2 Emma Lantschner, "History of the South Tyrol Conflict and its Settlement," in *Tolerance through Law: Self Governance and Group Rights in South Tyrol*, ed. Jens Woelk, Francesco Palermo and Joseph Marko (European Academy Bozen/Bolzano) (Leiden: Martinus Nijhoff Publishers, 2008), 3-15; Rolf Steininger, *South Tyrol: A Minority Conflict of the Twentieth Century* (Studies in Austrian and Central European History and Culture) (New Brunswick: Transaction, 2nd ed. 2009)

3 *Fine di un conflitto: Dieci anni dalla chiusura della questione sudtirolese*, ed. Andrea Di Michele, Francesco Palermo and Günther Pallaver (Bologna: il Mulino, 2003).

The successful settlement of the South Tyrol conflict is due to domestic factors, the two negotiation partners Austria and Italy as well as the international context.[4]

Today, the legal foundation of South Tyrolean autonomy is based on a widely branched out network of special domestic constitutional and international norms.[5] Along with the 1946 Paris Treaty and other framework conventions to protect minorities at European level Italy is a party of, the South Tyrolean autonomy statute enjoys constitutional backing and is based on the aforementioned Paris Treaty. There are further general domestic framework laws to protect minorities as well as a number of special norms. The legal convolute that aims at protecting the South Tyrolean minority amounts to 20.000 pages today with an upward trend.[6]

Along with the dense network of legal safeguards, there is also a wide political support framework for South Tyrolean autonomy. This is mainly true for Austria, who functions as a watchdog over South Tyrolean developments and regularly consults with the South Tyrolean political elites and, if necessary, with the Italian government in Rome. Legal security that goes beyond strictly legal foundations is first and foremost provided by the EU for the South Tyroleans.

A Federalist Foreign Policy?

The particularity of South Tyrolean autonomy consists among other things in the strong emotional and international law-based relationship between South Tyrol and Austria. However, the connection between South

4 Günther Pallaver, "Determinanten ethnischer Konfliktlösungen: Ein Vergleich zwischen Südtirol, Nordirland und dem Baskenland," *Canadian Review of Studies in Nationalism*, no. 1-2 (2002): 95-104; Idem, "South Tyrol's Consociational Democracy: Between Political Claim and Social Reality,"in *Tolerance through Law: Self Governance and Group Rights in South Tyrol*, ed. Jens Woelk, Francesco Palermo and Joseph Marko (European Academy Bozen/Bolzano) (Leiden: Martinus Nijhoff Publishers, 2008), 303-327; Günther Pallaver, "South Tyrol's Changing Political System: From Dissociative on the Road to Associative Conflict Resolution," *Nationalities Papers: The Journal of Nationalism and Ethnicity* 42, no. 3 (2014), DOI: 10.1080/00905992.2013.856393, 376-398, at <www.tandfonline.com/doi/pdf/10.1080/00905992.2013.856393> (10 March 2015); Stefan Wolff, "Complex Power Sharing as Conflict Resolution: South Tyrol in Comparative Perspective," in *Tolerance through Law: Self Governance and Group Rights in South Tyrol*, ed. Jens Woelk, Francesco Palermo and Joseph Marko (European Academy Bozen/Bolzano) (Leiden: Martinus Nijhoff Publishers, 2008), 329-370.

5 Ibid., 347.

6 Thomas Benedikter, *Autonomien der Welt: Eine Einführung in die Regionalautonomien der Welt mit vergleichender Analyse* (Bozen: Athesia, 2007), 90.

Tyrol and Tyrol is even stronger than that to Austria.[7] Tyrolean identity has been widely formed by the South Tyrol policy, for with the partition of Tyrol in 1918 today's federal state of Tyrol felt amputated in territorial and emotional terms.[8] This "national pain" led Tyroleans to fight even harder for their "brethren in the South," as they were referred to by the former Tyrolean Governor, Eduard Wallnöfer (1913-1989). This particular relationship between Tyrol and South Tyrol also has had spill-over effects on the foreign policy of other Austrian federal states. The Austrian federal states have pursued their own foreign policies since the 1989 constitutional reform, which gave the *Länder* the right to conclude international law treaties with their respective neighbors. The strongly developed checks and balances by the federal level, however, have led the federal states to hardly make use of these treaty-making powers, thus mainly resorting to their private-sector administration competences. The informal workings of the federal states' foreign policies are out of federal reach, which has contributed to the evolution of different forms of governance. The *Länder* well participate in federal European Union (EU) policy-making, however. This has caused the federal states to be able to successfully corepresent Austrian interests at European level.[9]

Another question, however, is whether federal states should have a strong say in federal foreign policy in a federal system like that of Austria, even including veto powers. It is true that there are strong coordination mechanisms between the federal and state levels in foreign policy affairs, however, it is also true that practice defies theory in that the federal states' involvement in foreign affairs is quite weakly developed.[10]

The federal state of Tyrol constitutes an exception in this respect, for South Tyrol enjoys some unwritten competences in South Tyrol matters and, thus, in a field that strongly affects Austrian foreign policy.

The Austrians never came to terms with the loss of South Tyrol after the First World War. This has been mainly due to Tyrol, who exerted pressure on Austrian foreign policymakers in Vienna as a result of a century-long union with South Tyrol in the former Tyrolean crown-land. Vienna's South Tyrol policy was strongly influenced by the essential contribution

7 Günther Pallaver, "Zwischen Kooperation und Konkurrenz: Zur Entwicklung der Beziehungen zwischen Nord- und Südtirol," in *Politik in Tirol: Jahrbuch 2013*, ed. Ferdinand Karlhofer and idem (Innsbruck: StudienVerlag, 2013), 109-132.

8 Michael Gehler, *Tirol im 20. Jahrhundert: Vom Kronland zur Europaregion* (Innsbruck: Tyrolia, 2009), 246.

9 Stefan Hammer, "Vorwort," in *Außenbeziehungen im Bundesstaat*, ed. idem and Peter Bußjäger (Institut für Föderalismus: Schriftenreihe 105) (Vienna: Braumüller, 2007), V-VII.

10 Peter Bußjäger, "Die innerstaatliche Koordination zwischen Bund und Ländern in auswärtigen Angelegenheiten," in *ibid.*, 31-40, p. 33.

of Tyrolean state and federal policymakers. South Tyrol was mainly a matter for Tyroleans themselves, which, to put it in exaggerated terms, was administrated by the Austrian government only for competence reasons. South Tyrol is the ultimate heritage of the Austrian republic, left over after the dismemberment of the Habsburg Empire and still forms a major item on the Austrian political agenda.[11]

Tyrol fulfills three functions in terms of the international law-based protective power role of Austria over the German and Ladin speaking minorities in South Tyrol: Austria's South Tyrol policy is essentially (co-) determined by Tyrol, which endows South Tyrol with a gatekeeper role. This is because South Tyrol tends to first consult with Tyrol and only then—jointly with Innsbruck—with Vienna. Austrian foreign policy does not operate without first including Tyrol and South Tyrol in deliberations. This means that South Tyrol impacts Austrian foreign policy when it comes to matters relating to herself.

The Austrian government in general and Austrian foreign policy in particular thus strongly focus on the needs and desires of Tyrol and South Tyrol in South Tyrolean matters. Tyrol and South Tyrol already once vetoed Austrian federal policy when the latter acted too unilaterally in South Tyroleans matters. This was the case in 1965 when the "autonomy package" negotiated by Austria's foreign minister, Bruno Kreisky, and his Italian counterpart, Giuseppe Saragat, was roundly rejected by Innsbruck and Bozen/Bolzano. Kreisky thus failed when confronted with the iron law of South Tyrolean policy: no solution to South Tyrolean problems without the consent by both Innsbruck and Bozen/Bolzano.[12]

The reasons for this will be outlined in this contribution, with several questions being additionally answered here: 1) Why did Austria so strongly focus on South Tyrol after the collapse of the Habsburg Empire while other extra-territorial German-speaking minorities at least deserved equal attention in terms of minority protection? 2) Austria fulfills the role of South Tyrol's protective power since the conclusion of the 1946 Paris Treaty. In which ways has this role changed over recent decades? 3) What is the role of Tyrol in the relations between South Tyrol and Austria and which (tacit and unwritten) procedures exist in this respect? 4) How have relations between Tyrol and South Tyrol developed in recent

11 Werner Wolf, *Südtirol in Österreich: Die Südtirolfrage in der österreichischen Diskussion 1945-1969* (Würzburg: Holzner-Verlag, 1972).

12 Michael Gehler, *Österreichs Außenpolitik der Zweiten Republik: Von der alliierten Besatzung bis zum Europa des 21. Jahrhunderts*, vol. 1 (Innsbruck: StudienVerlag, 2005), 323; *Unsere Sache ist gerecht: Südtirol als Thema der österreichischen Außenpolitik vor dem Hintergrund der europäischen Einigung*, ed. Markus Warasin (Bozen: Athesia, 2002).

years and what is the role of European integration therein? Regarding all these questions, we depart from the thesis that Tyrol (together with South Tyrol) has ever since had a tacit co-decision right in South Tyrol affairs including veto powers.

The Role of South Tyrol in Austrian Nation-Building

South Tyrol did not take up a special position when the Habsburg Empire collapsed. The Provisional National Assembly of the Republic of German Austria passed the "law on the size, borders, and relations of the state territory of German Austria" on 22 November 1918. Paragraph 1 said

> [t]he republic of German Austria exercises sovereignty over the closed settlements of Germans within the kingdoms and countries thus far represented in the Imperial Assembly. The republic comprises: The countries Austria below the Enns river including the German-Southern Moravian district and the German area of Neubistritz, Austria above the Enns river including German-Southern Bohemia, Salzburg, Styria, and Carinthia not including the closed Yugoslavian settlement areas, the county of Tyrol not including the closed Italian settlements, Vorarlberg, German Bohemia and the Sudetenland as well as the German settlements of Brno, Jihlava and Olomouc.[13]

Additionally, the law mentioned the German settlements in Western Hungary. The self-conception and bond with these minorities was considered self-evident because the Austrian republic was explicitly conceived as a German state.

However, German Austria was not able to successfully assert her claim for all these population groups residing outside of the territory of the new republic with the victorious allies. The 1919 Treaty of Saint Germain definitively established the borders of Austria as they still exist today. Nevertheless mutual ties did not just fade away, for the republic considered itself the natural protective power of the German (Austrian) minorities and competed with the German Reich in this respect. Austria, however, did not always act consistently vis-à-vis these minorities. The Austro-fascist regime

13 Gesetz vom 22. November 1918 über Umfang, Grenzen und Beziehungen des Staatsgebietes von Deutschösterreich, 1918, at <www.verfassungen.de/at/at18-34/gesetz40-1918.htm> (03 February 2015).

gave up on supporting the cause of the German speakers of South Tyrol when it strengthened its ties with the Italian fascist regime.[14]

When the German-speaking refugees fled from Eastern Europe to Austria in 1945 and 1946, the resurrected republic had long given up its protective power claims for these formerly Habsburg minorities; for Austria's policy was to distance herself from Germany after the horrific events caused by National Socialism, which soon led to national reorientation and thus a changed attitude towards the German minorities abroad. The same should have applied to South Tyrol if Austria had been serious about wanting to give up its protective power function for good. However, quite the contrary was the case. Austria demanded the right to self-determination for South Tyrol and the reunion with the republic. Federal Chancellor Leopold Figl (1902-1965) considered the return of South Tyrol part of his and every other Austrian's everyday prayers.[15] South Tyrol, however, was not affected by these new national trends. The difference between South Tyroleans and other Germans abroad was mainly based on Tyrol's self-conception, the identity of which was mainly grounded in the partition of the Tyrolean territory and the respective loss of South Tyrol. There had already been ideas about Tyrolean autonomy in the First Republic, with the reuniting of Tyrol being more important to Tyrolean decision-makers than the connection with Vienna.[16] Even today the Tyrolean people feel least attached to Austria (twenty percent) compared to the other federal states. However, their attachment to the proper Tyrolean homeland is strongest comparatively (forty-two percent).[17]

The deviating attitude towards the Austrian minority in South Tyrol from that toward the German Bohemians required explanation. The idea to define the republic as an Austrian ethno-nation and to extend this notion to a selection of other population groups outside of the country's borders was simply not tenable anymore after 1945, especially in political terms. Linguistic-cultural criteria played an increasingly less important

---

14 Leopold Steurer, *Südtirol zwischen Rom und Berlin 1919-1938* (Vienna: Europaverlag, 1980).

15 Rolf Steininger, *Los von Rom? Die Südtirolfrage 1945/46 und das Gruber-De Gasperi-Abkommen* (Innsbruck: Haymon Verlag, 1987), 27 and 36.

16 *Tirol und der Anschluss: Voraussetzungen, Entwicklungen, Rahmenbedingungen 1918-1938*, ed. Thomas Albrich, Klaus Eisterer and Rolf Steininger (Innsbrucker Forschungen zur Zeitgeschichte 3) (Innsbruck: Haymon Verlag, 1988).

17 Peter Bußjäger and Gilg Seeber, "Zwischen Föderalismus und Unitarismus: Das föderalistische Bewusstsein der Österreicherinnen und Österreicher nach der Föderalismusumfrage 2009," in *Föderalistisches Bewusstsein in Österreich: Regionale Identitätsbildung und Einstellung der Bevölkerung zum Föderalismus*, ed. Peter Bußjäger, Ferdinand Karlhofer and Günther Pallaver (Institut für Föderalismus: Schriftenreihe Politische Bildung 8) (Vienna: Braumüller, 2010), 27-49, p. 34.

role for Austria's national identity after the signing of the 1955 State Treaty.

Along with the extremely strong ties between Tyrol and South Tyrol, there have also been practical differences. The phenomenon of refugees from the east who were viewed with skepticism was not paralleled by the occurrence of refugees from South Tyrol. South Tyrol was a territorial question. If at all, the South Tyroleans would have taken their land to Austria with them. Aside from that, all parties could identify with the South Tyrolean problem. The Austrian People's Party (ÖVP) was able to appeal to patriotism and Catholicism, the Social Democrats (SPÖ) argued in favor of democratic fundamental rights for minorities, the Communists resorted to their theory on the national question, the right wingers and its preceding organizations used the German-national arguments to support the Tyrolean cause.[18] This cross-party consensus on South Tyrol played a pivotal role in Austria's evolution as a new nation. South Tyrol thus constituted a controversial challenge for the Austrian post-war state.[19] On the contrary: despite the occupation forces, supply constraints, and an insecure future, South Tyrol problem remained a top priority of Austrian foreign policy after 1945. In fact, it contributed to the identity-formation of the new nation of Austria and constituted the common ground between the Lake of Constance and Neusiedler See.[20]

The Treaty of Paris and Austria's Protective Power Role

Austria has functioned as a protective power over the German speaking (later including the Ladin speakers as well) minority in South Tyrol since 1946. The legal foundation of this protective power function constitutes the 1946 Paris Treaty, which ensures that the German-speaking population in South Tyrol "will be assured a complete equality of rights with the Italian-speaking inhabitants, within the framework of special provisions to safeguard the ethnic character and the cultural and economic development of the German-speaking element."[21] Austria

18 Wolf, *Südtirol in Österreich*, 96-119.

19 Peter Thaler, *The Ambivalence of Identity: The Austrian Experience of Nation-Building in a Modern Society* (Purdue, Indiana: Purdue University Press, 2001).

20 Karl Stuhlpfarrer, "Österreichische Südtirolpolitik," in ... *und raus bist Du! Ethnische Minderheiten in der Politik*, ed. Rainer Bauböck et al. (Österreichische Texte zur Gesellschaftskritik 37) (Vienna: Verlag für Gesellschaftskritik, 1988), 68-77, p. 74; Günther Pallaver, "L'erba del vicino: Italien–Österreich: Nachbarn in Europa," in *Österreich und die europäische Integration von 1945 bis zur Gegenwart*, ed. Michael Gehler and Rolf Steininger (Vienna: Böhlau, 2nd rev. ed. 2014), 235-277, p. 242.

21 Südtiroler Landesregierung, *Das neue Autonomiestatut* (Bozen: Tezzele, 2005), 12-13.

renounced claims for a reunion with South Tyrol with the conclusion of the Paris Treaty. Italy in turn agreed with not exerting full sovereignty over South Tyrol (that forms part of the Italian state's territory) while South Tyroleans factually dispensed with the right to self-determination. All parties involved in the conflict refrained from territorial changes, thus agreeing on internal self-determination.[22]

Austria is an external nation-state actor, the latter of which South Tyrol has relied upon since 1945/46. The protective power function goes beyond some problematic one-sided measures by kin states to protect or defend minorities in a given country that entertain kin relationships with them.[23]

The Paris Treaty assigned Austria the legal title of a protective power in favor of the South Tyrolean minority,[24] and Austria interfered on several occasion upon request by the minority, especially with the UN in 1960/61. Despite many difficulties, Austria kept on negotiating with Italy, encouraging the most representative South Tyrolean party, the South Tyrolean People's Party (SVP),[25] to hold on to the more realistic intra-Italian solution rather than external self-determination. Austria regularly consulted with the South Tyrolean minority and never acted against the latter's will. Austria refrained from any interference once a compromise was found between Rom and Bozen/Bolzano, as long as Austrian was not adversely affected.

Between Italy and Austria there have been substantial disagreements over Austria's role in terms of international law. Italy claimed that the Paris Treaty's aims were reached with the First Autonomy Statute of 1948, while Austria and South Tyrol considered the latter statute entirely insufficient.[26] Departing from this view, Italy continuously tried to depict minority protection as a purely domestic concession to the South Tyroleans in order to by-pass international law obligations. Italy also departed from this position when passing the Second Autonomy Statute in 1972. However,

22 Pallaver, "South Tyrol's Changing Political System."

23 OSCE High Commissioner on National Minorities, *The Bolzano/Bozen Recommendations on National Minorities in Inter-State Relations & Explanatory Note, 2008*, The Hague, at <www.osce.org/hcnm/33633?download=true> (20 February 2015).

24 Karl Zeller, *Das Problem der völkerrechtlichen Verankerung des Südtirol-Paketes und die Zuständigkeit des Internationalen Gerichtshofs* (Vienna: Braumüller, 1989).

25 Günther Pallaver, "The Südtiroler Volkspartei," in *From Protest to Power: Autonomist Parties and the Challenges of Representation*, ed. Elias Anwen and Filippo Tronconi (Vienna: Braumüller, 2011), 171-193.

26 Peter Hilpold, "Der Südtiroler Weg völkerrechtlicher Stufenlösung im europäischen Vergleich," in *1992: Ende eines Streits: Zehn Jahre Streitbeilegung im Südtirolkonflikt zwischen Italien und Österreich*, ed. Sieglinde Clementi and Jens Woelk (Baden-Baden: Nomos, 2003), 109-117, p. 110.

there were hardly any reservations concerning the international law basis of the autonomy statute. Austria just tried to push for further guarantees by securing the international law dimension via the Estoppel principle.[27]

The international law dimension of South Tyrolean autonomy and the protective power function guaranteed by the Paris Treaty were solidified by the 1992 dispute settlement, which ended the ongoing legal argument between Italy and Austria that existed since it was brought before the UN in 1960/61. The Italian government pointed to the fact that the South Tyrolean autonomy was to be interpreted as a minority protection measure as intended by the Paris Treaty.[28] The Austrian parliament recognized the Italian note and in turn included the dispute settlement declaration in the form of a *note verbale* that referred to the Italian note. This indirectly confirmed that South Tyrolean autonomy and all relating provisions were based on the Paris Treaty.

Austria's protective power function was expressed in the past by various diplomatic interventions with Rome, and even the UN. However, the European integration process and the confidence-building measures by its member states have also contributed to solving the South Tyrol problem beyond Austria's role.[29]

With the EU accession of Austria in 1995[30] and the resulting fact that Italy and Austria, both parties to the Paris Agreement, were now members of the EU, the centralist and uncooperative structures of the non-responsive state more and more started to fade. This non-responsive state was replaced by a responsive and cooperative one. Both Austria and Italy are today

27 "In public international law, the doctrine of estoppel protects legitimate expectations of States induced by the conduct of another State.... The typical effect of the doctrine is that.... a representing party is barred—estopped or precluded—from successfully adopting different, subsequent statements on the same issue, without regard to their truth and accuracy." See Thomas Cottier and Jörg Paul Müller, "Estoppel," in *Max Planck Encyclopedia of Public International Law*, ed. Rüdiger Wolfum, at <opil.ouplaw.com/view/10.1093/law:epil/9780199231690/law-9780199231690-e1401#law-9780199231690-e1401-div2-1> (25 February 2015).

28 Peter Hilpold, *Modernes Minderheitenrecht: Eine rechtsvergleichende Untersuchung des Minderheitenrechtes in Österreich und in Italien unter besonderer Berücksichtigung völkerrechtlicher Aspekte* (Vienna: Manz, 2001), 117.

29 Gebriel N. Toggenburg, "Regional Autonomies Providing Minority Rights and the Law of European Integration: Experiences from South Tyrol," in *Tolerance through Law: Self Governance and Group Rights in South Tyrol*, ed. Jens Woelk, Francesco Palermo and Joseph Marko (European Academy Bozen/Bolzano) (Leiden: Martinus Nijhoff Publishers, 2008), 177-200.

30 On the long Austrian way to come closer to the EC until finally becoming a member of the EU, South Tyrol again and again played a role not to be underestimated. Italy vetoed the Austrian association agreement with the EEC in the Council in 1967 as result of the fatal attacks on the Porzeschart that left four people dead. After adopting of the South Tyrol package of 1969, which formed the basis for the 1972 autonomy statute, Italy withdrew her veto. See Pallaver, "L'erba del vicino," 236.

featured by federal or strongly regional state structures, all of which has led to an increase in power of sub-national territorial entities.

The European integration process is based upon the recognition of state boundaries, thereby sanctioning once more what was agreed upon in the 1946 Paris Agreement. These boundaries, however, are relative against the background of the Schengen Agreement. Both Italy (1990) and Austria (1995) signed the agreement, with border controls becoming obsolete in 1997. It is true that the legal boundary between South Tyrol (Italy) and North Tyrol (Austria) is still in place. However, its significance is diminished in everyday life.

A further phenomenon the European integration process has not just enabled, but also promoted is cross-border cooperation in the framework of Euro-regions, which are, among other things, perceived as pillars of peace initiatives and as building stones of European integration.[31] Cross-border cooperation between the three regions of Tyrol, South Tyrol and Trentino, all of which together formed the Princely County of Tyrol until 1918, has been in place for more than fifteen years[32] and has been further intensified by the regulation of the Council and the European Parliament (2006) to establish the EGTC, the European Grouping of Territorial Cooperation.[33]

The friendly relations between Austria and Italy in the EU have helped solving South Tyrol-related issues informally. The South Tyrolean legislators in Rome meet with the Austrian ambassador once a month in order the exchange ideas; Austria's general consul consults Bozen/Bolzano once a month regarding the South Tyrolean situation; and South Tyrol's governor regularly informs the Austrian federal president and the national government in Vienna when visiting the Austrian capital.

How such potential conflicts are resolved by silent diplomacy is to be shown here by a particular example, which can be well used as a generalization of Austro-Italian relations: The Italian governing *Forza Italia* party lodged a proposal in the constitutional commission in 2004 that intended to grant Italians in South Tyrol minority status. This would have led to substantial changes to the autonomy and the institutional relations among the linguistic groups. The main supporters of this proposal were

31 Stefan Wolff and Karl Cordell, "Power Sharing," in *Routledge Handbook of Ethnic Conflict*, ed. idem (London: Routledge, 2011), 301-310, p. 303.

32 Alice Engl and Carolin Zwilling, "Cross-border Cooperation between Historical Legacies and New Horizons," in *Tolerance through Law: Self Governance and Group Rights in South Tyrol*, ed. Jens Woelk, Francesco Palermo and Joseph Marko (European Academy Bozen/Bolzano) (Leiden: Martinus Nijhoff Publishers, 2008), 161-176.

33 See the contribution of Alice Engl in this volume.

the Vice Minister President, Gianfranco Fini, Regional Minister, Enrico La Loggia, and Foreign Minister Franco Frattini. When the South Tyrolean People's Party had to realize it could not kill this proposal, it had a final consultation with the President of the Constitutional Committee, Bruno Donato. Since Donato did not envision anymore possibilities to interfere anymore, he pointed to the *Quirinal*, the seat of the Italian president.

The SVP contacted Austria's Federal President, Heinz Fischer, who got in touch with the Italian President, Carlo Azelio Ciampi. Federal Chancellor, Wolfgang Schüssel, intervened with Italy's Minister-President, Silvio Berlusconi, and the Austrian National Council President, Andreas Kohl, contacted the President of the Italian Chamber, Pier Ferdinando Casini. The proposal was withdrawn from the agenda within twenty-four hours. Casini, responsible for procedural questions, declared the proposal as unlawful.[34] The SVP, in turn, tries to represent Austrian interests in the Italian parliament whenever it can, as happened during the parliamentary debate over the "sanctions" of EU member states against Austria after the Freedom Party (FPÖ) joined government in 2000. The SVP then managed to substantially dilute the resolution against Austria.[35]

The international law character of the autonomy and the protective power function of Austria were underlined again in 2014. The consolidated friendship between Austria and Italy, both members of the EU, helped South Tyrol to negotiate a new financial agreement with Rome. The Italian Minister President, Matteo Renzi, informed Federal Chancellor, Werner Faymann, thereof in December of 2014, additionally referring to the 1992 *note verbale*. Werner Faymann responded in January 2015 in a letter that the announced measures constituted important steps forward in terms of implementing efforts by Austria and Italy for South Tyrolean autonomy. This exchange of letters contains vital mutual obligations to make sure agreement is reached regarding South Tyrolean autonomy questions. The

34 Manuel Massl and Günther Pallaver, "Interessenswahrnehmung selbständiger Landesparteien: Die Rolle der Südtiroler Volkspartei im römischen Parlament," in *Koalitionsregierungen in den Ländern und Parteienwettbewerb*, ed. Julia Oberhofer and Roland Sturm (Schriftenreihe des Zentralinstituts für Regionalforschung der Friedrich-Alexander-Universität Erlangen-Nürnberg 6) (Munich: allitera verlag, 2010), 251-276, p. 272-273.

35 Josef Berghold and Günther Pallaver, "Dire a nuora perché suocera intenda: Die Reaktion Italiens auf die schwarz-blaue Koalition," in *Österreich in der Europäischen Union/ Austria in the European Union: Bilanz einer Mitgliedschaft/Assessment of her Membership*, ed. Michael Gehler, Anton Pelinka and Günter Bischof (Schriftenreihe des DDr.-Herbert-Batliner-Europainstitutes: Forschungsinstitut für Europäische Politik und Geschichte 7) (Vienna: Böhlau, 2003), 575-594.

South Tyrolean autonomy thus constituted a norm that has international law backing and that enjoys dynamic character.[36]

Tyrol: The Driving Force Behind Austria's South Tyrol Policy

Whoever deals with the question of Tyrolean identity will soon realize that South Tyrol takes a central position therein. This was already reflected in the preamble to the 1989 Tyrolean constitution, which speaks of the "spiritual and cultural unity of Tyrol," clearly referring the composite parts of Northern, Eastern, and Southern Tyrol and the "historical heritage."[37] A similar formulation cannot be found in the South Tyrolean autonomy statute. The first item on each session of the Tyrolean government has conventionally been South Tyrol. This, in turn, is not true for the South Tyrolean government. These two indicators, the preamble and the daily agenda, as well as the difference to South Tyrol all insinuate that North Tyrol considers herself the protective power of South Tyrol along with Austria, thus feeling obliged to stand by South Tyrol's side regarding minority protection and autonomy questions.

There were cross-party protests for the reunion with South Tyrol in the immediate post-war years in Innsbruck. A Tyrolean delegation addressed the Allied Council in Vienna. In 1947, an external office of the federal chancellery was established in Innsbruck, thus forming a common triangle with Innsbruck and Bozen/Bolzano.[38] When Foreign Minister Karl Gruber (1909-1995), the first Tyrolean governor and signatory of the Paris Treaty together with Italy's then Minister-President, Alcide De Gasperi (1881-1954), stepped down in 1953, there were rising concerns in Tyrol over the loss of protection by Vienna.[39] His successor, Leopold Figl, soon became the target of criticism as a result of his appeasement policy over South Tyrol, with his successor, Bruno Kreisky (1911-1990), making South Tyrol his top priority.[40] In order to placate Tyrol, Kreisky placed the Tyrolean State Secretary, Franz Gschnitzer (1899-1968), on his side, who was later followed by Ludwig Steiner.

It was the pressure by Tyrol which convinced Kreisky to seek the UN in 1960 with Tyroleans (and informally South Tyroleans) dominating in the

---

36 Peter Hilpold and Christoph Perathoner, *Rom bekräftigt Österreichs Schutzfunktion gegenüber Südtirol*, at <diepresse.com/home/recht/rechtallgemein/4649393/Rom-bekraeftigt-Osterreichs-Schutzfunktion-gegenuber-Sudtirol> (20 February 2015).

37 Peter Pernthaler, *Die Identität Tirols in Europa* (Vienna: Springer, 2007), 63-64.

38 Gehler, *Österreichs Außenpolitik der Zweiten Republik*, 265.

39 Ibid., 271.

40 Bruno Kreisky, *Im Strom der Politik: Der Memoiren zweiter Teil* (Vienna: Kremayr & Scherian, 2007).

Austrian delegation in New York; and soon it became clear that, after the 1960 bombings in South Tyrol, there were a number of North Tyroleans in the liberation committee of South Tyrol who had close ties to the state government. The "Bergisel Union," founded in 1954 with its main seat in Innsbruck, led the propaganda efforts among Tyroleans for a "tougher course" to be taken in terms of South Tyrol.

After the failed bombing attacks which put a heavy strain on Austro-Italian relations,[41] it was self-evident that Tyrol had to be included in the autonomy negotiations and the implementation of autonomy. The corresponding "North-South Tyrol contact committee" usually held sessions in Innsbruck, not in Bozen/Bolzano. How central Tyrol was for South Tyrol affairs is shown by the fact that the strongest impulses for South Tyrol policy repeatedly came from Tyrol, and that—aside from the Kreisky era as foreign minister—the government in Vienna was usually considered the "executive arm of Tyrolean wishes in terms of South Tyrol."[42] This was also due to Tyrol's governor, Eduard Wallnöfer, who took office in 1963. Wallnöfer was born in South Tyrol, and he considered South Tyrol not only a political but also a personal matter. It was also Wallnöfer and his South Tyrolean counterpart, Silvius Magnago (1914-2010), who rejected the 1964 Kreisky-negotiated measure package as too insubstantial.[43]

A visible sign for and switchboard for intra-Tyrolean relations was the "South Tyrol department" in the Tyrolean state government, which gave logistical and financial support to South Tyrol. Federal and state funding from Austria was channeled through the department to South Tyrol, covering all spheres of life from culture, study allowances, agricultural subsidies to education. The lawyer fees of the bombing perpetrators in 1960s were also paid, just like perpetrators and their families were supported via the federal "South Tyrol account" in consultation with Tyrol bypassing control organs like the court of auditors and the state's *Landeskontrollamt*.[44]

The conclusion of the negotiations for the Second Autonomy Statute (1972) were followed by Wallnernöfer's 1972 *Arge Alp* initiative for cross-border cooperation between ten countries, provinces, regions and cantons of Austria, Germany, Italy, and Switzerland, including South and North Tyrol. Starting in 1970, the legislatures and governments (as of 1995) of Tyrol and South Tyrol convened on a regular basis (later joined by those of Vorarlberg

---

41 Hans Karl Peterlini, *Südtiroler Bombenjahre: Von Blut und Tränen zum Happy End?* (Bozen: Edition Raetia, 2005).
42 Gehler, *Österreichs Außenpolitik der Zweiten Republik*, 389.
43 Claus Gatterer, *Im Kampf gegen Rom: Bürger, Minderheiten und Autonomien* (Vienna: Europaverlag, 1968).
44 Gehler, *Österreichs Außenpolitik der Zweiten Republik*, 328.

and Trentino). Under the guidance of Wallnöfer and in consultation with Magnago, a permanent contact committee was established, which met at least twice a year. Under Tyrolean tutelage, the foreign minister, a representative from each the Tyrolean People's Party, other parties, and the South Tyrolean government (SVP party people mainly) convened regularly.

When the dispute was settled at the UN in 1992, a number of Tyrolean politicians exerted influence behind the scenes, mainly Ludwig Steiner and Andreas Kohl, who was a deputy of the Austrian People's Party back then. Kohl's parents were South Tyroleans and he also grew up there. The Tyrolean government, the Tyrolean legislature, and not only the National Council in Vienna, adopted a reaffirming declaration on the conclusion of the autonomy negotiations and thus the settlement of the dispute.[45]

Austria's accession to the EU and the preceding referendum in 1994 were combined with the South Tyrol policy in Tyrol at the time. Governor Wendelin Weingartner, whose mother was South Tyrolean, envisioned new cooperation opportunities with EU accession.[46] The first official act by Weingartner after Austria's EU accession was to remove the border posts at the Brenner on 2 January 1995 together with the South Tyrolean counterpart, Luis Durnwalder. It was also Weingartner who pushed for a Europe region of Tyrol,[47] which is today part of the European Grouping of Territorial Cooperation. Tyrol, South Tyrol and Trentino opened a common office in Brussels even before the Europe region was in place.

The special relation between Tyrol and South Tyrol with North Tyrolean predominance is particularly reflected in political symbolism. Many streets and places around the train station in Innsbruck carry the names of South Tyrolean towns and villages. Particularly interesting is the fact that the consul general of Milano, who is responsible for South Tyrol, usually visits the Tyrolean governor shortly after taking office. Austria's consul general is accredited by an Austrian governor! The first visit by South Tyrolean governors is usually done with the counterpart in Innsbruck, followed only then by Vienna to see the president and chancellor. South Tyrol's government representatives report to the chancellor, foreign minister, and

45 Ibid., 386.

46 Wendelin Weingartner, "1994: Ein spannendes politisches Jahr," in *Politik in Tirol: Jahrbuch 2015* (Innsbruck: StudienVerlag, 2015), 34-43, p. 36.

47 Günther Pallaver, "Europaregion Tirol-Südtirol-Trentino," in *Die Verfassung der Südtiroler Autonomie: Die Sonderrechtsordnung der Autonomen Provinz Bozen/Südtirol*, ed. Joseph Marko et al. (Minderheiten und Autonomien 7) (Baden-Baden: Nomos, 2005), 493-510.

president on a regular basis concerning the situation in South Tyrol and Italy, but also to the "South Tyrol committee," a subcommittee of the foreign policy committee of the Austrian parliament that deals with autonomy questions in South Tyrol. The committee chair is conventionally a Tyrolean.[48]

The Tyrolean parades are held in Innsbruck every twenty-five years to commemorate the Tyrolean insurgency of 1809 against Napoleon and the Bavarians.[49] Honorary medals of Tyrol are given to both Tyroleans and South Tyroleans in Innsbruck.[50] The annual Tyrol ball in Vienna is certainly also attended by the South Tyrolean governor. The national weather forecast by the Austrian Broadcasting Corporation (ORF) also includes the weather of South Tyrol by request of both parts of Tyrol, the North and the South. There are more examples to add.

South Tyrol's Emancipation Process

The 1957 manifestation by South Tyroleans at Sigmundskron castle close to Bozen/Bolzano included a claim for separation from Trentino in order to end regional autonomy together with the province of Trentino and to pave the way for the autonomous province of Bozen/Bolzano-South Tyrol, while the emancipation process of South Tyroleans from Tyrol began with the 1992 dispute settlement declaration. This process of emancipation has not changed the key aspects of the relations between Bozen/Bolzano, Innsbruck and Vienna, but elevated them to another level.

With the implementation of South Tyrolean autonomy, the normalization of Bozen/Bolzano-Rome relations, the European integration process and its impact on the relations between Austria and Italy as well between Bozen/Bolzano and Innsbruck (Trentino), South Tyrol developed her own regional identity. While South Tyrol was in a defensive political position until the 1992 dispute settlement and mainly focused on securing autonomy rights with the indispensable help provided by Austria and Tyrol, South Tyrol took a more offensive course after. Endowed with a strong autonomy status with sufficient financial backing, South Tyrol pursued independence at all levels, culturally, economically as well as in the fields of education and foreign relations.

48 Republik Österreich, Parlament, Südtirol, at <www.parlament.gv.at/PAKT/VHG/XXIV/A-AU/A-AU_00002_00282/index.shtml> (20 February 2015).

49 Hans Heiss, "Im Sog der Geschichtspolitik: Die Gedenkfeiern der Tiroler Erhebung 1909-2009," in *Politik in Tirol: Jahrbuch 2009*, ed. Ferdinand Karlhofer and Günther Pallaver (Innsbruck: StudienVerlag, 2009), 129-159.

50 Only the honorary crosses of Tyrol are awarded in Innsbruck and *Schloss* Tirol alternately.

This slow emancipation process from Tyrol,[51] sometimes even called "political separation,"[52] and South Tyrol's new self-consciousness is expressed in a number of ambitious projects, in which the interests of Tyrol do not matter that much anymore. Bozen/Bolzano established the European Academy Bozen/Bolzano (EURAC) and founded a trilingual university in Bozen/ Bolzano regardless of commitments made to the *Landesuniversität* Innsbruck.

South Tyrol expanded her airport in competition with that of Tyrol. South Tyrol founded her own state museum at Tyrol *Schloss* close to Meran/Merano along with the existing Ferdinandeum *Landesmuseum* in Innsbruck. South Tyrol asserted herself in the struggle for ownership over the mountain mummy, Ötzi, against Tyrol as a result of the national and thus national borders,[53] just to mention a few examples. The political desires of South Tyrol with Austria, such as the constitutional foundation of South Tyrol in a preamble to the Austrian constitution or the introduction of dual Italian-Austrian citizenship are not exclusively filtered by Tyrol anymore, but are more and more addressed directly between Bozen/Bolzano and Vienna. These claims by South Tyrol have not been fulfilled because they are politically undesirable.[54]

South Tyrol's development towards a self-conscious autonomous and independent entity did not leave Tyrol's South Tyrol policy unaffected. This has not just led to an almost complete halt of financial transfers to South Tyrol, but also to the dissolution of the "South Tyrol department," which was renamed to be called the "South Tyrol, Europe Region, and Foreign Relations Department." However, there were also common projects supported by South Tyrol and rejected by Tyrol. The prime example for that is the conflict over the establishment of a *Tirol Bank Holding*, a joint project between *Hypo Tirol Bank* and the *Südtiroler Sparkasse*, which was strongly supported by Governor Wendelin Weingartner, but killed by the Tyrolean state government.[55]

---

51 Michael Gehler, "Selbstbestimmung–kulturelle Landeseinheit–Europaregion? Die Tiroler Südtirolpolitik 1945-1998," in *Tirol: "Land im Gebirge:" Zwischen Tradition und Moderne*, ed. idem (Geschichte der österreichischen Bundesländer seit 1945) (Vienna: Böhlau, 1999), 569-726, p. 662 and 678.

52 Wendelin Weingartner, "Die Zeitgeschichte Südtirols im Zeitraffer," *Zett: Die Zeitung am Sonntag*, 8 July 2012, 8.

53 Pallaver, "Zwischen Kooperation und Konkurrenz," 113.

54 Republik Österreich, Parlament, *Österreichische Staatsbürgerschaft (doppelte Staatsbürgerschaft) für Südtiroler und Südtirolerinnen*, at <www.parlament.gv.at/PAKT/VHG/XXIV/AB/AB_09719/index.shtml> (22 February 2015). In 2014, eighty-three percent of Austrians agree with granting dual citizenship to South Tyroleans, according to a recent poll. See *Die Meinung der Österreicher zur Selbstbestimmungsthematik Süd-Tirol*, ed. Südtiroler Heimatbund, at <www.suedtiroler-freiheit.com/wp/wp-content/uploads/2015/01/SHB_Pressemappe-Wien-26.1.2015.pdf> (21 February 2015).

55 Benedikt Sauer and Michael Sprenger, *Dreierwatten: Banken, Macht und Politik rund um die Brennerachse* (Innsbruck: StudienVerlag, 2003).

Tirol has acknowledged South Tyrol's autonomy and increasingly focuses on the common goals within the Europe region Tyrol-South Tyrol-Trentino.[56] The issue of reunification has widely subsided in the Tyrolean parties' discourse.[57] Among the parties represented in the Tyrolean legislature, all parties except for the Freedom Party consider self-determination for Tyrol and thus reunification obsolete.[58]

Thanks to the accession of Austria to the EU and the European integration process, the state boundaries at the Brenner have become relative, having led to more and comprehensive cooperation between South Tyrol and Tyrol over the past two decades in the realms of politics, the economy, and culture most notably.[59]

Conclusion

South Tyrol is the only heritage of the Habsburg Empire over which Austria is a protective power according to international law today, based on the 1946 Paris Treaty between Austria and Italy to protect the German (and Ladin-speaking) minority in South Tyrol. The special relations between Austrian and South Tyrol are strongly connected to the relations between Tyrol and South Tyrol. The "land in the mountains" continues to hold on to the "cultural and spiritual unity of Tyrol." This particular Tyrolean role has led to a special Austrian foreign policy practice and conception. Although foreign policy is a federal domain, Tyrol has a tacit competence over South Tyrol issues reaching all the way to a veto power. For Tyrol, South Tyrol is first and foremost a Tyrolean matter, which is administrated by the federal level for competence reasons only.

As was seen in this contribution, Tyrol fulfills a threefold function when it comes to international law protective power function of Austria over the minority in South Tyrol: 1) Austrian South Tyrol policy is essentially (co-) determined in Tyrol. 2) Vienna foreign policy does not operate without first consulting Tyrol and South Tyrol in South Tyrolean affairs. 3) Tyrol has veto power in conflicts between Vienna and Innsbruck (Bolzano).

56 Land Tirol: Amt der Tiroler Landesregierung, Abteilung Südtirol, Europaregion und Außenbeziehungen, *Tirol in der Europäischen Union Erfahrungen und Perspektiven 2008/2010*, Vorlage an den Tiroler Landtag gemäß Entschließung des Tiroler Landtages vom 13. Oktober 1994, März 2011, at <www.tirol.gv.at/fileadmin/themen/tirol-europa/europa/238-11.pdf> (23 February 2015).

57 Manuel Fasser, *Ein Tirol–zwei Welten: Das politische Erbe der Südtiroler Feuernacht von 1961* (Innsbruck: StudienVerlag, 2009), 121.

58 The same poll (see fn 54) suggests that eighty-nine percent of Austrians agree with South Tyrolean self-determination and favor reunification with Austria.

59 Pallaver, "Zwischen Kooperation und Konkurrenz," 120-130.

Since the 1992 dispute settlement at the UN, there is an emancipation process from Tyrol to be observed in South Tyrol. This has an impact on Tyrol, which refocuses attention on the Europe region of Tyrol-South Tyrol-Trentino. This does not mean, however, that Austria does not fulfill her protective power function over South Tyrol anymore. The relations between Tyrol and South Tyrol have simply changed and can be qualified as intergovernmental as part of the European integration process, for the two Tyrols each behave as autonomous actors and their cooperation is more functional than it is emotional today, while the latter does not aim at state reunion. And yet, South Tyrol remains a matter of the heart for Austrians and Tyroleans, as was reaffirmed by the president, chancellor, foreign minister and the Tyrolean governors.[60]

60 *Südtirol ist eine Herzensangelegenheit: Medienbegleitheft zur DVD*, ed. Bundesministerium für Unterricht, Kunst und Kultur (Vienna: BMUKK, 2010), at <www.bmbf.gv.at/schulen/service/mes/12472_20091.pdf?4f2jk2> (22 February 2015).

Nontopical Essays

Books and Libraries as Witnesses of the Second World War and the Holocaust in Monuments: Vienna and Berlin

Moran Pearl

Introduction[1]

"The universe which others call the library"[2] are the opening words of Jorge Luis Borges' famous story "The Library of Babel." This metaphor could express the idea that in human history, events only took place if they were documented. Borges' words also emphasize the central role books assume in a society through their creation of collective memory. Like books, monuments are also thought of as agents of memory and representations of the human desire to preserve the past for future generations. In the past two decades, books and archives have frequently appeared as symbols in monuments for the Second World War and the Holocaust.[3] Paradoxically, the symbol of the book appears to be proliferating in a technological age in which media innovations render the printed book almost obsolete. Despite the increasing use of books and libraries as symbols in recent years, there is no comprehensive research that deals directly with this phenomenon. In order to understand the motivations behind the use of these symbols,

---

1 This essay is based on my Master's Thesis for the Hebrew University of Jerusalem under the supervision of Professor Bianca Kuehnel. I wish to express my deepest thanks to her and Dr. Guy Tal, for their support, wisdom, and dedication. I would also like to thank the Institute for Human Sciences in Vienna for granting me a five-month fellowship that allowed me to conduct key parts of this research.

2 Jorge Luis Borges, "The Library of Babel," in *Collected Fictions*, trans. Andrew Hurley (New York: Penguin, 1998), 112.

3 Books and libraries in art works about the Holocaust first appeared in Anselm Kiefer's work in the 1960s and later on in Micha Ullman's and Rachel Whiteread's work, both of which are discussed in this paper. Other key examples include the work of: Christian Boltanski, Clegg and Guttmann, Dvora Barzilai, Chanan De Langa, Moshe Safdie, and others which this essay is too short to include. In order to expand on some of those and on other examples see: Moran Pearl, "Books and Libraries as Agents of Memory in Monuments for the Second World War and Holocaust," M.A thesis, Hebrew University of Jerusalem 2013 (in Hebrew).

two monuments for the Second World War and the Holocaust will be compared—Rachel Whiteread's "Nameless Library," erected in Vienna in 2000, and Micha Ullman's "Empty Library," created in Berlin in 1995.

Figure 1. Rachel Whiteread, The "Nameless Library" (Memorial to the Victims of the Holocaust), 2000, negative casting, concrete. *Judenplatz*, Vienna (photo: Moran Pearl).

The "Nameless Library" was erected to remember the Austrian Jews who were killed by the Nazis (figure 1). Located on the *Judenplatz* (Square of the Jews), formerly the historical center of Jewish life in medieval Vienna, the monument is shaped as a rigid cubic library; its walls are constructed of a concrete cast of 7.000 books in rows, each of which is placed in a reversed position whereby the pages rather than the cover of the book are visible. The monument is seven meters wide, ten meters long, and four meters of height. On the one hand, these dimensions create a sense of comfort and contentment. On the other hand, the "library" also evokes discomfort by means of closed doors, which block the entrance and create a feeling of isolation like a "*Bunker*" situated in the middle of the square. Set upon a concrete base, the library bears the names of the forty-one sites across Europe where Jews perished at the hands of the Nazi regime and its allies. On the front of the monument, on the same base, an inscription is engraved in German, English, and Hebrew: "In memory of more than 65.000 Austrian Jews who were killed by the Nazis between 1938 and 1945."

Figure 2. Micha Ullman, "Empty Library" (in memory of the Nazi book burning), 1995, concrete, glass, and iron. *Bebelplatz*, Berlin (photo: Moran Pearl).

In contrast to the "Nameless Library" in Vienna, the "Empty Library" (figure 2) commemorates a specific event and does not directly address a specific group of victims. The "Empty Library" is located in the cultural heart of the Berlin capital in *Bebelplatz*. Its physical positioning in the middle of a large square surrounded by monumental and historical buildings—the State Opera, St. Hedwig's Cathedral, and the *Alte Bibliothek* of the Humboldt University Faculty of Law—emphasizes the fact that the monument symbolically commemorates the attack that came from a very educated and cultured society on fundamental liberal principles and values. Unlike the "Nameless Library," which protrudes above the ground, the "Empty Library" is an underground square room, each wall containing fourteen empty white concrete shelves. The room has the capacity to hold 20.000 books, which was approximately the number of books that were burned in that square on 10 May 1933, under the Nazi regime. The library is constantly lit, which makes it visible at night and allows it to embody the event it commemorates. A few steps away from the monument, an engraving in German appears on a bronze plaque: "That was but a prelude; where they burn books, they will ultimately burn people as well. Heinrich Heine 1820."[4] On the other side of the plaque, an engraving in German describes the historical event: "In the middle of this square on 10 May

4 The original German reads as follows: "DAS WAR EIN VORSPIEL NUR, DORT WO MAN BÜCHER VERBRENNT, VERBRENNT MAN AM ENDE AUCH MENSCHEN. Heinrich Heine 1820." It should be noted that this quote is taken from Heine's play *Almansor*, which was written in 1821, and not in 1820 as is engraved on the monument. See footnote 62.

1933 Nazi students burned the works of hundreds of independent writers, journalists, philosophers, and scientists."[5]

The comparative literature scholar Andreas Huyssen claims that society is obsessed with presenting memory in a visual way through the creation of archives and libraries that preserve the past.[6] Libraries appear to be an objective storage space of knowledge. However, as Jacques Derrida and Aleida Assmann both observed, the documented history they contain is driven by the political views of those in power; it is they who ultimately decide what will be remembered and what will be forgotten.[7] As will be demonstrated, the two monuments under study here have the ability to simultaneously expose and challenge the objectivity of archives. Both monuments offer an alternative to traditional Holocaust memorials through their unique design and their use of "negative aesthetics" and "empty spaces," which imbue them with a multiplicity of possible interpretations. Examination of the monuments' visual depiction will be vital to understand the memory they attempt to capture. For example, the depiction of inaccessible books and libraries in both monuments could be seen as symbolical representations of the difficulty in accurately presenting and remembering the Holocaust and experience during the Second World War. The book as a symbol will be observed through its uses in different ways of commemoration that depend on the monument's placement ("site specific"), and the local memory culture and political environment. Finally, the book will be examined in an attempt to determine whether the use of books and libraries in each site creates a representation of European and universal or specific memory.

Political Environment

Before 1986, the collective memory of World War II in Austria revolved around the "Anschluss," and presented the country as having been occupied and therefore, as a victim of the Nazis.[8] This self-image was supported by

5 The original German text: "In der Mitte dieses Platzes verbrannten am 10. Mai 1933 nationalsozialistische Studenten die Werke hunderter freier Schriftsteller, Publizisten, Philosophen und Wissenschaftler. Bibliothek–Denkmal Die Bücherverbrennung vom 10. Mai 1933. Von Micha Ullman, Gebaut 1994/95."

6 Andreas Huyssen, *Twilight Memories: Marking Time in a Culture of Amnesia* (New York: Routledge, 1995), 28-30.

7 See Jacques Derrida, *Archive Fever: A Freudian Impression (Religion and Postmodernism)*, trans. Eric Prenowitz (Chicago: University of Chicago Press, 1996); Aleida Assmann, *Cultural Memory and Western Civilization: Functions, Media, Archives* (New York: Cambridge University Press, 2011).

8 Matti Bunzl, "On the Politics and Semantics of Austrian Memory: Vienna's Monument against War and Fascism," *History and Memory* 17, no. 11 (1996): 7-35.

the Allies in the 1943 Moscow Declaration. During the Cold War, the Allies' concern was to keep Austria neutral by declaring Austria as "the first free country to have fallen a victim to Hitler's aggressive occupation."[9] This enabled Austria's "double discourse": on the one hand, Austrian foreign policy emphasized the resistance, and on the other hand, in terms of domestic policies, integrated former Nazi party members into the political system of the country.[10] This view prevented the Austrian government from taking responsibility for the fate of the Jews and from erecting an official monument for the Jewish victims.[11] In 1986, the Kurt Waldheim affair took place; it was discovered that presidential candidate Waldheim had been a Wehrmacht lieutenant in the Balkans and might have been aware of war crimes committed in the region.[12] Although Waldheim never faced trail, the affair revealed the inefficiency of Austria's denazification.[13]

The "Nameless Library" was the first official memorial in Vienna, dedicated to only the Austrian Jews who died in the Holocaust.[14] The project of the British artist Rachel Whiteread was chosen in 1995, following an international competition. The inauguration of the monument was planned for 9 November 1996, the 58th anniversary of the November Pogrom of 1938. However, it took another four years of debate until the dedication took place on 25 October 2000, in a modest ceremony with poor attendance. The continued disagreements and the long process that caused the delay expose the complexity and sensitivity that still existed regarding Austria's position in the Second World War.[15] The initiative to erect a Holocaust monument took place a year after the opening of the Jewish Museum in 1994 (in a

9 Heidemarie Uhl, "The Politics of Memory: Austria's Perception of the Second World War and National Socialist Period," in *Austrian Historical Memory and National Identity*, ed. Günter Bischof and Anton Pelinka (Contemporary Austrian Studies [CAS] 5) (New Brunswick, N.J.: Transaction Publishers, 1997), 64-94.

10 Christian Gerbel, "The Holocaust and the Politics of History in Austria's Second Republic," in *Clashes in European Memory: The Case of Communist Repression and the Holocaust*, ed. Muriel Blaive, Christian Gerbel and Thomas Lindenberger (Innsbruck: StudienVerlag, 2010), 99-116.

11 Uhl, "The Politics of Memory," 80.

12 Ibid., 72.

13 Anton Pelinka, "Taboos and Self-Deception: The Second Republic's Reconstruction of History," in *Austrian Historical Memory and National Identity*, ed. Günter Bischof and Anton Pelinka (CAS 5) (New Brunswick, N.J.: Transaction Publishers, 1997), 95-102.

14 For more information see: Andrea Schlieker, "A Book Must Be the Axe for the Frozen Sea within us," in *Judenplatz: Place of Remembrance*, ed. Gerhard Milchran (Vienna: Vienna Jewish Museum Judenplatz and Institute for Jewish History in Austria, 2001), 20-31.

15 For more information about the debate see Moran Pearl, "Books and Ash: The 'Nameless Library' as a Way to Read the Memory of the Holocaust–Austria's Jews Embodied in Monument," in *Transgressing Boundaries: Humanities in Flux*, ed. Marija Wakounig and Markus P. Beham (Vienna: LIT Verlag, 2013), 135-156.

central location, just a few steps away from the *Stephansplatz*). These events express a change in the Austrian political climate, which began in the 1990s. This change expresses Austria's desire to come to terms with its past and to integrate Jewish memory into its national consciousness.[16]

One reason behind the construction of the monument was to settle the controversy created by Alfred Hrdlicka's "Memorial against War and Fascism," erected in 1987 at the *Albertinaplatz*, and dedicated to all the victims of the Second World War with no specific mention of the Jews.[17] Hrdlicka's monument used a figurative depiction of "The Street Washing Jew" (figure 3), to commemorate the November Pogrom of 1938. This figure employed the same visual language as the anti-Semitic propaganda of the Nazis and was therefore considered to be offensive.[18] In contrast to Hrdlicka's monument, Whiteread's makes significant use of minimal and non-figurative language. The decision to erect Whiteread's monument was intended to create a positive image of the Jews by using the symbol of the book, which has positive connotations and associations with the tradition of enlightenment and Jewish education.

Figure 3. Alfred Hrdlicka, "Monument against War and Fascism," detail: Rebellions and The Street Washing Jew, 1987. *Albertinaplatz*, Vienna (photo: Moran Pearl).

Unlike Austria's initial conception of itself as a victim of the Nazis, West Germany felt an immediate responsibility towards the victims of the war, as well as a duty to remember and compensate, since its reestablishment as a democracy after 1945.[19] The *Erinnerungsarbeit* (memory work), the creating of monuments and museums began in the late 1980s and beginning of the 1990s, after German society had been gradually exposed to events such as the Auschwitz-Trial (1947), the Eichmann-Trial (1961), and the

16 Bunzl, "On the Politics and Semantics," 9-10.

17 The monument is dedicated to the Jews, members of the underground resistance, opponents of Hitler, and victims of the Allied bombings on the night of 12 March 1945.

18 Primarily, Hrdlicka's intention was to teach the Austrians to take responsibility for their acts, but the monument was not understood correctly. Bunzl, "On the Politics and Semantics," 13-16; James E. Young, *At Memory's Edge: After-Images of the Holocaust in Contemporary Art and Architecture* (New Haven: Yale University Press, 2000), 110.

19 For more information about the modes of remembrance and oblivion in Germany after the war see: Pearl, "Books and Libraries," 22-24.

screening of related TV series and films such as "Holocaust" (1979) and "Schindler's List" (1993) which portrayed the suffering of the victims.

The historian and Holocaust survivor Saul Friedländer claimed: "Germans found themselves in the last two generations on the border between the lack of desire to remember on the one hand, and the impossibility of forgetting on the other hand."[20] The conflict was demonstrated in 1985, on the 40th anniversary of the end of the Second World War:[21] On the one hand, the German President Richard Karl von Weizsäcker required the public to look bravely into the German past and to take responsibility for it,[22] while on the other hand, Cardinal Joseph Höffner insisted that the public should look to the future of the German people, rather than dwell in its past.[23]

This duality created a debate in West Germany about the "appropriate" modes of remembrance. Theodor Adorno claimed that "to write poetry after Auschwitz is barbaric."[24] Adorno's solution was "negative dialectics," a method of creating art that reflected the tensions of a culture, and the different layers of memory embedded within it. Accordingly, artists questioned the nature of the monument as a suitable vehicle of memory.[25] They criticized the monument as a frozen object that did not accurately reveal the past but rather encouraged the spectator to escape his own responsibility by remembering. They saw memory as dynamic and in constant flux, and therefore the traditional monument was seen as unsuitable for modern society.[26] Others raised questions regarding the aesthetics of monuments that echoed the fascist period.[27] For all of these reasons, artists began to use

20 Saul Friedländer, *Memory, History, and the Extermination of the Jews in Europe* (Cincinnati: Hebrew Union College Press in Association with the Leo Baeck Institute, 1994), 142.
21 Ibid., 8-12.
22 The German Federal President's website, Der Bundespräsident, <http://www.bundespraesident.de/SharedDocs/Reden/DE/Richard-von-Weizsaecker/Reden/1985/05/19850508_Rede.html;jsessionid=1D1F313C5339BD4043BC5E91B655998B.2_cid388> (20 March 2015).
23 Kardinal Joseph Höffner, "Predigt im Ökumenischen Gottesdienst im Kölner Dom am 8. Mai 1985," in *Erinnerung, Trauer und Versöhnung: Ansprachen und Erklärungen zum vierzigsten Jahrestag des Kriegsendes*, ed. Deutsche Bundesregierung (Bonn: Bundesregierung Verlag, 1985), 101-106.
24 The quote is from 1949 and was first published in 1951, Theodor Adorno, "Cultural Criticism and Society," in *Prisms*, trans. Samuel Weber and Shierry Weber (Cambridge, Mass.: MIT press, 1983), 17-34. The original German source was: "Kulturkritik und Gesellschaft," written in 1949, published in *Soziologische Forschung in unserer Zeit*.
25 James Young, *The Texture of Memory, Holocaust, Memorial and Meaning* (New Haven: Yale University, 1994), 5.
26 Rosalind Krauss, *The Originality of the Avant-Garde and other Modernist Myths* (Cambridge, Mass.: MIT Press, 1988), 280.
27 Lewis Mumford, *The Culture of Cities* (New York: Harcourt, Brace & world, 1938), 434-438.

negative aesthetics, in what they described as a "counter-monument."[28] As will be shown, the "Empty Library" is a realization of these new concepts and an expression of the German duality regarding the Holocaust.

Negative Aesthetic

The "Empty Library" and the "Nameless Library" both make use of "negative aesthetics," and were influenced by Adorno's thinking on how to express the void left in Europe after the Second World War and the Holocaust.

The "Empty Library" is an underground space that leaves the surface empty, unlike traditional monuments in public places that attract the spectator through their impressive size. The pedestrians in the square rarely notice the monument. From above the ground all that is visible is a square transparent window embedded within the floor. Approaching the window, the spectator will find it difficult to see the interior of the underground room due to reflections on the glass. With some effort, and by bending one's knees and covering one's eyes, it is possible to see white empty bookshelves reveal themselves like an archeological dig.

Most of Ullman's sculptures in the public sphere are located in pits in the ground and near the surface. Their unexpected locations lead ignorant spectators away, but invite others to approach and explore. Ullman describes himself as a "digging man," and the action of digging within his work represents the tension between life and death; the same action of digging a pit relates to planting trees and creating life, and also to death and digging a grave. This could be seen in the monument; the minimalist grid created by the white shelves, inside the ground, presents an image of catacombs and death, while the window's glass with its reflection of the sky and the busy square, expresses life and continuity.[29]

Ullman deals with the German past as a layer of memory that needs to be discovered. According to Ullman, digging a pit in a public space "exposes" the historical, political, and social levels of the site itself. The pit of the "Empty Library" marks the opening of a repressed memory. The memory of "The Night of the Book Burning" in 1933, which was an emblematic event, whose power demolished freedom of thought, is revealed every time one stops to look at the monument. This can be seen as an attempt to deal with

28 James Young was the first researcher to use these terms in his book *The Texture of Memory*, after examining the new artist's movement in Germany that had created new types of monuments from the 1980s on.

29 To expand on the idea of a negative space and its meaning of a dig in Ullmans works and in the "Empty Library" see Pearl, "Books and Libraries," 17-21.

"[t]he Nazi past [which] is too massive to be forgotten, and too repellent to be integrated into the normal narrative of memory."[30]

The "Nameless Library" also engages the spectator through its negative and disturbed aesthetics. At first glance, the "Nameless Library" seems to represent a very ordinary library, but on closer inspection, the viewer can recognize an unusual, almost absurd quality to it: a reversed room, revealing its inner content outside and reversed books (figure 4). The reversed position of the books presents the spectator with their pages rather than their cover, and their identity is kept hidden. This perspective creates a contradiction: a library that both reveals and prevents access. A second glance reveals the disturbing fact that the books are not supported by shelves, as they should be, but are floating in midair.[31] Moreover, the doors appear to be a negative casting of molded doors.[32] As a result, although the inside of the library is visible, the monumental doors keep this inner space sealed and unreachable.

Figure 4. Rachel Whiteread, "The Nameless Library," detail: one side of the monument, the gaps between the books Rows. *Judenplatz*, Vienna (photo: Moran Pearl).

Even though both monuments (figures 1 and 2) use negative aesthetics, they do so in very different ways. Describing his monument, Ullman said: "To express the unthinkable could be possible only by the absent."[33] In

30 Yigal Zalmona, "Hfr (dig), Hafor-root of dig," in *Micha Ullman: 1980-1988*, ed. idem, trans. Judy Levy (Jerusalem: Israel Museum, 1988), 6-8.

31 Stuart Morgan, "Rachel Whiteread," in *Rachel Whiteread: Shedding Life*, ed. Rosalind Krauss and Fiona Bradley (New York: Thames and Hudson and the Tate Gallery Liverpool, 1996), 19-31.

32 Negative casting is the first step in order to create the mold of the statue, from which, in the second step, a positive and three-dimensional object is cast. But Whiteread stops at the first step and in that way she challenges our confidence in the object, which becomes hard to identify. For more information on Whiteread's uses in negative casting see Pearl, "Books and Libraries," 54-60.

33 Micha Ullman, Interview with Moran Pearl in the artist's studio, Ramat Hasharon, 2013.

contrast, Whiteread claimed: "One can hardly build an invisible monument when 65.000 people were murdered."[34] Ullman expresses loss through a use of the void; the monument is hidden in the busy square and can be seen only by those who engage with it. And from a distance, one may see people gathering around a mysterious object, which is just out of reach (figure 5). One may therefore be attracted to the monument by a sense of curiosity created by the interest of others and not by the monument itself. It is only possible to truly view the "Empty Library" when one stands directly above it.

Figure 5. Micha Ullman, "Empty Library," *Bebelplatz*, Berlin (photo: Moran Pearl).

Whiteread's monument differs from the "Empty Library" in terms of its large size, which is visible in the small square. Through its negative form, the "Nameless Library" becomes an uncanny object that invites the spectator to reflect upon the memory it holds. These differences originate in the personal styles of the different artists, and also in their different political environments. In Germany, due to a feeling of obligation to commemorate and the continuous campaigns and debates about every monument erected, the public space, especially that of Berlin, is full of monuments. This could encourage artists and politicians to commemorate the Second World War through monuments that engage spectators but do not interfere with the urban space. In contrast, Austria avoided dealing with the past until the 1990s and therefore the erection of this monument was a monumental state event.

34 Rachel Whiteread, interview by "Diagonal," Ö1 Radio channel, 5 October 1996.

Empty Space

Based on ancient Greek memory techniques, Umberto Eco argued that in order to remember the past, the human mind must make a connection between past events and a figurative symbol. But the question remains: can absence be a sufficient figurative symbol?[35] The Egyptologist Jan Assmann believes that although there are no universal symbols for memory, there are icons that are based on common culture and memories, which allow us to remember specific events.[36] Ullman's goal is to visualize the concept of memory through absence, in this case, the absence of the books. "The Night of the Book Burning" was an act of "cultural cleansing" by the so-called Aryan "superior race" of its "degenerate" influences. The Nazi regime attempted to eliminate cultures that, in their eyes, were not consistent with their ideology. On 10 May 1933, while the books were set alight, Joseph Goebbels, the Minister of Propaganda, spoke the following words which show the full magnitude of this event: "The era of exaggerated Jewish intellectualism is now at an end.... and the future German man will not just be a man of books.... [In] this late hour [I] entrust to the flames the intellectual garbage of the past."[37] These words demonstrate the desire of the Nazi regime to create a new collective memory by erasing existing memories. The absence of books in the library invites the spectator to speculate upon books as vehicles of liberal and critical thinking both for individuals and societies. Although the monument does not officially refer to the Jewish Holocaust, both the fact that two thirds of the burned books were by Jewish authors and the placement of the plaque together with Heine's ominous words indicate a connection.[38] The absence of books in the library could therefore be seen as an analogy to the absence of Jews in German society.[39] The Jews were part of European culture and history, and their presence was felt in everyday life. After the Holocaust, their absence left a void in the public

35 Umberto Eco, "An Ars Oblivionalis Forget it?," *PALMA* 3, no. 3 (1980): 254-257.

36 Jan Assmann, "Ancient Egyptian Anti-Judaism: A Case of Distorted Memory," in *Memory Distortion: How Minds, Brains and Societies Reconstruct the Past*, ed. Daniel L. Schacter (Cambridge, Mass.: Harvard University Press 1995), 365-378.

37 Book burning: Historical film footage, retrieved from United States Holocaust Memorial Museum, at <http://www.ushmm.org/wlc/en/media_fi.php?ModuleId=10007978&MediaId=158> (24 October 2014).

38 To expand on the connection between the "Empty Library" and the memory of the Holocaust see Pearl, "Books and Libraries," 36-40.

39 Interestingly, the Hebrew word for void also refers to a soldier who died in battle and leaves a void in the nation.

space.[40] Therefore, the idea of immortalizing the lost ones by means of empty space is quite common in Europe.[41]

Empty space is also present in Whiteread's memorial in the gaps between books. In Whiteread's monument the book shows the void left by the Austrian Jews. The monument invites us to fill in the gaps with history and stories, but this cannot be realized since the books themselves are reversed and prevent us from accessing the knowledge they seem to offer. Wolfgang Kos, a historian and former director of the Vienna Museum, claims that these gaps are the core of the monument: "The void gaping between the rows of books reminds the viewer that none has access to the past or to history, and what remains is the memory, and memory is always in the present time."[42] A proposition had been raised to engrave the names of all those who had perished upon the monument,[43] but it was impossible as such a list was not available.[44] Therefore, the empty spaces separating the books grew to become a symbol, a restrained and quiet, yet powerful reminder of more than 65.000 Jews whose life stories could never be told.

40 An example of this is the Jewish Museum in Berlin, which was inaugurated in 2001, and built by architect Daniel Libeskind. The building contraction immortalizes those who passed away by means of a large, almost empty building. The permanent exhibition only occupies the upper levels of the building, leaving the entrance floor and the rest of the museum permanently empty. For more information about the use of void in Berlin see Andreas Huyssen, "The Voids of Berlin," *Critical Inquiry* 24 (Autumn 1997): 76-78; "The Jewish Museum Berlin: Between the Lines," Daniel Libeskind, 18 April 2007, at <http://www.daniel-libeskind.com/projects/pro.html?ID=2> (24 October 2014).

41 For more information on the memorialization of Jews in Europe by means of empty space see Shelley Hornstein, "Nothing to See: Private Art Mourning in Public Art," in *Memory and Oblivion*, ed. Adriaan Wessel Reinink and Jeroen Stumpel (Dordercht: Kluwer Academic Publishers, 1999): 1003-1110; Dagmar Richter, "Spazieren in Berlin," *Assemblage* 29 (April 1996): 72-85; Andreas Huyssen, "Monument and Memory in a Postmodern Age," in *The Art of Memory: Holocaust Memorials in History,* ed. James E. Young (Munich: Prestel Verlag, 1994), 57-81.

42 Wolfgang Kos, "Erinnerungspolitik und Ästhetik: Bemerkungen zu den Konflikten und nicht geführten Debatten um Rachel Whitereads Mahnmal für Wien," in *Projekt Judenplatz Wien: Zur Konstruktion von Erinnerung*, ed. Simon Wiesenthal (Vienna: Paul Zsolnay Verlag, 2000), 71-78.

43 Whiteread claimed that the idea of adding the list of names was inspired by the Vietnam Veterans Memorial by Maya Lin, see Craig Houser, "If Walls Could Talk: An Interview with Rachel Whiteread," in *Rachel Whiteread: Transient Spaces*, ed. Lisa Dennison and Craig Houser (Berlin: Deutsche Guggenheim, 2001), 57-61; Michael Kimmelman, "Out of Minimalism: Monuments to Memory," *The New York Times*, 13 January 2002.

44 Abigail Gillman, "Cultural Awakening and Historical Forgetting: The Architecture of Memory in the Jewish Museum of Vienna and in Rachel Whiteread's 'Nameless Library'," *New German Critique* 93 (2004): 145-173.

Site Specific

Figure 6. Micha Ullman, "Empty Library" at night, *Bebelplatz*, Berlin (photo: Moran Pearl).

Site specific is a term that refers to modern and contemporary works of art which were made for a specific location; they interact with their location and draw their meaning from it.[45] The two monuments can both be considered as site specific, but differ from one another in their use of this specificity.

The "Empty Library's" location is connected with the event it commemorates: "The Night of Burning Books." In daylight, the square buildings, which were the setting of the event, are reflected on the window of the monument. On that night in May 1933, students from the Humboldt University took books from their library and burned them. Today, one can see both the reflection of the old building representing the past, and one's own reflection with modern clothing representing the present. One must confront the monument, discover it, and then come to terms with the event commemorated in one's own time and perspective.

Figure 7. Austrian National Library–*Hof-Bibliothek* ("Imperial Library," 1349-1395). *Heldenplatz*, Vienna (photo: Moran Pearl).

At night, the monument is lit from the inside, allowing the library to be visible from a distance, and the shimmering light that glows from the monument draws wandering spectators (figure 6). The light works on our collective memory, bringing back images from films, photos, and textbooks

45 For more information on the definition of "site specificity" see Miwon Kwon, "One Place after Another: Notes on Site Specificity," *October* 80 (1997): 85-110.

that are engraved in our minds, helping us remember the horrific acts that took place in the square. The light and the surrounding buildings of the monument emphasize the site specific quality of the "Empty Library": it is inextricably bound to the *Bebelplatz*.

The "Nameless Library" is also site specific, but in a very different way; it is not situated in a place related to the Holocaust, but in a place connected to the Jewish history of Vienna. It is located a few minutes' walk from the National Library in *Heldenplatz* (figure 7). In contrast to the modest square and library in the *Judenplatz*, *Heldenplatz* presents the imperial cultural past through the glorious National Library and other imperial buildings and monumental statues in this square. But *Heldenplatz* is also remembered as the place where Hitler delivered a speech on 15 March 1938 after the "Anschluss" that inflamed the Austrian masses.[46] Whiteread insisted that the monument is site specific since it was planned for the *Judenplatz* in order to create a dialogue with its buildings and its historical layers. The first layer is the ruins of the medieval synagogue that was destroyed in the massacre of 1421; the ruins lie beneath the monument, accessible via the Jewish museum in the square. The monument was placed exactly above what was the mid-level synagogue's platform (*Bima*) where the Torah had been read (figure 8).

Figure 8. Remains of the medieval synagogue. Jewish Museum *Judenplatz*, Vienna (photo: Moran Pearl).

46 For more information about the connection between the two squares and the different libraries design see Pearl, "Books and Ash," 157-158.

The books of the monuments therefore refer to this act that ended with the destruction of the community. Moreover there is a wooden plaque with a Latin engraving embedded in one of the walls of the square, which describes the massacre and the disruption of Jewish life in the city 600 years before (figure 9).[47] The second layer is another memorial plaque, commissioned in 1998 by the Archbishop of Vienna, Cardinal Christoph Schönborn, following a public debate. It acknowledges the role of the church in the 1421 massacre through an engraving depicting the medieval persecution as an "early omen" of National Socialism.[48]

Figure 9. Plaque in memory of the Jewish pogrom of 1421, *Judenplatz*, Vienna (photo: Moran Pearl).

Lastly, in the square stands a statue of the famous poet Gotthold Ephraim Lessing created by Siegfried Charoux. Lessing, the famous Enlightenment playwright, who believed in freedom of thought and tolerance towards other religions, put forth his ideas in his play "Nathan the Wise," a play that some say was inspired by his relations with the Jewish-German scholar Moses Mendelssohn. The statue was unveiled in 1935, a few years before the "Anschluss," as a symbol of the integration of the Jews into the Viennese society in the 19th century. Lessing's statue was melted down by the Nazis in 1939 and was cast again by the same artist and revealed to the public one year after he passed away in 1968.[49] The roof of the "Nameless Library" is decorated with a rosette made through negative casting,[50] from a drain cover which blocks sunlight from entering

47 The writing on the plaque is as follows: The Flames of hate arose in 1421, raged through the entire city, and punished the terrible crimes of the Hebrew dogs. Translated from Latin in: Reinhard Pohanka, "Judenplatz after 1421," in *Judenplatz: Place of Remembrance*, ed. Gerhard Milchran (Vienna: Museum Judenplatz Vienna, 2000), 108-115.

48 Gillman, "Cultural Awakening," 170.

49 Rebecca Comay, "Memory Block: Rachel Whiteread's Holocaust Memorial in Vienna," in *Image and Remembrance: Representing and the Holocaust*, ed. Shelley Hornstein and Florence Jacobowitz (Bloomington: Indiana University Press, 2003), 251-271.

50 See footnote 32.

the library. The monument was designed so that the rosette could only be fully viewed from above and the statue of Lessing is the only object in the square high enough to see it (figure 10). This symbolically points to the culture of the modern Enlightenment that Lessing represented and the tragic fate of the integrated Jews, who were prevented from being part of German and Austrian society due to the ideology of the Nazis.[51]

Figure 10. Siegfried Charoux, Gotthold Ephraim Lessing monument, 1931-1932, reproduced 1962-65, *Judenplatz*, Vienna (photo: Moran Pearl).

The historian Reesa Greenberg referred to the monument as a "Topography of Horror," the horror being caused by the interaction of the "Nameless Library" with other monuments in the square. Because of this interaction, different periods of time became apparent and blurred at the same time, thus reflecting upon the complexity of Austrian history during the war while highlighting the Jewish victims.[52]

The Book as a European Symbol

In Jewish culture, due to religious reasons, the value of the written word is greater than that of visual images. The book was considered to be the cornerstone of the Jewish memory structure. This could be one of the reasons the Jewish communities chose to remember and to document the atrocities they experienced by means of *Izkor* books (remembrance books),

51 For more information about the Lessing monuments and the "Nameless Library" see Pearl, "Books and Ash," 146-148.

52 "Topography of Horror" is a term coined by Shelley Hornstein as a title for a session she organized at the annual meeting of the American Society for Aesthetics in 1997; see Reesa Greenberg, "The Jewish Museum, Vienna: A Holographic Paradigm for History and Holocaust," in *Image and Remembrance: Representation and the Holocaust*, ed. idem and Florence Jacobowitz (Bloomington: Indiana University Press, 2003), 235-250, p. 250.

which acted as portable private monuments. The book was also central in German culture, beginning with the invention of modern printing in the 15th century and in particular during the German Enlightenment in the 18th century. The Enlightenment tradition was also rooted in Austrian culture. Integrated Jews were, of course, a significant part of that culture. Therefore, the book can be perceived as a positive symbol that represents these three cultures simultaneously: the Jewish, the German, and the Austrian. For these reasons, the book and the library were chosen as symbols of the Holocaust in both monuments.

The archaeological excavations made in 1995 on the *Judenplatz*, which revealed the ruins of the ancient synagogue, led to discussions and debates on the nature of Jewish memory: what was the Jewish medium for memory? Was there even a need for a monument, or would the authentic ruins be enough to express memory? Was the book the most suitable image? Did the book represent the Viennese Jewish community as the "People of the Book," a representation which differentiated the Jews from their Viennese cultural surroundings? Did it represent modern Jews or just traditionally educated ones?[53]

Vienna, Berlin, Budapest, Prague, and Vilna were all centers of modern Jewish culture at the end of the 18th century and up until the beginning of the 20th, Jews were integrated and contributed to society in different areas as scientists, composers, writers and sociologists.[54] Robert Storr considers books to be part of the cultural richness of Vienna, in which the Jews undoubtedly took part.[55] However, the book as a symbol of Jewish identity also emphasizes the difference and uniqueness of the Jews.[56] According to the Jewish author Edmund Jabès, the real space of Jewishness is the book.[57] Jabès epitomizes an approach that was widely prevalent in Europe in different forms since medieval times, according to which the Jewish space

53 For more information see various essays written by historians, architects, philosophers and writers in *Projekt Judenplatz Wien: Zur Konstruktion von Erinnerung*, ed. Simon Wiesenthal (Vienna: Paul Zsolnay Verlag, 2000). See also Klaus Mosettig, "Das Mahnmal als in Auftrag gegebene Bewältigungsarbeit: Eine Untersuchung des sogenannten Holocaustmahnmals am Wiener Judenplatz," MA thes., Vienna University 2002.

54 For example: authors Arthur Schnitzler, Franz Werfel, Stefan Zweig, Franz Kafka, Heinrich Heine, Thomas Mann; philosophers and intellectuals such as Walter Benjamin, Karl Marx; composers such as Gustav Mahler and Arnold Schoenberg, psychoanalysts such as Sigmund Freud and scientists such as Albert Einstein.

55 Robert Storr, "Das Verbergen der Leere," in *Projekt Judenplatz Wien: Zur Konstruktion von Erinnerung*, ed. Simon Wiesenthal (Vienna: Paul Zsolnay Verlag, 2000), 22-28.

56 Gillman, "Cultural Awakening," 164.

57 Edmond Jabès, *La Question du livre L'écriture et différence* (Paris: Editions du Seuil, 1967), 99-116.

is not a real space, land or territory, but that of the book and of memory.[58] Therefore, some of the opponents to the monument argued that the book acted as an instrument that separated Jews from their environment.[59]

The book as the main motif of the "Nameless Library" generates an almost automatic tendency to interpret books as an explicit symbol for the Jews themselves. The spectator might interpret this monument as a verbal and visual expression of the Jews as the "People of the Book."[60] However, due to the negative aesthetics—the absence of books and reversed books—the question remains as to whether the book as a symbol can indeed evoke memory, or oblivion. The "Empty Library" and the "Nameless Library" make spectators ponder the historical narrative they deliver through an ambiguous aesthetic. The absence of books in the "Empty Library" is an absence of the repositories of knowledge and heritage, ordinarily passed down to future generations. This absence exposes the destruction of the legacy of Jewish authors, scientists and philosophers by German students and professors who burned their books. In the "Nameless Library," the pages within the books, which are usually unseen, are revealed to the viewer, but nonetheless fail to turn into living words and language.[61]

In both monuments, the library expresses the will to collect knowledge and make it accessible. However, by presenting inaccessible books and the void, the monument emphasizes the limitations of collecting documents about the past, and reminds us that our knowledge of the past is always fragmentary. Books and words provide knowledge and are, therefore, agents of memory. Even though there are many books and memories written about the Holocaust, and a great deal of documentation in many archives, the memories of the Holocaust remain hard to grasp. Therefore, books and monuments as agents of memory face an inherent difficulty in representing the Holocaust through the aesthetics of language and art. This great paradox is expressed in both monuments. By representing books in a monument—a visual vehicle—the knowledge they contain is no longer accessible, and thus the functionality of the book is symbolically destroyed.

Conclusion

The "Empty Library" in Berlin and the "Nameless Library" in Vienna are monuments depicting books and libraries as symbols of the Second

58 Ibid.
59 Gillman, "Cultural Awakening," 154-155.
60 Ibid.
61 Ibid.

World War and the Holocaust. This symbol appears to reflect a shared sense of perception. The choice of book imagery in both locations is an expression of European and even universal values that are manifested in books and libraries as symbols of memory. Books, like monuments, express the need to document and establish the past that must not be forgotten. Furthermore, books are attributed a positive image: they are the symbol of the tradition of education, scholarship, and the European Enlightenment. The book is a symbol that on the one hand has a connection to the Jewish tradition (The People of the Book) and on the other hand represents modern Judaism, which influenced and was influenced by the European Enlightenment. This dual symbolization led both locations to assume that books are viewed as positive objects able to show Jewish victims in a non-humiliating light, in contrast to the example of a Jewish street cleaner in the "Memorial against War and Fascism." However, books also have an ambiguous quality, since the same component that highlights the Jews' integration into their environment also shows their isolation. The complexity of using books—agent of written memory—as media for visual memory is evident from this paper's examination and discussion of monuments. When a book is presented in a monument, its contents are made unavailable and it becomes purely symbolic.

Using books and libraries in monuments raise questions regarding historical memory. However, the books featured in two of the monuments are used critically since they represent the public's longing for enlightenment and desire to make knowledge readily available. Gradually, the monuments point to the impossibility of fulfilling this desire because of the events they represent. Books become inaccessible and testify to the failure of language and art to comprehensively capture the Holocaust, and to transmit its memory to future generations. The inaccessibility of books and the use of negative aesthetics in both cases can be said to expose the fragmentary nature of memory, and the emptiness left in post-Holocaust Europe after the destruction of the Jewish communities.

Alongside the shared collective meaning expressed through book imagery in both monuments, both also used books and libraries to create specific meaning such as the memory of a historical event or an allegorical symbol of the Jewish people. These discrepancies are rooted in the unique cultural characteristics of each society, from the ethos of memory in each culture, to the location in which the monument is built, and of course to each artist. As was shown, Germany's political atmosphere called for an ethical obligation to remember, in contrast with a simultaneous desire to move on. This tension alongside the grand monuments already present in Germany is perhaps what caused decision makers to choose low-key structures for new memorials in order to keep difficult issues out of site. Austrian memory, conversely, and until the end of the 1980s, was characterized by the "victim thesis," which emphasized the suffering of the Austrian people as victims of Hitler's aggressive occupation, and, as such, did not deal with reparations or the suffering of other victims. For this reason, when an official monument depicting Jewish victims was finally erected, it was done so with the decision to create something memorable that would emphasize the great change in Austrian's collective memory as well as the will to integrate other victims into the Austrian public sphere and consciousness.

Finally, the "site specific" nature of these monuments transforms books into particular objects of memory, meaning that, if one were to disconnect the monument from its place and special circumstances, the viewer's understanding of the monument would be altered. In Berlin, the book depicts a historical event that occurred in the exact place in which the monument was erected, a place that allows one to draw conclusions about the Holocaust. The monument in Vienna is an expression of the "The People of the Book" and Jewish culture that perished in the Holocaust and is located in the place where the community lived and was twice destroyed in the Middle Ages.

In recent years, books as a medium have metamorphosed into a digital form that makes their content accessible online. This significant change might be the reason for the growing uses of the printed book as a symbol of the past. The inaccessibility of books depicted in both monuments through negative aesthetics is a powerful symbol that emphasizes the position of books as tools of human creation and memory, and also of destruction and a warning to future generations. In Heinrich Heine's words from his play *Almansor* in 1821: "Where they burn books, they will ultimately burn people as well."[62]

In the past ten years, with the expansion of European integration, we can see a search for a common identity. In particular, the Second World War and Holocaust shaped Europe after the Second World War, and as some scholars observed, led to the creation of common institutions, policies, laws and more.[63] In his book, Imagined Communities, Benedict Anderson defined processes and practices that turn a large group of people who are not

62 For the original citation see Heinrich Heine, "Almansor," in Gutenberg Project eBooks, ed. Erwin Kalischer and Raimund Pissin (Berlin: Deutsches Verlagshaus Bong & Co(, 21/244, at <http://www.gutenberg.org/files/45600/45600-h/45600-h.htm> (17 February 2015).

63 For more information on the establishment of this idea see Tony Judt, *Postwar: A History of Europe since 1945* (London: Vintage, 2010).

a natural community into a united community.[64] In his view, this can only be done by creating common symbols, monuments, and museums which shape the public sphere.[65] Despite artists' growing interest in the book as a symbol, no comprehensive research deals directly with this issue or examines the use of books in monuments. Such an examination would relate to other monuments for the Second World War and Holocaust across Europe, and could clarify this point and help us understand whether books can indeed be used as part of a shared European discourse and heritage that has the ability to present the Holocaust and the void the Jews left in Europe.

64 Benedict Anderson, *Imagined Communities: Reflections on the Origin and Spread of Nationalism* (London: Verso, 1991), 7-10.

65 The sociologist Maurice Halbwachs was the first scholar to develop the concept of collective memory, a comprehensive structure and convention based on shared memory and experience.

Austrian Victims and Austria as Victim in the "Short" 1940s: Visual Representations of the Nazi Past 1945-1947

Ina Markova

Introduction[1]

The quadripartite Allied occupation era (1945-1955) is of unequalled interest to those concentrating on Austrian postwar memory since it juxtaposes international and national players. It produced highly diverging and sometimes colliding worlds of images. 1947 may be singled out as a major turning point in the Austrian image canon. Cold War tensions contributed to silently acquitting Austrians from Nazi war crimes. From this period onward, newspapers failed to visualize Austria's Nazi past. This paper wants to examine the visual representations of the previous Nazi past in the immediate aftermaths of WW II 1945-1947 in different media such as newspapers, textbooks, and historical exhibitions. Various highly important canonical pictures will be examined. Those pictures have to be contextualized within the historical field they were used in; they have immensely shaped the society they have been disseminated in.

After 1945 it was crucial to make sense of a highly ambiguous Austrian World War II past, as has been argued elsewhere. This paper wants to elucidate that process of attributing meaning to the past by focusing on visual representations. Scholars have drawn attention to the fact that it was not until the onset of the Cold War that Austrian involvement in the crimes of the Nazi regime was denied in an outright manner, that the "anti-fascist consensus" collapsed.[2] Addressing the Nazi past in August 1945 vs. August

1 The author would like to thank Günter Bischof, Karin Liebhart, and Stefan Maurer for their comments on this paper; Günter Bischof's help with the English manuscript was particulary appreciated. UNO's CenterAustria generously funded a research trip to the National Archives in College Park, MD.

2 See Heidemarie Uhl, "Vom Opfermythos zur Mitverantwortungsthese: Die Transformationen des österreichischen Gedächtnisses," in *Mythen der Nationen: 1945–Arena der Erinnerungen*, ed. Monika Flacke (Berlin: Verlag Philipp von Zabern, 2004), 481-508.

1947 were two very different trajectories of historical memory—with two very different pictures of the past being painted.

This essay is based on the ideas articulated by scholars of the politics of history (*Geschichtspolitik*).[3] Following up on this body of thought, cultural memory is seen as shaped by socio-political and generally speaking antagonistic processes. What we call historical memory is best seen as a dynamic process—the temporary result of negotiations being passed on from generation to generation.[4] When analyzing the strategic uses and functions of historical photographs in Austria after the liberation from Nazism, two concepts lie at the core. On the one hand, I follow Stuart Hall's model of representation;[5] on the other hand, I use Gerhard Paul's notion of "canonical images" (*Bilderkanon*), which is closely connected to the ideas of critical discourse analysis. While a great variety of images can be used and verbal statements made, there are mechanisms constricting the field of what can be said and shown.[6] It is this field that will be analyzed in the following pages.

Rebuilding Austria: The Newspaper Scene

On 13 April 1945, the Red Army liberated the city of Vienna from the Nazi yoke; several weeks later, at the beginning of May, U.S., British, and French armies followed suit and overpowered the remaining Wehrmacht and SS forces in Austria's Western provinces. Up until this point, 65.000 Austrian Jews and 6.000 Roma and Sinti had been annihilated in concentration camps all over the European continent. Crimes had taken place on Austrian soil itself, not only in Mauthausen concentration camp, but also in Castle Hartheim, where 30.000 "handicapped" people were murdered in the so-called "euthanasia" program T-4. Furthermore, some 4.000-5.000 Austrians who had resisted the Nazi regime were executed

---

3 See *Umkämpfte Vergangenheit: Geschichtsbilder, Erinnerung und Vergangenheitspolitik im internationalen Vergleich*, ed. Petra Bock and Edgar Wolfrum (Göttingen: Vandenhoeck & Ruprecht, 1999); *Geschichtspolitik: Wer sind ihre Akteure, wer ihre Rezipienten?*, ed. Claudia Fröhlich and Horst-Alfred Heinrich (Stuttgart: Steiner, 2004); *Wie Geschichte gemacht wird: Zur Konstruktion von Erinnerungen an Wehrmacht und Zweiten Weltkrieg*, ed. Hannes Heer (Vienna: Czernin, 2003); *Geschichtspolitik und kollektives Gedächtnis: Erinnerungskulturen in Theorie und Praxis*, ed. Harald Schmid (Göttingen: V & R Unipress, 2009).

4 See Jeffrey K. Olick and Joyce Robbins, "Social Memory Studies: From 'Collective Memory' to the Historical Sociology of Mnemonic Practices," *Annual Review of Sociology* 25 (1998): 105-140.

5 Stuart Hall, "The Work of Representation," in *Representation: Cultural Representations and Signifying Practices*, ed. idem (London: Sage, 1997), 13-74.

6 See Gerhard Paul, "Das Jahrhundert der Bilder: Die visuelle Geschichte und der Bilderkanon des kulturellen Gedächtnisses," in *Das Jahrhundert der Bilder: 1900-1949*, ed. idem (Göttingen: Vandenhoeck & Ruprecht, 2009), 14-39.

for their acts of defiance.[7] Warfare had devastated Austrian cities and victimized numerous Austrian families. The World War II Austrian balance sheet records 250.000 soldiers killed in action and 30.000 civilians who perished as a result of the Allied bombing campaigns and combat operations in the final months of the war. However, identifying victims and victimizers in a country whose population had been *both* victims and perpetrators would preoccupy the Austrian mind for a long time after the war.[8]

After the end of the war, 537.632 Austrians had to register their Nazi affiliations in the denazification program unleashed by the Allied occupation powers. This group included people who had been members of the NSDAP, the SS, or other criminal organizations. 41.906 among them were labeled major offenders (*schwer belastet*) according to the *Nationalsozialistengesetz* in 1947.[9] Historian Bertrand Perz avers that many Austrians had been intensively involved in the Nazi occupation regimes throughout Europe; they had become complicit in committing war crimes; they were involved in both the expulsion of population and the dispossession of Jewish property; they had participated in committing "euthanasia" crimes and launching the Holocaust.[10] However, there was another, legal narrative to those years. Austrian politicians regularly drew attention to the fact that the "Anschluss" of Austria in March 1938 had been an act of German military aggression, immediately followed by massive persecution of Austrian Jews and the anti-Nazi political opposition, altogether victimizing some 50.000 people.[11]

Regardless of those moral and highly political questions of guilt, the Austrian postwar agenda encompassed the reorganization of Austria's political, economic, and intellectual life. The country had to be rebuilt after the wartime destructions and people and administrative structures needed to be denazified. Several important decrees were passed, among them the constitutional laws outlawing the National Socialist Party in the newly reestablished Austria on 8 May 1945, as well as the law persecuting war

7 Wolfgang Neugebauer, *Der österreichische Widerstand 1938-1945* (Vienna: Ed. Steinbauer, 2008).

8 Peter Berger, *Kurze Geschichte Österreichs im 20. Jahrhundert* (Vienna: Facultas.wuv, 2008), 232.

9 Karl Vocelka, *Geschichte Österreichs: Kultur–Gesellschaft–Politik* (Munich: Heyne, 2006), 302.

10 Bertrand Perz, "Österreich," in *Verbrechen erinnern: Die Auseinandersetzung mit Holocaust und Völkermord*, ed. Volkhard Knigge and Norbert Frei (Bonn: Bundeszentrale für Politische Bildung, 2005), 170-182, p. 172.

11 Oliver Rathkolb, *Die paradoxe Republik: Österreich 1945 bis 2005* (Vienna: Zsolnay, 2005), 20.

criminals (*Kriegsverbrechergesetz*), on 26 June 1945.[12] In addition, so-called "people's courts" (*Volksgerichte*) were created to prosecute the Austrian Nazi war criminals.[13] Punishing Nazis responsible for unspeakable war crimes was one thing. Yet in a country so thoroughly infused with Nazi ideology during the war, reeducating and re-democratizing the hundreds of thousands of Nazi fellow travelers and bystanders was equally important.

For the process of democratizing postwar Austria, the Allies felt that an independent press was paramount. Initially, the Allies diligently took on the task of supervising and administrating newspaper production themselves. A greater degree of liberty and less censorship was allowed shortly thereafter. The first Austrian post-liberation newspaper in print was published by the Soviet Information Service: The very first issue of the *Österreichische Zeitung* reached the newsstands as early as 15 April 1945, before the war had ended. It ran continuously until 31 July 1955. The U.S. forces followed a few months later with the launching of the *Wiener Kurier* on 27 August 1945. While the *Österreichische Zeitung* sold an average of 30.000-50.000 copies daily,[14] the *Wiener Kurier* quickly overtook the Soviet enterprise with some 250.000 papers published daily by January 1946. The *Kurier* became a major force on the Austrian newspaper scene, strongly influencing the development of the rest of the local newspapers in the postwar era.[15] U.S. policy makers were keenly aware of the *Kurier*'s propaganda value and took pride in being the "leading German daily in Austria."[16] Apart from democratizing the Austrian population, its anticommunist stance became more important as the Cold War was breaking out in Austria.[17] As early as in March 1946, the "policy of brotherly love" between the USA and the Soviet Union was finished. It became part of the Kurier's editorial agenda to "in a quiet way....snipe at the Soviets."[18]

12 StGBl. no.13/1945.
13 StGBl. no. 177/1945.
14 Wolfgang Mueller, "Die 'Österreichische Zeitung'," in *Die Wiener Tageszeitungen–Eine Dokumentation, Band 5, 1945-1955: Mit einem Überblick über die österreichische Tagespresse der Zweiten Republik bis 1998*, ed. Gabriele Melischek and Josef Seethaler (Frankfurt a. M.: Peter Lang, 1999), 11-56, p. 27.
15 Ulrike Harmat, "Medienpolitik der Alliierten," in *ibid.*, 57-96, p. 78-79.
16 Period Ending in 31 May 1947 (Headquarters United States Forces in Austria Information Services Branch APO-777), Chief ISB to Commanding General, U.S. Forces in Austria, Folder 221, Box 16, Operations Section, ISB, RG 260, National Archives and Records Administration [NARA].
17 Mission and Policy of the ISB (Headquarters United States Forces in Austria Information Services Branch APO-777), 29 April 1949, Folder 1, Box 1, Pictorial Section, ISB, RG 260, NARA.
18 History of the Wiener Kurier, Folder 55, Box 4, Press Section, ISB, RG 260, NARA.

Austrian media policy, however, was not only an Allied matter. Hans Fabris has pointed out that the political parties also played an important role in the immediate postwar period.[19] With Allied approval, the Socialist Party (SPÖ), the People's Party (ÖVP), and the Communist Party (KPÖ) all influenced the re-establishment of the postwar Austria media scene.[20] The Allied licensing policy placed the Austrian media under their control.[21] Only editors holding a license were allowed to publish newspapers; these much-desired permits were granted more easily to the political parties.[22] 5 August 1945 marked the first day Austria's postwar democratic parties were allowed to publish their own newspapers. The SPÖ launched the *Arbeiter-Zeitung* (AZ), the Communists the *Österreichische Volksstimme*, and the ÖVP the *Kleines Volksblatt*.

The launching of these party organs anteceded the formulation of the Allied media propositions of 1 October 1945, formulated as in the "Decision of the Allied Council Concerning the Democratic Press in Austria."[23] It handed "a maximum of possible freedom" to the Austrian press. But the press had to uphold principles such as fighting "against Nazi, pan-German and militaristic ideology and doctrines in all their forms and respects in political, social, cultural, and economic life." Also, publication of material directed against or undermining the Allied unity was prohibited. Newspapers and periodical publications were not subject to censorship, yet post-censorship could be inflicted upon those publications that did not meet these expectations. It is questionable whether Austrian postwar journalists were able to comply with these propositions. The media scholar Fritz Hausjell has estimated that 37.1 percent of all Austrian postwar journalists had laid the foundations of their careers during World War II. The baggage of their professional

19 See Wolfgang Pensold, "Vom Staatskanzler zum Medienkanzler: Drei Dogmen im medienpolitischen Diskurs der SPÖ nach 1945," *medien & zeit: Kommunikation in Geschichte und Gegenwart* 14, no. 3 (1999): 4-25; Theodor Venus, "'Wir sind wieder da:' Eine Dokumentation zur sozialistischen Pressepolitik in Österreich zu Beginn der zweiten Republik," *Medien & Zeit: Forum für historische Kommunikationsforschung* 6, no. 4 (1991): 17-33.

20 Hans Heinz Fabris, "Der 'österreichische Weg' in die Mediengesellschaft," in *Österreich 1945-1995: Gesellschaft, Politik, Kultur*, ed. Reinhard Sieder, Heinz Steinert and Emmerich Tálos (Österreichische Texte zur Gesellschaftskritik 60) (Vienna: Verlag für Gesellschaftskritik, 1995), 641-654, p. 647.

21 Oliver Rathkolb, "U.S.-Medienpolitik und die neue österreichische Journalistenelite," *Medien & Zeit: Forum für historische Kommunikationsforschung* 2, no. 2 (1987): 3-16, p. 6; see also idem, "Politische Propaganda der amerikanischen Besatzungsmacht in Österreich 1945 bis 1950," PhD thes., University of Vienna, 1981.

22 Harmat, "Medienpolitik der Alliierten," 57.

23 Decree of 1 October 1945 on Freedom of the Press of the Allied Council, Folder 223, Box 16, Operations Section, ISB, RG 260, NARA.

socialization and indoctrination in the Nazi period undoubtedly tarnished their postwar journalism.[24]

The *Salzburger Nachrichten* (SN) can serve as a case in point. Starting on 23 October 1945, it was first published by the U.S. Forces and later on by an independent board of Austrian journalists. After the SN was put under Austrian supervision, the tone of the news coverage changed drastically. Rene Marcic, its first postwar editor-in-chief, had made a name for himself as a cultural and press *attaché* in the fascist Croatian *Ustasha* regime. The well-known SN journalists Viktor Reimann, Ilse Leitenberger, and Alfons Dalma had been similarly compromised by their wartime affiliations.[25] The ISB's Press Scrutiny Section regularly had to interfere with the SN's "always very pro-German" coverage.[26] The SN preferred focusing on minor provincial matters "while playing down or not playing at all, stories which have much more significance, like the Nuremburg [sic] trials."[27]

Similarly, many important press photographers had started their careers in the Nazi era as well. Photo historian Anton Holzer ascribes such career paths in journalism to "old-boys networks."[28] Still, considerable efforts were made to train a new generation of democratic (and, in the course of the Cold war, also anti-communist) photojournalists. The ISB Pictorial Section, for instance, which had started out as a military organization during the war, developed into a highly professional civilian outfit after the war.[29]

24 Fritz Hausjell, "Die mangelnde Bewältigung des Vergangenen: Zur Entnazifizierung und zum Umgang von Journalistinnen und Journalisten mit der nationalsozialistischen Vergangenheit nach 1945," in *Die vierte Macht: Zu Geschichte und Kultur des Journalismus in Österreich seit 1945*, ed. Hans Heinz Fabris and idem (Österreichische Texte zur Gesellschaftskritik 53) (Vienna: Verlag für Gesellschaftskritik, 1991), 29-49, p. 40.

25 Harald Fidler, *Österreichs Medienwelt von A bis Z: Das komplette Lexikon mit 1000 Stichwörtern von "Abzockfernsehen" bis "Zeitungssterben"* (Vienna: Falter-Verlag, 2008), 533.

26 Headquarters United States Forces in Austria Information Services Branch APO-777, Priscilla Dall (Press Scrutiny Section) to Dr. Van Eerden, 5 February 1947, Folder 174, Box 12, Operations Section, ISB, RG 260, NARA.

27 Headquarters United States Forces in Austria Information Services Branch APO-777, Ted Kaghan (Ass't Operations Officer) to Dr. Van Eerden, 31 January 1946, Folder 298, Box 23, Operations Section, ISB, RG 260, NARA.

28 Anton Holzer, *Fotografie in Österreich: Geschichte, Entwicklungen, Protagonisten 1890-1955* (Vienna: Metroverlag, 2013), 176-177.

29 Hans Petschar, *Die junge Republik: Alltagsbilder aus Österreich 1945-1955* (Vienna: Ueberreuter, 2005), 11. On the ISB see Marion Krammer and Margarethe Szeless, "Yoichi Okamato and the 'Pictorial Section:' Austrian-American Relations in Press Photography," in *1914: Austria-Hungary, the Origins, and the First Year of World War I*, ed. Günter Bischof, Ferdinand Karlhofer and Samuel R. Williamson, Jr. (Contemporary Austrian Studies [CAS] 23) (Innsbruck and New Orleans: uno press and Innsbruck University Press, 2014), 275-292.

"Perpetrators in the Dock": The Visual Singling out of Traitors to the Fatherland

Three principal themes dominated key representations in postwar newspapers on Austria's immediate postwar past: 1) the homecoming of prisoners of war (*Heimkehrer*); 2) the visual record of the ruination and devastation of Austrian cities (*Trümmerbilder*); 3) dealing with Nazi perpetrators. The latter category comprised pictures taken of both Austrian Nazi war criminals prosecuted in the people's courts and the Nazi leadership in the docks of the elaborate Nuremberg war crimes trials. Cornelia Brink has analyzed these "perpetrators in the dock" as a part and parcel of a larger judicial postwar discourse.[30] Habbo Knoch has pointed out that these pictures were the harbinger of a genuine visual shock for postwar West Germans. They complied with "visual denazification" of the West German population, served as "propaganda of truth," and showed "pictures of the enemy."[31] Pictures of the crimes, however, were rarely present in Austria's immediate postwar years. Although a wide array of newspaper articles dealt with Nazi crimes in 1945/46,[32] they were usually not accompanied by visual representations of these crimes covered; there were only a few exceptions. On 19 September 1945, the AZ reproduced three photographs bearing the caption "Bone-Crushing Belsen–Nazi Germany's Eyesore" ("*Knochenmühle Belsen–der Schandfleck Nazideutschlands*"). The accompanying lead article talks about people sent to the gas in Auschwitz without even mentioning Jewish victims. Two of the pictures portrayed perpetrators—one depicting two male dead bodies, showing "what was done to people." While Viennese newspaper failed to reproduce pictures of Nazi war crimes, this was not true for "Western" papers still under direct supervision of the Allied forces.[33] In the beginning, the *Salzburger Nachrichten* was directly controlled by the U.S. occupation element and visually dwelt on topics such as memorial services

30 Cornelia Brink, *Ikonen der Vernichtung* (Berlin: Akademie Verlag, 1998), 14.

31 Habbo Knoch, *Die Tat als Bild: Fotografien des Holocaust in der deutschen Erinnerungskultur* (Hamburg: Hamburger Edition, 2001), 23-25.

32 See for instance "Der Massenmord an den Juden," *AZ*, 4 January 1946, 1; "Aufdeckung weiterer Judenmorde," *Neues Österreich*, 18 August 1945, 2; "Drei Todesurteile des Volksgerichtes: Abschluss des Prozesses gegen die Judenmörder von Engerau," *Neues Österreich*, 18 August 1945, 1; "Totenköpfe und Lampenschirme aus Menschenhaut in Nürnberg," *Wiener Kurier*, 14 December 1945, 1; "Bilddokumente des Grauens," *Österreichische Zeitung*, 20 February 1946, 1; "Menschenmassen wurden lebend verbrannt," *Österreichische Zeitung*, 31 January 1946, 1; "Der Massenmord von Engerau," *Österreichische Volksstimme*, 15 August 1945, 1.

33 For example the S*alzburger Nachrichten*, the *Oberösterreichische Nachrichten*, or the *Tiroler Tageszeitung* (TT); the TT was founded by the U.S. forces but later fell under the French zonal agenda.

in Mauthausen[34] as well as the fate of former inmates.[35] In addition, pictures of crematoria with piles of corpses and victims of the "euthanasia" crimes were printed in newspapers in the U.S. zone of occupation.[36]

While visual representations of the Nazis victims and Nazi war crimes were rare, "pictures of the enemy" were a recurring visual theme in the immediate postwar years, typically focusing on photos of high-ranking Nazi war criminals. There were also recurring iconic pictures like the one showing the eight defendants Hermann Göring, Rudolf Heß, Joachim von Ribbentrop, Wilhelm Keitel, Karl Dönitz, Erich Raeder, Baldur von Schirach, and Fritz Sauckel during the opening hearing of the Nuremberg war crimes trials. Often, Göring was the center of attention.[37] Focusing on the principal Nazi culprits allowed Austrians and Germans to exonerate themselves by way of criminalizing prominent perpetrators.[38] Similar visual strategies left their imprint on the many articles that covered the numerous trials of the Austrian people's courts.[39]

Credit: ÖNB / Obransky

34 Alfred Grüll, "An der Todesstiege von Mauthausen," *Oberösterreichische Nachrichten*, 13 May 1945, 6.
35 Stand-alone photo, *Salzburger Nachrichten*, 10 July 1945, 1; "Die Todesstiege von Mauthausen," *Salzburger Nachrichten*, 26 June 1945, 1; stand-alone photo, *Tiroler Tageszeitung*, 4 July 1945, 1.
36 "350.000 Zwangsverschickte nicht wiedergekehrt," *Tiroler Tageszeitung*, 1 October 1945, 1; "'Dachauer' herzlich empfangen," *Salzburger Nachrichten*, 30 June 1945, 1; "Kommission zur Ausmerzung wertlosen Lebens," *Salzburger Nachrichten*, 20 September 1945, 1.
37 "Göring beim Abendessen," *Wiener Kurier*, 14 December 1945, 1; "Neueste Bilder aus Nürnberg," *Wiener Kurier*, 21 March 1946, 6; "Selbstmord Görings," *Wiener Kurier*, 16 October 1946, 1.
38 Knoch, *Tat als Bild*, 285.
39 See "Vor dem Volksgericht," *Neues Österreich*, 15 August 1945, 4; "Drei Todesurteile des Volksgerichtes," *Neues Österreich*, 18 August 1945, 1; Stand-alone photo, *Neues Österreich*, 6 August 1946, 1; Stand-alone photo, Neues Österreich, 17 October 1946, 1; "Der Zertrümmerer des Elektronenmikroskops vor dem Volksgericht," *Österreichische Volksstimme*, 12 September 1945, 3; "Massenmörder Pilz war achtmal vorbestraft," *Österreichische Volksstimme*, 8 August 1946, 3.

Concentrating single-mindedly on the allegedly few "traitors to the fatherland" was a political strategy that had already left an imprint on the Preamble of the Declaration of Independence of the Second Republic, published by the SPÖ, ÖVP, and KPÖ on 27 April 1945.[40] The punch line charged that the "Anschluss" of March 1938 had been unleashed by an outside military force with the assistance of a small, treacherous stratum of the Austrian population; allegedly, this directly led to the war that a defenseless and destitute Austrian people would never have supported out of their own free will.[41]

This alleged "rape" of Austria claimed by Austria's political elite after the war subsequently became a pillar of the postwar narrative of "Austria as victim" (*Opferthese*).[42] Austria's postwar founding fathers were also eager to exploit a document proclaimed on 1 November 1943 by the Allied foreign ministers who had gathered in Moscow. Historians have termed this Allied declaration as Austria's "Magna Charta"[43] for the ensuing process of postwar Austrian nation-building; they have also considered this "Moscow Declaration" more a political stance than a document of international law.[44] Austria's postwar founding fathers took the declaration deliberately at its face value in 1945 and thereafter. In the "Moscow Declaration on Austria" the Allied foreign ministers came to the conclusion

> that Austria, the first free country to fall victim to Hitlerite aggression, shall be liberated from German domination.... They declare that they wish to see re-established a free and independent Austria.... Austria is reminded, however, that she has a responsibility which she cannot evade for participation in the war on the side of Hitlerite Germany, and that in the

40 Wolfgang Mantl, "Staatsvertrag, österreichische Identität und europäische Integration," in *Der österreichische Staatsvertrag 1955: Internationale Strategie, rechtliche Relevanz, nationale Identität,* ed. Arnold Suppan, Gerald Stourzh and Wolfgang Mueller (Archiv für österreichische Geschichte 140) (Vienna: Verlag der Österreichischen Akademie der Wissenschaften, 2005), 949-964, p. 954.

41 StGBl. no. 1/1945.

42 Günter Bischof, "'Opfer' Österreich? Zur moralischen Ökonomie des österreichischen historischen Gedächtnisses," in *Die politische Ökonomie des Holocaust: Zur wirtschaftlichen Logik von Verfolgung und "Wiedergutmachung"*, ed. Dieter Stiefel (Querschnitte 7) (Vienna: Verlag für Geschichte und Politik, 2001), 305-335, p. 308.

43 Thomas Albrich, "Holocaust und Schuldabwehr: Vom Judenmord zum kollektiven Opferstatus," in *Österreich im 20. Jahrhundert–Ein Studienbuch in zwei Bänden: Vom Zweiten Weltkrieg bis zur Gegenwart,* ed. Rolf Steininger and Michael Gehler (Vienna: Böhlau, 1997), 39-106, p. 56.

44 Robert H. Keyserlingk, "1. November 1943: Die Moskauer Deklaration–Die Alliierten, Österreich und der Zweite Weltkrieg," in *ibid.*, 9-38, p. 10.

> final settlement, account will inevitably be taken of her own contribution to her liberation.[45]

Initially intended by the Allies to boost morale and incite resistance in Nazi-occupied Austria, after her liberation Austrian political leaders took this propaganda statement on its face value and reinterpreted it as a legal statement that annulled the "Anschluss." The passage reminding Austria of her responsibility in participating in World War II was willfully ignored.[46] The onset of the Cold War reshuffled the cards for victims and perpetrators of the Nazi era alike. The Allies contented themselves with following the Austrian reading of the Moscow Declaration. Canadian historian Robert Keyserlingk has poignantly classified this turn of events as historical revisionism for reasons of political pragmatism.[47] Recognizing Austria's split identity as both victim of Nazi military aggression and willing perpetrator was a political nuisance. Even more, it might threaten Austria's international status and the much sought-after full political sovereignty. Contemporary Austrians and Allies alike harbored few illusions about the nature of Austrians' deep involvement in "Third Reich" criminal activities. Yet openly admitting Austrian complicity in war crimes would have been politically ill-advised. Chancellor Renner—not exactly an ardent resistance fighter—wanted to mention Austrian soldiers' participation in the gruesome crimes (*Barbareien*) of the Wehrmacht in a radio address in May 1945. But his staff told him to scratch the passage from the text, arguing that every hint of Austrian war crimes might imperil the Austrian pursuit of ending the occupation regime and regaining full sovereignty.[48] The Minister of Education, Ernst Fischer—a member of the Austrian Communist Party (KPÖ)—also mentioned Austrian complicity in war crimes and the need to atone for them. This might have pleased American journalists covering his speech in August 1945. Yet it really aggravated the diplomat Josef Schöner, who noted in his diary that such admissions were unwise from a "propaganda point of view."[49]

Make no mistake; the Allies were fully cognizant of the extent of Austrian involvement in war crimes. Were it not for the strategic importance

45 Idem, *Austria in World War II: An Anglo-American Dilemma* (Kingston: McGill-Queen's University Press, 1988), 207-208.
46 Albrich, "Holocaust und Schuldabwehr," 58.
47 Keyserlingk, "1. November 1943," 28.
48 See Günter Bischof, "Der wirtschaftliche, politische, moralische Wiederaufbau Österreichs nach der Katastrophe des Zweiten Weltkriegs," in *Österreich in der Zweiten Republik: Ein Land im Wandel*, ed. Philipp Strobl (Schriftenreihe Studien zur Zeitgeschichte 94) (Hamburg: Kovač, 2014), 13-33, p. 29.
49 Ibid., 30.

of keeping Austria separate from Germany, the high-ranking member of the British Foreign Office John M. Troutbeck noted in an internal assessment that "we would let this flabby country stew."[50] The Information & Education Section of the U.S. Forces in Austria stated straightforwardly that "[i]t was in part the Austrian people's fault that their country was overrun by the Germans and that they found themselves fighting in Hitler's armies. The fact that we have beaten Hitler gives them another chance. They are lucky."[51]

Trümmerbilder: Austrian Suffering Blamed on "Prussian War-Mongerers"

Credit: ÖNB / Hilscher

Many Austrians did not consider themselves very lucky, however. The vast devastation and ruination of their cities suggested to them that atonement had already been done. Among the many generic pictures, for which the German language coined thc tcrm "rubble images" (*Trümmerbilder*), one motif in particular combined the emotions hard to express. The iconic Austrian image, not only of the immediate postwar years but of the Second Republic at large, is Albert Hilscher's picture depicting St. Stephen's cathedral aflame in the final days of the war in April 1945.[52]

In the very first issue of the Red Army's *Österreichische Zeitung* on 15 April 1945, a drawing of the intact cathedral dominated the cover page. It announced that Austria was "Free again!" and also reproduced the text of the

50 See Robert Knight, "Besiegt oder befreit? Eine völkerrechtliche Frage historisch betrachtet," in *Die bevormundete Nation: Österreich und die Alliierten 1945-1949*, ed. Günter Bischof and Josef Leidenfrost (Innsbrucker Forschungen zur Zeitgeschichte 4) (Innsbruck: Haymon, 1988), 75-92, p. 77.

51 See Siegfried Beer, "Die Besatzungsmacht Großbritannien in Österreich 1945-1949," in *Österreich unter alliierter Besatzung: 1945-1955*, ed. Alfred Ableitinger, idem and Eduard Staudinger (Studien zu Politik und Verwaltung 63) (Vienna: Böhlau, 1998), 41-70, p. 44.

52 ÖNB / Hilscher, Sign. H 8951/2.

Moscow Declaration. The rebuilding of St. Stephen's during the occupation decade, financed by the entire country, cemented its symbolic value in the Austrian imagination. Meanwhile the representation of St. Stephen's in flames functioned as a visualization of the suffering of the Austrian people.

In years to come, pictures of the rebuilding of St. Stephen's allegedly testified to Austrian perseverance in mastering the past. The rebuilding of St. Stephen's as a collective national effort became symbolic of Austria's postwar reconstruction of the country.[53] What added further momentum to the church as Austria's premier *lieu de mémoire* was the engraving "O5" in the front section of the cathedral next to the main entrance. It symbolized the short-lived yet highly mythologized resistance group known as "O5." Its position on the outer wall of the cathedral made it the most important topographic place of a certain idea of the Austrian resistance.[54] Over time, St. Stephen's also came to symbolize the difference between the allegedly catholic, peaceful Austrian nation and its antipode, the pagan, anti-Austrian German Nazis and *their* war.[55] The Cold War, then, starting in Austria as early as November 1945 in the aftermath of the communists' electoral defeat,[56] helped to pave the way for Austria's strategy of demarcation vis-à-vis Nazism and West Germany. Central to this strategy was to portray Austria as a victim of Nazism—just as the Allies had suggested in the Moscow Declaration. Not being German was equal to not having been Nazis.[57]

Juxtaposing the peaceful Austrians with the belligerent Prussians was a recurring theme of the postwar era and was designed to help strengthen Austrian identity.[58] In this figment of the imagination the Nazi regime had been "foreign" (*volksfremd*); the "Prussians" were to be blamed for wartime terror and war crimes, as Hans Riemer, the city of Vienna's press officer, averred in a brochure entitled "Eternal Vienna" in 1945.[59] The average Austrian "Joe", Vienna's chief education officer Heinrich Gassner claimed, flinches in the eye of violence and brute force. Gassner boldly attributed

53 Karl Klambauer, *Österreichische Gedenkkultur zu Widerstand und Krieg: Denkmäler und Gedächtnisorte in Wien 1945-1986* (Innsbruck: StudienVerlag, 2006), 103.

54 Ibid., 110.

55 Ibid., 16.

56 See Hannes Leidinger and Verena Moritz, *Die Republik Österreich 1918/2008: Überblick, Zwischenbilanz, Neubewertung* (Vienna: Deuticke, 2008), 197.

57 Werner Suppanz, *Österreichische Geschichtsbilder: Historische Legitimationen in Ständestaat und Zweiter Republik* (Cologne: Böhlau, 1998), 6, 19.

58 Siegfried Mattl, "Geschlecht und Volkscharakter: Austria engendered," *Österreichische Zeitschrift für Geschichtswissenschaften* 7, no. 4 (1996): 499-515, p. 515.

59 Hans Riemer, *Ewiges Wien: Eine kommunalpolitische Skizze* (Vienna: Deutscher Verlag für Jugend und Volk, 1945), 58.

this character trait to Austrians being more relaxed in their emotional life than the "Northern Germans."[60] But not only the political backbenchers painted the Austrian character in the brightest of colors. None other than Chancellor Leopold Figl produced spurious claims such as scientists having discovered "traces of racial [!] comingling with Mongolian elements" in the "Prussians." According to Figl, this amalgamation could be traced back to the times of "Genghis Khan."[61] After the horrors of World War II, when they had been part of the Third Reich, Austrians needed to invent a new identity. They did this by discarding their prewar Pan-German one. Austrians had to embark on a steep learning curve to discover their new identity and had to overcome many obstacles—it was a "*Lernprozeß mit Hindernissen*," as Félix Kreissler aptly put it.[62]

The *Heimkehrer* and their Political Integration

The depiction of hundreds of thousands of Austrian Wehrmacht soldiers coming home from Allied prisoner of war camps (*Heimkehrer*) became another important visual icon in the structure of Austria's postwar national "visiography."[63] The *Heimkehrer* became the principal motif present in all the newspapers. Focusing on their release from Allied POW camps, newspaper articles usually presented the issue of discharged *Heimkehrer* who had been detained by one of the four occupation powers. Newspapers associated with the respective occupation power presented the case of POWs returning from camps entertained by that specific power. Thus the *Kurier* visualized the release of Austrian POWs from American camps, the *Österreichische Zeitung* and the *Volksstimme* reported on POWs returning from Soviet camps,[64] while the *AZ* and the *Kleines Volksblatt* depicted *Heimkehrer* from British camps.[65]

It was not clear yet how those years of military service in the Wehrmacht and subsequent imprisonment in the camps of the victorious Allies were presented to the public. In the immediate postwar years, Austrian

60 See Heinz P. Wassermann, *Verfälschte Geschichte im Unterricht: Nationalsozialismus und Österreich nach 1945* (Innsbruck: StudienVerlag, 2004), 21-22.

61 Leopold Figl, "Was ist Österreich?," *Österreichische Monatshefte* 1 (1945/1946): 89, p. 89; see Suppanz, *Österreichische Geschichtsbilder*, 35.

62 See Félix Kreissler, *Der Österreicher und seine Nation: Ein Lernprozess mit Hindernissen* (Vienna: Böhlau, 1984).

63 Knoch, *Tat als Bild*, 19.

64 Stand-alone photo, *Wiener Kurier*, 7 March 1946, 3; "Auch die Amerikaner entlassen Kriegsgefangene," *Österreichische Volksstimme*, 23 September 1945, 1.

65 Stand-alone photo, *Das kleine Volksblatt*, 26 September 1945, 1; "Kriegsgefangene kehren heim," *AZ*, 6 September 1945, 1.

government officials and historians had not yet constructed a credible master narrative about Austrians' World War II past. It was still a long way before some 300.000 Wehrmacht veterans began to gather in Austrian veterans' organizations—the *Kameradschaftsverbände*; only in 1953 did the occupation powers permit them to meet. The veterans' organization became a major influence in constructing a master narrative full of half-truths.[66] The founding political parties of the Second Republic—the ÖVP, SPÖ, and KPÖ—soon made a big effort to recruit the former soldiers returned home into their political camps. The *Heimkehrer* quickly became a force in domestic politics. Winning them over, however, was not easy. Some of those former prisoners of war, for instance, advocated the founding of a new rightist party,[67] an insistence which lead to the formation of such a "League of Independents" (*Verband der Unabhängigen*, VdU) in 1949. The new party became a "receptacle of former Nazis; a refuge for Pan-German ideologists; and advocates of those complicit in 'Aryianization.'"[68]

Credits: ÖNB / Blaha

The returning POWs also affected the population at large emotionally as almost every Austrian family had to take care of one in their midst. At

66 Alexander Pollak, *Die Wehrmachtslegende in Österreich: Das Bild der Wehrmacht im Spiegel der österreichischen Presse nach 1945* (Vienna: Böhlau, 2002), 22.
67 Robert Kriechbaumer, "Der lange Weg in die Moderne: Ein mentalitätsgeschichtlicher Essay zur Geschichte der Zweiten Republik," in *Österreichische Nationalgeschichte nach 1945: Der Spiegel der Erinnerung–Die Sicht von innen, Band 1*, ed. idem (Vienna: Böhlau, 1998), 17-48, p. 25.
68 Berger, *Kurze Geschichte Österreichs*, 287 (author's translation).

the end of the war some 750.000 Austrian Wehrmacht soldiers had been interned in Allied POW camps—the large majority of them in the Soviet Union.[69] In the immediate aftermath of the war, returning POWs were depicted in a generic way—an anonymous mass coming home. Rarely did newspapers feature individuals among those portrayed, a notable exception being Ernst Haas' pictures series of *Heimkehrer* returning to their families at Vienna's Southern railway station.[70] Habbo Knoch defines the *Heimkehrer* both as symbols of the German defeat and of heroic and thus "clean" warfare. The *Heimkehrer* as visual icon can therefore be linked to multiple layers of meaning such as the portrayal of heroism and suffering as well as of postwar anti-communism.[71]

Therefore, it comes a bit as a surprise that in 1947 the POWs coming home from Soviet camps were extensively covered in the communist party organs. Prior to the unveiling of the *Heimkehrer-Gedächtnismal*—an anti-communist and anti-Soviet memorial to Austrian soldiers returning home—constructed on Vienna's *Leopoldsberg*,[72] the KPÖ and the Soviet occupation element went to considerable length to shape public opinion on this topic. They deliberately sought to paint a positive picture of Soviet prisoner-of-war camps, showing smiling and cheerful Austrian POWs on their way home. As early as 1946, the movie *Der weite Weg*, produced by *Sowexport-Film*, tried to portray Soviet imprisonment as a hard, yet fair enterprise. A common feature of the communist representation of the *Heimkehrer* is their focus on individual POWs, who are often surrounded by children or welcomed back by their loving wives or mothers.[73] Ela Hornung has explained this motif as "Ulysses" finally coming home to his faithful "Penelope." Finally these sons and husbands, who had been gone for years, were coming home and might also be identified as harbingers of the restoration of traditional gender roles. Thus, they also became symbols of finally putting the burdensome wartime years to rest.[74]

Austrian families and newspapers alike were obsessed with the fate of POWs and their hardships behind barbed wire, but war and warfare were topics rarely covered by the postwar media. Only communist newspapers regularly devoted articles to the Red Army's liberation of Vienna in April

69 Ibid., 232.

70 "Soll all das wiederkommen?," *Salzburger Nachrichten*, 8/9 October 1949, 1.

71 Knoch, *Tat als Bild*, 322.

72 Klambauer, *Österreichische Gedenkkultur*, 67.

73 "Heimkehrer erzählen," *Österreichische Volksstimme*, 16 September 1947, 3; "Die Heimkehrer heute früh in Wien," *Österreichische Volksstimme*, 17 September 1947, 1; "Wieder sind 464 heimgekehrt," *Österreichische Volksstimme*, 23 July 1948, 1.

74 See Ela Hornung, "'Penelope' und 'Odysseus'," in *Eiszeit der Erinnerung: Vom Vergessen der eigenen Schuld*, ed. Ulf Brunnbauer (Vienna: Promedia, 1999), 65-83.

1945, thus creating a communist *lieu de mémoire*.[75] Both the *Österreichische Zeitung* and the *Volksstimme* featured an array of articles in their annual commemorations of 13 April 1945. These served as visual reminders to the amnesic Austrian public that the Red Army had liberated Vienna and paid a steep price in loss of lives.[76] The *Volksstimme* aimed at visually anchoring this day as Austria's "day of liberation" by establishing a visual narrative of cheerful crowds dancing around an Austrian flag. It was a difficult challenge to create the visual symbols for a liberation not wholeheartedly endorsed by the Viennese public at large.

Credits: ÖNB / Obransky

One man, however, bridged the gap between past and present. This was Austria's *pater patriae* Karl Renner, the first postwar provisional chancellor and then president.[77] The best-known picture regularly reprinted in the press featured Renner with a group of politicians walking on Vienna's inner ring road. The picture was taken on 29 April 1945, only two days

75 Klambauer, *Österreichische Gedenkkultur*, 88.
76 "Die letzten Kämpfe," *Österreichische Volksstimme*, 13 April 1946, 3; " ... im Kampf um die Befreiung Wiens," *Österreichische Volksstimme*, 13 April 1947, 3; "Im Kampf um Oesterreichs Befreiung," *Österreichische Zeitung*, 13 April 1947, 5.
77 Anton Pelinka, "Tabus in der Politik: Zur politischen Funktion von Tabuisierung und Enttabuisierung," in *Tabu und Geschichte: Zur Kultur des kollektiven Erinnerns*, ed. Peter Bettelheim and Robert Streibel (Vienna: Picus, 1994), 21-28, p. 25.

after the proclamation of the Declaration of Independence. Wilhelm Obransky's photo depicts Renner, the Viennese mayor Theodor Körner (and the communist leader Johann Koplenig, who was regularly visually and textually omitted) on their way from city hall to parliament, where the provisional government was to be reinstated.[78] This image of a "civil" postwar Austrian government visually connects the end of war with the rebirth of a democratic Austria—gone were the days of the "Anschluss" with its visual representation of hysterical Viennese masses welcoming Hitler to Austria and the country's absorption into Nazi Germany.

Never Forget: Austrian Resistance and the Holocaust

Soon after the liberation of Austria, official publications such as the 1946 *Rot-Weiß-Rot-Buch* established and reinforced a very specific interpretation of Austria's *Opferthese*. Austrians were portrayed as victims of the Nazi regime due to their seemingly relentless antifascist stance. Similarly, the exhibition *Niemals vergessen!* embodied this particular perspective of Austria's recent past in a masterly fashion. Wolfgang Kos has written extensively on this important exhibition. He categorizes it as a spontaneous manifestation of anti-fascist agitation, the planning of which had already started while the war was still raging.[79] Soviet officials encouraged *Niemals vergessen!*.

Meanwhile, U.S. forces in Austria started the production of exhibitions and graphic displays soon after the war ended. As early as June 1945, U.S. forces used graphic displays and posters in Salzburg to confront Austrians with Nazi crimes directly.[80] These displays moved on to Linz and were later turned into traveling exhibits. At least one display dealt with Nazi atrocities, namely photographs originating with the Office of War Information Exhibit Section in Rome and Life magazine. The American designers put particular emphasis on presenting an "Austrian point of view." Their main display carried the title "Austria is free from the Anschluss—Free from Connection (Anschluss) and Its Products." A smaller display bore the head "Austrians You Have Been Freed From

78 See Ernst Machek and Wilhelm Obransky, *Wie Wien wieder Wien wurde* (Vienna: Verlag Karl Kühne, 1945), 37; Bildarchiv Austria, Sign. O58/5, Obransky.

79 Wolfgang Kos, *Eigenheim Österreich: Zu Politik, Kultur und Alltag nach 1945* (Vienna: Sonderzahl, 1994), 950.

80 Report on Operations of Information Services Branch (Austria) for Week Ending 16 June, 1945 (Headquarters United States Forces in Austria Information Services Branch, APO-887), Chief ISB and P and PW Officer, 12th Army Group to Chief, PWD and SHAEF, 20 June 1945, Folder 121, Box 20, News Operations, ISB, RG 260, NARA.

this Culture." Austrians, however, were reminded of "their share of responsibility for the horrors depicted" by a panel carrying the heading "Supported? Tolerated? For 7 Years!"

Austrians apparently took a great interest in these posters, indicating that these war crimes on display were news to them. However, ISB officials saw such attempts of Austrians dissociating themselves from Nazi war crimes as disingenuous. They suspected that such responses of ignorance were "only half sincere and put on for the benefit of the passing soldiers." In August 1945, when these posters were displayed in Linz, they attracted a crowd of 600 onlookers.[81] One poster depicting the capitulation of high-ranking Nazi and Wehrmacht officials was put on display in a permanent information window. At the same time, Lieutenant Taquey's mobile graphic display unit focused on atrocity pictures exhibited in a show window of a local bookseller.[82] The display units later toured through the Upper Austrian provincial towns of Bad Ischl, Steyr, and Ried in the American zone of occupation.[83] In Bad Ischl, the pictures were intentionally shown to well-known Nazis in town. Their personal reactions were mute. These former members of the NSDAP supposedly had never heard of the "horrible" crimes of the "SS goon squads" (*Räuberbande SS*).[84]

Some of these postwar exhibits quickly thrown together, however, did not meet the expectations of Washington's propagandists in Austria. "The story we should tell now is not the story of our strength and wealth, but a projection of our system of government and of our achievements and plans in the field of foreign relations," observes a report.[85] Only four displays

81 Weekly Activity Report, no. 45/9 to August 10, 1945 (Headquarters United States Forces in Austria Information Services Branch: Unit no. 2 APO-777), Folder 117, Box 20, News Operations, ISB, RG 260, NARA.

82 Information Shop Weekly Report, August 4-10 (Headquarters United States Forces in Austria Information Services Branch: Unit no. 2 APO-777), Folder 117, Box 20, News Operations, ISB, RG 260, NARA.

83 Reports on Graphic Display Section, Activities from 5 August to 11 August 1945 (Headquarters United States Forces in Austria Information Services Branch APO-777), Charles H. Taquey, 1st Lt. F.A. Chief Graphic Display to Chief of Branch, Chief of Operations, Coordinator of Propaganda, "D" Section, 11 August 1945, Folder 117, Box 20, News Operations, ISB, RG 260, NARA.

84 Reports on Graphic Display Section, Activities from 5 August to 11 August 1945: Annex, Polizeiamt der Stadt Bad Ischl, 7 August 1945 (Headquarters United States Forces in Austria Information Services Branch APO-777), Charles H. Taquey, 1st Lt. F.A. Chief Graphic Display to Chief of Branch, Chief of Operations, Coordinator of Propaganda, "D" Section, 11 August 1945, Folder 117, Box 20, News Operations, ISB, RG 260, NARA.

85 Report on Graphic Display Section Activities from 18 August to 25 August 1945 (Headquarters United States Forces in Austria Information Services Branch APO-777), Charles H. Taquey, 1st Lt. F.A. Graphic Display Section to Chief of Branch, Chief of Operations, Coordinator of Propaganda, "D" Section, 25 August 1945, Folder 8, Box 20, News Operations, ISB, RG 260, NARA.

remained in use after the end of the war, namely displays showing "German atrocities" and the "defeat of the Wehrmacht."[86] U.S. propagandists considered the latter exhibit poster crucial in combating the recurrence of the old legend that Germany had never been beaten on the battlefield (the *Dolchstoßlegende* from the end of World War I). Some eighty pictures showed prisoners of war as well as capitulating German generals and high-ranking Nazi officials. Another display of seventy photographs depicted the "rise and fall of the Nazi party" and still another one visualized Austria's reconstruction efforts.

While these American exhibit posters were small and on display for only a few days, the planning for Austria's first large exhibit took more time and political deliberation. Exhibit designers expected the general population to embrace *Niemals vergessen!*, because it represented a joint effort on the part of three postwar democratic parties to come together with an explicitly antifascist message. *Niemals vergessen!* had "semi-official character"; it opened in the fall of 1946 in Vienna's *Künstlerhaus*.[87] With 260.000 visitors flocking to the exhibit in only fourteen weeks, *Niemals vergessen!* proved a resounding success.[88] Exhibit promoters also encouraged former Nazis to see the show by addressing letters of invitation to 125.000 former party members.[89] *Niemals vergessen!* later became a traveling exhibit; in 1947, it was also shown in the Western Austrian cities of Innsbruck and Bregenz.

The war was hardly over when the first working group who designed the exhibit met on 9 May 1945. Wolfgang Kos stresses that even at this early time of the postwar period the approach to the Nazi era was already highly ritualized. What Kos calls the balancing of "radical rhetoric and accepting postwar white lies and living with taboos" set in right away.[90] What had at first been a dynamic process was soon stifled by the institutionalization of a "political committee." From 1946 onwards, representatives from the three political parties demanded the right to examine all objects that would go

86 Report on Graphic Display Section Activities from 18 August to 25 August 1945, Annex I: A Report on Displays by Robert Harari (Headquarters United States Forces in Austria Information Services Branch APO-777), Charles H. Taquey, 1st Lt. F.A. Graphic Display Section to Chief of Branch, Chief of Operations, Coordinator of Propaganda, "D" Section, 25 August 1945, Folder 8, Box 20, News Operations, ISB, RG 260, NARA.

87 Wolfgang Kos, "Die Schau mit dem Hammer: Zur antifaschistischen Ausstellung 'Niemals vergessen!' in Wien 1946," in *Kunst und Diktatur: Architektur, Bildhauerei und Malerei in Österreich, Deutschland, Italien und der Sowjetunion 1922-1956*, ed. Jan Tabor (Baden: Grasl, 1994), 950-965, p. 951.

88 Idem, *Eigenheim Österreich: Zu Politik, Kultur und Alltag nach 1945* (Wien: Sonderzahl, 1994), 12.

89 Idem, "Schau mit dem Hammer," 963.

90 Idem, *Eigenheim Österreich*, 12.

on display and even censor the captions. As early as August 1945, plans for the exhibition lost their "antifascist" characteristics. Representatives from the Socialist Party insisted the what they called Austro-fascist interval coming before the Nazi era needed to be covered too. This was predictably rejected by the ÖVP—the successors to the Christian Social Party that had dismissed parliament in 1933 and built what they called the "*Ständestaat*." The SPÖ wanted to commemorate several members of the *Schutzbund* who had died in the course of the Austrian Civil War in 1934. The People's Party then insisted on honoring the former chancellor Engelbert Dollfuß, who was assassinated in 1934 by the Austrian Nazis.[91] Such partisan bickering over the politics of history threatened the shaky postwar truce between the former political adversaries. In the interest of rebuilding Austria, both parties decided to bury the hatchet and concentrate on the Nazi era and the years of the German occupation of Austria.

Niemals vergessen! was an exhibition financed by the Austrian government with a nation-building mission. The exhibit catalog was a compilation of dedications and short essays by Austria's postwar political elite. Most of these politicians expressed the usual platitudes by pondering the fate of the "small, peaceful Austria" in the past and in the present (Leopold Figl),[92] as well as referring to Austria as a country "abandoned by the whole world" (Oskar Helmer).[93] Most of these political leaders glossed over Nazi war crimes and the Holocaust; only Herbert Kohlich and Akim Lewit specifically mentioned these past tragedies that involved many Austrians, perpetrators and victims alike. The concentration camp ovens, Kohlich reminded Austrians, were "smoldering day and night."[94]

In the exhibition's visual narrative the Holocaust, in fact, played a prominent role. In June 1945, Leo C. Friedländer, head of the City of Vienna's Office for Cultural Activities, suggested a stand-alone section addressing the persecution of the Jews. Given the involvement of the political parties, the exhibit designers were susceptible to compromising regularly, but they still clung to the goal of "explaining, accusing and warning," as Wolfgang Kos has stressed.[95] Over time, however, the accusations were toned down. The preface of the catalog was adamant in pointing out that the exhibition did not intend to "eternalize hatred"; in the end, "we are all guilty," the

91 Idem, "Schau mit dem Hammer," 958.

92 Leopold Figl, " … und Österreich lebt!," in *"Niemals vergessen!:" Ein Buch der Anklage, Mahnung und Verpflichtung*, ed. Verwaltungsgruppe III Kultur und Volksbildung Gemeinde Wien and Viktor Matejka (Vienna: Verlag für Jugend und Volk, 1946), 19-21, p. 19.

93 Oskar Helmer, "Österreich–das erste Opfer des Nazifaschismus," in *ibid.*, 28-30, p. 30.

94 Herbert Kolich, "Der Strom der Heimatlosen," in *ibid.*, 56-59, p. 58; see also Akim Lewit, "Judenverfolgung–Judenvernichtung," in *ibid.*, 60-62.

95 Kos, "Schau mit dem Hammer," 952.

exhibit makers averred. Former resistance fighters thus played down their own suffering and compromised with their former tormentors in view of the ultima ratio of postwar Austrian political and economic reconstruction.[96]

Visual references to the Holocaust were concentrated in an entire room at the exhibition ("The Pillars of Fascism: Lies, Treason, and Violence"). Following up on the catchword "violence," a timeline demonstrated how during "each year of Hitler's rule" both Nazi terror and the number of victims increased.[97] Two highly potent visual motifs identifying the victims were intended to overwhelm visitors: one photograph depicted several civilians hanging on the gallows with their yellow stars clearly visible; the second picture showed children right after their liberation in Auschwitz, the little ones holding their arms tattooed with camp numbers directly into the Soviet liberators' camera. This image actually originated as a movie still.[98] Many Austrian visitors must have been familiar with this image as it was featured prominently in the U.S. "re-education" movie "Death Mills" (*Todesmühlen*).[99] "Death Mills" premiered on 26 April 1946 and was shown in many Austrian cities, including Vienna, Linz, Salzburg, and Graz.[100] We have no box office results recorded and viewing the documentary was (almost always) voluntary.[101] So it is hard to measure the movie's impact on Austrian audiences. However, given a broad advertising campaign in the leading newspapers *Wiener Kurier*, *AZ*, *Neues Österreich*, and *Weltpresse*, we may assume that the movie was widely known.[102]

Making a great visual impact, another room was dedicated to the theme "Persecution of Jews–Annihilation of Jews," which gave overview of the Jewish experience during the Nazi era. In a room dimly lit and with a lowered roof, two display cases were featured with photographs, documents, and models such as a crematoria oven.[103] 5.7 million murdered Jews were identified

96 *Niemals vergessen!*, ed. Verwaltungsgruppe III Kultur und Volksbildung Gemeinde Wien and Matejka, frontispice.
97 Ibid., non-paginated.
98 <http://en.auschwitz.org/m/index.php?option=com_ponygallery&func=detail&id=451&Itemid=3> (19 March 2014).
99 Michaela Anderle, "TODESMÜHLEN in Wien: Auf den Spuren eines Films im Dienste der Re-education," MA thes., University of Vienna, 2009, 71.
100 Ibid., 93, 132.
101 Ibid., 137. In her study on the Carinthian SPÖ's denazification endeavours, Doris Sottopietra avers that the Carinthian state government had made the viewing of the movie obligatory in April 1946. The student body under 16 years of age, all teachers, and those Austrians who had to register due to their former Nazi affiliations apparently had to watch "Todesmühlen." See Doris Sottopietra and Maria Wirth, "Die Länderebene der SPÖ," in *Entnazifizierung zwischen politischem Anspruch, Parteienkonkurrenz und Kaltem Krieg: Das Beispiel der SPÖ*, ed. Maria Mesner (Vienna: Oldenbourg, 2005) 77-145, p. 119.
102 Anderle, "TODESMÜHLEN," 91ff.
103 Kos, "Schau mit dem Hammer," 957.

as the victims of the Nazi terror, annihilated "by Hitler's command."[104] Representations of these victims included pictures of naked and almost-starved concentration camp survivors, especially children. This room illustrated instances of Nazi "plundering" and the "ostracism" of Jews, along with images depicting deportations. The images regularly photographically captured the perpetrators too, although the captions never dwelt on them. As the narrative of annihilation slowly captured the visitor, a section entitled "Death Mills Take on Their Work" grouped together several pictures depicting the execution of civilians and incinerated villages on the Eastern front. "The Most Rational System of Destruction Is Found" acted as the visual culmination, featuring pictures of deportees behind the now iconic cattle cars' wooden bars and images of concentration camp inmates in their makeshift bunk beds. On top of it, piles of corpses and the picture of an already decomposing body inside a crematorium made the visual spectrum of Nazi war crimes real. Looking at the overall trajectory of Austria's postwar memory of World War II, it is astounding that the topic of "war and genocide" was addressed so explicitly at this time. The exhibit *Niemals vergessen!*, along with the pictures printed in the Austrian newspapers, laid the foundation for the postwar Austrian visual archive—temporarily accessible yet soon made invisible. Cornelia Brink has pointed out that the vast majority of photographs available to visualize the Nazi past were at the public's disposal as early as in the summer of 1945. This visual archive was further enhanced by the postwar Nazi war crimes trials.[105] Notwithstanding the financial and material hardships of the immediate postwar period, *Niemals vergessen!* apparently had no problems finding these photographs of Nazi war crimes.

The visual record of the Austrian resistance was part and parcel of Austrian efforts to keep the World War II past alive. But the hard work of Austrian reconstruction took precedence over thorough introspection, Wolfgang Kos shrewdly observes.[106] One drawing in particular helped drive home this message. It showed a mason painstakingly building a wall; a woman assisted him with carrying the building materials. This scene takes place against the backdrop of the Viennese skyline in ruins and the remnants of Nazi devotional objects (e.g. swastikas) in the rubble. Postwar Austria found refuge in a sort of "nationalism light," political scientist Erika Thurner has suggested. Austria was part of the Western tradition of nationalisms associated with strict gender hierarchies. Reconstructing these

104 *Niemals vergessen!*, ed. Verwaltungsgruppe III Kultur und Volksbildung Gemeinde Wien and Matejka, non-paginated.
105 Cornelia Brink, "Bilder vom Feind: Das Scheitern der 'visuellen Entnazifizierung' 1945," in *Die Shoah im Bild*, ed. Sven Kramer (Munich: Ed. Text + Kritik, 2003), 51-70, p. 67.
106 Kos, *Eigenheim Österreich*, 8.

gender hierarchies after the war helped stabilize the country's reconstruction efforts.[107] The posture of the bricklayer and apparent physical strength relegated the female to the supportive role of an unskilled laborer.[108] Telltale was the fact that the foundations of the new democratic Second Republic were built upon the vestiges of the Nazi regime.

Educating Youth and Rewriting History: The Silences in Austria's School Textbooks

Secondary schools' Austrian history textbooks of the late 1940s may best be characterized as silencing the Nazi past. The Allies exerted a great degree of influence on the Austrian school system after 1945.[109] The Quadripartite Committee on Educational Affairs (renamed the Educational Directorate in 1947) oversaw school restructuring and curricula. It also was in charge of supervising the Austrian Ministry of Education. Denazification of people, curricula, and textbooks were of utmost importance during the early occupation period. On 1 May 1945, the 1929 constitution had been re-implemented, declaring all post-"Anschluss" laws null and void. There was also the *Rechts-Überleitungsgesetz* of 20 July 1945, which created a legal limbo in the educational arena. It demanded the abrogation of all decrees and laws alluding to "typical Nazi thoughts." However, curricula not thoroughly cleansed of Nazi content were taught until the introduction of the first postwar provisional curricula in 1946. The initial postwar phase was characterized by a legal grey area—a mental wasteland after years of totalitarian education with a teaching staff deeply mired in Nazi ideology and school systems aggravated by financial problems. Restarting a democratic Austrian education regime required all sorts of interim arrangements, such as harkening back to the prewar period by reinstating the 1926 and 1930 curricula.[110] A massive lack of resources[111] and the problematic contents of the provisional

---

107 Erika Thurner, *Nationale Identität & Geschlecht in Österreich nach 1945* (Innsbruck: StudienVerlag, 2000), 14.

108 Ibid., 54.

109 Ina Markova, *Wie Vergangenheit neu erzählt wird: Der Umgang mit der NS-Zeit in österreichischen Schulbüchern* (Wissenschaftliche Beiträge aus dem Tectum Verlag Reihe Geschichtswissenschaft 20) (Marburg: Tectum, 2013), 80ff.

110 Heinz P. Wassermann, *Verfälschte Geschichte im Unterricht: Nationalsozialismus und Österreich nach 1945* (Innsbruck: StudienVerlag, 2004), 13.

111 Freigabe von Kartoffelstärke für Buchbinderzwecke, no. 16.177-IV/12/Sch/46, Box 2198, 24-Lehrbücher, BMU, Archiv der Republik [AdR].

text books[112] made teaching difficult, not to speak of the remnants of Nazi ideology in the mental makeup of textbook authors. At least one case is known where the Ministry of Education refrained from licensing the approbation of a textbook that failed to grapple with the "hardships of the Nazi system; concentration camps; forced labor and the annihilation of the Jews."[113] School textbook approbation documents tell us about rejections of texts as a result of prominent Pan-German views.[114] The Western powers vested greater faith in Austrian textbook production than the Soviet officials did. The latter still brandished "harmful influences of Nazi, pan-Germanic, and 'unscientific' teaching" in textbooks as late as September 1950. The French High Commissioner General Béthouart, however, rejected such Soviet insinuations by mentioning Figl's and Hurdes' internment in Nazi concentration camps. "They could be trusted to guard against such dangers," Béthouart asserted.[115] Austrian textbook authors, however, were overwhelmed by the challenges of reinventing Austria's past. When the *Österreichische Zeitung* denounced the "fascist contamination of textbooks," the Ministry of Education replied with candor: "It has to be acknowledged that history textbook production suffers from a backlog.... [L]acking a clear and stable national consciousness (*Staatsbewusstsein*), historiography for the youth becomes a blurry line." Austria's new geopolitical situation leaves her without any guidelines to follow: "history must be rewritten."[116]

Early Attempts at Coming to Terms with the Past and the Onset of the Cold War

History indeed had to be rewritten. Contemporaries faced a period of geopolitical upheavals abroad and an ambiguous quest for a new identity and truthful history at home. Still, the depictions of *Heimkehrer* and

112 Ed. Hölzel Verlag, Wien, "Lehrbuch der Geschichte" von Zeehe-Nepomucky: Band I. und II. für die oberen Klassen der Mittelschule, um Zulassung, no. 5881-K/45, Box 2206, 24-Lehrbücher, BMU, AdR.

113 Walther Krenn, Wien IX, Rooseveltplatz 13: "Allgemeine Geschichte," hrsg. Walther Krenn, Verlag Leitner & Co., für Lehrerbüchereien an Haupt- Mittelschulen und Schülerbüchereien höherer Jahrgänge, no. 49 030/IV/15/50, Box 2199, 24-Lehrbücher, BMU, AdR.

114 Leitner & Co., Wels: "Geschichte in Tafelbildern und Zusammenfassungen" von Stöger, Approbation, no. 74.070-IV-15/55, Box 2226, 24E-Lehrbücher 1955-1956 (-85.000), BMU, AdR.

115 Press Release on Allied Council Meeting, 29 September 1950, Folder 106, Box 10, Press Section, ISB, RG 260, NARA.

116 Österreichische Zeitung, 28. Juni 1950: "Faschistische Verseuchung der Schulbücher," no. 2.30.955-IV/15/50, Box 2199, 24-Lehrbücher, BMU, AdR (author's translation).

returnees from POW-camps were rooted in the Austrian national imagery. This post-1945 imagery was needed to attribute meaning to the military service in the Wehrmacht—it was as basic to the reconstruction of Austria as "bread and coal."[117] In view of the four-power Allied occupation of Austria, an outright denial of Austrian involvement in Nazi war crimes was strategically inadvisable. Instead, in accord with the Declaration of Independence, individuals—an assortment of the "treacherous stratum of the Austrian populace"—were singled out and exhibited either in people's courts trials or in the docks at the Nuremberg War Crimes Trials.

1947 may be singled out as a major turning point in the Austrian image canon. Cold War tensions contributed to silently acquitting Austrians from Nazi war crimes. From this period onward, newspapers failed to visualize Austria's Nazi past; they began to ignore too those "treacherous" Austrians with a problematic past. In the immediate aftermath of the war, *Niemals vergessen!* proffered a very specific interpretation of the *Opferthese*. True, Austrians were victims, but they had been victimized because of their resistance, the reading went. In 1947, a full-fledged amnesty of the Nazi "small fry" (*Minderbelastetenamnestie*) followed. Lesser Nazi offenders like the lower echelon members of the NSDAP now went scot-free. More importantly, this amnesty returned active voting rights to this group. The partisan race for their votes characterized the 1949 elections.[118] Additionally, the number of trials against former Nazis declined by a staggering fifty percent in 1948.[119] This postwar spirit of pardoning the Nazis culminated in the far-reaching amnesty of 14 March 1957.[120] With the occupation powers gone, the Austrian government repealed important clauses of the *Nationalsozialistengesetz* and the *Kriegsverbrechergesetz*, and almost entirely shelved most legal disciplinary actions against Nazi war criminals in Austria.[121]

The Holocaust, Nazi war crimes, and the Nazi war of annihilation waged in Eastern Europe left only few visual traces in the postwar Austrian canon of images. Apart from early issues of the *Salzburger Nachrichten* or the *Tiroler Tageszeitung*, when they were under direct U.S. control, images depicting

117 Siegfried Mattl and Karl Stuhlpfarrer, "Abwehr und Inszenierung im Labyrinth der Zweiten Republik," in *NS-Herrschaft in Österreich: Ein Handbuch*, ed. Emmerich Tálos et al. (Vienna: öbv und hpt, 2000), 902-934, p. 914.

118 Sonja Niederacher, "Die Entwicklung der Entnazifizierungsgesetzgebung," in *Entnazifizierung zwischen politischem Anspruch, Parteienkonkurrenz und Kaltem Krieg: Das Beispiel der SPÖ*, ed. Maria Mesner (Vienna: Oldenbourg, 2005) 13-36, p. 23-24.

119 Perz, "Österreich," 173.

120 Bundesgesetzblatt 1957, 24. Stück, issued on March 29, 1957, 607-616.

121 Niederacher, "Entnazifizierungsgesetzgebung," 34ff; Winfried R. Garscha and Claudia Kuretsidis-Haider, "Die strafrechtliche Verfolgung nationalsozialistischer Verbrechen–eine Einführung," in *Holocaust und Kriegsverbrechen vor Gericht: Der Fall Österreich*, ed. Thomas Albrich, Winfried R. Garscha and Martin F. Polaschek (Innsbruck: StudienVerlag, 2006), 11-25, p. 13.

Nazi war crimes were totally absent in the Austrian media. Perpetrators may have been shown, but the victims remained in the dark. This is surprising as images and videos of Nazi war crimes were important pieces of evidence in the convictions of the Nuremberg War Crimes trials. Austrian newspapers extensively reported on these trials without printing pictures of the guilty parties.

The ISB's Press Scrutiny Office observed an "increase in the number of articles implying a sympathy for Nazis or National Socialism" in Austrian newspapers in March 1947, the SN being one of the "main culprits."[122] All in all, Austrian society refused to face Nazism and its legacies and Austrians' contributions to the Nazi war effort. The ISB conducted public opinion surveys in Vienna, Linz, and Salzburg.[123] The surveys revealed almost half of the Austrian population (45.6 percent to be exact) agreed with the provocative statement that "National Socialism, overall, had been a good idea but had been badly executed."[124] Salzburg in particular revealed itself to be a stronghold of diehard Nazi sentiments. In a May 1948 survey a staggering fifty-six percent of Salzburgers did not want to live in an apartment building where Jews were also welcome. After the annihilation of European Jews, seventy-five percent of the interviewees supported the statement that "too many Jews were living in Salzburg."[125] The sociologists Meinrad Ziegler and Waltraud Kannonier-Finster have highlighted that "the externalization of Nazism" gained momentum in the 1950s, after the State Treaty had been signed. As postwar Austrians cast aside their wartime German identity, they blamed Nazism on the Germans. Now Austrians began to revel in their snug identity of having been Nazi victims.[126] Only then, in the words of philosopher Günther Anders, who had himself been a refugee from the Nazis, did "fascism's afterlife" fully unfurl in Austria.[127]

---

122 Headquarters United State Forces in Austria Information Services Branch APO-777, Press Scrutiny Officer to Chief of Branch, 2 April 1947, Folder 24, Box 4, Communications Section, ISB, RG 260, NARA.

123 A good many of those surveys have been published in Martin F. Herz and Reinhold Wagnleitner, *Understanding Austria: The Political Reports and Analyses of Martin F. Herz, Political Officer of the U.S. Legation in Vienna 1945-1948* (Salzburg: W. Neugebauer, 1984).

124 Headquarters United States Forces in Austria Information Services Branch APO-777, Information Services Branch, Survey Action, APO 777-U.S. Forces, Bericht No. 41: Meinungen über den Nationalsozialismus, 4 May 1948, Folder 22, Box 1426, Foreign (Occupied) Area Reports 1945-54, RG 407, NARA.

125 Headquarters United States Forces in Austria Information Services Branch APO-777, Information Services Branch, Survey Action, APO 777-U.S. Forces, Bericht No. 43: Der Antisemitismus in Österreich, 13 May 1948, Folder 22, Box 1426, Foreign (Occupied) Area Reports 1945-54, RG 407, NARA.

126 Meinrad Ziegler and Waltraud Kannonier-Finster, *Österreichisches Gedächtnis: Über Erinnern und Vergessen der NS-Vergangenheit* (Vienna: Böhlau, 1993), 68.

127 Jason Dawsey, "Where Hitler's Name is Never Spoken: Günther Anders in 1950s Vienna," in *Austrian Lives*, ed. Günter Bischof, Fritz Plasser and Eva Maltschnig (CAS 21) (New Orleans, Innsbruck: uno press and innsbruck university press, 2012), 212-239, p. 214.

Forum:
World War I Literature and Memory

New Literature on Austria-Hungary and the First World War

Samuel R. Williamson, Jr.

Manfried Rauchensteiner, *The First World War and the End of the Habsburg Monarchy, 1914-1918*, trans. Alex J. Kay and Anna Güttel-Bellert (Vienna: Böhlau, 2014)

Hannes Leidinger et al., *Habsburgs schmutziger Krieg: Ermittlungen zur österreichisch-ungarischen Kriegsführung 1914-1918* (St. Pölten: Residenz Verlag, 2014)

***Grenzgang: Das Pustertal und der Krieg 1914-1918*, ed. Martin Kofler (Innsbruck: Haymon Verlag, 2014)**

Alma Hannig, *Franz Ferdinand: Die Biografie* (Vienna: Amalthea Signum Verlag, 2013)

On 28 July 1914, Austria-Hungary declared war on neighboring Serbia, launching what it hoped would be a local war to avenge the murders of Archduke Franz Ferdinand and his wife Sophie. For reasons of their own, Russia and Germany took military actions that converted the local war into a European war and then a world war. Four years later the Habsburg monarchy ceased to exist; the war to save it had instead destroyed it. For over a century participants, scholars, and commentators have written about the tragedy of the Great War, though the most serious scholarly attention to the Austro-Hungarian decisions has come in the last three decades. The four books reviewed reflect the new attention given Vienna and Budapest on the origins and conduct of the war. Other volumes will certainly come, including the long-expected studies sponsored by the Austrian Academy of Sciences, but these will remain valuable contributions.

Manfried Rauchensteiner's massive analysis, originally published in German in 2013 and now translated into English, stands apart from all other works, both for its exhaustive study of almost all aspects of the war and for its searing analysis of military decision-making. An expanded version of his *Der Tod des Doppeladlers: Österreich-Ungarn und der Erste Weltkrieg* (Graz: Verlag Styria, 1993), the new work incorporates much recent research, adds five new chapters, and revises some of the earlier sections. In assessing *Der Tod des Doppeladlers* for the *Austrian History Yearbook* in 1995, this reviewer called it "magisterial"; now that word should be "monumental." In a work that runs to 1.018 pages with 2.531 footnotes, no reviewer can do more than cite salient issues addressed and note areas of disagreement. At the same time, the scope of the volume makes it the perfect backdrop to consider the three other books, each a notable contribution to understanding why the war came, how it was conducted (especially in the border war against Italy), and the effect of war on the lives of both those who resided in the monarchy or who were its enemies.

Rauchensteiner's most significant change of emphasis focuses upon his insistence that Emperor/King Franz Joseph played a major and active part in the first decisions after Sarajevo. He sees the emperor setting the course, having few doubts that Serbia was responsible and required punishment. The roles traditionally assigned to Count Leopold Berchtold and István Tisza fade into background. This reviewer is not wholly convinced that the new emphasis has a strong evidentiary base, but the approach does render some of the strange aspects of the crisis more intelligible. Once the war starts, Rauchensteiner continues this focus on Franz Joseph and his close associates in the Military Chancellery. The chancellery's frequent unease over the strategy of Chief of Staff Franz Conrad von Hötzendorf receives attention, as do the emperor's repeated concerns about the wholesale dismissal of officers from their commands.

Yet in the end, Rauchensteiner's assessment of the monarch remains traditional. Franz Joseph was remote, virtually invisible during the war, comfortable in a set routine, and unwilling, having gone to war, to take any further political or strategic chances, including the dismissal of Austrian Minister President Karl von Stürgkh or the reconvening of the Austrian *Reichsrat*. Rauchensteiner states it graphically: "At the head of the Monarchy there was a vacuum that assumed ever more terrifying proportions" (p. 439). The long-term effect of this situation meant that all the actors believed they were "doing the right thing and, if this was not complied with, to paint a picture of impending disaster" (p. 440).

Franz Joseph lived long enough to see, in the weeks before his death, the virtual submission of Habsburg military power to its German ally. At various points in the book, Rauchensteiner offers masterful analyses of the

Austro-German tensions that began at the very start of the war, including colorful expressions of contempt showered by Conrad on the Germans and vice-versa. Whether strategy, or pleas for more German troops to rescue Habsburg forces, or disputes over war aims or peace efforts, eventually one ally clearly dominated the relationship. The very future of the monarchy was in doubt even if it won the war.

A skillful writer of military history, the author's narrative account of land and sea battles is superb, making it easy for readers to grasp the unfolding action. And he is unsparing in his critical analysis of key decisions, often made by Conrad, of the many failures in the field. The military chronicles are set amid chapters that address war finance, domestic food scarcities, and mounting labor strife as the war continued. But in a major omission by publisher and author, there are no adequate maps to follow the military narrative. By contrast, *Der Tod des Doppeladlers* had excellent maps; the endnote maps in the present volume (German and English editions) are simply not adequate.

Conrad remains the central military figure, of course, for much of the war. His erratic behavior, his ability to survive despite horrendous mistakes, and his consistent contempt for the Germans is amply documented. The general's disdain for the young heir-apparent, Archduke Karl Franz Joseph, would finally lead to his dismissal, though one can only wonder why it took so long for this to happen. It remains a mystery to this reviewer that so many fellow generals could have thought Conrad competent and would later defend him after the Great War. In this instance, one could wish that the author had offered his own final assessment on the most problematic but important figure in the end of the Habsburgs. Conrad's relationship with Gina von Reininghaus, both before and during the war, gets no notice, only an occasional reference to her presence at the headquarters where Conrad took tea with her every afternoon. After all, he went to the actual front less than five times during the entire war.

If the theme of military operations unites the book, Rauchensteiner pays extensive attention to the domestic political situation, especially in Austria. Put simply, the longer the war continued, the greater the friction among German-Austrians, Czechs, Poles, Ruthenians, and South Slavs. These frictions had already spilled over into the question of troop loyalty from the respective nationalities, though unit integrity remained far more intact than a casual observer would think possible.

But the situation changed dramatically when the new emperor allowed the *Reichsrat* to reconvene in May 1917. Almost immediately the Czechs pressed for concessions, while the German-Austrians reasserted their desire for dominance. The author puts it bluntly: "It was not in 1918 that the nations began to turn away from the Habsburg Monarchy, but already at the end of May 1917" (p. 712). Indeed, the aggrieved nationalities in 1917 and 1918 had a positive reason to keep the war going, since it assured them of a changed constitutional role in whatever monarchy survived. Even Tisza and the Hungarians had to make some accommodation to popular opinion, if only grudgingly and minimally.

Rauchensteiner pays special attention to the Italian campaign, first as a rallying cry for many in the monarchy who saw the Italians as traitors to the alliance, and second as a place where the military campaign usually produced more good news than bad. He details the final German-Austrian offensive at the end of 1917 as the last moment of military glory for the Habsburgs. Thereafter, the saga went downhill, including the ill-conceived final attack against Italy in the summer of 1918.

A special strength of the study, beyond its almost unbelievable detail, is the attention to issues that previously were pushed aside: the plight of refugees from the war zones as they poured into Austria and often Vienna (Hungary managed to deflect many), with consequent social tensions as the new arrivals needed food, housing, and jobs. Then there was the problem of housing and feeding nearly two million prisoners of war, a problem virtually unanticipated before the war. Even if some of the prisoners could be effective laborers, they still needed food, housing, and guards to keep them from fleeing, a task guards did not always fulfill. He pays less attention to the question of troops deployed in Serbia and in the east as occupation forces, though hundreds of thousands were on this duty.

The stern rule of the military over much of Austria (far less of Hungary) receives careful attention. Repeatedly, the civilian authorities tried to push back, with inconsistent success. For Conrad and his associates, a centralized Austria under military control suited them just fine, which meant no *Reichsrat* and an ineffective Stürgkh in power. And in this atmosphere, whether on the battlefield or the conquered areas, there were often reprisals against civilians, arbitrary executions, deportations, and a general insensitivity to the laws of war, though this eased after Karl became emperor.

Finally, Rauchensteiner portrays, almost as a novelist, the absolute chaos of the monarchy's last days. Even if you know the main turning points, the author has put them together so that you feel as if you are in the actual midst of chaos, with fear, uncertainty, mounting troop desertions, and peace beckoning even as the monarchy falls apart. The end becomes tragic. In a final church service in Vienna on 4 November 1918, to celebrate the name day of Karl, the mood was somber, not celebratory, and yet surprisingly wistful. As the author observes in the final sentence of the book: "But this entire scene was unreal" (p. 1010).

Any huge book will contain some factual errors and this study is not immune. Nor is the proofing always flawless and the translation, while readable, has far too many paragraphs starting with "However." Yet, for those teaching a course on the Habsburgs and the Great War, this is now an indispensable guide, either to preparing for lectures and seminars or simply exposing students to a prodigious product of a lifetime of work. The book will remain an essential reference.

I

Habsburgs schmutziger Krieg, an essay collection by four excellent Austrian historians, focuses upon a topic virtually ignored until very recently—the war crimes and savage reprisals conducted by Habsburg forces during the Great War. In 2009, Jonathan Gumz touched upon some of the issues in his study of the Habsburg army in Serbia, but his focus remained sturdily upon Serbia. Now, the canvas is expanded to include all fronts and the picture is sobering, indeed depressing.

Hannes Leidinger addresses, in two separate essays, why the topic has been neglected, while at the same time carefully phrasing the issues under discussion. He notes the swings of opinion from defense of the army and Emperor/King Franz Joseph to one of severe castigation of both institutions, with the legendary ruler now in our time labeled a "war criminal" (p. 11). Further, he sets the discussion in a transnational context, as the question of war crimes is being examined across Europe. The first and early studies focused on German atrocities in Belgium and France. Now all sectors of Europe are under examination. He carefully reminds readers of the problems caused by the confusion between civil and military relations, the problems of guerrilla warfare and who is the enemy, the impact of forced deportations, the summary executions often done with no procedural process, and all of this in the context of less than clear "laws of war." Much of this, he notes, could be called "war crimes," though one of the essays is especially clear in saying there is no issue of "genocide" in the Habsburg case.

After a chapter that tracks Vienna's decision to launch the war, Leidinger shows how quickly problems emerged for the army. Since it was widely assumed that Serbia had been responsible for the murders in Sarajevo, Serbs inside the monarchy and more importantly inside Serbia were suspect. But so also were Ruthenians in Galicia where Russophile groups had actively worked against Austria and Hungary before the war. The question became: who was loyal, who had betrayed us or might betray us, and who was in fact a soldier, a critical issue in Serbia where many of the army troops had no uniforms?

More crucially, once the armies began to operate in Serbia or in Russian territory, they were operating in a foreign environment where many residents were armed, prepared to resist, and often, because of language problems, unable to communicate. A further inflammatory situation arose in Serbia with wild talk of Serbian massacres of Habsburg forces, rumors that made it easy to arrest suspects, hang some as warning to others, and deport still others. Details of reprisals are explicit; in Lešnica, Serbia 109 persons were executed as a warning (p. 78).

In Galicia, thousands of residents were sent further inland in mass evacuations to avoid the actual fighting. Among those who stayed, especially around Przemyśl, the fighting meant casualties and official harassment. By 1917 some estimated that thousands of Ruthenians had been shot or arrested or deported (p. 85). Nor was the effort to mete out punishments just limited to the Army; in many instances Poles supported harsh countermeasures against the Ruthenians, nor were the Hungarians excessively merciful either.

If crimes against enemies were an issue, another noted also in the Rauchensteiner volume, was the deliberate deportation or internment of suspect populations. Verena Moritz puts things directly. For instance, perhaps as many as 46.000 South Slavs were interned in Doboj in Bosnia. The human tragedies represented by internments were compounded by catastrophic living conditions, little or no food, and frequent epidemics of disease. Similar in horror were the treatment of those who had merely fled the war. Their living conditions were also horrific, prompting wide complaints once the Austrian *Reichsrat* reopened in May 1917.

The mistreatment of war prisoners in many cases matched that of the civilians. The two million prisoners had many reasons to complain: harsh living conditions, punishments for minor infractions, work in dangerous conditions, and few distractions. Nor, ironically, did Habsburg soldiers, returning from Russian captivity receive a warm welcome; the authorities feared, correctly, that many had been infected by the radical Bolsheviks and

Two chapters address the legal aspects of Habsburg military authority as exercised during the war. If a virtual military dictatorship existed in much of Austria, with frequent military-civilian frictions over this relationship, the situation in Hungary was somewhat better, not least because Tisza blocked some of Conrad's most expansive claims of authority. Coupled with this problem was the actual administration of the Ukraine where the Habsburg military hoped for cooperation, gratitude, and food and got little in return. In part, Wolfram Dornik believes that the friction reflected the impact of colonial and imperial attitudes put into practice in the occupied areas, which for many residents let them fear that eventually they would fall under Habsburg rule.

The volume ends with a brief, useful sketch of the visual remembrances and portrayals of the war. Karin Moser notes the organized propaganda efforts made during the war, followed by attempts after the war to create myths on the one hand and ascribe guilt on the other—with Alfred Redl a favorite subject of movies. As the political squabbles in Austria accelerated in the interwar years, cinema productions shifted to inculcating the young with values of heroism and sacrifice. After 1945, attention went to families and the fate of family dynasties caught up in the war. Later television would turn its efforts to Austria and the war. And she provides a succinct summary of recent efforts by television productions before and during 2014 to address the centenary of the outbreak of the war. In short, she has given us a road map to study Austrian visual portrayals of the Great War as seen in movies and television. For foreign scholars, this is an exceptionally useful contribution.

Throughout the volume, the writers recognize the danger of using post Second World War standards to assess behavior after the first war. Yet they note that even during the war legal questions were raised about the treatment of civilians, especially once the *Reichsrat* reconvened. Nevertheless, from the start the Serbs got no benefit of the doubt and the memories of savagery of the Balkan Wars influenced those who now fought the Serbs. The "heat of battle" argument carries no weight for Leidinger, while he notes the widespread belief among Habsburg leaders of the Serbs as a "lesser" people or culture. Nor does he neglect the horrors committed on the Russian and Italian fronts, though the latter get less attention. But he also makes clear that the monarchy did not seek ethnic cleansing or genocide; it did not want to kill Serbs just to kill Serbs. Rather, it expected that the Serbs might be a part of a new and revamped monarchy after the war.

Finally, the book tracks, briefly, why no Habsburg leaders were held accountable after the war. Few wanted to revisit the past, veterans groups would have resisted any effort, and there was little incentive to do so. But now, with the collapse of the Soviet Union and access to new archival materials, it is possible to do a comparative analysis of the military actions of all of the powers. Further, the experiences in Bosnia in the 1990s when the brutality of war reached genocidal heights prompt new interest in all war crimes of the 20th and now 21st centuries. Different perspectives, new theoretical concepts, and more comparative data mean that the question of "dirty war" can be raised not only in regard to the former Habsburg monarchy, but also more broadly as it applies to all colonial wars and European countries.

War crimes are a feature of war; the heat of battle does cloud judgments, whether in Serbia or Galicia or Vietnam or Bosnia or Iraq. Reprisals do take place, sometimes accidentally, sometimes deliberately. The treatment of prisoners and refugees, whether in Syria or of Iraqis held in American prisons, is always problematic. This realization is the first step to putting limits into place, whether through a report on the Central Intelligence Agency and torture or by this book's daring attempt to bring Austro-Hungarian crimes into public discourse in the areas of the old monarchy. Some of their Austrian colleagues will surely be unhappy; the rest of us should congratulate them.

II

In mid-July 1914, General Conrad von Hötzendorf and his mistress, Gina von Reininghaus, spent a few days in Innichen high in the Dolomites, part of Vienna's deliberate strategy to lull the Serbs before the forthcoming ultimatum. The general loved the beauty of the Tyrol and enjoyed vacationing there as he hiked, sketched, and enjoyed the company of his future wife. Although he had more than once advocated war against his Italian ally, the war in 1914 saw Rome declare its neutrality. Few expected that to endure and the ones certain to lose were those who lived in the border land of Puster Valley, which was either to be negotiated away to Italy or to become the terrain of an eventual war. With Franz Joseph's adamant opposition to any land cessation, war came to the Dolomites with a fury. The entire area soon became one of the most heavily contested regions of the Great War.

Grenzgang: Das Pustertal und der Krieg 1914-1918 is a superb example of commemorative history, a conscious product of the centennial anniversary of the start of the Great War. Carefully edited by Martin Kofler, who had nearly a dozen collaborators, the volume makes full use of the extensive photographic collection of the *Tiroler Archiv für photographische Dokumentation und Kunst*, who created a second exhibition on the Pustertal at war. While many might see this as a catalog or coffee table book, that interpretation misrepresents its importance to historians. The essays provide a historical and economic framework of the area, followed by a set of complementary pictures. Then there are more narrative sketches, describing in one instance what happened to the town of Sexten in the midst of the war zone and, in another instance, analyzing life in support areas such as Lienz and Bruneck. Although there are scenes of forts, mountain redoubts, and occasional gruesome pictures of the actual front, the photographs mostly remind viewers of the fate of those caught in the middle of the fighting. And these photographs, along with the work of artists commissioned during the war, provide a nearly unique glimpse at the actual front lines; there are no counterparts to Serbia or Galicia for historians to consider.

The essays also provide reminders that the Tyrolean militia provided essential manpower in keeping the Italian army at bay. This was no easy task since the cream of the Tyrolean forces had died in the first weeks of the war in Galicia, on the far side of the monarchy. Indeed, of the 35.000 men who crossed the country, only a third remained after the disasters of September and October. These losses in turn meant that the *Standschützen*, the local militia, had to step forward to assist and buttress regular forces in 1915; they did so to the number of 32.000 men in May 1915 and remained essential for the rest of the war. To their credit, no Italian soldier reached Tyrolean land until the final collapse in 1918.

Regional histories represent building blocks in our understanding of the impact of wars and revolutions upon those who actually experience the events. In many instances, urban areas are well served by such histories, while rural and remote ones, even as beautiful as the Dolomites, are neglected. This volume rights the balance, while offering visual evidence of both the beauty of the land and the pain and suffering that it experienced. It is a remarkable achievement by a fine group of scholars. A final note: Conrad's beloved Innichen is now a part of Italy, the country he most wanted to fight; history and irony are always linked.

III

Alma Hannig's *Franz Ferdinand* offers scholars still another perspective on the *Thronfolger*, based on exhaustive research and the effective use of private archives. When juxtaposed with Jean-Paul Bled's *Franz Ferdinand: Der eigensinnige Thronfolger* (Vienna: Böhlau, 2013), these two works provide a comprehensive assessment of the assassinated archduke.[1] Access to the private papers of the Hohenberg and Hohenlohe families, as well as other collections, allow her to introduce personal comments never before seen.

1 On the Bled volume, see Samuel R Williamson, Jr., "The Odd Couple," in *1914: Austria-Hungary, the Origins, and the First Year of World War I*, ed. Günter Bischof, Ferdinand Karlhofer and idem (New Orleans, Innsbruck: UNO Press and iup, 2014), 351-356.

If Bled's volume is a more conventional biography, Hannig's study, after setting the historiographical context on Franz Ferdinand, addresses aspects of his life in serial fashion. Among the topics covered are his efforts to master Hungarian; family notebooks indicate serious efforts to learn the language, with more success in the written than spoken word; in this instance the private archive provides a rebuttal to the usual view of his language skills, though he did not know English. But his struggles with Hungarian were accompanied, as Hannig makes clear, by his dislike of Hungarians and his adamant refusal to meet Tisza.

The private archives also buttress our understanding of the archduke's trip around the world. Not only did he keep a diary, he privately published a two-volume commentary on his experience. Hannig sees little evidence that his exposure to the United States had any impact on his later consideration of a possible federal approach to the future of the monarchy. In fact, she makes it clear that he disliked Americans and his experiences in America. Moreover, she concludes that, despite the prolonged efforts to craft plans for the monarchy after Emperor Franz Joseph, that in fact few actual plans for constitutional change were settled in 1914. In this she and Bled more or less agree; Hungary was the chief problem and that could only be addressed incrementally.

The courtship and marriage to Sophie Chotek receive insightful attention as the archduke worked carefully to conceal his contacts with her before it became public. One new facet in the story emerges: concerns in Berlin that the archduke would marry suitably and fear that he might opt for a relationship that would hurt Germany. Eventually, *Kaiser* Wilhelm II had no cause for concern; indeed, over time he would pay special attention to Sophie. But Hannig correctly reminds readers that though the two men met often and shared many similar views such as naval power and love of hunting (Franz Ferdinand spent 200 days annually shooting), they had their differences. The *Thronfolger* wanted better relations with Russia, did not share Wilhelm's esteem for Tisza, and differed with him over Italy. Franz Ferdinand appreciated the importance of the German connection but did not allow it to becloud his own Habsburg views.

The impact of the marriage controversy on his relationship with Franz Joseph receives attention, as does his growing distance from his uncle in later years. In particular, Franz Ferdinand came to dislike the old monarch's failure to confront Hungary. On the other hand, she explores the emperor's decision to allow his nephew to have his own military chancellery and, over time, access to many of the state papers. Nor did he resist Franz Ferdinand's efforts to push forward men like Conrad and

Alois Lexa von Aehrenthal for key positions even if he personally may have had doubts about them.

Brief chapters explore Franz Ferdinand's relationship with the Catholic Church: respectful, devoted, but pragmatic and influenced by his hatred of Italy; his understanding of the modern role of the press and the need to have some support from the print media; and his scorn for political parties and his resistance to attempts to placate the Czech factions in the *Reichsrat*.

Her examination of the archduke's role in foreign policy tracks fairly familiar ground. He valued the alliance with Berlin but wanted closer relations with Russia; he saw the Balkans as a "*Lebenfrage*" issue, a view that Wilhelm did not understand; and wanted close ties with Romania since it might help in any confrontation with Hungary. He also had hopes for better relations with Britain, an area where his own personal visits to London, he hoped, would help, though in fact they appear to have had no impact on Sir Edward Grey and the Foreign Office, which by 1914 treated Vienna as an extension of Berlin.

In her analysis of the Balkan Wars, the author goes to great lengths to suggest that Franz Ferdinand wanted war against the Serbs in the fall of 1912 and worked for a while toward that end. This reviewer made this argument in the 1970s, as have others. To be sure he was no inveterate "peace prince," and as she recounts, he went to Berlin in November 1912 and got the *Kaiser* to back Vienna for a war. In this analysis Hannig makes excellent use of material from the diaries of Prince Gottfried zu Hohenlohe-Schillingfürst, who served in the diplomatic corps. Interestingly, there is no material from the archduke's military chancellery, which kept him well informed on the course of the Balkan fighting.

In any event, despite Franz Ferdinand's momentary bluster, she concludes that Franz Joseph and Count Berchtold brought his war caper to an end. The two men would also use Prince Hohenlohe as a conduit to help ease tensions with Russia during the spring of 1913. Thereafter, the *Thronfolger* backed Berchtold and supported a careful, cautious policy; indeed, he disliked the *démarche* sent to Belgrade in October 1913, though he showered praise on the foreign minister after its success. As most commentators have noted earlier, the *Thronfolger* realized that a war might be dangerous to the future of the monarchy, a view missing from the decision-making after his murder at Sarajevo.

Franz Ferdinand the man emerges in new details in this biography. Photographs from the Hohenberg private collection show aspects of the world trip, pictures of the archduke in civilian dress, and snapshots of personal moments off the public stage. His love for his family and his sense of honor were steadfast, even as he realized that in the wider world he was not especially loved. While he had many supporters and advisers, few loved him. Even some childhood friends, who remained closed to him and were important in court circles, had their reservations. For example, Gottfried Hohenlohe, scheduled to become the new Habsburg ambassador to Berlin in 1914 and one of those pressing for war in July 1914, appreciated the archduke's intellectual ability but found his mistrust of individuals, his temperament, and his strange sense of duty disturbing. As he scribbled bluntly in his diary in 1912: "Altogether not good qualities for a future ruler" (p. 242).

Hannig ends her study with a question often skirted: could Franz Ferdinand have rescued the monarchy had he lived? She tracks the pros and cons, noting the problems with Hungary and the Czechs. She doubts his reform plans would have been easy to implement and correctly stresses the changed geopolitical position of Austria-Hungary after the Balkan Wars. Nor could he have been sure how other governments—not least Germany—would have reacted to his plans, given his favorable views toward Russia. On the other hand, she believes he would have kept the peace if it served Habsburg interests. She concludes her study with the careful observation that we cannot know if he would have saved the monarchy; there were too many unknowns. But he might, she notes, have handled it exactly as Franz Joseph.

Alas, in 1914, Emperor/King Franz Joseph did not act as prudently as in the past. According to Rauchensteiner, he agreed, if not encouraged, a war of revenge against Serbia. This was not the earlier, careful, prudent ruler that had survived. Rather this was a ruler who put the fate of the monarchy on the gaming table, with few good cards and weaker prospects.

IV

This long review concludes with three quick observations. First, the current study of Austria-Hungary on the eve of war in 1914 and then during the war is vibrant, assertive, and imaginative. Diligent, gifted scholars are producing substantial studies. There has been success in locating new sources and new archives and a willingness to revisit older issues and personalities. Second, there are no topics that are now "off-limits" for historians, whether they are aspects of the dirty war or the competence of leadership or the self-serving actions of ethnic groups to further their own interests, whether they concern German-Austrian, Czechs, South Slavs, Poles or Hungarians. It was the genius of the Habsburg myth to keep these interactive forces in check and inside a single political grouping. A war almost certainly guaranteed some of this would change, yet the decision-makers blissfully went to war. A short war, they hoped, would do wonders; they never seemed to have considered the impact of a long war.

Finally, the emergence of regional histories and the use of photographic archives offer many opportunities for the interaction of narrative and visual commentaries, interactions that make history alive for those who want to study it. In an age where visual images and commentary join, whether on Facebook or Google or the print press, these new approaches offer ways to increase the public's appreciation of history. If historians could succeed in this task, we might be hopeful for the future of historians even as we can remain dismayed by the events of the Great War.

1914-2014: Austria's Commemoration of World War I

Martin Eichtinger

Introduction

During the "2014 Year of European Contemporary History" governments, media, historians, and the public have focused on and were inundated by commemorations and celebrations of major historic events: 100 years since the beginning of World War I, seventy-five years since the beginning of World War II, twenty-five years since the fall of the Berlin Wall, and the ten-year anniversary of the enlargement of the European Union (EU) to Central and Eastern Europe.

The two World War catastrophes of the 20th century as well as the shift of paradigms caused by the fall of the Iron Curtain shaped today's Austria, her role in the international community as well as her vision for the future of Europe.

While commemorating the events of 1914 which led to the unleashing of World War I, the Austrian government decided to focus on the lessons learned and to promote the idea that the view back on a common European history should reinforce the commitment of European Union member states to the European peace project, i.e. the European Union.

At the same time, the commemorations should remind European leaders that the region of WWI's inception still awaits its integration into the European Union. This paper will focus on the efforts of the Austrian government to offer an overview of current historical research on WWI by commissioning a committee of eminent historians who published a summary report prepared by Austrian researchers on the occasion of the centennial commemoration of the outbreak of WWI.

It will also summarize the events which Austrian institutions prepared in Austria and worldwide for 2014. Finally, the paper will report on

Austrian efforts to organize commemorative sessions at the European level, in the framework of the Council of Europe and in the institutions of the European Union.

Preparations for 2014

By 2011, preparations for the commemoration of World War I had started in the Austrian Foreign Ministry and other parts of the government. By that time, many of the big Austrian museums and cultural institutions, such as the Museum of Military History, the National Archives, the National Library—but also art museums and major cultural institutions in Austria's provinces—had already made plans for major exhibitions on the "the great seminal catastrophe of this century," as U.S. diplomat George F. Kennan called World War I in 1979.[1]

Over the decades, World War I, its roots and its course of events, had played a comparatively minor role in Austrian historical research, as the emphasis of Austrian historical writing was put on Austria's role during the Nazi period of WWII.

Early in 2012, the Austrian Foreign Ministry (today: Austrian Federal Ministry for Europe, Integration and Foreign Affairs), established an interministerial working group under my chairmanship with the goal of a regular coordination of WWI related events. Professor Manfried Rauchensteiner, an eminent historian on the subject of WWI, who published his much acclaimed book *The First World War and the End of the Habsburg Monarchy, 1914-1918* in July 2013,[2] repeatedly pointed to the fact that the Austrian government would have to officially take a position on World War I and Austria's role in 1914 during the commemorations in 2014.

The interministerial working group would commission historians to work on an analytical document that would serve as the basis for official statements to be delivered by the Austrian political leadership as well as by Austrian official representatives abroad. Some media had started to question Austria's role in World War I. In one instance, the demand was put forward that the Republic of Austria should use the centenary commemorations to come to grips with Austria's guilt as the party ultimately responsible for World War I and should beg forgiveness from the other parties involved in the war.

1 George F. Kennan, *The Decline of Bismarck's European Order: Franco-Russian Relations, 1875-1890* (Princeton: Princeton University Press, 1979), 3.

2 Manfried Rauchensteiner, *The First World War and the End of the Habsburg Monarchy, 1914-1918* (Vienna: Böhlau Verlag, 2014); see also Samuel Williamson's review essay in this volume.

In March 2013, the Australian professor of modern European history at Cambridge, Christopher Clark, published his meticulously researched book on World War I titled *The Sleepwalkers–How Europe Went to War in 1914*. This book very much influenced the ensuing debate of the history of World War I, in particular the question of guilt and responsibility for the war. Clark argues that none of the powers of the pre-war period really meant to wage an all-out war, but, rather, they sleepwalked into the catastrophe.

Let me quote from the speech that Christopher Clark delivered on 27 July 2014 on the occasion of the opening ceremony of the Salzburg Festival,[3] which also focused on the centenary in its festival program. As in his book, Christopher Clark did not accept the blame game to be played regarding the causes of World War I. I quote:

> The decisive element for the complexity of the events of 1914 were, however, the rapid changes in the international system.... these were no long-term historical transitions, no *forces profondes*, which had unfolded across generations, but short-term new alignments–*phénomènes de courte durée*....The Great War did not arrive slowly, his approaching was accelerated drastically by the brute force of the events.

And Clark continues and I quote again:

> There is no reason to look condescending upon the decision makers of the year 1914–in the sense of what E. P. Thompson called "the infinite condescension of posterity," as if these were the conceited representatives of an entirely overcome age. The complexity of the crisis of the year 1914 is to be attributed partially to human behavioural patterns which can still today be found on the political stage.[4]

Debates in the interministerial working group focused on the question of which key topics an Austrian official document on World War I would need to tackle?

Ambassador Christian Prosl, who was later appointed Special Representative of the Austrian Foreign Ministry for the Commemorations

3 See <http://www.salzburg.gv.at/festspielrede2014.pdf> (13 January 2015).
4 Ibid.

1914-2014 (see below), wrote a draft paper in which he outlined the most important elements for such a paper. Among those were:

- A brief summary of events
- Homage to the victims
- Remarks on the role of commemorations in a democratic society (*Erinnerungskultur*)
- Rejection of nationalistic celebrations
- Support of European, transnational, and international commemorations
- Lessons to be learned from WWI (analysis of the pre-war period, the war and its consequences)
- Forward-looking commitment to the project of European integration
- Austria's role (the question of responsibility for the war), also in view of its relations to the successor states of the monarchy)
- Organization of events in cooperation with media, special emphasis on the youth

The working group discussed all relevant aspects of national and international commemoration activities and projects. Originally, it was also tasked with deliberating on projects in the context of the 200th anniversary of the Congress of Vienna (1814-1815). However, it was soon decided that in view of the many commemorations and anniversaries during the year 2014, all major projects regarding the Congress of Vienna's anniversary would be shifted to 2015.

The discussions in the interministerial working group eventually shifted from the idea of an official document to a commissioned paper of historians in the form of a multifaceted presentation of research results. The six involved Austrian ministries (Foreign Affairs, Federal Chancellery, Culture and Education, Science and Research, Interior and Defence) finally agreed to commission contributions by historians to a basic document that would have the character of a modular collection of brief papers. This document, which was published in September 2013, was a valuable resource for politicians and diplomats that summarized which research topics the historians saw as most relevant.[5]

5 See <http://www.bmeia.gv.at/fileadmin/user_upload/bmeia/media/Vertretungsbehoerden/Belgrad/Grundlagenpapier_1914-2014_Englisch_Beidseitiger_Druck_01.pdf>; for the German version <http://www.bmeia.gv.at/fileadmin/user_upload/Zentrale/Kultur/Schwerpunkte/Grundlagenpapier_1914_-_2014.pdf> (13 January 2015).

Ten historians—Christa Hämmerle, Gabriella Hauch, Stefan Karner, Helmut Konrad, Wolfgang Maderthaner, Verena Moritz, Anton Pelinka, Oliver Rathkolb, Manfried Rauchensteiner, and Heidemarie Uhl—contributed to a comprehensive report (*Grundlagenpapier*) that earned high praise in European capitals.

The articles covered the following topics:

- Austria-Hungary and World War I: an overview
- Reflections on the question of war guilt
- Democracy, war, and peace: comments on the general framework of WWI
- The liberating element of the courageous deed: the "dark" side of modernity in Vienna around 1914
- Social militarization
- The war and the media
- Front experience
- Warfare and humanitarian consequences
- Women's and gender history of World War I
- Consequences of World War I, impact of the "front experience" of World War I on the development of Austria in the interwar period, and World War I in the memory of Austria and (Central) Europe – traditions of remembrance from a (trans)national perspective

The paper also includes an annex with the dates of major events of the period.

Starting in 2012, the Austrian Foreign Ministry also assembled and regularly updated three lists covering events dedicated to the commemoration of WWI. One list included exhibitions and conferences in Austria, one showed events to be organized internationally, and one focused on international projects with Austrian participation. The three lists grew at an enormous speed and it became difficult to keep them updated. However, they were used by all government agencies in Austria and by the Austrian missions abroad and became an indispensable tool for event planning and the dispersal of information to the media.

For all official commemorative events, the Foreign Ministry commissioned a special logo that was reprinted on a stamp which was issued on the occasion of the centenary.

International Preparations of the Commemoration and the Austrian Special Representative

Following the presentation of French Ambassador Joseph Zimet's report on the commemoration of the Great War in September 2011, the French Ministry of Defence invited a number of countries, including Austria, to a first stock-taking event on WWI activities in April 2012.

The report, which proposed that France should extend the commemorations to the period 2014-20, thereby including the Treaties of Paris, suggested that France should position itself as the center of the first worldwide commemorations in the age of globalization. The commemorations would concentrate on a reinforcement of Franco-German relations as the beginning of a new chapter in the relationship between the two countries. The report also saw the Western Front of WWI as the epicenter of the first global conflict of mankind and did not even mention the Austrian-Hungarian Monarchy and its role in WWI.

The German government appointed Ambassador Féaux de la Croix and Ambassador Andreas Meitzner as Special Representatives for the WWI commemorations. In March 2013, they published a brief position paper on the 100th anniversary of the beginning of WWI in which the German government stated that a major goal was the dignified commemoration of the millions of victims and to do this wherever possible jointly with international partners. According to the paper, the commemoration of the war should not divide nations, but rather unite them in common responsibility.

On 11 October 2012, British Prime Minister David Cameron presented the British plans for the commemoration of World War I at the Imperial War Museum and announced that the British government would dedicate funds of more than fifty million pounds to commemoration projects. The British program was to be organized in cooperation with the Imperial War Museum, the Commonwealth War Graves Commission, and the Heritage Lottery Fund. Additionally, a special homepage would be inaugurated for the First World War Centenary Partnership.[6]

At the annual Austrian Foreign Cultural Conference 2012, Austrian Vice-Chancellor and Foreign Minister Michael Spindelegger officially designated former Austrian Ambassador to Berlin and Washington Christian Prosl as Special Representative of the Foreign Ministry for the Commemorations 1914-2014.

Ambassador Prosl, who had only recently officially retired, immediately joined the international network of WWI coordinators. He participated in

6 See <http://www.1914.org> (13 January 2015).

several meetings of the international coordinators and actively contributed to all Austrian WWI activities. In a large number of meetings, he contributed to a national and international coordination of Austrian activities in 2014.

An important political goal of Austria's engagement in WWI activities was the desire to further an all-European commemoration of WWI in order to forge an ever-greater commitment to the European project for the future. This forward-looking attitude should complement legitimate national commemorations and focus on the future instead of the past. Already in January 2013, the Austrian Representative to the European Union in Brussels had been instructed to meet with the Chief of Staff of EU President Van Rompuy in order to discuss a European commemorative event during the European Council meeting in June 2014.

The non-paper which he submitted on this occasion read as follows:

> The European Union is indeed an outstanding example for the fact that the Nations of Europe have overcome their former attitudes of mistrust and belligerence. The EU has helped to transform Europe into a continent of lasting peace. It has consequently been awarded the 2012 Nobel Peace Prize. It is important to reaffirm that the EU will ensure peace and the well-being of peoples and nations also in the future. Therefore, it only seems natural to hold the 2014 key commemorative events in the framework or in the margins of a European Council meeting in Brussels, e.g. in June 2014. On this occasion, the importance and the success of the EU in ensuring peace in Europe and the World should be recalled. But we also will have to underline our responsibility in securing a peaceful and prosperous future for our continent as well as for the world as a whole. Such an event would highlight the link between past and future, in particular for the benefit of future generations.

Over the following months, this idea was repeatedly put forward, particularly by Ambassador Prosl, to several key actors of the EU. Eventually, on 11 March 2014, President Van Rompuy issued a press release under the heading of "EU leaders to commemorate World War I on 26 June 2014."[7]

> At the invitation of President Herman Van Rompuy, the June European Council will open with a commemoration of the

7 <http://www.consilium.europa.eu/uedocs/cms_data/docs/pressdata/en/ec/141440.pdf> (13 January 2015).

> outbreak of the First World War. This two-day meeting, held on the eve of the anniversary of the Sarajevo incident of 28 June 1914, will begin in Ypres on Thursday 26 June 2014 with a ceremony at the Ménin Gate starting around 17.00, followed by a dinner of the Heads of State or Government in the City Hall. The European Council meeting will resume its usual program in Brussels on Friday 27 June.

Finally, Austria's proposal had been recognized.

From November 2013 to May 2014, Austria held the Chairmanship of the Committee of Ministers of the Council of Europe. The Austrian Permanent Representative at the Council of Europe in Strasbourg introduced the idea of a joint statement on World War I by the Council of Europe to be approved at the Committee of Ministers meeting in Vienna on May 5-6, 2014. Although the text had been carefully drafted, the events in Ukraine made it impossible to get enough attention for the proclamation and the necessary support for such a statement.

The declaration would have also been reconfirmed at a Western Balkans conference the Austrian government invited to Vienna on 3 June 2014. Due to the political situation, the commemorative part of the conference (which would have included an introductory film and a music performance of a quartet of the Vienna Philharmonic playing compositions from the pre-war period from the region of Southeast Europe) had to be reduced to commemorative speeches by Austrian Foreign Minister Sebastian Kurz and EU Commissioner for Enlargement Štefan Füle.

The Austrian Commemorative Events in 2014

The extensive series of commemorative events of World War I started in January 2014 with an exhibition of WWI posters (focusing on the propaganda war) at the Federal Ministry of the Interior and a lecture by Professor Manfried Rauchensteiner at the Austrian Foreign Ministry on 29 January.

On this occasion the new Austrian Foreign Minister Sebastian Kurz expressed his hope that "the public commemoration will trigger more comprehensive preoccupation with World War I, which will help us understand the great potential of the European project and give us the opportunity to add our ideas to the advancement of Europe. Only if we know our own history will we be able to push Europe ahead with enthusiasm." He gave a brief introduction to the historic events and referred to their current relevance, above all for young people. He announced that in cooperation with different partners, the network of Austrian representations abroad would organize more than 120 events to mark the commemorative year. "I am confident that we will be able to make good use of the commemorative year to deal with the many facets of our history and to instill young people with enthusiasm for Europe," he said.

One of the premiere exhibitions which were organized for the centenary is the exhibition of the Austrian National Library "To my Peoples." It was officially opened in March 2014 and shows objects and documents from the First World War collection. On the occasion of the official opening, Federal President Heinz Fischer pointed to the fact that millions of people were helpless in light of a political elite who wanted to be victorious in the war. Eventually, there were only losers of the war who distinguished themselves by the degree of their losses. At the same time—so President Fischer remarked—"we look in disbelief at the testimonies of a war frenzy which carried away most people at the outset of the war. Hardly a voice was to be heard which stood up against this frenzy."[8]

Federal President Heinz Fischer also spoke on 18 June 2014 on the occasion of the official commemorative event "Peace and War" at the Austrian National Library, commemorating the 100th anniversary of the death of Nobel Peace Laureate Bertha von Suttner and the 100th anniversary of the outbreak of WWI. After a short show of still movies on the horrors of the war, accompanied by the eerie "Duo for Violin and Cello" composed by Hungarian composer Zoltan Kodaly in 1914, President Fischer touched on the issue of responsibility for the outbreak of World War I. He said:

> Today, a hundred years after the outbreak of the First World War, the question of who is responsible for the outbreak of this disaster of the century remains an issue of discussions. And still one can feel that the answer given from the point of view of the individual nations involved in this war, but also from the perspective of individual historians varies greatly or is—at least—characterised by different nuances and emphases. And what is more, this event still arouses emotions. It is true that the Austrian heir to the throne Franz Ferdinand—as

8 Austrian Federal President Heinz Fischer in his speech at the opening of the exhibition "To My Peoples" at the Austrian National Library on 12 March 2014, at <http://www.bundespraesident.at/newsdetail/artikel/eroeffnung-der-ausstellung-an-meine-voelker-der-erste-weltkrieg-1914-1918> (13 January 2015).

> already mentioned—was assassinated in Sarajevo. It is true that the ill-fated ultimatum of 23rd July 1914 was drawn up in Vienna. It is true that the Austrian-Hungarian Monarchy has a considerable share in the responsibility for the outbreak of the First World War. What is also true, however, is that other factors, other individuals, and other countries also have their respective share in the fatal course developments took 100 years ago. But all this does not prevent us today from enjoying excellent relations free from prejudice with what were the warring states of the First World War and naturally also with the young states of the Western Balkans. From Austria's point of view, the wounds suffered at the time should have healed—and healed they have.[9]

Between 2011 and 2014, Sarajevo was seen as the logical venue for major WWI commemorations. The City of Sarajevo had unsuccessfully bid for selection as European Capital of Culture in 2014, touting itself as the city in which the tragedy of WWI was triggered as well as the host of the Olympic Winter Games of 1984. Due to legal reasons, Sarajevo could not become European Capital of Culture in spite of major support by European cultural ministers. As compensation, the European Commission pledged considerable funds for commemorative projects in 2014 which were partially administered by the European Delegation in Sarajevo, partially by the foundation "Sarajevo–Heart of Europe."[10]

Plans for the events in Sarajevo included a meeting of heads of state and government on or around June 28, the date of the assassination of Archduke Franz Ferdinand and his wife in 2014, a meeting of ministers of culture of the EU, and much more.

The Vienna Philharmonic Orchestra played an extraordinary concert on 28 June 2014 at the historic city hall of Sarajevo, originally built by the Monarchy and renovated for the event. The concert, which was broadcast by the European Broadcast Union, was a major success and was shown in more than thirty countries in Europe. In a competition for the project money of the "Sarajevo–Heart of Europe" foundation, Austria was very successful: of approx. one million Euros which the Foundation

9 See <http://www.bundespraesident.at/newsdetail/artikel/100-todestag-von-bertha-von-suttner100-jahre-ausbruch-erster-weltkrieg> (13 January 2014); text in German language followed by the English translation.

10 See <http://www.sarajevosrceeurope.org> (13 January 2014).

administered on behalf of the European Commission, Austrian projects with a volume of € 260.000 were approved. Among them was the public viewing of the Vienna Philharmonic Orchestra's concert in Sarajevo, in order to allow those who could not get hold of tickets for the city hall to also watch the concert. Other projects included an art exhibition of Austrian and Bosnian artists ("SHARE–Too much history, more future!") and a conference of international historians ("The Long Shots of Sarajevo").

On 21 June 2014, the Austrian Foreign Ministry was co-organizer of an international event at Harmannsdorf Castle, home of the Austrian peace activist and Peace Nobel Prize winner Bertha von Suttner, on the occasion of the 100th anniversary of her death.

Both the Salzburg Festival and the Bregenz Festival saw a focus on World War I at the opening speeches. The commemoration of the centenary of the outbreak of World War I constituted an important focus of Austria's cultural work in all cultural fora, embassies, and consulates abroad. More than 120 events were organized or co-organized in Belgium, Bosnia and Herzegovina, Croatia, the Czech Republic, France, Hungary, Lithuania, Poland, Russia, Serbia, Sweden, Switzerland, Turkey, Ukraine, United Kingdom, the United States, and many other countries. A special emphasis was put on projects with the enemies of WWI. The list of events included exhibitions, conferences, symposia, education programs, and artistic projects. My directorate general developed a traveling exhibition, "1914–The eventful lull before the storm," reflecting the developments in Austria immediately before WWI in politics, society, arts, and culture which was shown in several locations and countries during this year.

The list of commemorative projects, events, and exhibitions in Austria is too long to be discussed here in detail. I would just like to point to major exhibitions at the Austrian National Library, at Schallaburg Castle in Lower Austria and Artstetten Castle (where Archduke Franz Ferdinand and his wife are buried), at the Military History Museum and the *Wien Museum* in Vienna, and in many provincial museums. Of all the conferences and symposia that were held in Austria, "Homefront–Women, Media and the War. On Role Models and Myths from WWI to today" at the Austrian parliament should be mentioned.

Many commemorative events took place in Austria's federal provinces. For example, the European Region Tyrol-South Tyrol-Trentino organized an event in the Polish city of Cracow in which the governors of all three provinces and 400 students from the region committed themselves to the message of "Never Again" and the Carinthian government invited students and youth to a commemorative *enquête* in the Carinthian archives, to name just a few of a large number of commemorations. In addition to thousands of media articles and documentaries, hundreds of new books have been published during the year 2014 in Austria. Among several award-winning productions was the documentation series by the Austrian Broadcasting Corporation ORF called "14–Diaries of the First World War."

Conclusion

In Austria, the centenary commemorations of the beginning of World War I showed an unprecedented interest in its roots, its horrors, and its consequences for the history of the 20th century. Hardly an institution, be it museum or other public institution, did not include a commemorative exhibition in its program.

World War I, which has been dealt with by Austrian historical researchers and institutions to a much lesser degree than WWII, became the focus of major Austrian official events and initiatives. The commemoration of World War I reached an unexpected intensity, including not only political events, historical conferences, scientific publications and exhibitions, but also events associated with the media and the cultural sector.

Although the federal government did not issue an official declaration on the centenary of the assassination of Archduke Franz Ferdinand or on the centenaries of the declaration of war and the beginning of the war, official statements by Federal President Fischer and members of the Austrian government on several commemorative occasions dealt comprehensively with Austria's role in World War I. While Austria's responsibility was clearly acknowledged, all statements reflected the historical analysis that other countries and individuals also had their respective share in the tragic course of those events 100 years ago.

Austria's decision to focus on transnational, international, and European commemorations of the centenary, rather than confining it to a national retrospect, certainly contributed to the efforts of reaching a common European narrative of World War I. Despite its limited resources, Austria organized and co-organized a large number of important contributions to the worldwide commemorations.

Austria's diplomatic efforts to initiate European commemorative events and declarations—which also included a clear commitment to the European integration process as the greatest peace project in Europe—only partially succeeded due to political developments in Europe. Austria would have liked to see a declaration by the former war-parties that WWI was—although tragic and sad—a period of European history that is behind us; events such as the ones that occurred in WWI are, fortunately, unthinkable in today's European Union (the events in Ukraine conjure up some of the nasty ghosts of the past as far as the rest of Europe is concerned), and the EU should reinforce Europe's commitment to European integration and to the success of the European project. Even from a perspective of 100 years later, questions of who was responsible for the outbreak of WWI led to heated debates in some European countries and did not allow full reconciliation. A common European narrative of World War I still needs to be developed.

Book Reviews

Frank Trommler, *Kulturmacht ohne Kompass: Deutsche auswärtige Kulturbeziehungen im 20. Jahrhundert* (Cologne: Böhlau Verlag, 2014)

Emil Brix

There is no doubt that it is very valuable to write a study about an important aspect of international relations which is—in spite of the groundbreaking works of Joseph Nye and Samuel Huntington on the crucial role of culture as "soft power"—neither well documented nor thoroughly researched. Therefore, the history of cultural diplomacy and the role of culture as a "soft power" for national identity building as well as for the reputation and position of individual countries in an international context rightfully deserve our attention. What makes this topic complicated for any researcher is the fact that it demands an inter- or even transdisciplinary approach which covers the grounds of diplomatic and political history as well as institutional history—the history of ideas and cultural studies. In the book under review, it is obvious that the author is well aware of this challenge, but it may be fair to say that the book is an interesting hybrid between a pertinent long-winded polemical essay (732 pages) and a compilation of facts taken from the political and institutional history of German cultural diplomacy and nation building.

Frank Trommler wrote this book with an ambitious double objective. It is not only the first comprehensive study of German cultural diplomacy in the 20th century but also an attempt to understand the significant role of different perceptions of "German culture" in the long and difficult process of German nation building. The grand narrative of this book is impressive. The idea of Germany as a cultural power ("*Kulturmacht*") has been flawed from its conception in the early 1900; however, in spite of the catastrophes of two World Wars, the Nazi regime, and decades of two separate German states, there has been more continuity in the official political use of "culture" than one would expect after all these developments. His arguments are convincingly presented by interweaving the institutional development of German cultural diplomacy from the German Empire to the reunification of Germany after 1989 with broader questions of German political identity and how it has been perceived in other countries. Also the comparison with developments in the cultural diplomacy instruments of other large countries strengthens his argument that the political use of "culture" provides an interesting perspective on processes of national self-understanding.

For Germany, Trommler portrays the 1960s as a turning point away from the idea of a "*Kulturmacht*" towards an identity with less mobilization of national traditions and values. He presents in quite some detail how much the notion of Germany as a superior civilization or culture is a part of official German policies and thinking before and during both World Wars. Additionally, he touches on how much changing attitudes in society depend on generational issues and on the strength of civil society. Regarding politics of image and reputation, German cultural diplomacy has come a long way from its beginning in the empire as a statement of the superiority of German scientists and science to its modern day activities which aim to create platforms for cultural dialogue in order to present Germany worldwide as a liberal modern democracy.

The book also tries to answer the intractable question of what the author calls the mental and geographical territory of German culture. The often manifold and changing identities of German-speaking populations in the Habsburg Monarchy and later in Austria, of German-speaking minorities in other countries, and of the Central European Jewish population are described in their contribution to mobilizing German culture. These parts of the book are the least convincing because they are written from a German perspective without taking into account most of the relevant research on Austrian identity building, on Jewish intellectual history, on anti-Semitism, on Zionism, and on the sociology of language minorities.

It is certainly of interest to describe the growing dilemmas of German-speaking Austrian intellectuals around 1900—many of them of Jewish origin—who felt more and more driven to decide whether they felt "German" or "Austrian." But official Austrian cultural policies at the end of the Habsburg Monarchy showed none of the imperialistic national fervor the German Empire thrived in. Austria-Hungary was a multinational state that had to make sure—for its very existence—that it offered alternatives to ethnic national mobilization. It is equally interesting to discuss the Jewish "assimilation" to German culture in the 19th Century and how this helped to modernize German culture. In this context, one might also discuss why a large number of "assimilated" German and Austrian Jews did not want to identify themselves with the notion of a specific Jewish culture and at the same time why it was not in Germany but in multinational Austria-

Hungary where Zionism as an ethnic ideology started. But these chapters in the book are not really conclusive, do not add much to the grand narrative of the book, and give the impression that the author simply deplores the loss of Austrian multinational traditions and Jewish modernizing traditions within a common German culture. This feeling of loss would be a good starting point for a polemical essay rather than a thorough analysis of the history of German cultural relations.

Both Austrian history and Central European Jewish history are topics in their own right and should not be alluded to merely to prove an allegedly special relationship with German culture. The increase of ideas of ethnic identity building in the late Habsburg Monarchy from Herzl to Hitler had more to do with the political challenges of a multinational state at the beginning of mass politics than with the mobilization of culture in German politics. This also holds true for the intellectual responses of German-speaking Austrian writers such as Hofmannsthal and Musil. It is interesting that the author spends more time describing intellectual life in Vienna around 1900 than he does describing the development of cultural policies in the German Democratic Republic. Admittedly, "Vienna 1900" was more fascinating, but the history of the GDR is certainly more topical in a study about German international cultural relations.

About Austria, Trommler rightfully comments that its national identity officially changed from being "the second or better German state" after the First World War to being a "*Kulturstaat*" after the Second World War. And his criticism of Austria's official denial from 1945 until the early 1990s of any responsibility for the deeds of the Nazi regime is correct. But, again, why should these facts have a prominent place in a history of German international cultural relations? The author seems to think that because Austrian identity developed out of a common German history, an enlightened German cultural diplomacy should have every right to see Austrian culture as something other than fully "foreign." To a certain extent, this view is supported by the fact that there is no "Goethe Institute" in Vienna today. At least from a Viennese perspective, many traditions in German culture feel much more "foreign" than those in our neighboring countries in Central and South Eastern Europe.

The book ends with the German reunification and thus does not answer the tempting question of how Germany, which by now has been unified for about twenty-five years and has become the dominant political force in Europe, formulates its cultural diplomacy today. What the study does show is a strong continuity from the interwar period until today in the fragmented set-up of institutions (often at "arm's length" from government) responsible for cultural promotion abroad and a strong tradition to give priority to language promotion. Given its history in the 20th century, it does not seem unwise to me that a politically and economically re-energized Germany plays the “cultural fiddle” softly.

Philipp Strobl, *Innsbrucker Wirtschaftsgeschichte* (Veröffentlichungen des Innsbrucker Stadtarchivs: Neue Folge 52) (Innsbruck: StudienVerlag, 2013)

Franz Mathis

The economic development of the city of Innsbruck may well be regarded as a success story. It began as a small trading place between Upper Germany to the north and Upper Italy to the south of the Alps in the Middle Ages and developed into a modern, diversified center for all kinds of economic activities. This is mainly due to the fact that, in the 15th century, the city was established as the capital of the Habsburg province of Tyrol. From then on, it was no longer interregional trade and traffic, but rather the presence of nobles and public servants that fostered demographic growth and local consumption. Innsbruck became a center of administration, attracting more people from the outside than other cities did. And yet, for a long time, population numbers remained relatively low with less than 10.000 inhabitants. It was not before the 19th and early 20th centuries that—partly due to the incorporation of nearby villages—the population grew at a more rapid pace, reaching its peak of about 120.000 inhabitants in the 1970s, followed by a kind of stagnation with still-growing numbers in the suburbs.

Innsbruck is no longer only an administrative center. Now, it is also the seat of several middle-sized and large companies serving regional, national, and global markets—including hotels, shops, and restaurants that cater to tourists from all over the world. Although it was little affected by the large-scale industrialization process of the 19th and 20th centuries, with the help of several educational establishments including a university, the city's economy has so far succeeded in meeting the challenges of the modern, global world.

All this and much more is depicted by Philipp Strobl in considerable detail. Although he devotes about a third of his study to the early economic life of the city, the focus lies on the 20th century when structural changes were most profound. A great number of tables and charts support his arguments; numerous pictures help illustrate them. Exemplary stories of individuals or selected firms are hardly included, since they would have exceeded the space available. Instead, the various branches of the economy, their ups and downs, are described as groups which determined the structure of Innsbruck's economy in the course of the centuries. In order not to be lost in too much minutiae, Strobl has added several short summaries between the larger chapters and an overall conclusion at the end, thus helping the reader focus on the central findings of his book. Beyond mere description, he tries to search for the causes of continuity and change—external as well as internal, regional, and even global as well as local. Especially in modern times, growing competition from both within as well as outside the city resulted in a decline of traditional branches of economic activity, while at the same time rising incomes and purchasing power encouraged the emergence and flourishing of new ones. In general and notwithstanding certain exceptions, manufacturing tended to decline, whereas services of all kind—personal, social, and public—were on the rise. To ask in what way Innsbruck resembled other cities and the economic development in general or whether it differed from them might have allowed the author to arrive at an even better picture of the peculiar features of the city's development.

Walter Manoschek, *"Dann bin ich ja ein Mörder!": Adolf Storms und das Massaker an Juden in Deutsch Schützen* (Göttingen: Wallstein Verlag, 2015)

Karin Liebhart

From July to September 2008, Walter Manoschek, a professor of political science at the University of Vienna and an expert in contemporary history with a focus on National Socialism and the Holocaust, conducted a series of interviews (altogether about fifteen hours) with SS junior squad leader (*Unterscharführer*) Adolf Storms. Storms was very probably co-responsible for the massacre of fifty-seven Jewish slave laborers from Hungary, which took place in March 1945 in Deutsch Schützen, a village located in the Eastern part of Austria, in the province Burgenland. Moreover, Storms most likely shot a Jew who was too exhausted to move on on a death march soon thereafter. Two eyewitnesses bore testimony to the latter crime.

The author became aware of Adolf Storms in the course of one of his student's research activities. Andreas Forster found Storms' name and address in the German telephone directory. Walter Manoschek called and visited him, and subsequently recorded detailed interviews with Storms. During these interviews, the eighty-nine year old man, who as a volunteer in the *Waffen*-SS Division "*Wiking*" was a committed National Socialist during World War II, provided elaborate accounts of his wartime experiences. However, when Manoschek began to ask questions related to the murderous events in Deutsch Schützen, Storms' memory suddenly became faint and showed major gaps.

Walter Manoschek first compiled the video-taped interviews and then turned them into a documentary movie. This startling documentary was released in 2012 and was—amongst others—highly praised by the Austrian author and nobel prize winner Elfriede Jelinek. The DVD of the documentary is enclosed in the book.

The book version improves on the documentary in two significant ways. First, it includes a lot of background material and provides crucial historical information about the *Waffen*-SS and their crimes. Moreover, it provides insight into crimes committed by other representatives of the Nazi regime during the final phase of World War II—particularly as regards the "*Todesmärsche*" (death marches) and the treatment of forced laborers who were coerced to build the Southeast rampart („*Südostwall*"). Manoschek also includes interviews with survivors of the massacre in Deutsch Schützen as well as members of the *Hitlerjugend* who were involved in these gruesome crimes. Secondly, Manoschek reflects on a central question. Why did Storms speak to him at all after so many years, but was not willing (or able) to talk about the Deutsch Schützen massacre? Did the former SS man perhaps want to make a late confession before he passed away? Was he struggling with his personal memories? Or did he want to use the researcher as a test person in preparation of a possible murder trial? Eventually, Adolf Storms was indicted for murder and accessory to murder in Dortmund in 2009. Shortly before the beginning of the trial, Storms died in June 2010.

The book also sheds light on the indifferent attitude of official Austrian and German authorities. The mass grave of those killed in Deutsch Schützen had been discovered in 1995 and the Austrian ministry of the interior installed a memorial plaque on the site. But no one in Austria bothered to find the culprits responsible for this mass murder in the final days of World War II. For sixty years, Adolf Storms had lived unharmed in his house on the outskirts of Duisburg. After his role became known, it was German authorities who put him on trial.

What is particularly remarkable about the book is the attitude of the author. Walter Manoschek is an expert in the field of Holocaust studies and World War II war crimes. From 1995 to 1999, he participated in conceptualizing of the exhibition "Vernichtungskrieg: Verbrechen der Wehrmacht 1941-1944" ("War of Extermination: Crimes of the German Armed Forces 1941-1944"). He also edited a volume dedicated to the victims of Nazi military justice,[1] as well as an anthology about the massacre of Hungarian Jews in Rechnitz, another village in Burgenland, in the final days of the war.[2] Elfriede Jelinek calls him "somebody, who knows," and, nevertheless, "aims at understanding." Manoschek is very clear in his questions and statements, but refrains from accusing his interview partner. He attempts to initiate and, respectively, support the process of remembering. Hower, in the end, he did not succeed as Adolf Storms did not deliver a consistent and informative account concerning the events in Deutsch Schützen in March 1945.

1 *Opfer der NS-Militärjustiz: Urteilspraxis, Strafvollzug, Entschädigungspolitik in Österreich*, ed. Walter Manoschek (Vienna: Mandelbaum, 2003).

2 *Der Fall Rechnitz: Das Massaker an Juden im März 1945*, ed. idem (Vienna: Braumüller, 2009).

The fact that Storms eventually failed to recollect the crimes of Deutsch Schützen does not adversely affect the publication. Manoschek's book is persuasive due to its compassionate approach to Storms—he tries to explain what happened *sine ira et studio.*

Wolfgang Neugebauer, *The Austrian Resistance 1938-1945* (Vienna: Edition Steinbauer, 2014)

Evan B. Bukey

Readers of this meticulously researched study may wish to consider the author's somber conclusions before delving into the text. In six brief pages Neugebauer takes pains to stress that Austrian independence was restored not by patriotic freedom fighters, but by unwelcome conquering Allied armies, that 700.000 Austrians had belonged to the Nazi party, and that in the decades following 1945 the Alpine Republic was dominated by those who had fought for the Greater German Reich or themselves belonged to Hitler's movement. Further, while claiming victim status for Austria, officials of the Second Republic tended to discount or ignore the efforts of those who had opposed Nazi rule. Today we know that while no mass resistance movement arose between 1938 and 1945, at least 110.000 Austrians lost their lives and 100.000 others were jailed, imprisoned, or dispatched to concentration camps for political crimes. The objective of this study is to document and explore the behavior of those courageous men and women who for multiple reasons dared to speak out or actively resist a popular tyranny.

In a superb historiographical introduction, Neugebauer modestly emphasizes that he is not the first to undertake a scholarly study of the Austrian resistance. Nor does he take issue with conclusions reached in 1984 by Radomír Luža, viz. that the Communists put up the most stubborn, often suicidal, opposition primarily in Styria and Vienna, that for the most part the Social Democrats stayed out of the fray, and that disparate legitimist and Catholic groups were most active in Tyrol and Vienna. On the other hand, Neugebauer does fault Luža for omitting "non-organized resisters," such as Ella Lingens, incarcerated in Auschwitz for assisting Jews, as well as the Christian martyrs Sister Maria Restituta and Franz Jägerstätter. Indeed, some of the most nuanced, textured, and gripping pages in Neugebauer's book recount the fate of ordinary people who spontaneously denounced the Nazis in public, posted graffiti, or like the more famous Otto and Elise Hampel in Berlin, were beheaded for simply writing subversive postcards.

Neugebauer begins his account by providing a detailed description and analysis of the machinery of repression, focusing on the structure and personnel of the SS/police complex and the judicial system. He stresses that the Gestapo was staffed by highly intelligent Reich German and Austrian detectives who were able to recruit talented informants to penetrate Communist cells and spy on malcontents disrupting the war economy and others engaged in subversive activities (*Heimtücke*). The judicial system tended to be more cumbersome and less effective, Neugebauer writes, primarily because of "inherited judicial norms." This oblique point neglects to mention that the Austrian legal order remained in place between 1938 and 1945 so that the judiciary retained a measure of autonomy, most notably in criminal cases. Even so, Austrian judges dominated both the Higher Regional Courts and the Special Courts, rarely hesitating to mete out death sentences for trivial offences such as postal theft or insulting a Nazi official.

In shifting to the main topic of resistance, Neugebauer scrutinizes the judicial records of 6.300 individuals tried by the Higher Regional Courts in Vienna and Graz and the Senate of the People's Court (*Volksgerichtshof*). His decades of painstaking research substantiates Luža's findings that the Communist-Party-dominated organized resistance, primarily in factories but also within the Wehrmacht, that eighty-five percent were former Social Democrats, and that the movement's highly centralized structure enabled the Gestapo to penetrate and crush most cells by 1943. While much of the information here is well known, Neugebauer provides many fascinating personal details, for example, on women refugees who returned from France to influence French workers or on youngsters who distributed flysheets or infiltrated the Hitler Youth only to fall prey to the Gestapo. Combining arrest lists with court records, Neugebauer calculates that three quarters of those engaged in active resistance to Nazi rule in Austria were affiliated with the KPÖ (Austrian Communist Party), although sometimes only marginally—such as the eighteen-year old Josef Landgraf who distributed flysheets based on BBC radio broadcasts. The author also quite correctly stresses that KPÖ militants, unlike Communists elsewhere in Europe and the United States, stepped up their opposition to the Nazi regime following the Hitler-Stalin pact in 1939. This highly significant point has been noted by others, but remains insufficiently explored.

While the efforts of Communist resisters may have received inadequate attention during the Cold War, those of Catholic conservatives and legitimists have tended to be exaggerated, even though Cardinal Theodor Innitzer and the Austrian episcopate had endorsed the "Anschluss" regime. This helps to explain how and why a fair number of the lower clergy and active laity found it difficult to express antipathy to Nazi rule in, for example, situations such as the case of Franz Jägerstätter, whose decision to choose death over service in the Wehrmacht met the disapproval of the archbishop of Linz. Still, Neugebauer reminds us that the Rosary Festival of October 1938 constituted the largest mass protest ever staged in Greater Germany and that during the "Anschluss" era 724 priests were imprisoned and fifteen sentenced to death. Over one hundred perished in concentration camps, while 208 others were banished from their parishes. Although sixty-nine Catholics gave their lives for their faith, Neugebauer provides evidence that Nazi judges treated youthful Catholic protesters more leniently than members of the Communist Youth League, nearly all of whom were sentenced to death.

A number of active Catholic resisters tended to be monarchists associated with clusters scattered throughout incorporated Austria. As former supporters of the hated Dollfuß-Schuschnigg dictatorship, they garnered relatively few adherents though their social structure was astonishingly wide-ranging—from professionals, to businessmen, housewives, and a large number of female domestic servants. Neugebauer surveys sixteen of these groups, whose activities generally consisted of circulating subversive poems and distributing pamphlets calling for a Habsburg restoration. The most important in the author's judgment was a group founded in 1938 by a trade unionist, Johann Müller, who had known Otto von Habsburg. Using a network of couriers, he established contacts both at home and abroad. The Nazis broke up the group in late 1939, eventually sentencing its members to long prison terms. Less fortunate were individuals belonging to other groups of monarchists. Among these was Leopold Eichinger, beheaded in 1944 for distributing roughly 80.000 anti-German flysheets. Also executed or murdered were the curate Heinrich Maier, the *Semperit* executive, Josef Messner, and the forester Walter Caldonazzi whose contacts provided the Office of Strategic Services in Switzerland with valuable intelligence on war production in the "*Ostmark*." Although far fewer legitimists resisted Nazi rule in incorporated Austria than dedicated Communists, they were indisputably patriotically motivated, as were 10.000 exiles fighting in Allied armies. Sadly, Neugebauer reminds us, many of those who had fled abroad sincerely believed that their homeland had been invaded by the German Reich, unaware or unwilling to admit that a majority of their countrymen had embraced National Socialism or benefitted from its racist policies. That Herbert Steiner, founder of the *Dokumentationsarchiv des österreichischen Widerstandes*, directed by the author between 1983 and 2004, believed the "victim myth" speaks volumes.

One of Neugebauer's most interesting findings is the prominent role women played both within autochthonous monarchist groups and Slovenian armed battalions operating in the Carinthian and Styrian borderlands. Whether Hitler's officials considered females as weaker, non-dangerous figures may seem problematic to some. But the evidence adduced here demonstrates that women were essential in providing intelligence, food, lodging, and other services for those engaged in resistance. To this may be added an ironic footnote that between 1933 and 1938 girls and women had provided invaluable aid and assistance to "illegal" Austrian Nazis.

In surveying the issue of military resistance Neugebauer covers well-trodden ground. He briefly recounts the well-known story of Carl Szokoll's undetected involvement in the Stauffenberg bomb plot, the brief success of the coup in Vienna, and the subsequent executions of Robert Bernardis and Rudolf Maragona-Redwitz for their role in the conspiracy. Without casting aspersions on the leaders of the famous O5 cross-party resistance movement, including the courageous Molden brothers, the author deflates the myth that O5 was an umbrella group coordinating all organized Austrian resistance. This observation leads readers into some of the most fascinating, often stomach-churning examples of individual opposition and non-conformist behavior, primarily on the part of ordinary citizens. In examining the records of 10.000 cases tried by Hitler's Special Courts, Neugebauer emphasizes that Austrian judges prosecuted persons apprehended for making defeatist remarks, insulting Nazi officials, or aiding persecuted minorities just as severely as they did members of underground movements. Although the sentences meted out tended to be relatively mild, those convicted were frequently dispatched to concentration camps upon release from prison. Further, a number of individuals caught listening to foreign radio broadcasts or providing assistance to Jews were sentenced to death.

On balance, it is difficult to criticize Neugebauer's impressive study, felicitously and precisely translated by Jon Nicholson and Eric Canepa. One may quibble whether resistance in Nazi Austria was significantly distinctive or different from other regions of Greater Germany; one may also wonder why no mention is made of three Upper Austrian farming families who in 1945 hid or sheltered Soviet escapees from Mauthausen following the vicious "*Mühlviertler Hasenjagd*." While Neugebauer modestly concludes that much of Austria's Nazi past remains to be explored, his own book will surely stand as the authoritative work for decades.

Robert Kriechbaumer, *"... ständiger Verdruss und viele Verletzungen": Die Regierung Klima/Schüssel und die Bildung der ÖVP-FPÖ-Regierung. Österreich 1997-2000* (Vienna: Böhlau, 2014)

Alexander Smith

After more than ten years of a grand coalition between the Austrian Social Democratic Party (SPÖ) and the conservative People's Party (ÖVP) under the social democratic Chancellor Franz Vranitzky, both parties were increasingly exhausted by constant internal bickering. Viktor Klima, who succeeded Vranitzky in January 1997, promised a new style of government and better cooperation with the ÖVP at the beginning of his chancellorship. Klima's intent, however, did not materialize. On the contrary, as the title of Robert Kriechbaumer's book aptly describes, the grand coalition years of the Klima-Schüssel government were in fact marked by "constant frustration and many hurt feelings." Chapters II to V of the book elaborate on the main divides that led to a veritable alienation of the two parties at the end of the 1990s. Most notably, SPÖ and ÖVP locked horns over the future of the long-established *Creditanstalt* bank, a pension and fiscal reform, and the country's security policy.

In the narrow-minded Austrian party-political thinking, the Vienna-based *Creditanstalt-Bankverein* was considered part of ÖVP's domain. The bank's acquisition by the SPÖ-dominated *Bank Austria* shattered the relationship between the two coalition partners and brought the government to the brink of collapse at the beginning of 1997. According to Kriechbaumer, the ÖVP regarded the takeover as "a declaration of war." Vice-Chancellor Wolfgang Schüssel "never got over this humiliation." Schüssel felt betrayed by Klima, which put a strain on their relationship (pp. 59-65). The Social Democrats and the Conservatives clashed over other issues as well. While the latter advocated Austrian membership both in the Western European Union (WEU) and the North Atlantic Military Alliance (NATO), the SPÖ adamantly adhered to the "myth of neutrality" and threatened to exploit the question of NATO membership in its election campaign (p.

114). Despite escalating costs and a burgeoning government debt, a major reform of the pension system failed in 1997 because of the strong resistance from the Austrian Trade Union Federation (ÖGB) and its major influence on the SPÖ. For largely the same reason, all efforts for a structural reform of the tax system were to no avail (p. 133). The tax relief bill adopted only a few months before the general elections of October 1999 demonstrated the grand coalition's inability to meet future challenges, casting doubt on its legitimacy. By this point, the Klima-Schüssel government had reached an impasse. The honorable Heinrich Neisser, who had always advocated cooperation with the Social Democrats, came to the conclusion that "the grand coalition has had its day" (p. 277).

Klima flirted with the social democratic Third Way and placed himself on the same level with Tony Blair and Gerhard Schröder, but in reality he never was. His ambitions to modernize the SPÖ and its program failed in the face of opposition by leftist ideologues within the party and the "structural conservative" proponents of the status quo in the Austrian Chamber of Labor (*Arbeiterkammer*) and the ÖGB. Under these circumstances a political renewal of the SPÖ had no reasonable chance. Also the People's Party was in a gloomy state by the end of the 1990s. More than twelve years in a grand coalition government with the Social Democrats resulted in an ever decreasing share of the vote. The ÖVP was tired of playing the thankless role of the junior partner under a social democratic chancellor. While, from their own viewpoint, the ÖVP was the driving force behind the reforms, the SPÖ gained the credit. Opinion polls before the parliamentary elections of 3 October 1999 showed the ÖVP only in third place, behind Jörg Haider's right-wing populist Freedom Party (FPÖ).

The FPÖ was on the upswing. Haider won a landslide victory in the provincial government elections in Carinthia on 7 March 1999 and returned as governor in Klagenfurt eight years after he was forced to step down in 1991 following his inglorious praise of the employment policy of the Third Reich. The rise of the FPÖ was largely at the expense of the ÖVP. The latter found itself in a difficult position in the run-up to the October elections. In order to encourage conservative voters to go to the polls, Schüssel made the announcement that he would lead the ÖVP into opposition if the party came third in the vote. The SPÖ received 33.2 percent of the vote and remained the strongest party in the *Nationalrat*. The FPÖ came second in the 3 October ballot with 26.9 percent. For the first time ever in parliamentary elections, the ÖVP ended up third by a narrow margin of 415 votes. The election result left the country in a delicate political situation.

Kriechbaumer's analysis of the SPÖ-ÖVP and ÖVP-FPÖ coalition negotiations that followed the ballot largely reflects the traditional conservative perspective. He mainly replicates the ÖVP's interpretation of events and their ultimate outcome. The SPÖ's side of the story is not given sufficient consideration. The book also lacks a critical assessment of Schüssel's controversial coalition building with Haider's extreme right-wing FPÖ. For these reasons, Kriechbaumer's narrative shows some analytical imbalance. Since a number of leading ÖVP and FPÖ representatives are given plenty of chances to make their case, the chapters on the negotiations and the formation of a coalition government between the two parties read like a story of inevitability. The SPÖ's, or rather the ÖGB's, unwillingness to implement structural reforms made a continuation of the grand coalition for the ÖVP highly unattractive. Klima refused to form a coalition with the FPÖ and Haider declined to back a SPÖ-led minority government. By going into opposition, Schüssel would therefore be forced to support a minority government headed by Chancellor Klima, if he wanted to avoid snap elections. Considering the party's low approval ratings in the polls, an early ballot was not in the ÖVP's interest at all. Along these lines, Schüssel, who is widely recognized as a superb negotiator and political strategist, had no reasonable choice but to create a government with the FPÖ.

Kriechbaumer describes the SPÖ-ÖVP dispute in the final stages of the negotiations in January 2000 as a clash of conflicting positions. In this sense, it was basically disagreement over the political roadmap for the country's future that prevented the coalition talks to succeed. Thereby, it is suggested that the ÖVP did engage in serious negotiations with the SPÖ and that Schüssel was sincerely willing to conclude an agreement. Since leading SPÖ trade unionists, most notably the uncompromising Rudolf Nürnberger, refused to sign the coalition agreement, the ÖVP had no alternative but to put an end to the talks in late January and enter into negotiations with the FPÖ. Based on Schüssel's post-election behavior, Kurt Richard Luther argues, by contrast, that the ÖVP leader had already "by December at the latest decided upon governmental collaboration with the FPÖ." Luther thus holds that Schüssel, in fact, had no intention to conclude a final agreement with the Social Democrats. Knowing that the SPÖ would not accept them, the ÖVP made a series of additional demands at the last minute in a bid to cause the negotiations to collapse.[1]

With the support of his ally Hans Dichand, editor of the infamous

1 Kurt Richard Luther, "Governing with Right-Wing Populists and Managing the Consequences: Schüssel and the FPÖ," in *The Schüssel Era in Austria*, ed. Günter Bischof and Fritz Plasser (Contemporary Austrian Studies 18) (New Orleans and Innsbruck: UNO Press and iup, 2010), 85.

tabloid *Kronen Zeitung*, President Thomas Klestil strongly pressed for a government headed by Klima. Despite numerous efforts, he failed to prevent the far-right FPÖ from entering the government. On 4 February 2000, the first ÖVP-FPÖ coalition under Chancellor Schüssel was sworn in by a grim-faced president. According to Kriechbaumer, Klestil played an "active role" in the imposition of political measures by European states against the new Austrian government (p. 404). The so-called "sanctions" of the EU-14 against the Austrian ÖVP-FPÖ coalition government are portrayed as "partially aggressive" measures arising from domestic political considerations in Germany, France, and other countries rather than the troubling statements and character of Haider and his extreme right-wing Freedom Party (p. 387). Kriechbaumer's assessment of the EU-14 measures reflects the rejectionist stance that still dominates the discourse on the "sanctions" in Austrian media and academic writing.[2]

Kriechbaumer provides a detailed account of the incidents that created an increasing rift between SPÖ and ÖVP and led to a personal alienation between Klima and Schüssel. The FPÖ was the main beneficiary of this process that eventually resulted in the controversial inauguration of the first ÖVP-FPÖ federal government. Kriechbaumer's study is based on a thorough examination of hundreds of newspaper articles, published primarily between 1997 and 2000 in *Die Presse*, *Kurier*, *Der Standard*, *Salzburger Nachrichten*, *Format*, and others. As criticized by Hans Werner Scheidl, "the author nobly confines himself to quoting newspaper articles" and does not offer "any interviews with the key people involved." For this reason, the volume "remains a collection of journalistic commentaries."[3] Kriechbaumer, indeed, makes use of lengthy quotes from news articles throughout the book.

Unfortunately, the book contains a number of typographical errors (especially in the preface) and mistakes in names (e.g. Hubert instead of Alfons Gorbach on p. 10; Richard instead of Rudolf Nürnberger on p. 344). Kriechbaumer's lucid story of the Klima-Schüssel years and the controversies associated with the formation of the ÖVP-FPÖ government in February 2000 deserves better copy-editing.

It is sobering how close the author's description of past events resembles today's political situation in Austria. Ideological stupor among the ruling parties still largely dominates over constructive and sustainable problem

2 A different perspective on the issue is offered, for instance, by *Sanktionen–10 Jahre danach: Die Maßnahmen der Länder der Europäischen Union gegen die österreichische Regierung im Jahr 2000*, ed. Martin Strauß and Karl-Heinz Ströhle (Innsbruck: Studienverlag, 2010).
3 Hans Werner Scheidl, "'Wie Hund und Katz': Story einer Entfremdung," *Die Presse*, 31 May 2014.

solving. Despite decades of discussion and numerous proposals, SPÖ and ÖVP are as far as ever from agreeing on fundamental administrative reforms. With regard to the recent controversy between the Social Democrats and the People's Party about a fiscal reform, it seems as if nothing has changed since the discordant days of the Klima-Schüssel government. With the current political debates in mind, reading the book may result in an unpleasant feeling of déjà vu.

Christian H. Stifter, *Zwischen geistiger Erneuerung und Restauration: US-amerikanische Planungen zur Entnazifizierung und demokratischen Reorientierung und die Nachkriegsrealität österreichischer Wissenschaft 1941-1955* (Vienna: Böhlau, 2014)

Thomas König

Other than in Western Germany, there was no reeducation in Austria. At least that is the conventional wisdom. Historical evidence, however, has been sparse. And there are contradictions. The idea of Austria as the first victim of Nazi Germany was present in the discourse of exile groups in Washington and London, all right; but it became a powerful concept and the ideological base of Austrian identity only after the war. For the Americans thinking about postwar scenarios, Austrian society must have been similarly problematic to that of Germany (if they even thought of them as two distinctively different cultural entities, which was not always the case).

So, was there really no reeducation? In more than 660 pages, Christian H. Stifter's study provides a more nuanced picture of the overall process, including American plans, actual implementation, and the effects on the ground. Plans for reeducation (or reorientation) existed; however, their implementation was impeded and overruled by other considerations—which is why the effects, if any at all, were rather contrary to the initial ideas. Tackling all three questions is a daring undertaking, not only because of the methodological and conceptual challenges that are addressed in the introduction, but also because each of them deals with many shifts and changes over a rather short (and, to say the least, tumultuous) period of time, from the U.S. entry to war until the end of the occupation period in 1955.

The starting point of Stifter's study is the negative image of Americans in European cultural discourses since the 19th century, and the inability of European elites to accept that education and (what would be called today) "life-long learning" has always been deeply ingrained in American culture (even though it is difficult to speak of the latter in the singular); indeed, the very notion of a democratic society, in the U.S., relies on education. Different U.S. institutions—the State Department, think tanks, the U.S. Army—started drafting policy papers on how to shape the postwar societies in the (former) German Reich. Nonetheless, for a surprisingly long time the American government remained undecided about how to proceed with the former enemies. Stifter's succinct analysis of the (mostly) domestic quarrels about how to proceed belongs to the best descriptions of that complex matter. Austria, in particular, was not taken into consideration even after the Moscow Declaration announced that the Allies would annul the country's 1938 annexation to Germany.

Once on the ground, the policies were changed quickly again, mostly due to the confrontation with the Soviet Union. At this point, Stifter focuses on academia as a case study: de-nazification of Austrian universities and democratization of university teachers and students have been one of the core goals of postwar U.S. policy. Those efforts failed almost completely. Why? American officials quickly retreated to a policy of "non-interference" with an autochthonous academic culture that was as conservative as it was keen to propagate its "autonomy." Seldom has that latter concept been more of a hollow, purely political nature than in this period of university history.

The consequences are well known: Austrian universities remained an intellectual wasteland until the late 1960s. More generally, as Stifter notes with a hint of irony, it was not top-down measures, but U.S. pop culture ("Coca-Colonization") spreading across the Atlantic that had the greatest impact on Austrian society in the first decades after the war.[1] This we know, as most of the findings of Stifter's study are not surprising per se. Its accomplishments are twofold. One, it processes an impressive number of archival documents and literature, although, at times, unfortunately, the author confuses details (on page 642, referring to my own book on the Fulbright Commission in Vienna, Stifter mentions that only about 140 Austrians benefited from the U.S. academic exchange program in total—that number actually only entails the small group of Austrian scholars, but not the much larger group of high school teachers and students).[2] Second, it strives to overcome the "methodological nationalism" that still drives most studies in the field of cultural diplomacy and Americanization. For anyone interested in the two latter topics, this study is a must-read.

---

1 Reinhold Wagnleitner, *Coca-Colonisation und Kalter Krieg: Die Kulturmission der USA in Österreich nach dem Zweiten Weltkrieg* (Vienna: Verlag für Gesellschaftskritik, 1991).

2 Thomas König, *Die Frühgeschichte des Fulbright Program in Österreich: Transatlantische "Fühlungsnahme auf dem Gebiet der Erziehung"* (transatlantica 6) (Innsbruck: StudienVerlag, 2012), 128-136.

Günter Bischof, *Relationships/Beziehungsgeschichten: Austria and the United States in the Twentieth Century* (TRANSATLANTICA 4) (Innsbruck: StudienVerlag, 2014)

Nicole M. Phelps

This excellent collection of ten essays written over the past fifteen years provides important insights into specific aspects of 20th century U.S.-Austrian relations, as well as an impressively cohesive overview of that relationship from the interwar period through the Cold War and into the much more recent history of Wolfgang Schüssel's government and Arnold Schwarzenegger's term as governor of California. The volume also serves as a valuable teaching tool for exploring aspects of the historical profession.

The cover image effectively captures many of the book's key themes. The picture shows a American GI in uniform holding hands with an Austrian woman; the GI looks at her and smiles benevolently while she gazes on a statue that evokes both the classical period as well as more modern Austrian artistic styles. The image reflects the importance of an official U.S. government presence in Austria, bringing to mind U.S. efforts to keep the country unified and non-communist during the 1945-55 Allied occupation and the Marshall Plan's impact on Austrian economic recovery—an impact that Bischof convincingly argues persists to this day in the form of the Austrian government's ERP-Fond, which uses credits earned under the Marshall Plan to provide long-term, low-interest loans. The GI is less interested in the statue itself than in the Austrian woman's reaction to it, which resonates with American efforts to interest Austria in Western democracy and capitalism. One might also read it as American interest in Austrian reactions to American culture, whether that be attempts at high culture, which many Austrians were skeptical about, thus producing American apprehension and insecurity, or the popular culture of jazz, rock and roll, and consumer goods that so many post-World War II Austrian young people avidly embraced, in part as an act of rebellion against their parents.[1]

1 In making this argument, Bischof draws heavily on Reinhold Wagnleitner, *Coca-Colonization and the Cold War: The Cultural Mission of the United States in Austria after the Second World War* (Chapel Hill: University of North Carolina Press, 1994).

In the photo, we cannot see the woman's face, so her feelings—Austrian feelings—about the situation are unknown. On the one hand, that suggests ambivalence, which appears in the volume as the mutual presence of an Americanized Austrian culture and expressions of Austrian anti-Americanism, as well as in many Austrians' ambivalence about Nazism in the country's history. On the other hand, the fact that the woman's opinions are unknown to the viewer brings to mind the methodological challenges historians face when trying to reconstruct the past experiences of everyday people, a theme that Bischof explores in multiple essays, especially the one on World War II prisoners of war in the United States. Bischof points out that the U.S.-Austrian relationship is much more than high politics, and even more than economic and cultural exchanges; the migration of people between the two countries, be they permanent immigrants or short-term visitors, has been the key element in shaping that relationship. That definition of "foreign relations" makes the cover image even more fitting: the photo depicts everyday people, not high-level officials, and the GI had to travel a considerable distance to be in the same physical location as the Austrian.

The cover image, of course, is clearly gendered, with the United States represented as masculine and Austria as feminine. Though Bischof does draw our attention to some specific women in the U.S.-Austrian relationship—most especially the importance of Eleanor Lansing Dulles and Margarethe Ottilinger in shaping the Marshall Plan in Austria—he does not offer a gendered analysis of the U.S.-Austrian relationship. Such an analysis, perhaps following the models laid out by Frank Costigliola or Petra Goedde, would be fruitful.[2] When either Americans or Austrians talked about Austria as the first victim of the Nazis, were they envisioning a feminized Austria? As U.S. leaders emphasized the importance of NATO membership in the post-Cold War world, were their depictions of neutral Austria gendered? What did American observers have to say about Jörg Haider's masculinity, or Austrians about that of George W. Bush?

In pointing out the absence of gender analysis, my point is not to find fault with Bischof's work, but rather to call attention to the vast range of topics in the U.S.-Austrian relationship that remain uninvestigated by scholars. Bischof's essays here are generally written to pack a great deal into a small space—and often for non-academic audiences—and so they are rife with mentions of people and incidents that warrant more in-

2 Frank Costigliola, "The Nuclear Family: Tropes of Gender and Pathology in the Western Alliance," *Diplomatic History* 21, no. 2 (1997): 163-83; Petra Goedde, *GIs and Germans: Culture, Gender and Foreign Relations, 1945-1949* (New Haven: Yale University Press, 2003).

depth study. (The excellent notes and bibliography are also valuable assets for those looking to pursue these topics.) Studies of the Marshall Plan's application in Austria and the 1955 Austrian State Treaty have provided important insights about the European Recovery Program and the Cold War more generally, and other U.S.-Austrian topics could also be framed to capture that broader significance. The personal papers of Peter Moser, Austrian ambassador to the United States from 1999 to 2003, which have been donated to Center Austria at the University of New Orleans, are a particularly tantalizing source base. The scholarly community would also be very well served by a study that focused on change over time in Americans' tendency to conflate Austria with Germany and the advantages and disadvantages that conflation has presented to the Austrian government—and Austrian migrants—at various points in history.

Besides its exploration of U.S.-Austrian relations, the volume is of tremendous pedagogical value because of the opportunities it presents to talk about historical writing and careers in academic history. In the introduction to the book, Bischof notes that academics are always responding to requests and invitations to contribute to volumes or panels. The volume is a collection of pieces written to fulfill those requests; there are contributions to *Festschriften* and interdisciplinary edited volumes, an exhibition catalog done for a museum display on the Marshall Plan, an essay first presented as a speech to the Austrian Diplomatic Academy, and an essay interpreting recent scholarship on America as empire for Austrian audiences. One essay involves family history; several require using the skills and contextual knowledge of the historian to interpret recent events for which there is not yet archival evidence to consult. In the United States, graduate students in history are trained to read and write monographs, journal articles, and book reviews; many will also have a chance to develop lectures aimed at undergraduates and present papers at academic conferences. Those are, of course, absolutely essential genres to master for a historian, but they are not the only things historians write. The essays in Bischof's volume each begin with a paragraph explaining the context in which they were originally created, thus offering readers an opportunity to think about the constraints presented by the assignment and how effectively the pieces would have reached their intended audiences. There is ample opportunity to discuss when it is appropriate to synthesize other scholars' work, when original analysis is vital, and when one wants to stick closely to a detailed, facts- and statistics-heavy narrative of what happened. The challenges and opportunities of using personal history could also be discussed, along with crafting responsible interpretations of recent history. Bischof's career trajectory has been rather unique—few historians are quite so alone in their field, or so effectively immersed in multiple countries and academic cultures—but there is much here for graduate students working in a variety of historical subfields to learn from and emulate.

Cornelius Lehnguth, *Waldheim und die Folgen: Der parteipolitische Umgang mit dem Nationalsozialismus in Österreich* (Studien zur historischen Sozialwissenschaft 35) (Frankfurt a. M.: Campus Verlag, 2013)

Günter Bischof

In 2001, late but not too late, the Socialist/Social Democratic Party of Austria (SPÖ) commissioned the Institute of Contemporary History of the University of Vienna to investigate how many higher party functionaries of the post-World War II era had been member of the Nazi Party (*Nationalsozialistische Deutsche Arbeiterpartei* = NSDAP). A year later a study of some 1.021 SPÖ functionaries established that 10.3 percent had been members of the NSDAP. The conservative People's Party (ÖVP) and the right-wing Freedom Party (FPÖ) refused to do such self-studies, claiming that few of their party leaders had been Nazi Party members. Yet the SPÖ study averred that 12.8 percent of the postwar ÖVP members of parliament had been members of the NSDAP (10.7 percent of SPÖ parliamentarians) (pp. 454f). In the FPÖ's predecessor party *Verein der Unabhängigen* (VdU) some eighty percent of the party leaders had been Nazi party members (p. 456). The long-term FPÖ leader Friedrich Peter had been a member of the 1st SS Infantry Brigade that had been involved in committing war crimes on the Eastern front (p. 67). Jörg Haider, one of his successors, came from a Nazi family and always tried to pooh-pooh Nazi policies and the extent of their war crimes. Meanwhile the Green Party—in parliament since 1986—and the short-lived Liberal Forum (LIF) had acted as mouth pieces for a more critical Austrian mastering of its World War II past and restitution and compensation payments to Austria's true victims of the war—Jews, Roma and Sinti, handicapped, homosexuals, "asocials," and Wehrmacht deserters. The differentiation and fine-tuning of the often bitter partisan discourses ("memory politics") about Austrians' role in World War II constitutes the strength of this book.

Cornelius Lehnguth's thorough study of Austria's postwar historical memory of the Nazi era (1938-45) in general and the political parties' responses to Austrians' involvement in the crimes of National Socialism in particular is a book long overdue. Lehnguth's University of Leipzig dissertation in political science is based on some archival material, fifteen personal interviews with Austrian party leaders, parliamentary debates and the partisan public discourses (esp. anniversary speeches and official reports), a broad reading of the Austrian press, and deep immersion in the extant secondary literature. Lehnguth provides the first broad survey of Austria's "politics of history"—the country's partisan political efforts to master its World War II past from the heated Waldheim debates in 1986 to the present. He focuses on the paradigm shift of Austrian World War II memory politics from the "victims doctrine" dominating the postwar years to the critical "shared responsibility" thesis defining discourses since the 1990s, often sparked by pressure from the international community.[1] He attributes the paradigm shift specifically to generational changes after the war. Without going into the heated debates of the 1980s about whether Austria needs to be considered one of the three "succession states" to the Third Reich (eg. Federal Republic of Germany, German Democratic Republic, Austria),[2] Lehnguth implicitly argues that in the field of World War II legacies and memories of Hitlerite war crimes it willy-nilly is.[3]

Lehnguth establishes the context of Austria's historical memory by summarizing the tortured trajectory of the country's postwar politics of history in a long chapter reaching up to the turning point of Kurt Waldheim's election as president in 1986.[4] Based on the Allied 1943

---

1 This paradigm shift in historical memory was part and parcel of a larger paradigm shift in the party political arena spawned with the rise of the Haider FPÖ and the Green Party's election into parliament in 1986. See Anton Pelinka, *Austria: Out of the Shadow of the Past* (Boulder, CO: Westview, 1998).

2 The Erdmann-Stourzh debate can be followed in Karl Dietrich Erdmann, *Die Spuren Österreichs in der deutschen Geschichte: Drei Staaten, zwei Nationen, ein Volk?* (Zurich: Manesse, 1989); Gerald Stourzh, *Vom Reich zur Republik: Studien zum Österreichbewusstsein im 20. Jahrhundert* (Vienna: Edition Atelier, 1990).

3 Here Lehnguth is not alone: *Schwieriges Erbe: Der Umgang mit Nationalsozialismus und Antisemitismus in Österreich, der DDR und der Bundesrepublik Deutschland*, ed. Werner Erbmann, Rainer Erb and Albert Lichtblau (Frankfurt a. M.: Campus, 1995); Jeffrey Herf has compared East and West German World War II memories in *Divided Memory: The Nazi Past in the Two Germanys* (Cambridge, MA: Harvard University Press, 1997). Lehnguth does not really use the German term "*Vergangenheitsbewältigung*," maybe because the Nazi past is "unmasterable" as Charles S. Maier suggests. See *The Unmasterable Past: History, Holocaust, and German National Identity* (Cambridge, MA: Harvard University Press, 1988).

4 Albeit, others have done so before, but none so thoroughly, eg., see Konrad Paul Liessmann, *Die Insel der Seligen: Österreichische Erinnerung* (Österreich – Zweite Republik 11) (Innsbruck: StudienVerlag, 2005); Günter Bischof, "Victims? Perpetrators? 'Punching Bags' of European Historical Memory? The Austrians and Their World War II Legacies," *German Studies Review* 27 (2004): 17-32; Heidemarie Uhl, "From Victim Myth to Co-Responsibility Thesis: Nazi Rule, World War II, and the Holocaust in Austrian Memory," in *The Politics of Memory in Postwar Europe*, ed. Richard Ned Lebow, Wulf Kansteiner and Claudio Fogu (Durham: Duke University Press, 2006), 40-72.

Moscow Declaration, the postwar political leadership eagerly seized the opportunity to claim Austria's status as "Hitler's first victim."[5] The political elite incorporated the entire citizenry of civilians and returning soldiers in this universal "victims collective" rather than allowing Jews or *emigrés* a special victim status. The two principal parties, ÖVP and SPÖ, garnered more than ninety percent of the votes in the November 1945 election. This "elitist cartel" then clung to the "foundational myth" of the victims doctrine as "a compromise riddled with memory gaps;" both parties soon included former Nazis in the "antifascist victim's narrative" (p. 40). They simply ignored the Austrian "responsibility clause" of the Moscow Declaration. Rejecting any shared responsibility[6] for Hitlerite war crimes, the "victims doctrine" quickly took on a life of its own in domestic politics. Serious "denazification" efforts stopped in the late 1940s with the outbreak of the Cold War. By the early 1950s public memory culture depoliticized the Wehrmacht and thus turned it "clean"; the Mauthausen concentration camp became a principal place of memory, allowing Austrians to "silence" the Holocaust (and their role in it) (p. 67); the Austrian government dealt with the vast complex of restitution ("*Wiedergutmachung*") by passing numerous laws taking care of political "victims" such as Austrian resistance fighters (and soon Wehrmacht soldiers), wiggling out of paying substantive restitution to Jews and Roma and Sinti, who came low on the totem pole of the Austrian hierarchy of victims (pp. 71f); no effort was made to return art works stolen by the Nazis that had ended up in Austrian museums (or in a monastery filled with "heirless" art works) to their rightful owners, amounting to a "second aryanization" (p. 74) of properties that had been "aryanized" after the "Anschluss" in 1938.

Lehnguth shows at great length the clear-cut partisan dividing lines in the postwar "politics of history" and "politics of memory." While the regular coalition partners ÖVP and SPÖ soon after the war came to agree on silencing Austria's National Socialist period from history books, they never agreed on how to incorporate the period of Austrofascism (1933-38) into their postwar consensus narrative. The ÖVP kept insisting that the "*Ständestaat*" was the first entity to fight Nazism in Europe. The SPÖ averred that Dollfuss and Schuschnigg headed "fascist" regimes. Both parties refused to address Austria's role in the Holocaust or battle traditional anti-Semitism in their own ranks. Both wanted to end the purge of Nazis in Austrian society quickly, as they were vying with the FPÖ for

5 *Die Moskauer Deklaration 1943: Die Wiederherstellung Österreichs*, ed. Stefan Karner and Alexander Tschubarjan (Vienna: Böhlau, 2015).

6 I have translated "*Mitverantwortung*" as "shared responsibility" (eg. responsibility shared with the Germans) rather than the awkward "co-responsibility."

incorporating the large reservoir of more than half a million former Nazis into their parties. The Communist Party (KPÖ) was part of the first postwar Austrian coalition governments (until 1947). The KPÖ simply blamed the Holocaust and anti-Semitism as being "products of finance capitalism" (p. 82); they pleaded for strict denazification but only wanted to restitute small properties—not large fortunes to "capitalists." The German national camp VdU/FPÖ made the incorporation of former Nazis its wherewithal and did not join the "anti-fascist consensus" of the coalition parties (p. 86).

1986 and 1988 were the "hinge years" in Austrian postwar memory (p. 178). Waldheim's election as president in 1986 and the 50th anniversary of the "Anschluss" in 1988 rung in the demise of the Austrian victims paradigm. Waldheim's meek self-defense of simply having "done his duty" as a Wehrmacht soldier during World War II was no longer a credible defense, especially with the generations born after the war. Some of the Austrian media and the World Jewish Congress suggested criminal involvement in his war record; after Waldheim's election, the U.S. Department of Justice placed him on their "watch list." Thus the former General Secretary of the United Nations was barred from entering the United States. An international commission of historians produced a report on Waldheim's wartime record. While no direct involvement in war crimes as a Wehrmacht intelligence officer in the Balkans could be proven, the historians' verdict was that Waldheim had been well-informed about the progress of the war; he also "consulted and supported repression measures" against Jews and Yugoslav partisans (pp. 108f), an assessment that did not exactly clear his name. Waldheim's personal amnesia reminded the world about Austria's larger national amnesia when it came to facing up to her World War II past. The "victims doctrine," at last, was revealed to be Austria's "opportune living lie" (p. 112). While the ÖVP defended their candidate against the SPÖ's "smear attacks" and clawed onto the victims doctrine as Austria's hegemonic narrative of the past, the SPÖ no longer dwelt on Waldheim's past after his election—their strategy of discrediting Waldheim had misfired. The FPÖ was happy to finally get rid of the victims doctrine, which they had never believed in. Meanwhile the new Green Party, supported mainly by young voters, was thrilled about the implosion of the victims myth. Lehnguth goes off on a long tangent covering the role of the "Republican Club"—a new group of artists and intellectuals representing Austrian civil society and their role in attacking and ridiculing Waldheim's unmastered past.

The rapid erosion of the victims doctrine became clearly visible during the commemorations of the 50th anniversary of the "Anschluss" in March 1988.[7] After the U.S. "watch list" and the tepid report of the historians' commission, Waldheim himself began to acknowledge Austrian shared responsibility for Hitlerite war crimes. In a television address to the nation on the eve of the "Anschluss" commemorations on 10 March 1988, he apologized as the head of state for "National Socialist war crimes committed by Austrians" (p. 119). Snubbed by the Greens, he was not invited to the commemoration ceremonies of the Federal Assembly (eg. the federalist *Bundesversammlung* = the two parliamentary bodies *Nationalrat + Bundesrat*) and the government in Vienna's *Hofburg*. Most of the political speeches reduced the old victims doctrine to what one might call "the victims doctrine light," namely the legal argument that the state had been a victim of Nazi aggression in March 1938. Waldheim himself broke the ice in his television address by introducing the new formula that Austrians had been both "victims and perpetrators" ("*Opfer und Täter*"),[8] finally admitting that many of the worst Nazi perpetrators had in fact been Austrians. Politicians conceded for the first time that many Austrians had enthusiastically welcomed the "Anschluss." Lehnguth speaks of a "modified official history narrative" (p. 156) in which the responsibility of Austrian perpetrators was admitted and the old domestic consensus shattered. While the Greens welcomed this admission of Austrian responsibility, Haider's FPÖ denounced it as "Austro-masochism" (p. 171). Meanwhile as a first step towards atonement and reconciliation vis-à-vis the victims of racial persecution, the government set up two funds for restitution payments to people persecuted by the Nazis.

In 1988, also, two talented Austrian *agents provocateurs* raised the heat in the ideological wars over the politics of the past in the cultural arena. The controversial "Monument against War and Fascism" by the famous Viennese sculptor Alfred Hrdlicka was unveiled on 24 November 1988; the ÖVP and the FPÖ detested the memorial and boycotted the unveiling ceremony. Both had wanted to hide such a monument in a dark corner of the first district rather than give it the prominent venue on the *Albertinaplatz*. Jewish critics of Hrdlicka's *Mahnmal* complained

7 Lest anybody forget the criminal activities many Viennese Nazis inflicted on their Jewish neighbors, read the reports the U.S. minister in Vienna sent to Washington to document these "Anschluss" crimes. See Günter Bischof's essay "Austria's Loss—America's Gain: *Finis Austriae*—The 'Anschluss' and the Expulsion/Migration of Jewish Austrians to the U.S.," in *Relationships/Beziehungsgeschichten: Austria and the United States in the Twentieth Century*, ed. idem (Innsbruck: StudienVerlag, 2014), 57-82; see also Nicole Phelps' review of this book in this volume.

8 On the complexity of victim-perpetrator narratives, see Ernst Hanisch, "Opfer/Täter/Mythos: Verschlungene Erzählungen über die NS-Vergangenheit in Österreich," *zeitgeschichte* 33, no. 6 (2006): 318-327.

about Austrian soldiers being commemorated next to the "street-cleaning Jew" of 1938 (p. 1989). Hrdlicka's provocations were outdone by Thomas Bernhard's play "Heldenplatz"—referencing the square in front of Vienna's court castle, where Hitler was enthusiastically welcomed by hundreds of thousands of Viennese on 15 March 1938. Claus Peymann, the German director of Vienna's venerable old *Burgtheater*, had commissioned the play. Thomas Bernhard had been acting as the *enfant terrible* of the Austrian literary scene for a while and fully lived up to his reputation as the "artist of exaggerations." Unceasing Austrian media attacks elevated the play to a scandal. Bernhard hero's was a Jewish Oxford professor who returned to his flat on *Heldenplatz* in his native Vienna in 1988 and promptly committed suicide by jumping out the window. Quotations such as "Austria, 6.5 million morons" were taken out of context and agitated the local press and public opinion to no end—both demanding the play to be censored and not performed (pp. 191f). Bernhard's provocations were ultimately allowed onto the famous *Burgtheater* stage—the heated debate about his play contributed to further deconstruction of Austria's hegemonic victims myth.

SPÖ-Chancellor Franz Vranitzky strengthened the new paradigm of Austrians as both "victims and perpetrators" in two signal speeches—one delivered before parliament in 1991 and the other at Hebrew University in Jerusalem. On 8 July 1991, Chancellor Vranitzky addressed the Austrian parliament in a speech on the unfolding crisis in Yugoslavia. After Waldheim, the more credible Vranitzky was the second official Austrian representative to mention Austrian responsibility for the grief that Austrians had inflicted on other peoples. He conceded that Austrians had enthusiastically welcomed the "Anschluss" and supported the Nazi regime. Many Austrian had contributed to Nazi persecutions. For the first time also a high representative of the Austrian republic broadly defined which groups had been "victims" of the NS-regime: Jews, mentally handicapped (=euthanasia victims), homosexuals, and other minority groups (such as Roma and Sinti, or Jehovah's Witnesses). Vranitzky admonished the Austrian public to face up to all the dates in their national past and all the "deeds" of Austrians—the good and the bad, apologizing for the bad. Vranitzky was also the first high-level Austrian politician to mention that Austria still had a debt to these victims and needed to pay restitution ("*Wiedergutmachung*") for all the damage done in the past (pp. 206f). In June 1993, the Hebrew University in Jerusalem bestowed an honorary doctorate on Vranitzky for his historic admission of Austrian shared responsibility for the crimes of National Socialism. Vranitzky was the first representative of the Second Republic to visit Israel officially. In his speech, he returned to the themes of his 1991 speech. He rejected the notion of "collective guilt" for Austrians but conceded both "collective" and "moral responsibility"; he also averred that the memory of the Holocaust needed to be part of Austrian national and "collective" memory across the generations. Vranitzky mentioned that Austria had tried to pay restitution to the victims but there were still "gaps and deficiencies" in "*Wiedergutmachung*" that needed to be filled (pp. 232f). A year later President Thomas Klestil (ÖVP) picked up many of the same themes in speech for the *Knesset* in Jerusalem. He spoke of Austrian "victims and perpetrators," mentioned that some of the "worst perpetrators" in the Nazi dictatorship had been Austrians, and addressed the "difficult legacies" of Austria's history (pp. 232f).

Lehnguth's multi-dimensional analysis of this turning point in Austria's postwar politics of history is persuasive. He recognizes both international and domestic factors that contributed to this paradigm shift in postwar memory politics from the victims doctrine to admitting shared responsibility for Hitlerite war crimes. In July 1989, Austria applied for membership in the European Economic Communities (EC, soon to be named European Union, EU). "Euphoria for Europe" allowed Austria an escape from the endless "Waldheim affair." The EC accession debate replaced the difficult discourses about the past and offered an end to Austria's isolation (p. 216). The Vranitzky and Klestil speeches showed the outside world that Austria finally was trying to master its difficult World War II past, which eased EU-accession in 1995. At the same time, the end of the Cold War in the years 1989 to 1991 contributed to "bursting of dam" in historical memory—in Eastern Europe even more than in the West. The Holocaust became the symbol of universal World War II memory. Admitting guilt and paying restitution became part of a new "international morals" (E. Barkan). Vranitzky's speeches suggested that Austria was joining this "new political culture" in Europe (pp. 220f). In other words, coming clean of the Nazi past may well have been part and parcel of EU expectations before Austria joined the Union.

Next to this "cosmopolitan dimension" there was also a "domestic political dimension." Haider's outrageous statements about the Nazis' "fair employment policies" ("*ordentliche Beschäftigungspolitik*") probably helped spark Vranitzky's attempts to counter the negative image of some Austrians still wallowing in their Nazi past. Prominent voices from civil society such as journalist Hugo Portisch admonished Austrians to admit to their shared responsibility and face more restitution payment; this contributed to Vranitzky's confessions and the early 1990s paradigm shift in historical memory.

Lehnguth might also have considered that the 1990s were a transitional moment in Austrian postwar remembrance of the war. Fifty years after the end of World War II, Austrian memory quietly slipped from "communicative" to "cultural" memory. In the memory theory of Jan Assmann, "communicative" social memory refers to everyday modes of direct communication, whereas "cultural" social memory is conveyed through monuments, cultural artifacts, and media discourses that outlast generational shifts. The World War II generation was passing away and with them their personal memories of the war.[9]

These prominent Austrian voices speaking of shared responsibility unleashed a wave of restitution efforts in the 1990s. On the occasion of the 50th anniversary of the end of World War II, the Austrian parliament installed a 500 million Austrian Schillings fund for those persecuted by National Socialism. A year later some 27.000 applicants registered for payments from the National Fund (*Nationalfonds*). The Green Party acted as the main advocate for "*Wiedergutmachung*." Apart from brave voices such as Heinrich Neisser, the ÖVP tried to block it. The Greens insisted Roma and Sinti, homosexuals, and the handicapped (=victims of euthanasia crimes) should be included next to Jews. Meanwhile the FPÖ countered by serving its constituencies; it demanded that former Wehrmacht soldiers be compensated as "victims of forced labor" (!) (p. 251) as well as Sudeten German expellees. With the beginning of class action suits against Swiss banks and German and Austrian companies that had utilized forced labor during the war, the issue of "Holocaust era assets" came to the fore of restitution politics. After a multi-billion dollar settlement with the Swiss banks, the Federal Republic of Germany set up a mega-fund to compensate tens of thousands of forced laborers mostly in Eastern Europe. Austria followed suit in 2001, after setting up a historians' commission (*Historikerkommission*) in the fall of 1998 to investigate the entire complex of property looted during the "Anschluss" era and the extent of restitution and compensation paid for the loot (p. 283). On top of it, art restitution became a hot-button issue after two Klimt pictures from the Leopold Collection in Vienna were impounded in New York where they had been on display in the Modern Museum of Art. Eventually thousands of works of art in Austrian museums, storage places, and private collections came under scrutiny. Again the Greens pushed the Socialists to continue with their restitution program based on Austrian responsibility, again the ÖVP tried to block these efforts.

9 I follow here David Reynolds, who has captured the same transition of British remembrance of World War I in the 1960s in his brilliant book *The Long Shadow: The Legacies of the Great War in the Twentieth Century* (New York: W.W. Norton, 2014), 311.

With the formation of new ÖVP/FPÖ coalition government by Wolfgang Schüssel in February 2000, Austrian restitution efforts were further sped up as a result of the international isolation of this controversial government, which included the right-wing Haider party. The EU "sanctions" isolated the Schüssel government internationally like the "watch list" decision had kept Waldheim from travelling ("Waldheim remixed," pp. 304ff). Schüssel wisely chose a forward defense strategy and established commissions to quickly arrive at broad agreements on the issue of compensating slave laborers and making up for "gaps and deficiencies" in payments to Jewish victims who had lost apartments, art treasures, and personal effects during the "Anschluss" days ("aryanizations"). This constituted one of the most remarkable breakthroughs in the postwar restitution practice. Was it an inheritance of the more sensitive consciousness about Austria's past established by the Vranitzky government, or did the FPÖ's inclusion in the government serve as a "catalyst" (p. 313)? Lehnguth cannot answer this question. It was probably both, with enormous international pressure on Austria to face up to its Nazi past and the loss of prestige in the world being in the mix as well.[10]

During all of these debates, the long-standing question of who needed to be included in the Austrian collective of Nazi victims was answered. The Green Party had been defining Austrian victimhood very broadly; in 1999 they began to push the agenda for rehabilitating and compensating Wehrmacht deserters (eg. "victims of the Wehrmacht judicial system" = "*Opfer der Wehrmachtsjustiz*").[11] The FPÖ fought compensation for Wehrmacht deserters who they outrageously attacked as "traitors" and "murderers of their comrades" ("*Kameradenmörder*") (p. 329). In a very convoluted legislative process lasting from 2005 to 2009, deserters were eventually included in updates to the *Opferfürsorgegesetz*. At the same time, the FPÖ watered this legislation down by compensation payments to all "victims of war," including Austrian prisoners of war (even if they had been involved in SS or Wehrmacht crimes) and "*Trümmerfrauen*" (women who cleaned up the rubble in 1945). World War II POWs had already received symbolic payment for their "lost" war years from the Schüssel government. At the same time, homosexuals and "asocials" were included in the *Opferfürsorge* as

10 Günter Bischof makes the argument for international pressure being the main source for Schüssel's "forward defense." See "'Watschenmann der europäischen Erinnerung'? Internationales Image und Vergangenheitspolitik der Schüssel/Riess-Passer-ÖVP/FPÖ-Koalitionsregierung," in *Österreich in der Europäischen Union: Bilanz seiner Mitgliedschaft*, ed. Michael Gehler, Anton Pelinka and idem (Vienna: Böhlau, 2003), 445-78 (esp. 457-59).

11 On deserters see also Thomas Geldmacher, "Von der Verweigerung des Gleichschritts: Deutsche und österreichische Wehrmachtsdeserteure," *Wiener Zeitschrift zur Geschichte der Neuzeit* 8, no. 2 (2008): 72-87.

well but now as "victims of justice" (p. 333). In the end, paying long overdue compensation to some victims meant that the definition of "Nazi victims" was expanded so much in the bitter partisan ideological discourses that almost everybody fit the bill (SS butchers included).

In the final chapter of the book, Lehnguth analyzes the transition in the paradigm shift from the "victims doctrine" to the "shared responsibility" thesis through four case studies on historical memory and monuments discourses (i.e. "cultural" social remembrance). In 1992/93, a private initiative launched efforts to build a monument to the Austrian Wehrmacht soldiers that had perished in the battle of Stalingrad. Critics of the memorial raised the issue that these Wehrmacht "victims," in fact, might have been perpetrators involved in war crimes committed by the 6th Army on the road to Stalingrad. The 6th Army involvement in the Holocaust was one of the themes addressed in the controversial travelling exhibit "War of Annihilation: Crimes of the Wehrmacht 1941 to 1944" ("*Wehrmachtsausstellung*") shown in thirty-three German and Austrian cities between 1995 and 1999 (p. 356) with many raw pictures of Hitlerite war crimes.[12] The left-liberal postwar generation in Austria welcomed the deconstruction of the myth of the "clean Wehrmacht"; this pitted it against the conservative wartime generation that still desperately defended the Wehrmacht. Predictably, the Greens supported the showing of this exhibit in Austria while the FPÖ strictly opposed it. The ÖVP and SPÖ coalition partners sat on the fence, trying not to offend their wartime-generation voters. It was civil society again that pushed the envelope and raised funds to bring the exhibit to Austrian provincial capitals. Veterans' associations denounced it as "abject falsification of history" and "crypto-communist agitation" (p. 371).

In October 2000, Austrian politicians opened a new Holocaust memorial in the Jewish Square of Vienna, dedicated to some 65.000 Austrian Jews killed in the Holocaust. Years of vigorous and often nasty debates about the need for such a memorial, its location, design, and cost preceded the dedication. Unlike the unending and vicious partisan debate about building a "House of Tolerance/House of History" (see below), these arguments ended with British artist Rachel Whiteread's ingenious Holocaust memorial design of a library turned inside out eventually built and completed.[13] Since the late 1990s the building of

12 See Miriam Y. Arani, "'Und an den Fotos entzündete sich die Kritik:' Die 'Wehrmachtsausstellung,' deren Kritiker und die Neukonzeption. Ein Beitrag aus fotohistorisch-quellenkritischer Sicht," *Fotogeschichte: Beiträge zur Geschichte und Ästhetik der Fotografie* 22, no. 85/86 (2002): 97-124.

13 On the Vienna Holocaust Memorial and its "book metaphor", see also the essay by Moran Pearl in this volume.

such a museum of contemporary history had been debated. Whereas historians affiliated with the ÖVP such as Stefan Karner wanted to build a museum dedicated to Austria's history of the twentieth century without paying much attention to the era of National Socialism, the SPÖ asked political scientist Anton Pelinka to do a feasibility study of a "house of tolerance" mainly dedicated to the Holocaust and practices of discrimination. Both Karner and Pelinka had also served as prominent historical consultants in the debate about the Stalingrad monument. In the end, the cream of Austrian historians of contemporary history attacked both concepts as a "strapping history into a museum" ("*Musealisierung der Geschichte*") (p. 412). Various governments unsuccessfully tried to mediate an agreement between the two partisan sides for ten years before the project was put on ice in 2009. This may have been one of the most scurrilous memory debates in a nation never short of such discourses. In the end, the disagreement may well be a result of Austria's failure to reach a national consensus regarding the narrative of its trajectory in the twentieth-century, especially its inability to historicize the contentious era of "authoritarian government-dictatorship" ("*autoritäre Regierungsdiktatur*"[14]) and National Socialism (1933/8-1945) and find its proper place in Austria's grand historical narrative.

Finally, in the "memory year" 2005 (what Chancellor Schüssel proclaimed a "year of reflections" = "*Gedankenjahr*") the political parties went at it again, attempting to interpret the meaning of the 60th anniversary of the end of World War II, the 50th anniversary of the signing of the Austrian State Treaty, and the 10th anniversary of Austria entering the European Union.[15] Particularly Chancellor Schüssel and ÖVP politicians took the occasion to revive the old victims narratives of the late 1940s (p. 433). The SPÖ tried to obstruct the ÖVP from establishing a "monopoly on history" (the partisan monopolization of Austria's historical grand narrative ultimately was also the issue in the design of the "House of Tolerance/History"). The new FPÖ leadership refused to accept the paradigm of shared responsibility and some of the hardliners in the party even tried to deny the Holocaust by raising doubts about whether "gas chambers" had really existed (pp. 435f). Karner organized a symposium on Austrian World War II resistance as an "alibi" to buttress the old victims doctrine (p. 439). Were it not for the return of the

14 Stourzh's term in *Vom Reich zur Republik*, 7.

15 See also the essays by Katharina Wegan and Günter Bischof in the FORUM "Memory Boom: 'The Year of Reflection' 2005," in *Contemporary Austrian Studies [CAS]* 15 (2007), 172-237; see also the essays in *rebranding images: Ein streitbares Lesebuch zu Geschichtspolitik und Erinnerungskultur in Österreich*, ed. Martin Wassermair and Katharina Wegan (Innsbruck: StudienVerlag, 2006).

Socialists into an SPÖ/ÖVP governing coalition, Schüssel's revival of the old victims myth may have stuck. But brave voices such as the President of the Austrian Parliament, the late Barbara Prammer (SPÖ), insisted in the 2008 "Anschluss" commemorations that the victims doctrine was "fiction" and that Austria shared in the responsibility of Nazi war crimes (thus accepting what Lehnguth calls the "*kritische Mitverantwortungsthese*"—pushed by the Greens since their arrival as a political force) (p. 441). In this climate, the legislation acknowledging and rehabilitating deserters and other persecuted minorities as victims finally passed (what oddly became known as the *NS-Aufhebungsgesetz* of 2009) (p. 445). Presumably, these partisan battles can be revived at any time.

Lehnguth's study relentlessly—and, as is the case with thesis-driven dissertations, even repetitively—identifies the various political parties' stances in all these controversial historical debates. Cumulatively, this becomes tedious as the partisan "politics of history" have been so predictable over the past 70 years. The two principal coalition partners, ÖVP and SPÖ, constructed the victims myth after the war for opportunistic reasons and were reluctant to abandon it after the fiasco of Kurt Waldheim's election as president—the ÖVP more so than the SPÖ. The FPÖ, with its reservoir of German nationalist and former Wehrmacht voters, embraced the "Anschluss" and considered the old soldiers as the real "victims" of the war. They never bought into the postwar anti-fascist consensus. Were it not for consistent pressure from new progressive parties such as the Greens and the Liberal Forum, as well as relentless international pressure since 1986, the codes of the victims doctrine might never have been cracked. Lehnguth is particularly good at identifying specific generational support for these parties and their politics of history. One element entirely missing in Austrian memory politics is the Austrian churches. The Catholic Church had been deeply involved in the politics of the First Republic and supported the "*Ständestaat*" and the "Anschluss" in 1938. Even though it retreated from the political arena after the war, the Catholic Church has remained a moral force in the country and an important influence in the ÖVP. How did the Catholic Church come to terms with this past? What role did it play in supporting the victims doctrine within the ranks of the ÖVP? How could a "Christian" party such as the ÖVP be so callous in its politics of the past and deny Austrians' deep involvement in Hitlerite war crimes for so long? How could it ignore the Holocaust and its legacies? Lehnguth has absorbed an enormous amount of literature but failed to consult with the long-standing and consistent coverage of Austrian politics of history in the pages of this journal.[16] Given the vast ambition of Lehnguth's study to cover the entire trajectory of Austrian World War II memory, these are minor quibbles. This insightful book is a must-read for everybody interested in World War II memory studies in general and Austria's tortuous path of the post-war politics of memory in particular.

16 The politics of history is the issue CAS covered most consistently starting with volume I. See Thomas Albrich, "Jewish Interests and the Austrian State Treaty," in *CAS* 1 (1993), 137-164; John Haag, "Austrian Jews from Emancipation to Holocaust," in *CAS* 2 (1994), 222-237; Jonathan Petropoulos, "The Importance of the Second Rank: The Case of the Art Plunderer Kajetan Mühlmann," in *CAS* 4 (1996), 177-222; see the articles by Heidemarie Uhl, Anton Pelinka, Brigitte Bailer, and Robert Edwin Herzstein, and the review essay by Günter Bischof, "Founding Myths and Compartmentalized Past: New Literature on the Construction, Hibernation, and Deconstruction of World War II Memory in Postwar Austria," in *CAS* 5 (1997), 64-135, 302-341; FORUM "Austria and the Ghost of the New Europe" [on Haider and the FPÖ], in *CAS* 6 (1998), 120-173; FORUM "The Long Shadow of World War II: The Politics of Historical Memory and Art Restitution," in *CAS* 7 (1999), 190-243; Richard Mitten, "Jews and Other Victims: The 'Jewish Questions' and Discourses of Victimhood in Postwar Austria," in *CAS* 10 (2002), 223-270; FORUM "World War II Crimes against Jews and Their Persecution in Austrian Courts after the War," in *ibid.*, 271-309; FORUM "Commissioning History: Austria and World War II Restitution and Reconciliation," in *CAS* 11 (2003); 212-266; Evan Burr Bukey, "New Literature on Nazi Austria and the Holocaust," in *ibid.*, 267-280; Robert E. Herzstein, "The Waldheim Matter: Old Issues and Perplexing Questions," in *ibid.*, 281-286; Jonathan Petropoulos, "Provenance Research as History: Reconstructed Collections and National Socialist Art Looting," in *CAS* 14 (2006), 361-372; many of the essays in *New Perspectives on Austrians and World War II*, in *CAS* 17 (2009); Günter Bischof and Michael Maier, "Reinventing Tradition and the Politics of History: Schüssel's Restitution and Commemoration Policies," in *CAS* 18 (2010), 206-35; Winfried Garscha, "Ordinary Austrians: Common War Criminals during World War II," in *CAS* 21 (2012), 304-326.

Annual Review

Austria 2014-2015

Reinhold Gärtner

EU Parliamentary Elections

Elections in Vorarlberg

Parliamentary Enquiry Committee

Cabinet Reshuffle

Barbara Prammer 11 January 1954–2 August 2014

Economic and Statistical Data

EU Parliamentary Elections

The European Union (EU) parliamentary elections were held in May 2014. Since 1979, the EU parliament is elected every five years in all EU member states. The 2014 elections were held between 22 and 25 May 2014. The EU parliament consist of 751 MEPs, eighteen of them are from Austria.

The MEPs are organized in political groups:

	2014	2009
EEP Group of the European People's Party	221 - 29.43 %	274 - 35.77 %
S&P Group of the Progressive Alliance of Socialists and Democrats in the European Parliament	191 - 25.43 %	196 - 25.59 %
ECR European Conservatives and Reformists	70 - 9.32 %	57 - 7.44 %
ALDE Alliance of Liberals and Democrats for Europe	67 - 8.92 %	83 - 10.83 %
GUE/NGL European United Left/Nordic Green	52 - 6.92 %	57 - 7.44 %
Left		
Greens/EFA The Greens/European Free Alliance	50 - 6.66 %	35 - 4.57 %
EFDD Europe for Freedom and Direct Democracy Group	48 - 6.39 %	31 - 4.05 %
NI–Non attached members; members not belonging to any political group	52 - 6.92 %	33 - 4.31 %

Source <http://www.europarl.europa.eu/elections2014-results/en/election-results-2014.html> (12 March 2015).

In Austria, nine parties ran for the election, five of them were successful in gaining seats in the newly elected EU parliament: ÖVP (member of EPP) 5 (- 1), SPÖ (S&P) 5 (- 1), FPÖ (NI) 4 (+ 2), *Grüne* (Greens) 3 (+ 1) and Neos (ALDE) 1 (+ 1). Voter turnout was at 45.4 % (46.0 % in 2009).

The Austrian results were not really surprising; on the European level, however, some remarkable results occurred:

In the United Kingdom, the UKIP (United Kingdom Independent Party) was a surprising winner with 26.77 % (24 seats), followed by Labour (24.74 %; 20 seats) and the Conservatives (23.31 %; 19 seats). UKIP not only opposes European integration (which is not very surprising in the UK) but wants a UK exit from the European Union.

Other EU skeptical parties were very successful in France and Italy. In France the right wing populist *Front National* (FN) received 24.86 % (23 seats); and in Italy Beppe Grillo's populist *Movimento 5 Stelle* (M5S) with 21.15 % (17 seats) was runner up to the Social Democratic *Partito Democratico* (PD) with 40.81 % (31 seats).

Most alarming were the gains for some rightwing extremists' movements (not to say neo-Nazi) parties like *Chrysi Avgi* (Golden Dawn) in Greece with 9.39 % (3 seats) or the *Nationaldemokratische Partei Deutschlands* (NPD) in Germany with 1 % (1 seat). Hungary's

Jobbik received 14.67 % of the votes (3 seats). In 2009, *Jobbik* had already gathered 14.77 %. Besides these extremist parties, many right wing populist parties managed to get seats in the Parliament, for example the Belgian *Vlaams Belang*, the Swedish *Sverigedemocraterna* (Swedish Democrats), and *Dansk Folkepartie* (Danish People's Party) or Austria's FPÖ.

Another alarming result was the voter turnout: the overall EU turnout was 42.61 percent, in Slovakia it was at 13.05 percent; in the Czech Republic 18.2 percent, in Poland 23.83 percent and in Slovenia 24.55 percent.

Elections in Vorarlberg

The elections in the Austrian *Land* Vorarlberg were held on 21 September 2014. Because of the Neos candidacy in Vorarlberg it was expected that the ÖVP would lose its absolute majority. The ÖVP lost 9 percent of the vote and received 41.79 percent, followed by the FPÖ (23.42 percent; - 1.7 percent) and the *Grüne* (17.14 percent; + 6.46 percent). SPÖ—traditionally weak in Vorarlberg—received 8.77 percent only (- 1.25 percent) and the Neos 6.89 percent.

Markus Wallner thus stayed as governor of Vorarlberg as the head of an ÖVP-*Grüne* coalition government.

Parliamentary Enquiry Committee

Up to 2014, investigative committees could be installed by parliamentary majorities only. As these committees are basic instruments of parliamentary control, for years parliament debated whether a minority should have the right to appoint such a committee. Finally, in fall of 2014 the Austrian parliament decided to make it a minority right to appoint such committees.

One aspect of this decision was the never-ending political debate about the failed Carinthian bank *Hypo Alpe Adria*, Austria's current financial disaster.

Cabinet Reshuffle

In August 2014, the luckless ÖVP chairman Michael Spindelegger resigned. Spindelegger had become chairman of the ÖVP in 2011. Since 2008, he had served as Federal Minister for

Europe and Foreign Affairs. After the 2013 election, he became Federal Minister of Finance in the new SPÖ-ÖVP government. His colorless performance, though, was criticized by more and more ÖVP representatives (like the governors of Vorarlberg, Tirol, and Salzburg). Finally, in August 2014, the ÖVP replaced Spindelegger as party chairman with the Federal Minister of Science, Research, and Economy Reinhold Mitterlehner. Johann Georg Schelling was sworn in as new Minister of Finance. Harald Mahrer became State Secretary within the Ministry of Science, Research and Economy; Sabine Oberhauser Federal Minister of Health; Alois Stöger replaced Doris Bures in the Federal Ministry of Transport, Innovation and Technology. Bures succeeded Barbara Prammer, who passed away in 2014, as First President of the *Nationalrat*.

Barbara Prammer 11 January 1954–2 August 2014

In August 2014 Barbara Prammer (SPÖ), the President of *Nationalrat* died of cancer. From 1997 until 2000, Prammer was Minister for Women's Affairs, and after the inauguration of the ÖVP-FPÖ government in February 2000, she became leader of the SPÖ parliamentary group. In 2004, the SPÖ appointed her Second President of the *Nationalrat* and, in 2006, First President of the Austrian parliament. She was the first woman in Austria to hold this office.

Economic and Statistical Data

In 2014, inflation stood at 1.70 percent (compared to 2.0 percent in 2013), HICP was at 1.5 percent (compared to 2.1 percent in 2013). The public deficit amounted to 1.5 percent in 2013 (2.3 percent in 2012) and public debts amounted to 81.2 percent in 2013 (81.7 percent in 2012).

In 2013, the GNP reached a per capita average of € 38.050 (compared to € 37.650 in 2012); economic growth amounted to 0.2 percent in 2013 (compared to 0.9 in 2012).

In 2013, Austria imported a meagre € 130.700 million worth of goods (€ 93.170 million from the EU) and exported € 125.800 million (€ 86.740 million to the EU). Imports from NAFTA were € 5.026 million; exports to NAFTA € 8.536 million.

In 2013, 4.175.000 people in Austria were employed; according to the International Labour Organization (ILO) the rate of unemployment was at 4.9 percent in 2013 (on average 4.3 percent in 2012). According to national data estimates the rate of unemployment was at 7.6 percent (7.0 percent in 2012).

At the beginning of 2014, 8.507.786 people were living in Austria (8.579.747 at the beginning of 2015), among them 1.066.114 foreigners (and among them 527.369 from the EU/EWR/Switzerland). In 2013, 79.330 children were born alive in Austria and 79.526 people died. In 2013, Austrian life expectancy was 78.45 years for men and 83.56 years for women.

List of Authors

Günter Bischof is the Marshall Plan Professor of History and the Director of Center Austria: Austrian Marshall Plan Center for European Studies at the University of New Orleans (UNO).

Emil Brix is the Austrian Ambassador in the Russian Federation and in Belarus and deputy chairman of the Institute for the Danube Region and Central Europe in Vienna.

Evan B. Bukey is a professor emeritus of history at the University of Arkansas.

Peter Bußjäger is professor at the department for Public Law at the University of Innsbruck, head of the Institute of Federalism in Innsbruck and a researcher at the Liechtenstein-Institute in Bendern/Liechtenstein.

Martin Eichtinger is the Austrian Ambassador to the United Kingdom of Great Britain and Northern Irland, former director general for Cultural Policy at the Austrian Federal Ministry for Europe, Integration, and Foreign Affairs.

Alice Engl is a senior researcher at the Institute for Minority Rights of the European Academy Bozen/Bolzano.

Annegret Eppler is an assistant professor at the Department of Political Science at the University of Innsbruck

Franz Fallend is a senior scientist at the Department of Political Science at the University of Salzburg.

Reinhold Gärtner is an associate professor in the Department of Political Science at the University of Innsbruck.

Ferdinand Karlhofer is an associate professor and chair in the Department of Political Science at the University of Innsbruck.

Thomas König is a researcher at the Institute for Advanced Studies, Vienna.

Karin Liebhart is a senior lecturer at the Department of Political Science at the University of Vienna; in 2014/15, she was the Austrian Marshall Plan chair at UNO.

Ina Markova holds an ÖAW doctoral fellowship and works at the University of Vienna; in 2014/2015, she was Austrian Ministry of Science fellow at UNO's Center Austria.

Franz Mathis is a professor of economic and social history emeritus of the University of Innsbruck.

Heinrich Neisser is Jean Monnet Professor emeritus at the Department of Political Science at the University of Innsbruck.

Günther Pallaver is a professor at the Department of Political Science at the University of Innsbruck and president of the South Tyrolean Political Science Association.

Moran Pearl is a PhD candidate at the DAAD Center for German Studies at Hebrew University of Jerusalem.

Anton Pelinka is a professor of political science and nationalism studies and the Center European University in Budapest.

Nicole M. Phelps is an associate professor in the Department of History at the University of Vermont.

Margit Schratzenstaller is a senior researcher (public finance) at the Austrian Institute of Economic Research (WIFO), Vienna.

Alexander Smith is a doctoral candidate in economic history and political science at the University of Innsbruck.

Fritz Staudigl is managing director of the External Relations Department at the Office of the Tyrolean Government.

Samuel R. Williamson, Jr. is president and professor of history emeritus of the University of the South.

Contemporary Austrian Studies

Günter Bischof, Anton Pelinka/Fritz Plasser/Ferdinand Karlhofer, Editors

Volume 1 (1992)
Austria in the New Europe

Volume 2 (1993)
The Kreisky Era in Austria
Oliver Rathkolb, Guest Editor

Volume 3 (1994)
Austria in the Nineteen Fifties
Rolf Steininger, Guest Editor

Volume 4 (1995)
Austro-Corporatism: Past—Present—Future

Volume 5 (1996)
Austrian Historical Memory & National Identity

Volume 6 (1997)
Women in Austria
Erika Thurner, Guest Editor

Volume 7 (1998)
The Vranitzky Era in Austria
Ferdinand Karlhofer, Guest Editor

Volume 8 (1999)
The Marshall Plan in Austria
Dieter Stiefel, Guest Editor

Volume 9 (2000)
Neutrality in Austria
Ruth Wodak, Guest Editor

Volume 10 (2001)
Austria and the EU
Michael Gehler, Guest Editor

Volume 11 (2002)
The Dollfuss/Schuschnigg Era in Austria: A Reassessment
Alexander Lassner, Guest Editor

Volume 12 (2003)
The Americanization/Westernization of Austria

Volume 13 (2004)
Religion in Austria
Hermann Denz, Guest Editor

Volume 14 (2005)
Austrian Foreign Policy in Historical Perspective
Michael Gehler, Guest Editor

Volume 15 (2006)
Sexuality in Austria
Dagmar Herzog, Guest Editor

Volume 16 (2007)
The Changing Austrian Voter

Volume 17 (2008)
New Perspectives on Austrians and World War II
Barbara Stelzl-Marx, Guest Editor

Volume 18 (2009)
The Schüssel Era in Austria

Volume 19 (2010)
From Empire to Republic: Post-World War I Austria

Volume 20 (2011)
Global Austria: Austria's Place in Europe and the World
Alexander Smith, Guest Editor

Volume 21 (2012)
Austrian Lives
Eva Maltschnig, Guest Editor

Volume 22 (2013)
Austria's International Position after the End of the Cold War

Volume 23 (2014)
1914: Austria-Hungary, the Origins, and the First Year of World War 1
Samuel R. Williamson, Jr., Guest Editor